FISCAL SURVEY OF PANAMA
Problems and Proposals for Reform

JOINT TAX PROGRAM OAS/IDB

FISCAL
SURVEY
OF PANAMA

PROBLEMS AND PROPOSALS FOR REFORM

PUBLISHED FOR THE JOINT TAX PROGRAM OF THE
ORGANIZATION OF AMERICAN STATES AND THE
INTER-AMERICAN DEVELOPMENT BANK
BY
THE JOHNS HOPKINS PRESS
BALTIMORE, MARYLAND

JOINT TAX PROGRAM OAS/IDB

Committee of Alternates

Alvaro Magaña (OAS)
James A. Lynn (IDB)

FISCAL MISSION TO PANAMA

Members of the Mission

Milton C. Taylor, Mission Chief
(*Michigan State University*)

Raymond L. Richman
(*University of Pittsburgh*)

M. Slade Kendrick
(*Cornell University*)

Raúl Gochez
(*Pan American Union*)

Marco Baeza
(*Seton Hall University*)

Editor of the Fiscal Survey

Marto Ballesteros
(*Chief, Public Finance Unit, Department of Economic Affairs, Pan American Union*)

Preface

THE JOINT TAX PROGRAM of the Organization of American States (OAS), the Inter-American Development Bank (IDB), and the United Nations Economic Commission for Latin America (ECLA) was organized a few months before the August, 1961, Conference of Punta del Este, with the objective of uniting the efforts of these three organizations for the purpose of contributing to strengthening the fiscal systems of Latin America.

The Charter of Punta del Este gave special emphasis to the programming of development, economic integration, the solution of the problems of basic products, and the adoption of structural reforms. Among the structural reforms fiscal reform has an important role, and the Charter indicates that it should be oriented to achieve a more equitable income distribution, to increase public revenues, to create conditions favorable to a more efficient utilization of financial resources together with other measures that contribute to maintaining the stability propitious to development.

Fiscal reform, which is the result of a frequently slow process—from the creation of a climate favorable for the adoption of appropriate measures to the point of preparation of legal texts—has been the ultimate objective of the Joint Tax Program. In order to contribute to this objective, two closely related activities have been undertaken during the last two years which have already shown positive results in various countries.

The first activity involved two conferences: the first, on tax administration, took place in Buenos Aires, Argentina, in October, 1961; and the second, on fiscal policy, took place in Santiago, Chile, in December, 1962.

The Santiago Conference produced a document of extraordinary importance, namely, the Summary and Conclusions which established the general guidelines for the tax reforms that should be undertaken by the countries of Latin America to accelerate their development. In accordance with original plans, the participation of ECLA in the activities of the Joint Tax Program ended with the realization of these two conferences.

The Program's second type of activity is involved with the preparation of detailed studies of the fiscal systems of the individual Latin American countries. Through these surveys it is hoped to point out salient characteristics and problems, thus permitting the formulation of concrete proposals for reform. The study of the effects of a tax system on the over-all economy, the effectiveness of incentive programs, and the analysis of other fiscal policy problems provides the information necessary for the formulation of reform measures oriented to the achievement of a more equitable distribution of income and an acceleration of the development process.

The agencies sponsoring the Joint Tax Program are pleased to present the first volume of these studies covering Panamá to those interested in fiscal reform in Latin America.

A distinguishing feature of these studies is that they not only display adequate comprehensiveness and technical competence, but also that they are oriented to the objectives of the Charter of Punta del Este and to the guidelines offered by the Santiago Conference. The specific recommendations contained in this work are the joint product of the members of the Mission and the Public Finance Unit of the Pan American Union, who sought to apply these general principles to the particular fiscal problems existing in Panamá

The present study could not have been concluded without the extraordinary collaboration of Panamanian authorities. The President of the Republic, Roberto F. Chiari, established a Coordinating Committee at a high level to collaborate with members of the Fiscal Mission. The Committee, which contributed in great measure to facilitate the tasks of the Mission, was composed of David Samudio A., Director General of Planning and Administration, Gilberto Arias, Minister of the Treasury, and Alejandro Remón Cantera, Comptroller General of the Republic. It is virtually impossible to list all of the officials who lent assistance to the Mission, but mention should be made of Messrs. Jorge Riba and Rodrigo Núñez of the Department of Planning and Administration, who maintained close contact with the Mission throughout its labors and thus made a special contribution to the preparation of this study. We take this opportunity to acknowledge to all of these officials the valuable assistance received.

Principal responsibility for the present survey belongs to the Chief of the Fiscal Mission, Professor Milton Taylor of Michigan State University. Collaborating closely in most phases of the research was Professor Raymond Richman of the University of Pittsburgh. Professor M. Slade Kendrick of Cornell University was also a principal contributor. Assistance in certain parts of the study was rendered by Mr. Raúl Gochez of The Pan American Union, and Professor Marco Baeza of Seton Hall University.

The representative of the Inter-American Development Bank to the Joint Tax Program, Dr. James A. Lynn, has collaborated in setting the general directions of the Program and in the specific orientation of the tax studies.

ALVARO MAGAÑA (OAS)

Joint Tax Program

OAS/IDB

February, 1964

Table of Contents

LIST OF TABLES

CHAPTER 1

The Fiscal Problems and Proposals for Reform

THE ECONOMY OF PANAMÁ

PANAMÁ HAS BEEN inaptly referred to as a small, poor country "sliced in half by a canal." The country is small, with a population of only 1,100,000, but compared to some countries in Latin America that are yet to awake from a century and a half of stagnation and others in which the per capita income has actually been declining during the last decade, Panamá is relatively well off. In 1961, Panamá had the fifth highest per capita income among nineteen Latin American republics.

Not only this, but the economy is booming. In 1961, the gross domestic product increased by 7.5 per cent, and about the same growth rate is indicated for 1962. The increase in domestic product in 1961 exceeded the annual average growth rate of 3.3 per cent for the preceding 16 years, the average growth of 5.3 per cent from 1951 to 1961, and even the very substantial increase for 1960 of 6.4 per cent. With an estimated population increase of 2.8 per cent per annum, the net increase in per capita gross domestic product in 1961 was 4.6 per cent. Considering that the goal of the Alliance for Progress is to achieve an average annual increase in per capita income of 2.5 per cent in Latin America, Panamá,

quite obviously, is ahead of schedule under the Alliance.

But having made these favorable observations on the economy of Panamá, it is difficult to find anything else that is cause for satisfaction. Stating the domestic product in terms of a per capita average obscures the fact that an unequal distribution of income in Panamá results in a part of the population being no better off than if they lived in the poorest and most stagnant economy in Latin America. While the average family income is about B/2000,[1] approximately 16 per cent of the family units have an income of less than B/1000. The relatively high per capita income means nothing to the nearly 10 per cent of the nation's labor force that is unemployed, or to the one worker out of five unemployed in the cities of Colón and Panamá; it means nothing to the 63 per cent of all farm operators that are squatters and live like pioneers of the eighteenth century; it means nothing to the thousands of urban slumdwellers. To resolve these problems, Panamá needs to sustain the current growth rate indefinitely; but probably more important, it needs to distribute the nation's wealth and income more equitably. It needs to insure that the gains achieved by a rising output

[1] Although the official monetary unit is the "balboa," the U.S. dollar, equivalent in value, is the circulating cash medium of exchange.

1

will be used for alleviating material privation instead of providing additional opportunities for conspicuous consumption on the part of the upper income groups.

A few statistics will demonstrate the need for a leveling of income and wealth. In Chapter four, dealing with the property tax, it is shown that one hundred individuals or companies own one-third of the agricultural land, and 34,936 operate the remaining two-thirds. According to estimates made by the Department of Planning and Administration, 16 per cent of the families at the lower end of the income scale received 6 per cent of the national income in 1960, while 13 per cent of the families at the higher end of the scale received 32 per cent. And inevitably associated with this unequal distribution is a concentration of political power and control, for economic and political oligarchies feed and sustain each other.

The Republic has few conventional means of sustaining a high level of growth. Panamá is relatively poor in natural resources, while a lack of transportation facilities and an unequal distribution of land inhibits the full exploitation of the available land resources. While 42.5 per cent of the population is engaged in agriculture, this industry in 1961 contributed only 19 per cent of the gross domestic product. Manufacturing has been similarly neglected, with the result that the country is self-sufficient in relatively few manufactured products. Manufacturing in 1961 contributed only 11 per cent of the gross domestic product. Even the tourist trade has not been exploited effectively. Although the economic growth rate has been relatively high during the past decade, there is little evidence of this increased product in the basic economic infrastructure. When one looks for tangible signs of development, these are to be found principally in the high level of commercial activity (16.2 per cent of the gross internal product in 1961) and in construction (7.2 per cent of the gross internal product).

But Panamá has the canal, its principal, and in fact, only important "natural" resource. To Panamá, the canal is as valuable as oil is to Venezuela. It is primarily the canal that accounts for Panamá's relative well being; it is the canal that has made the nation a trader, an entrepôt, an international merchant; it is the canal that generates the invisible earnings that make a very unfavorable balance of visible trade tolerable. In fiscal year 1962, Canal Zone expenditures for goods and services from the Republic of Panamá totaled B/75 million, about 16 per cent of the nation's gross internal product. Over 20,000 Panamanians were employed in the zone, earning about B/33 million. Expenditures in Panamá by various agencies and organizations in the zone totaled B/23 million, while Canal Zone residents spent an additional B/17 million. Obviously, it is not a matter of coincidence that the total of these expenditures increased by 9 per cent in fiscal 1962 while Panamá's gross internal product rose at nearly the same rate.

But the old adage that one does not get something for nothing is true of the canal. It is a tremendous source of political tension and distraction, continuously raising basic issues involving sovereignty, the rights of Panamanian workers, and smuggling. These problems became clearly evident during the early months of 1964.

Partly because of geographic location and the influence of the canal but also because of the political influence wielded by commercial interests, Panamá has developed a mercantilist mentality. And with this long-run emphasis on commerce, there has been an unbalanced utilization of resources. Very conspicuous in the past and even in the present has been an economic philosophy that little else needs to be done but to exploit the nation's geography. There is a tendency to view Panamá as unique in Latin America —as Switzerland is in Europe. There is a tendency to follow a "fast-buck" approach to economic development with incentives to tax-haven corporations, numbered bank accounts to attract foreign capital, tax-exemption for the registry of ships, and casinos (but very little else) to attract tourists.

These efforts do not constitute the real substance of economic development. They do not provide the foundation for the type of an economic society that is likely to have consistent growth and one in which the fruits will be shared equitably. Rather, they result in the type of economy that Panamá has, one that advances in fits and starts, depending on such variables as the level of canal traffic and the number of new tax-haven corporations. And for this type of economy, it matters little for much of the population whether the economy as a whole is advancing or standing still. The Panamanian economy reminds one of a ballgame in which only the stars are allowed to play. One cannot help but wonder how long the other contestants will be content to sit on the bench.

THE DEVELOPMENT PROGRAM[2]

Panamá's new development program promises a different and better future for the country. This plan, covering the five-year period from 1962 to 1966, establishes as its goal an average annual increase in per capita income of 2.5 per cent.[3] To attain this objective, it has been determined that a total public sector investment of B/213 million will be necessary. Additional objectives of the development program are the diversification of economic activities in order to decrease dependence on the canal, to alleviate the chronic and severe trade deficit and unfavorable balance of payments, and to reduce the high unemployment rate. For these reasons, the projected public investment expenditures touch every aspect of the economy. Of the B/213 million projected for public investment, B/93 million will be spent on agrarian reform, housing, education, and public health; B/109 million on agricultural development,

transportation, electrification, industrial development, tourism, and planning; and B/11 million will be invested in public buildings and penal institutions.

Agrarian reform and agricultural development are emphasized, with a planned expenditure of B/35.7 million. Chapter four on the property tax demonstrates that there is justification for this emphasis, for there are pressing problems involving the need to redistribute land to squatters, to improve the primitive technology of most farmers, and to provide for the general economic and social integration of the rural population. These objectives will be served by settling 18,000 families on 75,000 hectares of unused land, and by providing roads, marketing and distribution facilities, land and resource surveys, and credit to small-farm operators. Since there are about 70,000 rural squatters, these efforts will not resolve the problem of the landless, but at least they constitute a beginning in the right direction.

Several measures are planned to meet the critical needs for housing. Besides conventional low-cost public housing, they include a self-help program, the establishment of financial institutions to induce savings and financing for private home construction, and an FHA mortgage-type insurance institution. By 1966 it is expected that these efforts will result in the construction of ten thousand houses. Once again, however, this achievement will represent only a first step in resolving the housing problem, for two-thirds of the population currently is housed in overcrowded and unsanitary conditions.

Although the general health of the population in Panamá is somewhat better than that of the people in other Latin American countries, health and sanitation problems are still severe. Life expectancy is only fifty-two years, infant mortality is 60 per 1,000 live births, and the incidence of tuberculosis is 173.4 per 100,000. Much of the rural population is without any hospital or clinical facilities. Panamá's five-year plan has programmed an expenditure of B/8.7 million on hospitals and clinics and an additional B/12.3 million on

[2] A new development program was completed in 1963 after this section was written. Although the new program is more comprehensive and extends over a longer planning period, the basic characteristics of the two programs are similar.

[3] Since the net increase in per capita gross domestic product in 1961 was 4.6 per cent, it could be argued that a goal of 2.5 per cent in Panamá's case is unduly modest, even if it represents a sustained rate of increase.

TABLE 1.1

Sources of Funds for the Development Program

(Millions of Balboas)

	1962	1963	1964	1965	1966	Total
Grants	12.5	12.5	12.5	12.5	12.5	62.5
Loans	16.6	17.2	17.8	18.4	16.5	86.5
Budgetary contributions	9.3	10.7	12.2	13.9	18.0	64.1
TOTAL PUBLIC INVESTMENT	38.4	40.4	42.5	44.8	47.0	213.1

Source: Departamento de Planificación, *Informe Económico*, Febrero, 1962, pp. 42–43.

the improvement of water and sewer systems. By 1966, it is expected that 80 per cent of the rural population will have preventive and curative medical services available.

Considering that the literacy rate is below 50 per cent in several Latin American countries (e.g., it is only 30 per cent in Guatemala), Panamá's rate of 70 per cent is relatively high. Nevertheless, 30 per cent of the children between seven and fifteen years do not attend school because of a lack of facilities. Although the government is already spending one-quarter of its budget on education, the five-year development plan allots B/18.4 million for education, primarily for new schoolrooms.

These brief observations on a few parts of the development program are sufficient to explain the general character and magnitude of the plan. It is not the purpose of this survey to inquire into the adequacy of the program. Suffice it to say that a hasty review warrants the conclusion that the planned expenditures appear minimal in terms of their need. It is within the purview of this study, however, to inquire whether sufficient financial resources appear to be available for its fulfillment.

In formulating the financial plans for the development program, it was first assumed by the planners that the Government of Panamá, "because of its unique relationships with the United States," would be able to receive an annual grant of B/12.5 million. With this total given for each year, it was then proposed to obtain the remainder of the annual investment needs through a combination of loans and budgetary contributions.

This balance between loans and budgetary contributions was arranged in such a way that the loans would be relatively more important than contributions at the beginning of the program period, but contributions would rise to become a more important source of investment funds than loans by the end of the period. Table 1.1 shows that the results of these assumptions are that B/62.5 million (29.3 per cent) of the program will be financed by grants, B/86.5 million (40.6 per cent) by loans, and B/64.1 million (30.1 per cent) by budgetary contributions.

Grants and loans as sources of investment funds are self-explanatory, but the term budgetary contributions requires an explanatory comment. As this term is used in the development program, it means investment funds made available by all government revenues and receipts, including both ordinary government revenues as well as the receipts of independent agencies. Thus, budgetary contributions to the development program is the residual remaining, if any, after total public sector consumption expenditures are deducted from total public receipts.

In considering whether these plans for financing the development program are realistic, it is beyond the scope of this report to pass judgment on the assumption with respect to the level of expected grants. Attention will therefore be confined to the relative shares of the program to be financed by borrowing and budgetary contributions. For this analysis, it is necessary to consider Panamá's historical record of revenues, expenditures, and borrowing.

RECENT AND PROSPECTIVE
FISCAL PERFORMANCE

From 1951 to 1961, the ordinary revenues of the government increased from B/32.7 million to B/62.5 million, or by 91.4 per cent, while government expenditures, including interest on the public debt but excluding amortization, rose from B/35.0 million to B/86.1 million, or by 146 per cent. In the ten-year period from 1952 to 1961 inclusive, deficits resulted in each year except two, with the total deficit amounting to B/73.3 million for the decade.

Revenues

For convenience, Panamá's revenues may be classified into three groups: indirect taxes, direct taxes, and proprietary income. While this classification is traditional, and is the way the revenue statistics are reported in Panamá, it should be borne in mind that the distinctions are arbitrary from an analytical point of view. Indirect taxes are assumed to be shifted, while direct taxes are believed to resist shifting. However, taxes on improved real estate, a direct tax, are believed to be shifted at least in part to renters. Income taxes on corporations likewise may be shifted in part to consumers. On the other hand, business license fees, an indirect tax, probably are not shifted. Even proprietary income may be partially an indirect tax if the price exceeds the economic cost of the service. In this study, the traditional classification is employed for convenience only, and does not imply shifting or non-shifting of the taxes.

Panamá relies heavily on indirect taxes, although their relative importance has declined compared to a decade ago. In 1961, indirect taxes, including taxes on foreign commerce, produced B/33.0 million or 52.8 per cent of total ordinary revenues, while in 1951 they accounted for B/19.0 million or 58.2 per cent. Customs duties alone were nearly 37 per cent of total ordinary revenues

and 70 per cent of total indirect taxes in 1961.

Taxes on alcoholic beverages, gasoline, and automobiles are the most important among the import duties. Alcoholic beverages, tobacco, stamp taxes, and a meat slaughtering tax are the most important among the domestic excises. Except for automobiles, owned by a relatively small proportion of the population, and imported liquors, few luxury goods are taxed (the principal reason being the importance of the tourist trade), including sales to Canal Zone residents. Nevertheless, except for a few items like wheat, tobacco, beer, and meat, the products bearing indirect taxes are not consumed by the lower income groups, and therefore the burden of the indirect taxes is quite tolerable. Much more oppressive are the protective tariffs, which do not bring in revenue, but which produce a burden in the form of higher prices on many products of mass consumption, many of which are nutritionally important.

Special problems are created for the administration of the customs by the existence of the Canal Zone, where many Panamanians live and may shop in stores that sell goods free of Panamanian duties. Customs enforcement is also complicated by the existence of the Free Zone of Colón, which is alleged to be a source of contraband activity.

Direct taxes, principally income and property taxes, have been growing in importance, rising from B/5.8 million or 17.7 per cent of ordinary revenues in 1951 to B/14.6 million or 23.3 per cent in 1961. However, they rose to a peak of 28.6 per cent of ordinary revenues in 1955.

The income tax is based on the gross income of individuals and the net income of corporations. Personal exemptions determine whether one is liable to the tax, but if income exceeds the basic exemptions, the base of the tax is the entire income without deductions. The same rate schedule applies to individuals and corporations, except that the rates are increased by a 40 per cent surtax for corporations, a 10 per cent surtax for

TABLE 1.2

Ordinary Government Revenues of the Republic of Panamá, 1951 and 1961

(Thousands of Balboas)

	1951	Percentage of Total Revenue	1961	Percentage of Total Revenue	Change from 1951 to 1961 (Per Cent)
Indirect taxes	19,022	58.2	33,036	52.8	73.7
Foreign commerce	13,377	40.9	23,099	36.9	72.7
Domestic excises	5,645	17.3	9,938	15.9	76.0
Direct taxes	5,794	17.7	14,594	23.3	151.9
Income	4,064	12.4	10,672	17.1	162.6
Property	1,522	4.7	3,257	5.2	114.0
Inheritance and gift	208	0.6	665	1.1	219.7
Proprietary and miscellaneous	7,856	24.1	14,908	23.9	89.8
National services and monopolies	6,784	20.8	11,431	18.3	68.5
Rent and royalties	129	0.4	237	0.4	83.7
Canal annuity	430	1.3	1,930	3.1	348.8
Miscellaneous	513	1.6	1,310	2.1	155.4
Ordinary revenues	32,672	100.0	62,538	100.0	91.4

Source: Contraloría General de la República, Dirección de Estadística y Censo, *Hacienda Pública y Finanzas*, 4° trimestre, 1960 y 1961.

married couples, and a 25 per cent surtax for bachelors.

The relatively low yield of the income tax is attributable to modest rates and the narrowness of the base. The rates begin at two per cent on the first B/2400 of income, with no liability imposed on married couples if their income is less than B/1800. Effective rates are relatively low, only 2.73 per cent on an earned income of B/5000, 4.73 per cent on B/10,000, and 15.72 per cent on B/100,000. In addition, the base has been narrowed by the use of the income tax for incentive purposes, the exclusion of income earned abroad, the exemption of capital gains on assets held for more than two years, and the exclusion of dividends at the personal income tax level. In spite of the low rates, there is evidence of widespread evasion. How poorly the enforcement staff is supported may be gauged by the fact that the Minister of Finance and the Treasury has never levied an income tax penalty for negligence or fraud.

The property tax, in a country which derives much of its non-wage income from land and real estate, is surprisingly unproductive. In 1961, the tax produced only B/3.2 million or 5.2 per cent of ordinary revenues. The absence of a significant tax burden is reflected in extremely high land values, since the price of land is not deflated by tax capitalization to any appreciable degree. Consequently, the cost of land represents a disproportionately high share of the initial cost of housing. This condition is being remedied gradually in the City of Panamá by a general reassessment that has been in progress since 1953. New construction is exempt from real estate taxes until December 31, 1967. This exemption, amounting to approximately 18 per cent of 1959 collections, adds a subsidy to land speculators in addition to the benefits landowners receive through low assessments. Collections are also weak, with the accumulated total of delinquency for ten years being about equal to the annual revenue. Only 54 per cent of property owners pay the tax on time.

In addition to the income and property taxes, there are inheritance and gift taxes which produce a relatively small amount of revenue. The progressivity of the death tax is reduced by basing the levy on the inherited shares rather than on the estate, and by exempting life insurance, government bonds, and foreign assets. The rates of the inheritance tax are also quite low, and the productivity is eroded further by a discount of 30 per cent of the tax. The average effective rate was only 9.3 per cent on all estates probated during the period from 1957 to 1961 inclusive, and only 16.6 per cent on estates with a gross value of B/500,000 to B/1,000,000.

A relatively large proportion of revenue, about 24 per cent, is derived from proprietary activities of the government, including the post office, water charges, the operation of the national lottery and other gambling activities, the annuity for the canal paid by the United States government, the sale of land and mineral rights, and other miscellaneous activities. These sources yielded B/14.9 million in 1961 compared to B/7.9 million in 1951, the proportion of ordinary revenues remaining about the same during the decade.

From this brief review of the revenue system, representing merely an insight into the ensuing twelve chapters of this study, three conspicuous faults and weaknesses are apparent: 1) Panamá has played "give-away" with the tax system, which has resulted in an excessive narrowness of nearly every tax base. 2) Tax administration has suffered from a long period of neglect. 3) There is an excessive reliance on indirect taxes that has a regressive effect.

In coming to the conclusion that the tax system is excessively regressive, it must be admitted that no incidence study of the whole of the revenue system was attempted, principally because of the absence of necessary data. But this omission does not appear to be very important. Whether a tax system is unduly regressive or not depends on a policy conclusion with respect to the prevailing distribution of income and wealth. If the conclusion is that this distribution is undesirably unequal, it follows that the tax system should be made more progressive as a corrective.

Expenditures

The expenditures of the national government completely dominate the public sector. In 1961, these expenditures amounted to B/86.1 million, including interest on the public debt, subsidies, and transfers. On the other hand, the spending of all municipalities amounted only to B/3.2 million. It is to be expected, therefore, that the national government would perform many of the tasks that are often undertaken by local governments in other countries. These include most of the responsibility for education, public works, water, sewage, and police and fire departments. Historically, this development is probably due to the dominance of the capital city, and to a reluctance to share power and control. Whatever the reason, however, social and economic forces probably will operate to decentralize government activities. These problems are discussed in the chapter on municipal finance.

Ranked in order of amounts spent, the four regular government departments with

TABLE 1.3

National Government Expenditures, 1951 and 1961

(Millions of Balboas)

Departments	1951	1961
National Assembly	416	1,071
Controller General	504	1,405
Presidency	1	683
Government and Justice	6,249	8,141
Foreign Relations	696	1,169
Finance and the Treasury	1,965	1,930
Education	7,568	15,991
University of Panamá	546	1,152
Public Works	7,464	23,658
Agriculture, Commerce and Industry	1,364	1,474
Office of Price Regulation	—	89
Labor, Social Welfare and Health	6,361	14,101
Judiciary	1	692
Public Attorney	1	393
Electoral Tribunal	—	329
TOTAL	33,133	72,278
Subsidies and extraordinary	1,303	10,733
Interest on public debt	543	3,067
TOTAL	34,979	86,078

[1] Included within Government and Justice.
Source: Contraloría General de la República, Dirección de Estadística y Censo.

TABLE 1.4

Consumption and Investment Expenditures of the Public Sector, 1952 to 1961

(Millions of Balboas)

| | Public Sector | | | Gross Private Investment | Gross Domestic Product (Adjusted)[1] |
	Consumption Expenditures (Adjusted)[1]	Investment Expenditures (Adjusted)[1]	Total		
1952	35.4	10.9	46.3	21.3	296.0
1953	33.9	9.0	42.9	26.6	310.2
1954	37.1	8.1	45.2	27.5	320.9
1955	39.1	12.6	51.7	26.5	344.0
1956	45.2	23.0	68.2	32.6	361.7
1957	44.7	7.5	52.2	51.0	389.9
1958	49.3	14.2	63.5	46.7	395.8
1959	51.6	19.7	71.3	46.3	420.9
1960	55.6	16.3	71.9	61.3	445.8
1961[2]	64.4	29.4	93.8	65.1	496.3
	456.3	150.7	607.0	404.9	3,781.5

[1] Consumption and investment expenditures of the public sector have been adjusted upward from those reported in the national accounts to include salaries paid by autonomous agencies and investment expenditures charged against loans. It was also necessary to adjust the gross domestic product by the same amounts. The data, therefore, differ from those in *Ingreso Nacional*, 1950–58, 1955–59. All data are from the Dirección General de Estadística y Censo.

[2] Preliminary.

the highest expenditures in 1961 were the Ministry of Public Works, the Ministry of Education, the Ministry of Labor, Social Welfare and Health, and the Ministry of Government and Justice. Together, these four accounted for 85 per cent of the expenditures of regular government departments. Table 1.3 shows the changes in expenditures of regular departments for the period from 1951 to 1961.

The importance of public sector expenditures in the economy may be gauged by comparing total public sector expenditures on goods and services with the gross domestic product, and public investment with private investment. For the decade 1952 to 1961, total public sector expenditures on goods and services increased from 15.6 per cent to 16.1 per cent of the gross domestic product. Both public and private investment increased greatly over the decade, the former just short of tripling and the latter more than tripling. Public investment represented 37.2 per cent of private investment for the period, with no clear tendency for this percentage to increase or decrease. As it may be seen from Table 1.4, it was a decade of consider-

able economic growth with gross domestic product rising by about 80 per cent from 1952 to 1961 inclusive.

Table 1.4 also shows that the capital expenditures of the public sector for the decade amounted to B/150.7 million, or nearly 25 per cent of total public sector expenditures on goods and services. This percentage increased from 23.5 per cent in 1952 to 31.3 per cent in 1961. And if expenditures on education and health are considered as investments in human capital, public sector investment shows a further increase for the decade. The expenditures of the Ministry of Education and the Ministry of Labor, Social Welfare and Health increased from B/13.8 million in 1951 to B/30.1 million in 1961, or by 173 per cent (see Table 1.3).

There is no question that the growth in public investment during the past decade has had beneficial effects on the economy. In anyone's scale of the factors that contribute to economic growth, the role of capital formation would be placed high on the list. The investments in public works, roads, communications, education, and public health have contributed to a rising national income.

Yet complacency would be out of order. Illiteracy, poor health, poverty, unemployment, inadequate housing, and a generally deficient economic infrastructure are so apparent that the increased emphasis on investment expenditures during the past decade can be considered merely as an initial deposit on the necessary level of public investment.

The Public Debt

From 1952 to 1961 inclusive, government expenditures, including interest on the public debt, exceeded government revenues by B/73.3 million. In only two years, 1953 and 1954, were there surpluses. In the latter part of the decade, 1959 to 1961, very sizable deficits occurred, accounting for roughly two-thirds of the total deficit for the ten-year period. As a result, the total debt of the national government increased from B/38.3 million at the end of 1952 to B/111.1 million at the end of 1961. In addition, the debt of the autonomous institutions increased from B/7.0 million in 1952 to B/12.06 million in 1961. With these rather consistent deficits, and not an insignificant increase in debt, it is somewhat ironic to hear Panamanian officials claim that the budget is always in balance.[4]

A large amount of the public debt is held by the Social Security System. On December 31, 1961, the System held B/29.4 million of national government bonds and B/9.8 million of obligations of the autonomous institutions. Thus, of the total national government debt outstanding on December 31, 1961 of B/111.1 million, the Social Security System held 26.5 per cent. This debt is in the nature of an intra-governmental loan, financed by taxes, euphemistically called contributions.

Of the total national government debt of B/111.1 million on December 31, 1961, the external debt amounted to B/39 million, and the internal debt, including current obligations (floating debt), to B/72 million. To

place these magnitudes in perspective, the public debt amounted to 27.2 per cent of the national income of B/407.3 million in 1961 as compared to 15.8 per cent of the national income in 1952. The external debt on December 31, 1961 represented 9.6 per cent of the national income, while the total debt owned by the public, i.e., excluding the holdings of the Social Security System, amounted to 20 per cent of the national income. While there are no absolute standards for measuring the burden of the debt, these ratios do not appear to indicate an unusual or dangerous state of affairs. Compared to most industrialized countries, the ratios are quite low.

Nor does the burden of carrying the debt appear to be serious at the present time. The total interest expense in 1961 amounted to B/3.1 million, of which B/1.6 million was paid on external debt and B/1.5 million on internal debt. In addition, the amortization requirements of the foreign debt were B/0.6 million and of the internal debt B/1.2 million, excluding payments of current obligations. Total interest expense represented 3.6 per cent of government expenditures, while amortization costs amounted to an additional 2.1 per cent.

But there is cause for concern arising from the higher deficits recorded in the period from 1959 to 1961. Table 1.5 shows a deficit of B/22.8 million in 1961, approximately double the size of the deficit in 1960. Maintenance of deficits of this magnitude would undoubtedly have some adverse repercussions eventually.

Another cause for concern is the excessive amount of current obligations (floating debt). In addition to the aforementioned amortization requirements in 1961, payments of current obligations amounted to B/11.5 million, while new current obligations of B/16.2 million were incurred. The total amount of current obligations at the end of 1961 amounted to B/24.9 million, of which B/15.7 million were to be charged against new-funded debt. The amount of current obligations used to pay contractors depressed the market for

---

[4] Some Panamanian officials consider the budget to be balanced whenever actual borrowing does not exceed anticipated borrowing.

TABLE 1.5

National Government Operations and the Public Debt, 1952 to 1961

(Millions of Balboas)

	Receipts Excluding Borrowing	Expenditures Excluding Debt Operations	Interest and Miscellaneous Debt	Surplus or Deficit (−)[1]	Internal Debt	External Debt	Total Public Debt[1]
1952	36.3	41.5	.7	−5.9	26.5	11.6	38.3
1953	41.4	40.0	1.1	.3	30.0	11.4	41.4
1954	42.7	40.4	1.1	1.2	30.4	11.1	41.5
1955	45.3	46.5	1.2	−2.4	32.4	11.8	44.1
1956	48.5	57.8	1.3	−10.6	40.6	12.6	53.2
1957	50.3	50.0	1.6	−1.4	42.3	13.9	56.4
1958	53.1	55.8	2.2	−4.9	36.7	28.1	64.9
1959	51.4	64.2	2.4	−15.3	50.6	29.2	79.8
1960	57.6	66.0	3.0	−11.5	54.4	36.4	90.8
1961	63.2	83.0	3.1	−22.8	72.0	39.0	111.1

[1] Totals do not equal because of rounding-off.

Source: Hacienda Pública y Finanzas, 4° trimestre, 1961; and *Informe del Contralor General*, October, 1962.

government bonds in 1962, resulting in a temporary fall in price of about 20 per cent. This was simply a mechanical problem of an excess issuance of debt, which could not be absorbed by the market, and which could have been avoided by sounder debt management. Nevertheless, this experience demonstrates a need for more orderly marketing of short-term obligations and for anticipating deficits on current account.

The deficits of B/73.3 million incurred by the national government from 1952 to 1961 could be justified as a necessary stimulus to an economy suffering from extensive unemployment. In 1951, 8.4 per cent of the labor force was unemployed. By 1955, unemployment had risen to 10.5 per cent, and in 1961 had fallen only to 8.8 per cent. The continuing heavy unemployment persists despite the fact that the economy expanded considerably during the decade. National income rose about 80 per cent, and nearly 60,000 more persons were employed at the end of the period than were employed at the beginning.

What is surprising in view of the large deficits (relatively speaking), and the significant increase in private investment, is that inflation did not result. The price index used to deflate private consumption expenditures in the national income accounts shows a rise of only 3.8 per cent from 1950 to 1960.

The answer appears to lie not in a low marginal propensity to consume—it is 90 per cent or more—but in the institutional characteristics of the economy. Considering the extensive use of the United States dollar as a means of exchange, government deficits that are not financed by foreign loans affect the money supply only to the extent that bank loans may increase as a result of the deficits. The reserves of the banks are not affected directly. As a result of a relatively high propensity to import goods and services, deficits not financed by foreign loans will actually tend to reduce the reserves of the banks. Aside from the monetary effects, increased purchases of foreign goods and services tend to reduce the secondary effects of the deficit. Finally, to the extent that government deficits are financed by the Social Security System, their inflationary effect is offset by current savings.

The evidence of the past decade indicates that it would not be wrong for the government to finance its increased burdens in part by borrowing. But a continuation of the deficits of the past few years would appear to be a threat to price stability.

Revenue Projections and Needs

The increase in revenues during the decade 1952 to 1961 was due to an increase in the rates of several taxes, to the adoption of a few minor new taxes, and to higher levels of economic activity. If these changes continue into the future, revenues will continue to grow. In order to estimate the increase in revenues, the annual data for each major source of revenue for the period 1952 to 1961 were correlated with the national income by the least squares method and the linear relationships were determined. The choice of the national income as the independent variable was made on the assumption that the principal determinant of governmental revenues is the level of economic activity.

In Table 1.6, the values of the relationships obtained by this method are indicated in Columns 1 and 2, and the correlation coefficients are shown in Column 3. The values in Column 3 suggest very high correlations of the national income with revenues from foreign commerce, other indirect taxes, the property tax, national services and monopolies, and total ordinary revenues, but only fair correlations of the national income with the income tax and the inheritance and gift taxes.

By comparing Columns 2 and 4, an indication may be obtained of the trend as compared to the existing relationship. Column 4 indicates the ratios of each revenue source to the national income in 1961, while Column 2 shows the trend of the ratios. The entries in Columns 2 and 4 indicate that total government revenues will tend to decrease as a percentage of the national income. Among the particular revenue sources, taxes on foreign commerce and national services and monopolies will tend to decline, inheritance and gift taxes will remain about the same, while the others will tend to increase.

Estimates of government revenues for the years 1962 to 1967 were obtained by using the linear relationships shown in Table 1.6 and by assuming an annual growth in the national income of 5.5 per cent. These estimates are shown in Table 1.7. They indicate that the ordinary revenues of the national government will increase, depending on the method of estimating used, to B/84.7 million or B/87.4 million by 1967. The first estimate (I) was obtained by summing the results of the several estimates for the specific revenue sources shown, while the second (II) was obtained directly from the linear relationship of total ordinary revenues to the national income.

But government expenditures as well as revenues may be expected to increase substantially over the next few years. In addition to the increased development expenditures shown previously in Table 1.1, the ordinary government expenditures may be expected to increase substantially due to higher salaries and wages, additional services, and the expanding needs of a rapidly growing population.

TABLE 1.6

Linear Relationships between Revenues and the National Income, 1952 to 1961

Revenue Source	(1) "a" Values (Millions of Balboas)	(2) "b" Values	(3) Correlation Coefficients (Per Cent)	(4) Ratios of Revenues to National Income, 1961
Foreign commerce	3.5073	.0484	93.4	.0567
Other indirect taxes	−0.5454	.0251	96.0	.0244
Income tax	−0.7956	.0312	66.0	.0262
Property tax	−0.4324	.0084	94.0	.0079
Inheritance and gift taxes	−0.2653	.0016	60.7	.0016
National services and monopolies	33.1074	.0202	94.4	.0366
Total ordinary revenues	1.5087	.1528	97.3	.1535

TABLE 1.7

Estimates of Ordinary Government Revenues for 1962 to 1967

(Millions of Balboas)

Revenue Source	1962	1963	1964	1965	1966	1967
Foreign commerce	24.3	25.4	26.6	27.9	29.3	30.7
Other indirect taxes	10.2	10.8	11.4	12.1	12.8	13.5
Total indirect taxes	34.5	36.2	38.0	40.0	42.1	44.2
Income tax	12.6	13.3	14.8	14.9	15.8	16.7
Property tax	3.3	3.5	3.7	4.0	4.2	4.5
Inheritance and gift taxes	0.4	0.5	0.5	0.6	0.6	0.7
Total direct taxes	16.3	17.3	19.0	19.5	20.6	21.9
National services and monopolies	11.8	12.3	12.8	13.3	13.9	14.5
Other[1]	3.6	3.7	3.8	3.9	4.0	4.1
Total proprietary and miscellaneous income	15.4	16.0	16.6	17.2	17.9	18.6
Total ordinary revenues I	66.2	69.5	73.6	76.7	80.6	84.7
Total ordinary revenues II[2]	67.2	70.8	74.6	78.6	82.9	87.4
Assumed national income	429.7	453.3	478.2	504.5	532.2	561.4
Ordinary revenues I as a percentage of the national income	15.41	15.33	15.39	15.20	15.14	15.09
Ordinary revenues II as a percentage of the national income	15.64	15.62	15.60	15.58	15.58	15.57

[1] Because of the importance of the canal annuity in this category, an increase is assumed of only B/0.11 million per annum. This is the average annual increase in the remainder of the category.

[2] Based on the linear relationship shown in Table 1.6.

In making estimates of future government expenditures, it was assumed that the dynamic growth in education expenditures would continue through 1966 at an annual rate of 11.0 per cent, double the assumed growth in the national income of 5.5 per cent. Public works will be affected mainly by the new development program, but existing expenditures were assumed to increase at a rate of 3.25 per cent per annum. Labor and welfare expenditures, other than those included in the new development program, as well as "other" government expenditures, were assumed to increase at the modest annual rate of only 2.5 per cent. Special expenditures (subsidies, advances, and extra-budgetary) were estimated at the same rate of increase as the assumed annual increase in the national income of 5.5 per cent. Interest expense for 1962 was assumed to increase by 6 per cent of the 1961 deficit, while for the years 1963 to 1966 it was assumed to increase at the rate of 6 per cent of the projected borrowing of the previous year.

The results of these projections are shown in Table 1.8. As it may be seen, government expenditures, including the planned investments under the development program, are expected to increase from B/100.5 million in 1962 to B/132.0 million in 1966.

These projected expenditures now may be related to estimated revenues and the assumption for financing the development program shown previously in Table 1.1. Subtracting estimated revenues and grants from the projected expenditures leaves a series of deficits rising from B/21.8 million in 1962 to B/38.9 million in 1966. Subtracting further the projected borrowing in the development program leaves additional revenue needs rising from B/5.2 million in 1962 to B/22.4 million in 1966. *Unless these additional revenues are provided through the tax system, it is unlikely that the development program can be completed under the assumed methods of financing.* Moreover, the additional revenue needs will be much greater than those shown if the assumed annual grants of B/12.5 million do not materialize.

FISCAL POLICY FRAMEWORK

In assessing Panamá's fiscal system and its capacity to make economic and social development a realizable goal, the characteristics and objectives of a desirable revenue system should be made explicit. It is these criteria relative to the faults and shortcomings of the system that result in the recommendations for fiscal reform appearing in this survey. The criteria underlying the recommendations fall into two groups: those that apply in general to the revenue system, and those that refer to particular taxes.

General Propositions

1) Panamá is in need of additional government revenue. This revenue is necessary to provide the investment needs of the de-velopment program, to finance rising levels of government consumption expenditures, and to reduce budgetary deficits.

2) The raising of additional government resources is more important in terms of promoting economic development in Panamá than the maintenance of generally low tax rates as an encouragement to private savings and investment. At the same time, however, efforts should be made to adjust the tax system in such a way that it will be conducive to private savings and investment.

3) The tax system, while not the only means for mitigating economic and social inequality, is a powerful means to this end. One can even go so far as to say that tax reform should be used in Panamá for promoting a better distribution of income and wealth even in the absence of a need for additional government revenue. Accordingly, revisions in the revenue structure should emphasize more effective levies on the owners of land and capital, and a reduction of taxes that have a regressive effect. Another way of saying this is that tax reform in Panamá should involve a development of

TABLE 1.8

Projected Government Expenditures and Revenue Needs, 1962 to 1967

(Millions of Balboas)

Expenditure Category	1961 (Actual)	1962	1963	1964	1965	1966
Education	15.991	17.750	19.703	21.870	24.276	26.946
Public works	23.658	24.427	25.209	26.028	26.874	27.747
Labor and welfare	14.101	14.454	14.815	15.185	15.565	15.954
Other	18.527	18.990	19.465	19.952	20.451	20.962
Special (subsidies, advances, extra-budgetary)	10.733	11.323	11.946	12.603	13.296	14.027
Interest	3.067	4.437	5.433	6.465	7.533	8.637
TOTAL	86.077	91.381	96.571	102.103	107.995	114.273
Projected increase in development expenditures	—	9.100	11.400	13.200	15.600	17.700
TOTAL PROJECTED GOVERNMENT EXPENDITURES		100.481	107.971	115.303	123.595	131.973
Projected government revenues		66.200	69.500	73.600	76.700	80.600
Projected grants		12.500	12.500	12.500	12.500	12.500
Estimated deficits		21.781	25.971	29.203	34.395	38.873
Projected borrowing		16.600	17.200	17.800	18.400	16.500
Additional revenue needs		5.181	8.771	11.403	15.995	22.373

direct taxes and a de-emphasis of indirect taxes.

4) There is ample capacity in Panamá to increase public revenues. This is evident from the relatively low percentage of the national income that is obtained in public revenue. The capacity of the country to bear a heavier tax burden is also enhanced by an unequal distribution of income and wealth.

5) The tax system should have stability in the sense that it is a dependable source of revenue, but it should also have flexibility, or the capacity to be productive of more revenue as the economy grows and expands.

6) Both for compliance and enforcement purposes, the tax system should not be complicated and obtuse. In other words, the venerable tax maxims of simplicity and certainty should be acknowledged.

7) Strengthening the fiscal resources of local governments is desirable on the grounds that it fosters democratic processes and, in some instances, is the most efficient way of providing public services.

8) It is recognized that tax incentives have a legitimate place in an over-all development program for the purpose of inducing resources into more desired uses and impeding their use in less desired areas. Historical experience suggests, however, that tax incentives should be used with caution and restraint in order to prevent undue revenue losses.

9) Autonomous agencies should not be so independent that they are free of executive control. When undertaking activities of a proprietary nature, they should be operated so as to be self-sustaining.

10) Strengthening the administration of a tax system is equally as important as perfecting its structural design. However, the improvement of administration is a long-run and gradualistic undertaking and should not be viewed as a substitute for structural changes in the tax system. In the final analysis, adequate tax administration depends on the employment of more and better staff resources.

Particular Taxes

1) Because of its interpersonal equity, broad base, and progressive features, the personal income tax is viewed as the keystone of an equitable and productive tax system. There is a presumption in favor of a unitary income tax, encompassing all forms of income, including the taxation of dividends and capital gains.

2) A progressive rate schedule should be avoided in the application of a corporate income tax, for progressive rates detract from the growth of corporations and result in the splitting of corporate entities.

3) A progressive inheritance tax is desirable as a means of reducing the importance of inherited wealth in the distribution of wealth and income. This tax should be complemented by a similar tax on *inter-vivos* gifts.

4) There is a presumption in favor of extending the liability for income taxation to income received from foreign countries. Foreign assets should also be included for purposes of inheritance taxation.

5) The taxation of urban real estate, levied at a progressive rate, has a convincing rationale both as a means of taxing an important form of wealth and as a levy on a luxury consumption item.

6) A progressive property tax should also be applied to agricultural land in order to increase the efficiency of land use and to promote the objectives of agrarian reform.

7) Indirect taxes, though undesirable in principle in terms of equity and their undesirable economic effects in distorting the price system, may be improved by simplification, by substituting *ad valorem* for specific taxes, and by the special taxation of luxury consumption items.

PROPOSALS FOR REFORM

Literally hundreds of recommendations for the reform of the Panamanian revenue system are advanced in the ensuing analytical chapters of this study. Since these recommendations are explained later in detail, and are also summarized at the end of each chapter, it would be repetitious to list all of them. Therefore, it is necessary merely to restate the principal recommendations, and then to demonstrate that they are designed to achieve the general objectives of a desirable revenue system.

Principal Recommendations

1) *The Income Tax.* There should be a shift in emphasis from corporate to personal income taxation. This may be accomplished by substituting a flat-rate tax on corporations for the present progressive schedule, and by taxing dividends at the personal level. Incentives should be improved by the provision of a carry-over of losses, liberalized depreciation, and the provision of more generous business deductions. On the other hand, loopholes such as the reserve fund for bad debts and the special insurance company reserves should be eliminated.

The base of the personal income tax should be broadened by the inclusion of foreign income and capital gains. Personal exemptions should be reduced, but their availability should be liberalized administratively so that they are freely obtainable. The principle of tax discrimination in favor of earned income should be abandoned and replaced by a system of taxing all income neutrally. Progressivity should be increased by raising the income tax rates on middle and upper income groups. The administration of the income tax should be strengthened by doubling the existing auditing staff and by obtaining technical assistance for the training of auditors in accounting and auditing procedures.

2) *Property Taxation.* For the rationalization of the urban real property tax, the base of the tax should be broadened by eliminating the exemption for new construction and by terminating the policy of granting a freeze of the property tax rate as an incentive to new firms. Property tax rates should be raised and made more progressive. The revaluation of property should be accelerated through foreign technical assistance. Property tax collections may be improved by eliminating the 10 per cent discount for paying the tax within thirty days, by adding an interest charge of 1 per cent per month to the amount of delinquent taxes, and by selling the property of delinquent taxpayers promptly.

When sufficient progress has been made on the revaluation of rural land, the B/30 per hectare minimum assessment of titled land and the B/.50 per hectare tax on the possession of untitled land should be repealed, and the property tax should be based on market value assessments. Public land should be distributed to the *campesinos* by gift rather than by sale, with a property tax exemption provided until the close of the second year.

3) *Inheritance and Gift Taxation.* The base of the tax should be broadened by altering the rule of tax jurisdiction from the source or location of the property to the residence of the heirs, by reducing the exemption of life insurance to B/10,000, and by terminating the issuance of tax-exempt government bonds. The revenue productivity and the progressivity of the tax should be strengthened by eliminating the 30 per cent reduction in the amount of the tax, and by increasing the tax rates on all inherited shares of more than B/25,000 by 50 per cent. The tax also should be simplified by classifying heirs into three instead of six groups. Administration may be improved by the valuation of estates, inherited shares, and gifts exclusively by personnel in the Ministry of Finance and the Treasury, and by their valuation at market value.

4) *Customs Duties.* Customs duties should be made less regressive in their incidence by substituting *ad valorem* for specific rates, and by utilizing direct subsidies instead of protective duties for nutritionally important foods consumed by low income groups. On the other hand, luxury goods should be subject to higher duties, but a system should be introduced for those goods that are important for the tourist trade so that tax-free purchases would be available for tourists.

Duties on capital goods should be reduced or eliminated, but the exemptions from other duties should be restricted. For purposes of simplification, the existing duties should be consolidated.

5) *Indirect Taxes.* Stamped paper, except where the tax is a charge for a service rendered by the government, should be eliminated, while the stamp taxes that are retained should be related to the cost of the service. *Ad valorem* excises should be substituted for specific taxes in the case of the slaughter tax, theatre admissions, and business license fees. The schedule of fees for registering corporations should be revised so that it is less regressive with respect to capital, and the base of the tax for registering transfers of real estate should be the sales price, or the fair market value, whichever is higher.

6) *Alcoholic Beverages. Ad valorem* instead of specific excises should be used as the basis for the internal excise taxes on beer and liquors of higher alcoholic content, and the tax discount for storing rum more than three years should be eliminated. The customs duty on imported beer should be reduced to promote more competition for the domestic brewing industry. To eliminate the smuggling of liquor from the Canal Zone to Panamá, all liquors of higher alcoholic content consumed in the Zone should be subject to the full amount of Panamanian taxes. The administration of liquor taxes would be improved by extending civil service to include tax collectors.

7) *Autonomous Agencies.* The status of autonomous agencies should be reserved for proprietary activities that have the likelihood of generating their own revenues, and denied to agencies that have merely control or regulatory functions. Also, specialization of function or responsibility should be the rule in establishing autonomous agencies. The same standards of accountability, personnel selection, job security, and freedom from political patronage that apply to regular government departments should be required of autonomous agencies. All financial resources of the Social Security System should be invested in government bonds. The purpose of government-operated lotteries and games of chance should be to make gambling available but not to encourage that activity through advertising and propaganda.

8) *Tax Incentives.* Because of a serious loss of revenue, the income tax concessions granted for twenty-five years to firms under the 1950 law should be restricted. This may be done either by limiting the exemption to fifteen years for each firm or by taxing the dividends of *all* corporations at the personal income tax level. A new tax incentive law should be enacted providing for a maximum period for contracts of five to ten years, granting income tax and customs duty exemptions, and providing limited and diminishing tariff protection.

9) *Colón Free Zone.* Subsidies to the Colón Free Zone by the national government should be terminated, and the Free Zone also should assume responsibility for the payment of grants to the city of Colón. Firms should not be allowed to operate in the Free Zone unless at least 60 per cent of their sales are made to foreign countries. Domestic sales, as well as those made to ships in transit and to the Canal Zone, should be subject to the full amount of Panamanian taxes, while foreign sales should be subject to a 75 per cent reduction of the current income tax rates.

10) *Municipal Finance.* The municipalities of Panamá should be given additional expenditure responsibilities as well as provided with greater revenues. Municipal governments should assume most of the responsibility for primary education, health services, the construction and maintenance of city streets, and garbage removal. To undertake those services, a doubling of tax revenues is needed. Additional revenues should be obtained by a steeply progressive registration fee on vehicles and by either a property tax or income tax "supplement." The current taxes on commercial and industrial establishments should be abandoned.

11) *Net Wealth Taxation.* Consideration should be given to the adoption of a net

wealth tax when adequate *cadastral* values of real property are available.

Achievements

1) *Additional Revenues.* The additional revenues that would result from the adoption of all of the recommendations is impossible to calculate for several reasons. For example, in many instances, such as the taxation of capital gains and dividends under the income tax, there is an absence of data necessary for revenue estimating. In other cases, the proposals involve such broad structural changes—such as the taxation of corporations at a flat rate under a corporate income tax—that only the general direction and not the specifics of the reform may be indicated. Further, the recommendations are so comprehensive that they could only be implemented in their entirety gradually and over the long run.

Although no upper limit on additional revenues may be indicated, it is possible to demonstrate that the recommendations probably satisfy the test of fiscal adequacy. During the course of the research, a number of specific proposals based on the research were prepared for consideration by the executive branch of the government. These proposals involved only the income, property, and inheritance taxes. Despite the fact that these reforms covered only a relatively small number of all proposals for tax reform, and merely represented a first step toward an improved revenue system, estimates indicated that their adoption would result in approximately B/4.5 million in additional revenue, an increase of close to 10 per cent of 1961 total tax revenues. From this evidence, it is apparent that the tax reform proposals in their totality provide ample opportunities for Panamá to obtain all the government revenue that would be needed to achieve its economic and social goals.

2) *Mitigation of Economic and Social Inequality.* Several recommendations serve to promote a better distribution of income and wealth. Among the more important are an increase in the progressivity of the income, inheritance, and property taxes, the taxation of dividends and capital gains under the income tax, the inclusion of foreign income under the income tax and foreign assets under the inheritance tax, higher taxes on luxury consumption goods, and a revision of indirect taxes so as to reduce their regressive impact. These measures would serve to place a relatively heavier tax burden on the owners of capital, and would also recast the tax system so that there would be more reliance placed on direct as compared to indirect taxes.

3) *Encouragement of Private Savings and Investment.* Beyond the fact that private saving and investment are encouraged generally by a tax system that is equitable, orderly, and rational, specific efforts have been made to promote private enterprise and initiative by recommending the elimination of the special surtax on unearned income (business enterprises), by substituting a flat-rate corporate income tax for the current progressive schedule, by proposals for strengthening the personal income tax and lightening the tax burden at the business level, and by such specific measures as a carry-over of losses, accelerated depreciation, and a more liberal policy with respect to business deductions.

4) *Stability and Flexibility.* Stability of the revenue system has been developed by proposals that would broaden the bases of the major taxes through closing loopholes and eliminating exemptions. Flexibility has been promoted by a greater reliance on the personal income tax, which is elastic with respect to yield as the national income rises.

5) *Simplicity and Certainty.* Proposals that serve to make the tax system less complicated and arbitrary include the elimination of the differential surtaxes on earned and unearned income under the income tax, a simplified system of classifying heirs under the inheritance tax, the elimination of nuisance taxes such as stamped paper, the substitution of *ad valorem* for specific excises, and the recommended elimination of business license taxes at the municipal level.

CHAPTER 2

The Income Tax —
Statutory Provisions and
Functional Problems

STATUTORY PROVISIONS

THE INCOME TAX was introduced in Panamá by presidential decree in 1934, but in a rudimentary form that was narrowly applied. This early law was superceded in 1941 by a much broader legislative statute that in revised form is the present income tax law.[1] Before elaborating in greater detail on certain features of the present income tax, a few of its basic elements may be presented in outline form:

1) There is a single income tax law, with the same progressive rates applying to the income of individuals, partnerships, and corporations. Partnerships are taxed on the totality of their income rather than on the basis of individual shares. 2) A distinction is made between earned and unearned income, with the latter bearing a heavier surtax. 3) Another surtax is levied on single individuals who have no obligation under the requirements of the *Civil Code* to support

dependents. 4) Because personal exemptions have very limited application, and there are no privileged personal deductions, Panamá's income tax is close to a gross income levy on salaries and wages; however, it has the characteristics of a net income tax on profits. 5) Corporate earnings are construed to be taxed in full at the business level; therefore, dividends are not subject to taxation at the individual level. 6) Income tax liability is based on source rather than on residence, with all income arising within Panamá taxable and all income arising outside Panamá exempt.

Exemptions and Exclusions

Gross taxable income is defined broadly to cover all forms of compensation for personal services, profits, rent, and interest. At the same time, however, there is a lengthy list of exemptions: 1) the net income of single individuals and of all business entities which does not exceed B/900 annually, the income of married couples which does not exceed B/1800, and the exemption of B/100 per dependent minor; 2) capital gains, if they do not constitute a regularly recurring

---

[1] For the early history of income taxation in Panamá, see Simeon E. Leland, *A Report on the Revenue System of Panamá*, A Report to the President and Members of the Economic and Fiscal Commission, June 15, 1946, pp. 92–115.

source of income and if they are realized on assets held for more than two years; 3) dividends received by shareholders; 4) interest derived from Panamanian government securities, and from savings accounts maintained in commercial banks; 5) income which is exempt from the income tax by virtue of special contracts with the government; 6) income derived from maritime commerce by merchant vessels registered in Panamá; 7) income received from foreign countries; 8) lottery prizes and other income from games of chance administered by the Panamanian government; 9) income received by charitable, religious, and other nonprofit institutions; 10) amounts received as compensation for labor accidents and all insurance payments; 11) social security payments; 12) salaries and fees paid to personnel of the diplomatic corps; and 13) inheritances.

In the application of the B/900 exemption for single individuals, partnerships, and corporations, and the exemption of B/1800 for married couples, any income received in excess of these exempt amounts renders the totality of the income taxable. In other words, an income of B/900 received by a single individual is exempt, but an income of B/901 is taxable on the whole of this amount.

The exemption of B/100 for each dependent minor is restricted to minors under the age of 21 years, unless the dependent is incapable of self-support or is continuing studies at the expense of the taxpayer. There are no exemptions for dependent relatives other than children, and no privileged personal deductions as for medical expenses or for contributions. The use of exemptions for minors does not serve to render a taxable income exempt, even though the income is reduced below the exemption limit. For example, a married couple receiving B/1900 and utilizing four exemptions totaling B/400, would have an income subject to tax of B/1500, even though an income of B/1800 would be exempt for a couple with no minor dependents.

Capital gains are excluded from taxation if they do not constitute a regularly recurring

source of income and are realized on property or investment held for more than two years. Gains on assets held for less than two years are taxed as other income. All capital gains are treated similarly, whether arising from the sale of land, buildings, corporate stock, or other assets.

Dividends and interest receive different tax treatment. Dividends are exempt when received by individuals, on the theory that they have already been taxed at the corporate level. On the other hand, interest payments on the bonded indebtedness of a corporation are deductible before application of the tax at the business level, and are taxable at the individual level. Interest received from an individual is taxable, but interest earned on government bonds or received from savings accounts in commercial banks is exempt.

Panamá taxes on the basis of source of income rather than on the residence or domicile of the recipient, with the result that all income arising within Panamá is taxable, and all income arising outside the country is exempt. Thus a Panamanian individual or corporation receiving income from abroad is not subject to the Panamanian income tax, but a United States citizen or corporation earning income in Panamá is subject to taxation. It is possible, however, for a corporation to have an office and employees in the Republic, and still not pay a Panamanian income tax, if the office merely directs the purchases and sales and the merchandise does not physically arrive in Panamá.

Normal and Surtax Rates

A basic or normal income tax rate is applied to the net income of all taxable individuals, partnerships, and corporations. Within recent years, the normal rates, shown in Tables 2.1 to 2.4 of this chapter, have been increased in 1953 and 1962. The change in 1953 was significant, altering a progressive schedule rising from 2 per cent on incomes up to B/2400 to 16 per cent on incomes of more than B/1,000,000, to a schedule of rates of from 2 to 34 per cent on the same brackets of income. (See Tables 2.1 and 2.2.) More moderate was the change in 1961 (Table 2.3), when the tax brackets were revised, and the progression was increased to one of 2 per cent on incomes of less than B/2400 to 35 per cent on incomes of more than B/750,000.

In addition to the normal tax, unearned income (principally profit earned by business entities) is subject to a surtax. Business entities were subject to a 20 per cent surtax during the period from 1941 to 1961, with this rate being increased to 40 per cent in 1962. There was no surtax on the earned income of individuals (wages and salaries) until the imposition of a 10 per cent levy in 1962, an additional tax restricted in its application to incomes in excess of B/1,799.

When the surtax on business entities was increased from 20 to 40 per cent in 1962, a ceiling was placed on the combination of the normal and surtax rates so that the effective rate of the two taxes would not exceed 42 per cent. In effect, this means that business

TABLE 2.1

Income Tax Rates, 1946 to 1952

Taxable Income Brackets (Balboas)		Normal Tax Rates[1] (Per Cent)	Normal Tax Rates Plus Surtax on Business Entities[1] (Per Cent)
Up to	2,400	2.0	2.4
2,400–	3,600	2.5	3.0
3,600–	4,800	3.0	3.6
4,800–	6,000	3.5	4.2
6,000–	8,400	4.0	4.8
8,400–	12,000	4.5	5.4
12,000–	16,800	5.0	6.0
16,800–	22,800	5.5	6.6
22,800–	30,000	6.0	7.2
30,000–	38,400	6.5	7.8
38,400–	50,000	7.0	8.4
50,000–	60,000	8.0	9.6
60,000–	70,000	9.0	10.8
70,000–	80,000	10.0	12.0
80,000–	90,000	11.0	13.2
90,000–	100,000	12.0	14.4
100,000–	250,000	13.0	15.6
250,000–	500,000	14.0	16.8
500,000–	1,000,000	15.0	18.0
Over 1,000,000		16.0	19.2

[1] Both earned income (principally wages and salaries) and unearned income (principally profits, and roughly synonymous to the earnings of business entities) were subject to the normal tax rates, while unearned income was subject to a surtax of 20 per cent.

TABLE 2.2

Income Tax Rates, 1953 to 1960

Taxable Income Brackets (Balboas)		Normal Tax Rates[1] (Per Cent)	Normal Tax Rates Plus Surtax on Business Entities[1] (Per Cent)
Up to	2,400	2.0	2.4
2,400–	3,600	2.5	3.0
3,600–	4,800	3.0	3.6
4,800–	6,000	4.0	4.8
6,000–	8,400	5.0	6.0
8,400–	12,000	6.0	7.2
12,000–	16,800	7.0	8.4
16,800–	22,800	8.0	9.6
22,800–	30,000	9.0	10.80
30,000–	40,000	10.25	12.30
40,000–	50,000	11.50	13.80
50,000–	60,000	12.75	15.30
60,000–	70,000	14.00	16.80
70,000–	80,000	15.25	18.30
80,000–	90,000	16.50	19.80
90,000–	100,000	17.75	21.30
100,000–	150,000	19.25	23.10
150,000–	200,000	20.75	24.90
200,000–	300,000	22.50	27.00
300,000–	400,000	24.25	29.10
400,000–	550,000	26.25	31.50
550,000–	750,000	28.50	34.20
750,000–	1,000,000	31.00	37.20
Over 1,000,000			

[1] Both earned income (principally wages and salaries) and unearned income (principally profits, and roughly synonymous to the earnings of business entities) were subject to the normal tax rates, while unearned income was subject to a surtax of 20 per cent.

entities are taxed progressively up to an income of B/1,064,200, but incomes in excess of this amount are taxed at a flat rate of 42 per cent. Apparently, the ceiling on the effective rate was established in order to provide relief for a few very large corporations.

There are certain problems and inconsistencies in the application of the surtax on unearned income. For individuals receiving income from both salaries and profits, a specific allocation between the two must be made in order to levy the heavier surtax on profits. Although a surtax of 10 per cent is imposed on professional workers such as doctors, lawyers, or architects, even if these persons form partnerships for business purposes, a surtax of 40 per cent is levied on a group of engineers operating an engineering firm. A conspicuous exemption from the surtax is rental income, even though it may

TABLE 2.3

Income Tax Rates Applicable for 1961

Taxable Income Brackets (Balboas)	Tax Rates[1] (Per Cent)	Normal Tax Rates Plus Surtax on Business Entities[1] (Per Cent)
Up to 2,400	2.0	2.4
2,400– 3,600	2.5	3.0
3,600– 4,800	3.0	3.6
4,800– 6,000	5.0	6.0
6,000– 8,400	6.0	7.2
8,400– 12,000	7.0	8.4
12,000– 20,000	9.0	10.8
20,000– 40,000	11.0	13.2
40,000– 60,000	15.0	18.0
60,000– 80,000	18.0	21.6
80,000– 100,000	21.0	25.2
100,000– 150,000	24.0	28.8
150,000– 300,000	27.0	32.4
300,000– 500,000	30.0	36.0
500,000– 750,000	33.0	39.6
Over 750,000	35.0	42.0

[1] Both earned income (principally wages and salaries) and unearned income (principally profits, and roughly synonymous to the earnings of business entities) were subject to the normal tax rates, while unearned income was subject to a surtax of 20 per cent.

TABLE 2.4

Income Tax Rates Applicable for 1962

Taxable Income Brackets (Balboas)	Normal Tax Rates[1] (Per Cent)	Normal Tax Rates Plus Surtax for Individuals[1] (Per Cent)	Normal Tax Rates Plus Surtax on Business Entities[1] (Per Cent)
Up to 2,400	2.0	2.20	2.80
2,400– 3,600	2.5	2.75	3.50
3,600– 4,800	3.0	3.30	4.20
4,800– 6,000	5.0	5.50	7.00
6,000– 8,400	6.0	6.60	8.40
8,400– 12,000	7.0	7.70	9.80
12,000– 20,000	9.0	9.90	12.60
20,000– 40,000	11.0	12.10	15.40
40,000– 60,000	15.0	16.50	21.00
60,000– 80,000	18.0	19.80	25.20
80,000– 100,000	21.0	23.10	29.40
100,000– 150,000	24.0	26.40	33.60
150,000– 300,000	27.0	29.70	37.80
300,000– 500,000	30.0	33.00	42.00
500,000– 750,000	33.0	36.30	46.20
Over 750,000	35.0	38.50	49.00

[1] Both earned income (principally wages and salaries) and unearned income (principally profit, and roughly synonymous to the earnings of business entities) were subject to the normal tax rates. A surtax of 10 per cent was levied on earned income in excess of B/1,799 and a surtax of 40 per cent on unearned income. The combination of the normal tax and surtax on unearned income, however, cannot exceed an effective tax rate of 42 per cent.

arise from the operation of a large apartment house.

Another surtax of 25 per cent has been imposed continuously and without change since 1941 on single individuals who do not contribute to the support of an immediate relative. For purposes of administering this surtax, the requirements for the support of relatives in the *Civil Code* are followed; i.e., if an individual contributes to the support of a relative whom he has an obligation to support under the *Civil Code,* he may claim exemption from the 25 per cent surtax. No statistics are available on the application of the surtax to single individuals, but since *any* degree of support for an eligible relative makes exemption from the surtax possible, it seems likely that few individuals are subject to the surtax.

Deductions

There are no privileged personal deductions, and individuals receiving salaries and wages are not permitted to deduct any incidental costs involved in earning income, such as membership fees in professional societies. As a result, the deductions from gross income are limited to taxpayers operating a business entity.

Allowable business deductions are not explicitly stated in the income tax law. Rather, all ordinary and necessary business expenses are allowable deductions, *except* for seven categories of nondeductible expenses enumerated in Article 699 of the income tax law: 1) Taxpayers may not deduct the cost of any personal expenses. 2) The cost of repairs made to real or personal property is not deductible if depreciation is allowable on the same property. 3) The cost of any improvement made to real or personal property must be depreciated rather than deducted in full. 4) Amounts allotted to reserve funds are not deductible, except to reserves established for depreciation and bad debts. 5) Expenses are not deductible if incurred for recreation trips, or for contributions not directly related to the business activity of the firm. 6) Bonuses paid to employees are deductible providing that they do not exceed the amount of one month's salary. 7) Any other business expense may be disallowed as a deduction if the expense cannot be verified to the satisfaction of the income tax administration.

Article 699 was revised by Law No. 63 of December 11, 1961, and although the final implications of the changes are still uncertain, the effects could be important. Previous to this revision, the prologue of Article 699 stated that certain business expenses were not deductible "in the production of income," and then listed seven nondeductible expenses as indicated above. In the revised statute, however, the phrase "in the production of income" was changed to read "in the production of income and on account of interest paid." It appears that the purpose of this amendment was to permit the deduction of interest charges incurred for personal expenditures, in addition to interest deductions previously allowed for business purposes. If this is the correct interpretation, the revision would mean that interest on personal debts would be deductible, and accordingly, all individual taxpayers incurring interest charges in 1962 could claim tax refunds. There is some doubt, however, as to the correct interpretation of the revision, for the first limitation of Article 699 prohibits *all* deductions of a personal nature. As of July, 1962, the amendment had not been interpreted by the Supreme Court.

The income tax law (Article 696) permits special deductions from rental income. First, gross rent may be reduced by an arbitrary percentage established by law in lieu of deductions for repairs, depreciation, and bad debts. There are two of these percentages, 35 per cent for rooming houses and 20 per cent for apartment houses. Second, owners of rental property may deduct management commissions of up to 10 per cent of the gross rent, property taxes, interest and land rental expenses, and power and light costs, when the latter utility expenses are incurred for services communal in nature, such as those of an elevator.

In the depreciation of assets for income tax purposes, a straight-line method is required. The specific allowances have been determined by administrative regulations, and the ones presently in effect have been used without change since 1947. Taxpayers may propose alternative depreciation schedules for consideration, and faster write-offs are permitted when adequately justified.

The Filing of Returns and Payment of the Tax

According to the income tax law, all recipients of income have an obligation to file an income tax return. Returns may be filed on a fiscal year basis only if adequate justification is offered. Tax returns are due on March 15 for those filing calendar year returns, or two and one-half months after the close of a fiscal year. If a taxpayer has a capital of more than B/100,000, or sales exceeding B/50,000, the return must be prepared and signed by a certified public accountant.

Withholding on wages and salaries was introduced in 1934, and the procedure is presently administered in such a way as to retain the full amount of the tax. By administrative order, taxpayers subject to withholding, who do not receive more than one salary or another type of income, are absolved from the requirement to file tax returns. This exemption was introduced as an administrative convenience, because of the shortage of personnel in the income tax division. The tax is also withheld on all payments to a nonresident of Panamá, except from dividends, which are construed to be taxed in full at the corporate level.

Taxpayers not covered by withholding have been subject to the current payment of income taxes since 1953. Under this system, a taxpayer is required to file a final tax return on March 15 for the preceding calendar year, and to pay any residual tax liability on the preceding year's income by June 30. By March 15, the taxpayer must also estimate his current year's income. This estimated income cannot be less than the previous year's actual income. There is no penalty for an underestimate of income, provided that the estimated income is not less than the preceding year's actual income. The tax on the estimated income may be paid in full on or before June 30, or in three equal installments, on or before June 30, September 30, and December 31. Thus, by June 30, a taxpayer must pay the remainder, if any, of his preceding year's tax as well as at least one-third of his current year's tax. The tax is paid on the basis of a notice presented to the taxpayer, and the notices for the June 30th payment are usually mailed by April 30.

When a husband and wife both receive income, separate returns must be filed. In the filing of separate returns, the husband must claim all of the exemptions for minor dependents.

For the late payment of the tax, there is a penalty of 10 per cent of the tax, regardless of the duration of the delinquency. In the event that legal proceedings for collection of the tax are instituted, an additional penalty of 10 per cent is applied plus enforcement costs.

The statute of limitations is two years for the auditing of returns, and five years if no returns have been filed, or if fraud is proven. There is also a limit of five years on the collection of delinquent income taxes.

If a taxpayer objects to an assessment, several stages of appeal are available. He may first establish an initial claim, an action that must be initiated within fifteen days of the issuance of the assessment notice. On failing this first attempt at redress, the taxpayer may ask for a reconsideration, after which he may then appeal to the General Administrator of Internal Revenue. If the taxpayer is still dissatisfied with the decision, he may appeal to the President of the Republic, and finally to the Supreme Court.

Panamá has a unique enforcement device for the income tax in the form of the *Paz y Salvo* certificate. This certificate is required for a large number of transactions and activities, such as departure from the country, the withdrawal of merchandise from customs, and the registration of public deeds. The income tax division is charged with the issuance of these certificates, and they are given only to firms and individuals who have fulfilled their income tax liabilities.

Penalties

Panamá took a long step forward in 1961 in order to provide more effective penalties for income tax evasion. The statutory change was very simple, but its potential significance is great. Article 752 of the income tax law, enacted in 1956, provided penalties for fraud, but it required that the *intent* to defraud must be proved. Not a single case of fraud was prosecuted successfully under this article, however, because of the inability to prove "intent." But under the new legislation of 1961, it is only necessary for the income tax administration to prove the existence of certain infractions in order to apply the various penalties available.

The infractions specified under Article 752 cover the gamut of income tax evasion practices, including the under-reporting of income, the exaggeration of expenses, delinquency in depositing withheld payroll taxes, refusal to provide information, providing of false information, the maintenance of two sets of books, the destruction of records, or any other attempt to defraud the government. For any one of these infractions, a penalty of from two to ten times the amount of the tax may be levied together with imprisonment for a duration of from one month to a year. The actual penalty levied within these limits is discretionary on the part of the General Administrator of Internal Revenue. No cases have been prosecuted under this revised article as of July, 1962, because it does not have retroactive effect for income years prior to 1962. It is reported, however, that two or three cases are being prepared.

Although the penalties for fraud are the most comprehensive and severe available for application in the administration of the income tax, several other penalties may be levied for particular offences:

1) *Article 751.* Every business activity in Panamá must be registered. This requirement is for the purpose of maintaining adequate records for income tax compliance and enforcement purposes. There is no charge for the registration of businesses with a capital of less than B/500, and of professional workers, but all other businesses must pay a stamp tax of one cent for each accounting page used to maintain necessary accounting records. The income tax administration is required to impose a penalty of B/25 to B/100 on a business that is not registered and that does not maintain adequate records.

2) *Article 753.* This article provides a penalty of from B/10 to B/1000 for the late filing of a return, with the amount of the penalty depending on the extent of the delinquency, the level of taxable income, and whether or not the offense has been repeated.

3) *Article 755.* A penalty of B/10 to B/500 may be levied on a taxpayer who does not make his records available to the income tax administration.

4) *Article 756.* A penalty of B/5 to B/50 may be levied on a public employee who denies information to the income tax authorities.

5) *Article 710.* A penalty of B/25 to B/1000 may be levied on a chartered accountant who falsifies returns.

6) *Article 758.* A penalty of from two to five times the amount of the tax may be levied on an employer who is delinquent in forwarding withheld payroll taxes to the government.

7) Another penalty for the late payment of withheld taxes provides for a surcharge of 5 per cent of the amount due if the payment is made within thirty days after the due date, with an additional surcharge of 1 per cent for each month or fraction of a month of delinquency beyond the initial period of thirty days. This penalty is an alternative to the one for fraud. If attachment proceedings must be resorted to in order to collect the tax, there is an additional surcharge of 10 per cent.

8) The income tax authorities are empowered to invoke a section of the *Commercial Code,* which provides for a penalty of B/25 for each month that business records are not currently maintained.

It is important to note that none of the above penalties provides for the application of an interest charge in addition to the imposition of penalties.

FUNCTIONAL PROBLEMS

Income Tax Collections

As explained in Chapter 1, the income tax should play a central role in the evolution of an improved revenue system in Panamá. To repeat briefly, progress in improving the Panamanian revenue structure consists primarily of a shift from a tax system that is overly dependent on customs duties and internal indirect taxes on consumption and production, to one in which a larger proportion of revenue is obtained from direct taxes. And of the relatively few direct taxes that may be extended and strengthened, the income tax, because of the breadth of its base and the several economic and social goals which it serves, should constitute the dominant single source of revenue. Thus, without income tax reform in Panamá, there can be no appreciable rationalization and improvement of the tax system as a whole.

From the point of view of the revenue contributed, there has been retrogression rather than progress in the development of Panamá's income tax from 1955 to 1961. This contention is supported by the data presented in Table 2.5, which compares income tax collections both to total ordinary government revenues and to total tax revenues for the period from 1951 to 1961. For each of these comparisons, the statistics show rather dramatic improvement in income tax collections from 1952 to 1955, but then a gradual deterioration from 1956 to 1961. This deterioration is not minor in degree, for income tax collections were only 22.41 per

TABLE 2.5

Income Tax Collections, 1951 to 1961

	Income Tax Collections[1] (Balboas)	Income Tax Collections as a Percentage of Ordinary Government Revenues	Income Tax Collections as a Percentage of Total Tax Revenues
1951	4,063,700	12.44	16.37
1952	4,112,000	11.32	15.24
1953	7,461,500	18.18	24.03
1954	8,371,200	19.61	25.34
1955	10,843,200	23.96	30.33
1956	10,215,300	20.95	27.75
1957	7,543,600	14.89	19.90
1958	12,212,700	23.09	30.56
1959	8,135,500	15.76	21.41
1960	10,751,500	18.54	24.26
1961	10,672,200	17.06	22.41

[1] New tax rates were adopted effective in 1953 and 1961.

cent of total tax collections in 1961 as compared with 30.33 per cent in 1955. Even as far back as 1953, the income tax was a more important source of total tax revenues than in 1961. The conclusion is warranted, therefore, that the income tax during the past several years has not maintained its relative importance in the revenue system. As will be explained later, special circumstances explain this developing weakness.

Considerable improvement in income tax collections was anticipated during 1962, when total collections were expected to rise to B/14,082,680 as compared with B/10,-672,200 in 1961 (Table 2.6). For the most part, this increase was attributable to higher surtax rates effective during 1962 and to larger earnings on the part of one particularly large firm. Although this increase of 32 per cent within one year is substantial, it represents merely the type of progress that needs to be effected annually for several years. This is evident because income tax collections are expected to be 26.3 per cent of estimated total tax collections of B/54.1 million in 1962. An improvement over the comparable percentage of 22.4 per cent in 1961 is thus indicated, but the yield of the tax is still far removed from the point at which the income tax constitutes the dominant impost in the revenue system.

It would be quite unrealistic to say that income tax collections may be improved easily and quickly. That there are pervasive inhibitions to the further development of the income tax are evident from the basic characteristics of the economy. As shown in Table 2.7, approximately 50 per cent of the labor force is engaged in agriculture, forestry, and fishing. Many of the persons employed in these enterprises, because they live close to a subsistence level, must be discounted as potential payers of a personal income tax. In other words, the income tax in the foreseeable future cannot be viewed as a mass tax in the sense of covering nearly all the gainfully employed. Another problem evident from the data in Table 2.7 is the unemployment rate of 10 per cent in the Republic.

Further, Panamá is not physically large, populous, or rich. The estimated population in 1962 is only 1,100,000 persons, and the gross internal product is but B/447.6 per capita. Stating the internal product in terms of a per capita average also obscures a fact of central importance, namely, that an unequal distribution of income and wealth results in a significant proportion of the population having incomes so low as to be outside the pale of an income tax.

Not the least of the problems in developing the income tax is inadequacies in compliance and enforcement. These defects are important, and will be analyzed subsequently. It

TABLE 2.6

Estimated Income Tax Collections for 1962[1]

Amounts already paid and receipts issued for payment	B/10,269,661
Royalties	157,195
Estimated receipts from fiscal returns	725,824
Additional assessments from audits	100,000
Receipts expected from one large firm	330,000
Canal Zone employees	200,000
Withholding	2,300,000
TOTAL	B/14,082,680

[1] These estimates were made by the Income Tax Division of the Ministry of Finance and the Treasury in October, 1962.

TABLE 2.7

Labor Force by Type of Economic Activity,
1960 Census

Type of Activity	Number Employed	Number Unemployed	Total Labor Force
Agriculture, forestry, fishing	153,058	2,632	155,690
Extractive industries	360	90	450
Manufacturing	22,079	3,435	25,514
Construction	9,312	5,052	14,364
Public Service industries	1,500	183	1,683
Commerce	27,482	3,239	30,721
Transportation and communications	8,571	1,431	10,002
Personal services	58,560	9,103	67,663
Canal Zone employees	16,261	2,587	18,848
Other	2,203	2,680	4,883
TOTALS	299,386	30,432	329,818

Source: Division of Statistics and Census, Comptroller General of Panamá.

is sufficient to say at this point that an income tax is essentially a voluntary levy, which is dependent upon its acceptance by taxpayers and the ability of the income tax administration to "encourage" them to meet their obligations. Neither condition is conspicuously present in Panamá.

These problems, however, are not unique to Panamá. Every country encounters the same difficulties in the development of an income tax, but some countries do a much better job of overcoming them than others. Table 2.8 shows the derivation by source in 1960 of tax revenues for nineteen Latin American countries. This table indicates that the income tax varies in importance—from Colombia, which obtained 51.7 per cent of its total tax revenue from the income tax in 1960—to Guatemala, which received only 7.1 per cent of its governmental income from this source.[2] Panamá, perhaps, has done relatively well, ranking eighth among the nineteen countries with 18.6 per cent of its tax revenues supplied by an income tax. But Panamá's per capita gross national product in 1960, which is an important indication of

[2] This comparison is imprecise because the data reported for Colombia include collections from a net-wealth tax.

the ability to utilize an income tax successfully, was the fifth highest among the nineteen countries of Latin America. If Colombia and Peru are able to obtain 51.7 and 47.1 per cent, respectively, of their tax revenues from an income tax, it could be said that only a lack of effort in the future would prevent a similar attainment in Panamá.

The Breadth of the Tax Base

One of the faults of the Panamanian income tax, and one that must be corrected if income tax revenues are to be increased appreciably, is the narrowness of the tax base. This problem has several manifestations, such as the relatively small number of taxpayers, the comparatively light income tax burden borne by wages and salaries, and the high percentage of total income tax collections derived from a relatively small number of taxpayers.

Before analyzing some of these problems, it should be observed that statistics of income tax collections are not maintained adequately or currently in Panamá, with the result that the data assembled for the purpose of this study leave much to be desired. The statistics have two basic shortcomings: 1) Since taxpayers with only a single employer are not required to file a tax return, dependable and complete information cannot be obtained for collections due to withholding. This also means in general that "tax returns" in Panamá refer to the returns of business entities. 2) All taxpayers not subject to withholding are required during each calendar year to make a final payment on their preceding year's tax, as well as pay an estimated tax on their current year's income. Most of the data for this study could only be obtained for the estimated tax. As a result, the statistics available are not directly comparable to collections made during a calendar year period.

Data obtained for 1961 afford an approximate insight into the importance of withholding on wages and salaries. It is known for this year that total tax collections from withholding were B/2,300,000. Of this

TABLE 2.8

Distribution of Tax Revenues by Source in Latin America, 1960

Country	Total Taxes	Income Taxes (Per Cent)	Sales, Turnover, and Excise Taxes (Per Cent)	Customs Duties (Per Cent)	Monopoly Receipts (Per Cent)	Other Taxes (Per Cent)
Venezuela	100.0	38.4	39.8	11.0	9.0	1.8
Chile	100.0	32.3	41.6	21.8	—	4.3
Argentina	100.0	29.3	32.7	32.1	—	5.9
Uruguay	100.0	7.3	25.6	37.2	—	29.9
Panamá	100.0	18.6	18.6	44.2	11.6	7.0
Costa Rica	100.0	16.9	13.6	57.6	6.8	5.1
Mexico	100.0	36.8	29.2	27.5	—	6.5
Colombia	100.0	51.7	9.8	33.8	.7	4.0
Brazil	100.0	31.6	43.3	11.8	—	13.9
Dominican Republic	100.0	17.7	22.6	43.6	—	16.1
Ecuador	100.0	16.5	10.6	41.2	17.6	14.1
Peru	100.0	47.1	22.5	21.1	4.2	5.1
Nicaragua	100.0	9.1	18.2	60.6	3.0	9.1
Honduras	100.0	14.7	29.4	55.9	—	1
El Salvador	100.0	11.4	19.7	60.7	—	8.2
Guatemala	100.0	7.1	21.4	53.6	1	17.9
Paraguay	100.0	12.5	25.0	20.8	1	41.7
Bolivia[2]	100.0	14.2	23.4	50.6	1.8	8.0
Haiti	100.0	9.1	15.1	65.2	—	10.6

[1] Less than 0.05 per cent.

[2] Total does not add to 100 per cent due to errors in original data.

Source: Hearings, Committee on Foreign Affairs, House of Representatives, 87th Congress, March, 27–29, 1962, p. 477.

amount, B/505,324 was withheld from taxpayers who filed returns because they had two salaries, or because they had other income in addition to their salary. As a result, the difference between B/2,300,000 and B/505,324, or B/1,794,676, is attributable to taxes withheld from taxpayers who had no liability to file returns. Thus, it may be said that approximately 22 per cent of the Panamanian income tax represents revenue attributable to withholding on salaries and wages (on the part of both taxpayers who file returns and those who do not), and about 17 per cent of the total income tax collections is obtained from taxpayers who are subject to withholding and do not file tax returns. Although these percentages undoubtedly vary somewhat from year to year, they at least demonstrate that the Panamanian income tax is predominantly a levy on unearned rather than on earned income.

In the light of this, it is important to examine, for purposes of comparison, the factor components of the national income in 1960.[3] For this year, the total national income was B/366.5 million. Subtracting from this total the amount of income earned on government property, and other similar components not included in the aggregate income tax base, there remains a total of B/357.4 million. Of this amount, in turn, wages and salaries constituted B/250.1 million, or 70 per cent of the total possible exploitable base of an income tax in Panamá, while the sum of profits, interest, and rent represented the remaining 30 per cent. As a result, associating the actual source of income tax collections in 1960 with the factor components of the national income, it may be said that Panamá obtained roughly 22 per cent of its income tax revenues from a source (wages and salaries) which represented 70 per cent of the national income. Conversely, about 78 per cent of the income tax revenue was obtained from interest, rent, and profits, the

[3] At the time that this research was undertaken, national income data of the type needed were not available for 1961.

TABLE 2.9

Declared Income and Tax Payments of the Twenty Taxpayers with the Highest Taxable Incomes
in 1959 with Comparable Figures for 1960

Taxpayer Number	Declared Income (Balboas)		Tax Payments (Balboas)		Cumulative Percentages of Total Income Tax Collections	
	1959	1960	1959	1960	1959	1960
1*	8,858,978	4,981,288	2,643,600	1,494,386	32.5	13.9
2	2,952,271	2,963,334	1,099,391	1,103,905	46.0	24.2
3*	1,158,193	1,282,450	194,656	218,439	48.4	26.2
4	1,199,279	610,152	38,588	94,556	48.9	27.1
5	806,946	973,734	215,850	277,452	51.5	29.7
6	824,600	930,708	237,350	276,830	54.4	32.2
7*	837,867	90,523	94,235	12,762	55.6	32.4
8	662,518	621,300	179,946	165,845	57.8	33.9
9	546,684	652,257	141,050	176,436	59.5	35.5
10*	444,971	538,169	65,484	82,113	60.4	36.3
11*	383,577	347,042	89,435	78,803	61.5	37.0
12*	339,391	351,520	76,577	80,106	62.4	37.8
13	321,862	286,391	71,476	69,374	63.3	38.4
14	279,475	421,168	29,984	100,749	63.6	39.4
15*	228,103	212,363	45,702	41,454	64.2	39.7
16	202,535	216,790	38,799	50,748	64.7	40.2
17	165,318	125,410	15,489	19,048	64.9	40.4
18	133,923	175,162	21,951	31,930	65.1	40.7
19*	121,644	192,216	12,705	23,714	65.3	40.9
20	117,881	141,359	12,631	23,241	65.5	41.1

* Firms having contracts with the government which affect their income tax liabilities.

sum of which represented only 30 per cent of the national income.

Another indication of the narrowness of the income tax base is the percentage of total income tax collections which is attributable to a relatively small number of taxpayers. Table 2.9 presents the declared income and tax payments in 1959 of the twenty taxpayers with the highest taxable income. Shown in the table also are the comparable figures for these taxpayers in 1960. The data indicate that these twenty taxpayers accounted for 65.5 per cent of total income tax collections in 1959 and 41.1 per cent in 1960. Five of the twenty taxpayers represented more than 50 per cent of total income tax collections in 1959, and the taxpayer with the highest income accounted for nearly one-third. But in 1960 the situation was quite different, with the first five taxpayers accounting for only 29.7 per cent of the total collections, and the highest taxpayer for only

13.9 per cent. Under these circumstances, total income tax collections obviously are related directly and closely to the incomes of a mere handful of taxpayers.

One important effect of this dependence on a few large taxpayers for an undue proportion of the total income tax collections is that the level of revenue from this source moves capriciously from year to year, which causes budgetary problems. Another effect, as shown in Table 2.10, is that there is no close and dependable relationship between total collections and the national income. For example, it is possible for income tax collections as a percentage of the national income to fall from 3.5 per cent in 1956 to 2.4 per cent in 1957 despite an appreciable rise in the national income between the two years. On the other hand, if the base of the income tax were broader in Panamá, income tax collections and the national income would move in the same direction, and the collections would rise even more than proportionately to the increase in the national income, because of the progressivity of the rates.

Most of the instability of income tax collections is attributable to variations in the profits of one large corporation. This firm influences the revenue from the Panamanian income tax so greatly that its tax payments relative to total collections are somewhat like the tail wagging the dog. If the tax payments of this firm are subtracted from total income tax collections for each year from 1954 to 1961, the residual revenues

show an increase from B/6,054,575 in 1954 to B/10,558,927 in 1961. Table 2.11 also shows that these residual revenues reflect an increasing percentage of the national income, rising from 2.3 per cent of the national income in 1954 to 2.7 per cent in 1961.

It is evident from Table 2.12 that the distribution of taxable income is like a pyramid, a few taxpayers with high incomes forming a sharp and narrow peak, but 72 per cent of the taxpayers having a taxable income of under B/6000. This table also shows that the total taxable income within the brackets from B/901 to B/10,000 is B/21,171,745, which is almost as great as the total of B/24,216,084 from all tax brackets between B/10,001 to B/100,000. Further, if the taxpayers subject to withholding and not filing returns were included in this table, the preponderance of taxable income at the lower end of the income scale would be even more pronounced.

Finally, it may be determined that the taxable base of the income tax in 1961 represents only about 36 per cent of the national income. Assuming that the average effective rate of the income tax was 2.2 per cent on the total of B/1.8 million of income tax withheld from wages and salaries, the tax base for this portion of the income tax collections was B/81.8 million. To this amount may be added the declared income from all tax returns of B/63.8 million, which

TABLE 2.10

Comparison of Income Tax Collections
to the National Income, 1951 to 1961

	Income Tax Collections (Millions of Balboas)	National Income in Current Prices (Millions of Balboas)	Income Tax Collections as a Percentage of the National Income
1951	4.1	223.4	1.8
1952	4.1	242.5	1.7
1953	7.5	255.4	2.9
1954	8.4	258.1	3.2
1955	10.8	277.5	3.9
1956	10.2	287.4	3.5
1957	7.5	315.9	2.4
1958	12.2	326.7	3.7
1959	8.1	348.0	2.3
1960	10.7	366.5	2.9
1961	10.7	398.2	2.7

TABLE 2.11

Total Income Tax Collections Minus the Tax Payments of One Large Firm

	Total Income Tax Collections (Millions of Balboas)	Total Income Tax Collections Minus the Payments of One Large Firm (Millions of Balboas)	Income Tax Collections as a Percentage of the National Income	Total Income Tax Collections Minus the Payments of One Large Firm Expressed as a Percentage of the National Income
1954	8.4	6.0	3.3	2.3
1955	10.8	6.4	3.9	2.3
1956	10.2	6.1	3.5	2.1
1957	7.5	8.1	2.4	2.6
1958	12.2	8.5	3.7	2.6
1959	8.1	9.2	2.3	2.6
1960	10.7	9.0	2.9	2.5
1961	10.7	10.6	2.7	2.7

results in a total income tax base of B/145.6 million. This total, in turn, represents about 36 per cent of the national income of B/407.3 million in 1961.

Three conclusions of importance for purposes of income tax policy emerge from the foregoing analysis: 1) It is apparent that the Panamanian income tax is largely a levy on unearned rather than on earned income. 2) An undue amount of income tax revenue is obtained from a relatively small number of taxpayers. 3) If the Panamanian income tax is to become a more productive and dependable source of revenue, the tax base must be broadened, particularly by obtaining a greater share of collections from the lower end of the income scale.

TABLE 2.12

Distribution of Income Tax Returns by Income Brackets for 1961[1]

Taxable Income Brackets (Balboas)	Number of Returns	Declared Income (Balboas)	Tax Liability (Balboas)
901 to 2,000	2,537	3,459,988	75,600
2,001 to 4,000	1,938	5,542,735	125,030
4,001 to 6,000	1,001	4,916,616	131,364
6,001 to 8,000	559	3,892,475	136,434
8,001 to 10,000	377	3,359,931	142,608
10,001 to 12,000	245	2,680,638	128,572
12,001 to 14,000	158	2,059,802	112,314
14,001 to 16,000	119	1,792,475	109,205
16,001 to 18,000	103	1,751,515	112,868
18,001 to 20,000	61	1,157,980	77,742
20,001 to 25,000	103	2,310,403	180,656
25,001 to 30,000	60	1,645,348	136,915
30,001 to 35,000	50	1,618,995	150,718
35,001 to 40,000	25	924,878	87,247
40,001 to 45,000	28	1,182,709	114,272
45,001 to 50,000	36	1,704,444	187,724
50,001 to 60,000	27	1,469,549	162,093
60,001 to 70,000	18	1,187,124	162,537
70,001 to 80,000	16	1,189,714	166,566
80,001 to 90,000	9	764,446	114,853
90,001 to 100,000	8	776,064	127,904
100,001 to 250,000	33	4,966,732	989,202
250,001 to 500,000	7	2,811,511	600,070
500,001 to 1,000,000	5	3,799,454	958,852
Over 1,000,000	3	6,798,783	2,165,087
TOTALS	7,526	63,764,309	7,456,433

[1] The data refer only to the estimated tax for 1961. As a result, the statistics do not include two types of tax payments: (1) those made by taxpayers who are subject to withholding but do not file tax returns; and (2) final payments of 1960 income taxes paid in 1961.
Source: Ministry of Finance and the Treasury.

Tax Rates

Panamá has not been unaware of the need to increase income tax rates, with heavier imposts being levied in 1953, 1961, and 1962. But the net result of these increases has two basic shortcomings: 1) There have been no increases in tax rates on the lower levels of earned income since 1946. 2) Although the tax rates have been increased considerably on the middle and upper income groups, the effective tax rates are still very moderate.

Tables 2.13 and 2.14 have been prepared in order to demonstrate the effective rates of taxation on both earned and unearned income at various levels of gross taxable income. Considering first the tax burden on earned income, it may be seen from Table 2.13 that incomes below B/1800 have experienced no increase in taxes since 1946. At the level of B/5000 in gross income, the effective rate of taxation has increased from 2.42 per cent in 1946 to 2.73 per cent in 1962; at B/10,000 the rate has increased from 3.24 per cent to 4.73 per cent; and at B/100,000, the rate has risen from 7.77 per cent to 15.72 per cent. It is apparent from these changes that an attempt has been made to increase the progressivity of the rate structure.

Unfortunately, there is no best "scientific" progressive income tax schedule. A decision on the desirability of a particular rate schedule essentially involves the whole context of social, political, and economic goals. This much can be said, however, with some certainty: 1) That any person in Panamá who currently pays an income tax, even if his income is taxable at the beginning marginal rate, is in a relatively privileged economic position. 2) Much heavier tax burdens will have to be borne by every taxable person if the income tax is to fulfill its role as an instrument of social and economic change.

More specifically, considering that the national income was only B/366.5 per capita in 1960, a gross income of B/1500 represents a considerable degree of financial security not enjoyed by much of the population, yet the effective income tax rate at this level of income is only 2.0 per cent. With an income of B/5000, a married couple in Panamá has a high middle-class standard of living, yet the effective income tax rate in 1962 on this income is only 2.73 per cent. Should it not be as high as 10 per cent? On B/100,000, which represents a very high income in Panamá, the effective rate of tax is 15.72 per cent. If a peaceful revolution is to mean anything besides high-sounding phrases, should not this rate be as high as 25 per cent?

In 1962, surtaxes of 10 per cent were levied on earned income and of 40 per cent on unearned income. The effect of these two surtaxes, through some "political arithmetic,"

is to make the difference between the effective rates of taxation on earned and unearned income somewhat less than 30 per cent. Thus, as shown in Table 2.14, an individual proprietor with a net taxable income of B/5000 pays an effective rate of tax of 3.47 per cent as compared to 2.73 per cent if the same income had been received in the form of a salary. The difference between these two effective rates is 27 per cent rather than 30 per cent.

Although unearned income is assigned the heavier tax burden, there appears to be considerable latitude for heavier taxation on the income of business entities. On a net income of B/10,000, a business firm pays an effective

TABLE 2.13

Effective Income Tax Rates on Earned Income for Representative Years[1]

Gross Taxable Income (Balboas)	1946		1953		1961		1962	
	Total Tax (Balboas)	Effective Rate (Per Cent)	Total Tax (Balboas)	Effective Rate (Per Cent)	Total Tax (Balboas)	Effective Rate (Per Cent)	Total Tax (Balboas)	Effective Rate (Per Cent)
1,000	20	2.00	20	2.00	20	2.00	20	2.00
1,500	30	2.00	30	2.00	30	2.00	30	2.00
2,000	40	2.00	40	2.00	40	2.00	44	2.20
2,500	50	2.00	50	2.00	50	2.00	56	2.24
3,000	63	2.10	63	2.10	63	2.10	69	2.30
4,000	90	2.25	90	2.25	90	2.25	99	2.48
5,000	121	2.42	122	2.44	124	2.48	136	2.72
6,000	156	2.60	162	2.70	174	2.90	191	3.18
7,000	196	2.80	212	3.03	234	3.34	257	3.67
8,000	236	2.95	262	3.28	294	3.68	323	4.04
9,000	279	3.10	318	3.53	360	4.00	396	4 40
10,000	324	3.24	378	3.78	430	4.30	473	4.73
15,000	564	3.76	708	4.72	840	5.60	924	6.16
20,000	830	4.15	1,090	5.45	1,290	6.45	1,419	7.09
30,000	1,416	4.72	1,962	6.54	2,390	7.97	2,629	8.76
40,000	2,074	5.19	2,987	7.47	3,490	8.72	3,839	9.60
50,000	2,774	5.55	4,137	8.27	4,990	9.98	5,489	10.98
60,000	3,574	5.96	5,412	9.02	6,490	10.82	7,139	11.90
70,000	4,474	6.39	6,812	9.73	8,290	11.84	9,119	13.03
80,000	5,474	6.84	8,337	10.42	10,090	12.61	11,099	13.87
90,000	6,574	7.30	9,987	11.10	12,190	13.54	13,409	14.90
100,000	7,774	7.77	11,762	11.76	14,290	14.29	15,719	15.72
200,000	20,774	10.39	31,762	15.88	39,790	19.90	43,769	21.88
300,000	34,274	11.42	54,262	18.09	66,790	22.26	73,469	24.49
400,000	48,274	12.07	78,512	19.63	96,790	24.20	106,469	26.62
500,000	62,274	12.45	104,762	20.95	126,790	25.36	139,469	27.89
750,000	99,774	13.30	174,887	23.32	209,290	27.90	230,219	30.70
1,000,000	137,274	13.73	252,387	25.24	296,790	29.68	326,469	32.65

[1] No allowance is made for dependent children because of the infrequent claims for these deductions. The effective rate is the percentage of the total tax to the gross taxable income.

TABLE 2.14

Effective Income Tax Rates on Unearned Income (Business Entities) for Representative Years[1]

Net Taxable Income (Balboas)	1946 Total Tax (Balboas)	1946 Effective Rate (Per Cent)	1953 Total Tax (Balboas)	1953 Effective Rate (Per Cent)	1961 Total Tax (Balboas)	1961 Effective Rate (Per Cent)	1962 Total Tax (Balboas)	1962 Effective Rate (Per Cent)
2,000	48	2.40	48	2.40	48	2.40	56	2.80
3,000	76	2.53	76	2.53	76	2.53	88	2.93
4,000	108	2.70	108	2.70	108	2.70	126	3.15
5,000	145	2.90	146	2.92	149	2.98	174	3.48
6,000	187	3.12	194	3.23	209	3.48	244	4.07
7,000	235	3.36	254	3.63	281	4.01	328	4.69
8,000	283	3.54	314	3.93	353	4.41	412	4.55
9,000	335	3.72	382	4.24	432	4.80	504	5.60
10,000	389	3.89	454	4.54	516	5.16	602	6.02
15,000	677	4.51	850	5.67	1,008	6.72	1,176	7.84
20,000	996	4.98	1,308	6.54	1,548	7.74	1,806	9.03
30,000	1,699	5.66	2,254	7.51	2,868	9.56	3,346	11.15
40,000	2,486	6.22	3,584	8.96	4,188	10.47	4,886	12.22
50,000	3,329	6.66	4,964	9.93	5,988	11.98	6,986	13.97
60,000	4,229	7.05	6,494	10.82	7,788	12.98	9,086	15.14
70,000	5,369	7.67	8,174	11.68	9,948	14.21	11,606	16.58
80,000	6,569	8.21	10,004	12.51	12,108	15.14	14,126	17.66
90,000	7,889	8.77	11,984	13.32	14,628	16.25	17,066	18.96
100,000	9,329	9.33	14,114	14.11	17,148	17.15	20,006	20.01
200,000	24,929	12.46	38,114	19.06	47,508	23.75	55,706	27.85
300,000	41,129	13.71	65,114	21.70	80,148	26.72	93,506	31.17
400,000	57,929	14.48	94,214	23.55	116,148	29.04	135,506	33.88
500,000	74,729	14.95	125,714	25.14	152,148	30.43	177,506	35.50
750,000	119,729	15.96	209,864	27.98	251,148	33.49	293,006	39.07
1,000,000	164,729	16.47	302,864	30.29	356,148	35.61	415,506	41.55
2,000,000	356,729	17.84	710,864	35.54	776,148	38.81	840,000	42.00[2]
3,000,000	548,729	18.29	1,118,864	36.30	1,186,148	39.54	1,260,000	42.00[2]

[1] In addition to the normal tax, a surtax of 20 per cent was levied from 1946 to 1961 and one of 40 per cent in 1962.

[2] The application of the normal tax and the surtax cannot exceed an effective rate of 42 per cent.

rate of tax of only 6.02 per cent, while a firm with a net income of B/100,000 has an effective rate of 20.01 per cent.

On the basis of the evidence presented in Tables 2.13 and 2.14, there probably would be no serious objection to the policy conclusion that middle and upper income groups should bear a heavier income tax burden. Some objection can be anticipated, however, to the proposition that the tax rates should also be increased at the lower end of the present rate schedule, and that consideration should even be given to a reduction in exemptions. Some of the protests that probably will be made are: that married couples with children who have an income of B/2000 are already suffering severe economic hardships by having to pay an income tax of

B/40; that these families are living on the verge of subsistence; that families with an income of B/2000 are heavily in debt for consumer goods, and so have no tax capacity; that in the light of these tax burdens on lower income groups, it would be folly to reduce the exemption limit for a married couple from B/1800 to perhaps B/1200; that exemptions for most married couples are inoperative in practice because they pay the tax if their income exceeds B/900; and that it is politically very difficult to increase tax burdens on lower income groups.

As will be explained later, it is true that most couples in Panamá actually pay an income tax if their incomes exceed B/900, because of the way the exemptions are administered. This is a serious fault that should be corrected. But this irregularity also has an advantage in terms of the feasibility of reducing exemptions for married couples, for most of these taxpayers are already accustomed to bearing an income tax.

On the issue of the political difficulty of increasing income tax burdens on lower income groups, there can be no rebuttal; it probably will take considerable political courage to induce more of the population to make a sacrifice for economic development openly and directly through income taxation rather than covertly through indirect taxes or inflation. But the sacrifice must be made, for the essence of economic development is short-run hardship for the benefit of long-run gain. And since a sacrifice only on the part of the middle and upper income groups will never be enough to bring about accelerated economic growth, is it not better to assess the cost of economic development openly and equitably from those groups who are relatively well off? And the statistics on income distribution demonstrate that a family with an income of B/1500, and even one with an income of B/1200, *is* relatively well off in Panamá.

Data developed for the *Informe Económico*[4] show that 54.8 per cent of Panamanian families have annual incomes of less than B/2000 and only 3.6 per cent of the families have incomes greater than B/6000 (see Table 2.15). These data demonstrate that a family with an income of B/2000 may not be financially secure, but that it is better able to bear an increased tax burden than are 54.8 per cent of the families in Panamá. The data show that even if the exemption limit for a married couple were reduced to B/1200, the total families included under an income tax would have higher incomes than about 25 per cent of the family groups in Panamá. The data reveal that by Panamanian standards an income of B/1200 represents what could be called a low middle-class income.

Economic hardship is relative. Even if families with an income of B/1200 are economically hard-pressed, they are better off than approximately 25 per cent of the families in Panamá with even lower incomes. And if the Panamanian income tax is to become a more productive and dependable source of revenue—if the levy is to become more of a mass tax both for the purposes of achieving equity and additional revenue—those families with *relative* economic well-being must bear a heavier income tax burden.

Tax Evasion

There is a widespread impression on the part of most informed persons in Panamá that sizable amounts of income tax revenue are lost because of low levels of compliance and enforcement. But to present quantitative evidence supporting the alleged loss of revenue is more difficult than to voice vague impressions. There are perhaps three ways in which it is possible to gain an insight into evasion. One is to compare the totals of taxable income as reported in income tax returns with national income aggregates. Using this method in the United States, it has been determined that total income tax evasion results in a loss of federal income tax

TABLE 2.15
Distribution of Income by Family Groups
in Panamá

Income Groups (Balboas)	Average Income (Balboas)	Percentage of Families
Less than 500	358.98	2.0
500 to 999	788.61	13.8
1,000 to 1,499	1,253.23	20.5
1,500 to 1,999	1,732.29	18.5
2,000 to 2,499	2,245.06	11.4
2,500 to 2,999	2,705.18	11.1
3,000 to 3,999	3,465.54	10.0
4,000 to 4,999	4,427.18	5.8
5,000 to 5,999	5,405.30	3.3
6,000 to 7,499	6,618.08	2.0
7,500 and over	10,123.26	1.6

Source: Informe Económico, Departamento de Planificación, Dirección General de Planificación y Administración, Febrero, 1962, p. 39.

---

[4] Departamento de Planificación, Dirección General de Planificación y Administración, Febrero, 1962, p. 39.

revenues of approximately 10 per cent. This procedure is impossible to follow in Panamá, however, for the base of the income tax represents only about 36 per cent of the national income. Accordingly, the total factor return to profits in the national income accounts could not be compared to profits reported in income tax returns, because of the numerous exclusions of profits from the income tax base for one purpose or another.

A second method of measuring the quantitative degree of evasion is to analyze the parts rather than the whole; that is, to analyze intensively a particular sample of taxpayers or a portion of reported income with the idea in mind that the evidence obtained may be meaningful for purposes of generalization. As will be shown later, a modest effort along these lines was undertaken in Panamá for the purposes of this survey.

The third insight that may be gained into evasion is through what might be called presumptive or circumstantial evidence. The data presented in Table 2.16 for the distribution of income tax returns by provinces in 1961 provide this type of evidence. These data show that 67.1 per cent of all tax returns, 81.9 per cent of the declared income, and 92.2 per cent of the total tax payments were attributable in 1961 to the province of Panamá. One would imagine from this evidence that there was such a high concentration of employment and business activity in the province of Panamá that there was very little economic activity anywhere else in the Republic.

There is no question that the province of Panamá dominates business activity in the Republic, but there are grounds for believing that the income tax statistics exaggerate the concentration. There are no data available for the derivation of the national income by provinces, but agriculture alone in 1961 represented approximately 20 per cent of the net internal product, and the vast majority of this agricultural output is produced outside the province of Panamá. And while manufacturing is concentrated in the province

of Panamá, 38 per cent of the total value of industrial output in 1960 was derived from the group of provinces exclusive of Panamá. Table 2.17 shows that approximately 70 per cent of total income taxes withheld from wages and salaries, exclusive of public employees, is attributable to the province of Panamá. On the other hand, the census data for 1960 show that the province of Panamá had only 39.3 per cent of the total labor force.

Thus, on the basis of the foregoing circumstantial evidence, it may be hypothesized that income tax collections reflect a high concentration of employment and business activity in the province of Panamá, but this is due in part to higher levels of income tax compliance and enforcement in this province. This hypothesis is supported by the income tax administrators, who admit that enforcement activities in most provinces, other than Panamá, are very weak.

There are also grounds for questioning the relatively small number of taxable income tax returns in Panamá. In 1961, there were only 7,526 tax returns for all individuals, partnerships, and corporations reporting a taxable income. One reason for this low

TABLE 2.16

Distribution of Income Tax Returns by Province, 1961[1]

Province	Number of Returns	Declared Income (Balboas)	Tax Liability (Balboas)
Bocas del Toro	128	431,805	15,873
Coclé	180	529,942	17,292
Colón	870	4,841,011	285,023
Chiriquí	624	2,628,788	150,043
Herrera	271	847,792	30,672
Panamá	5,050	52,260,128	6,876,207
Darién	199	603,761	21,708
Veraguas	162	419,417	14,131
Los Santos	21	52,380	1,685
Colón Free Zone	21	1,149,283	43,799

[1] The data refer only to the estimated tax for 1961. As a result, the statistics do not include two types of tax payments: 1) those made by taxpayers who are subject to withholding but do not file tax returns: and 2) final payments of 1960 income taxes paid in 1961.

Source: Division of Statistics and Census, Comptroller General of Panamá.

TABLE 2.17

Source of Withheld Income Taxes on Wages
and Salaries for 1961

Private Business and Autonomous and Semi-autonomous Government Agencies, by Provinces	Amount Withheld (Balboas)
Panamá	1,184,318
Colón	202,656
Coclé	19,500[1]
Bocas del Toro	61,923
Chiriquí	67,312
Los Santos	4,018
Herrera	7,030
Veraguas	7,880
	1,554,637
Public employees	750,615
TOTAL	2,305,252

[1] Estimated for the last six months of 1961.
Source: Division of Statistics and Census, Comptroller General of Panamá.

number is that taxpayers subject to withholding and not receiving another salary or other income are not required to file income tax returns. Even so, the number of taxable returns appears minimal. Consider, for example, the category listed as "professional" in Table 2.18. This category includes not only the professions such as medicine, law, engineering, and accounting but also all skilled artisans like carpenters and mechanics, and certain self-employed persons like taxi and bus drivers. As shown in Table 2.18, there were only 920 taxable returns from this group in 1961, yet it was determined by a check of professional associations that six categories of professional workers had total registrations in 1962 of 1,053.[5] Similarly, there were 2,239 manufacturing and 6,984 commercial establishments as of July 31, 1960, yet Table 2.18 shows only 3,369 taxable returns from commerce and industry in 1961.

Data obtained from the 1960 census provide an opportunity to approximate the number of taxpayers who either should be subject to withholding or who should file a tax return classified in Table 2.18 under "salaries." The census data show the wage rates of all

[5] This group includes doctors, lawyers, dentists, engineers, architects, and public accountants.

employed persons, and whether the employees have full-time or part-time jobs. Taking a conservative approach, and counting only those employees shown by the census to have full-time employment, it was determined that 58,400 employees had an income above the withholding tax level of B/900 in 1960. On the other hand, Table 2.18 shows that 2,412 income tax returns were filed in 1961 by taxpayers who had two salaries or one salary and other income. Therefore, the difference between the 58,366 employees with an apparent tax liability according to the census, and the 2,412 returns filed by taxpayers receiving a salary, which amounts to 55,988 taxpayers, represents the *approximate* number of employees who should be subject to withholding but are not required to file tax returns.

The income tax division does not maintain a record of the number of employed persons subject to withholding, but a special count undertaken for this study disclosed that the total number was 49,180 in July, 1961, and 51,513 in December, 1961. Comparing these totals with the 55,988 full-time employees who should be covered by withholding according to census data, leaves a gap of some 5000 to 7000 untaxed but taxable employees. Therefore, presumptive evidence once again suggests that not all taxable employees are covered by the income tax.

Within recent years, the income tax administration has been concerned over the amount of evasion and has taken action to tighten enforcement. An office audit of all professionals and lottery vendors in the provinces of Panamá and Colón was initiated in 1960, with 3,752 cases assigned for office audit and 2,791 completed. (This total of 3,752 assigned cases may be compared to the total of only 920 taxable returns from professional workers in 1961 shown in Table 2.18.) These office investigations resulted in total additional tax assessments of B/114,074. A census of professional workers was also undertaken in Chiriquí Province, which disclosed a total of 244 workers.

Table 2.18

Distribution of Income Tax Returns by Type of Taxpayer for 1961[1]

Taxable Income Brackets (Balboas)	Salaries		Rental Income		Commerce and Industry		Professional	
	Number of Returns	Tax Liability (Balboas)	Number of Returns	Tax Liability (Balboas)	Number of Returns	Tax Liability (Balboas)	Number of Returns	Tax Liability (Balboas)
900 to 2,400	971	64,584	816	109,868	1,559	81,228	557	61,550
2,401 to 6,000	932	150,711	509	631,222	878	130,727	246	46,827
6,001 to 8,400	227	73,612	113	86,645	220	74,614	40	16,790
8,401 to 12,000	171	83,709	90	93,514	194	115,984	46	28,657
12,001 to 30,000	106	112,388	117	1,167,097	299	462,169	24	25,298
30,001 to 50,000	4	14,286	15	52,979	100	411,518	6	18,978
50,001 to 100,000	1	6,034	3	16,574	72	699,288	1	6,173
100,001 to 500,000	0	0	2	349,272	39	1,567,405	0	0
500,001 to 1,000,000	0	0	0	0	5	958,852	0	0
Over 1,000,000	0	0	0	0	3	2,165,087	0	0
TOTALS	2,412	505,324	1,665	2,507,171	3,369	6,666,872	920	204,273

[1] The data refer only to the estimated tax for 1961. As a result, the statistics do not include two types of tax payments: 1) those made by taxpayers who are subject to withholding but do not file tax returns; and 2) final payments of 1960 income taxes paid in 1961. There is a certain amount of double-counting in this table, since a return showing two types of income was split to differentiate the income and was thus counted as two returns. As a result, the table shows a total of 8,411 returns whereas there were actually only 7,526 returns.

Source: Ministry of Finance and the Treasury.

These efforts were followed by an enforcement drive on a group of thirty-nine medical doctors undertaken in February, 1962. This sample was drawn by singling out a group of thirty-nine doctors whose declared incomes appeared to be unduly low. All the doctors in the sample were field-audited, and *each* of the investigations resulted in an additional tax assessment. The average *additional income* assessment for the group in 1960 was B/2,016, but one doctor was given an additional income assessment of B/7,979 and another one of B/7,021.

Returning once more to circumstantial evidence of evasion, Table 2.19 presents the results of a sample drawn for the purposes of this study. This sample, selected at random from the classified section of the telephone directory, included one hundred professional workers, twenty-five each from the four categories of medical doctors, accountants, engineers and architects, and lawyers. Relatively good results were obtained in finding the tax returns of these one hundred professional workers in the income tax office, with only one instance in which a return could not be located. The incomes reported as being attributable to professional services, however, were suspiciously low. Forty-four out of the one hundred taxpayers had a professional income which was below the exemption limit of B/1800 for a married couple, while only nine had a professional income exceeding B/10,000. The average net professional income varied from B/2,724 for the twenty-five accountants to B/4,956 for the twenty-five lawyers.

For the honest taxpayer who is uninformed about income tax compliance and enforcement, tax evasion may mean merely some slight under-reporting of income, some trivial exaggeration of expenses, or an unintentional misinterpretation of the income tax law. Therefore, it is instructive to demonstrate that there is such a thing as large-scale evasion, which by its very nature shows an intent to defraud the government. For example, one large landowner simply ignored his records in filing his tax returns, and reported a taxable income of B/19,982 as compared to a corrected income of B/182,-913. An investment firm created an illegal reserve of B/100,000, reporting an income of B/41,881 instead of B/141,881. Contrary to the requirements of the income tax law, another firm maintained its accounts on an accrual rather than on a cash basis, reporting a loss of B/31,000 instead of a profit of B/76,270. A commercial firm had no receipts to substantiate its expenditures, with the result that its net income was raised from B/7,074 to B/40,939. One businessman entered his total costs twice, so that his real taxable income was B/77,685 instead of B/17,980. With another firm, customs records were checked with imports shown on the income tax returns, which resulted in a taxable income of B/72,819 instead of B/23,253. How extensive is this form of blatant evasion in Panamá? No one really knows. There is only the certainty that the income tax division has never reached the point of diminishing returns in their enforcement activities.

The Canal Zone

The Canal Zone has important income tax implications, principally because of the sizable number of Panamanians employed in the zone. Before a revision of the Canal Zone Treaty in 1956, all Panamanian citizens working in the zone were exempt by treaty provision from the Panamanian income tax. Since the treaty revision in 1956, however, all Panamanian citizens employed in the zone are taxable.

According to information returns supplied to the income tax division by the United States government, approximately 30,700 Panamanian citizens were employed during 1961 by either the Panamá Canal Company or by the United States Armed Forces. Many of these employees, however, had total earnings below the income tax exemption limits because of part-time employment. In the Panamá sector, 10,115 employees out of about 20,700 were taxable, while 6,859 workers were taxable out of about 10,000 employees in the Colón sector. Thus, in 1961 there were 16,974 taxable Panamanian employees working for agencies of the United States government.

In addition, there are two types of Panamanian employees in the Canal Zone about which very little is known. The first is a sizable group of domestic servants who work for United States citizens. Most of these, however, probably have earnings below the income tax exemption limits. Second, there is a group of employees working for private businesses operating in the Canal Zone, such as commercial banks, oil companies, and construction firms. These firms are accorded tax immunity because of their location in the zone, but their Panamanian employees have been taxable since the canal treaty was revised in 1956. There are no statistics available in the income tax division on the number of Panamanian employees working for private

TABLE 2.19

Professional Income Declared by a Sample of Taxpayers in 1960

Declared Net Taxable Income or Loss[1] (Balboas)	Medical Doctors (Number of Returns)	Accountants[2] (Number of Returns)	Engineers and Architects (Number of Returns)	Lawyers (Number of Returns)
Loss	3	2	0	1
0 to 1,800	7	12	7	12
1,801 to 2,999	6	4	7	5
3,000 to 4,999	3	3	4	4
5,000 to 9,999	3	3	5	0
10,000 and over	3	1	2	3
TOTALS	25	25	25	25

[1] Only income from professional services is included.
[2] The tax return for one accountant could not be found in the income tax office, so the sample was completed by the addition of one more taxpayer.

businesses in the zone, since the latter do not furnish information returns. The labor unions representing the workers claim that private firms operating in the Canal Zone employ 7000 workers, but other estimates are as low as 4000.

The most important income tax problem arising from the Canal Zone is the absence of withholding on the approximately 17,000 taxable Panamanian employees. It is alleged that the Canal Zone employers have refused to introduce withholding on Panamanian employees, and this has forestalled adequate income tax enforcement. On the other hand, the United States government provides information returns on employees in the zone, and there is little evidence to suggest that these have been used effectively. Moreover, it is possible that the absence of withholding is attributable more to a lack of Panamanian initiative to prosecute the issue, because withholding would reduce the real income of the workers. Whatever the reason for the absence of withholding, however, the tax evasion of Panamanian citizens employed in the zone constitutes a serious income tax problem that should be corrected immediately through the institution of withholding.

A few statistics will demonstrate the need for immediate action. By administrative order, Panamanian citizens employed in the Canal Zone are required to submit to a system of "self-withholding" with voluntary monthly payments. Although there were 10,115 taxable employees in the Panamá sector during 1961, as of July, 1962, only 1,450 employees were current in their payments. In the Colón sector, only 589 out of 6,859 taxable employees were current in their payments. As a result, only about 12 per cent of those Panamanian citizens working in the Canal Zone with a demonstrable tax liability actually meet their tax obligations. In 1961, B/131,000 was collected from Canal Zone employees, but the total tax liability was probably close to B/1,000,000.

It should be observed also that a more effective utilization of information returns should not be viewed as a realistic alternative to the introduction of withholding. Most of the information returns presently received are inadequate for identification purposes, with many providing only the business address of the employer rather than the residence of the employee. The information returns are also incomplete, because the private businesses in the zone refuse to provide information on the earnings of their employees. Moreover, an effective utilization of information returns would divert the meager resources of the income tax division away from even more pressing responsibilities.

The tax status of private businesses operating in the Canal Zone also should be given attention, for at the present time many of these firms have an unwarranted exemption of taxes. The Panamanian National Council of Foreign Affairs has given consideration to the tax status of these firms and has concluded that the income of any business in the Canal Zone should be taxable when it results from "activities not directly or immediately related to the operation, maintenance, sanitation, and protection of the canal." [6] This appears to be a reasonable rule, and one that should be implemented through discussions on the part of Panamanian and United States officials.

---

[6] A letter from Vice President Carlos Sucre C. to Aquilino E. Boyd, Minister of Foreign Affairs, dated January 28, 1958.

CHAPTER 3

The Income Tax —
Structural Problems, Administration, and
Summary of Recommendations

STRUCTURAL PROBLEMS

The Taxation of Individuals, Partnerships, and Corporations

THE MOST BASIC structural income tax issue that should be raised in Panamá is the implicit assumption in the income tax act that both partnerships and corporations should be taxed as entities in themselves, separate and distinct from the taxation of their owners. Following this principle, Panamá subjects both partnerships and corporations to progressive income tax rates, and then excludes partnership shares and dividends from further taxation at the individual level apparently on the theory that these earnings already have been taxed in full.

There is no question that partnerships, and more especially corporations, have an individuality in themselves that is somewhat separate and distinctive from their owners. There is also some truth in the claim that these forms of business have a tax capacity related in some degree to the size of their net income. But on the other hand, to ignore the fact that partnerships and corporations are owned by individuals, and not to realize that the earnings of partnerships and corporations, in the final analysis, redound to the benefit of individuals, represents an essentially erroneous concept of the nature of these enterprises, and frustrates the application of a progressive net income tax to individuals.

Considering a partnership first, the case is convincing that tax capacity rests with the individual shares rather than with the income of the firm before distribution. Consider, for example, the situation of two lawyers, each of whom has an individual practice and a net income of B/10,000, and compare these two taxpayers with two lawyers who have equal shares in a partnership that has a net income of B/20,000. Despite the fact that each one of these four lawyers in reality has the same personal income of B/10,000, the Panamanian income tax law exacts a greater tax from the two lawyers associated together as partners. The law is thus discriminatory in the sense that it does not follow the basic principle that individuals in similar circumstances should be taxed equally. Moreover, by taxing the partners at a higher rate of taxation, the law discriminates without justification against the partnership form of business.

39

What is true of partnerships is to some degree also true of corporations, for the latter represent larger numbers of persons (shareholders) associated together for business purposes. And to ignore what lies behind "the corporate veil" causes serious unneutralities in taxation. If corporations are subject to progressive rates, low-income shareholders of large corporations are over-taxed, while high-income shareholders of small corporations are undertaxed. If corporations are subject to progressive rates, a large corporation would be taxed at a relatively high effective rate though the taxable income might represent an average or low rate of profit on the invested capital of a large number of individuals. Thus, it is apparent that the concept of ability to pay, at least as measured by a progressive income tax, relates more to individuals and cannot be applied rationally to corporations.

Subjecting partnerships and corporations to progressive rates also results in maneuvers in order to circumvent the progressive impact of the tax. There is a tendency for partners to associate together informally rather than formally in order to avoid having the income of the firm taxed in its totality. More serious is the tendency to split corporations, which is reported to be quite widespread in Panamá. It is alleged that a large manufacturer recently formed a separate corporation for sales purposes, and that a retail firm was split into ten corporations, one for each sales outlet.

For these reasons, Panamá should give consideration to an approach that would de-emphasize the partnership and corporate structures in the application of the income tax, and instead, place more of the tax burden on the individual owners of these entities. The solution for a partnership is relatively simple, for it is necessary merely to attribute all of the earnings, whether distributed or retained, to the partners according to their ownership participation for taxation at the individual level. For corporations, another approach is necessary and desirable: the imposition of a flat-rate income tax at the business level, and the taxation of dividends at the individual level.

The proposal to tax corporate income at the business level and then again at the individual level through the taxation of dividends at once raises the issue of the so-called "double" taxation of corporate profits. There is no discounting that this double imposition results in a somewhat heavier impact of taxation on the corporate form of business organization than on other forms of business. And if neutrality of tax treatment is established as a high priority, it follows that the double tax burden should be ameliorated. Integration of the corporate and individual income taxes in order to reduce the impact of the tax burden on corporate earnings is also feasible from a technical and administrative point of view, as there are several methods of integration, and it is merely necessary to select the one most appropriate for Panamá.[1]

But corporate tax policy is more than a matter of achieving tax neutrality. More fundamental, it would appear, is the need to shift a greater part of the over-all tax burden borne in Panamá to the owners of wealth. In other words, a high priority is to use the tax system for the promotion of a more equitable distribution of income and wealth. On the other hand, any procedure of integrating the corporate and individual income taxes would have, as its net effect, the provision of tax relief to corporate owners, who undoubtedly represent the income élite in Panamá. Furthermore, an integration procedure in Panamá is inhibited by an extensive development of foreign share ownership.

---

[1] If the integration of the corporate and individual income taxes were considered a desirable policy in Panamá, the type of dividend-received credit used in Great Britain would appear to be the most appropriate. Under this procedure, a flat-rate tax is imposed on the net income of corporations, whether the income is retained or distributed as dividends, but the portion of the tax falling on dividends is considered to be a withholding tax. When the stockholder determines his tax liability, he includes the dividends with his other income as well as the tax paid on them by the corporation, but also takes a credit for the tax paid on the dividends by the corporation. Then depending on the level of the taxpayer's income, he may either have an additional tax to pay on the dividends, or be entitled to a refund.

Dilemmas such as these, in which the achievement of different goals point in opposite directions, are not unusual in tax policy. When confronted with them, there is no alternative but to establish priorities for the goals, and in this case the promotion of a more equitable distribution of income and wealth appears to take precedent. Accordingly, integration of the corporate and individual taxes does not appear to be warranted, at least in the short-run period.

If the taxation of partnerships and corporations is rationalized along the lines suggested, bearer or unregistered corporate stock would have to be eliminated. Since the owners of these stocks cannot be identified, the taxation of dividends on bearer stocks would be very difficult to enforce. Bearer stocks could be eliminated simply by requiring corporations to substitute common for bearer stocks.

The Taxation of Earned and Unearned Income

Panamá discriminates deliberately in favor of labor income by imposing a surtax of 10 per cent on earned income above B/1800 as compared to a surtax on every level of taxable unearned income of 40 per cent. This discrimination may be justified in several different ways: 1) that unearned income has more stability; 2) that workers are allowed no depreciation on their productive capacities; and 3) that tax evasion is more extensive on the part of the receivers of unearned income.

Although there is some merit to these arguments, they may also be rebutted. It is true that labor income is uncertain, but there are other and probably better ways, like unemployment insurance, of ameliorating this uncertainty. Similarly, social security is probably a superior way of providing for the depletion of human productive capacities. And on the issue of relative ease with which unearned income may evade the income tax, is it not better to strive toward a goal of applying the income tax uniformly to all forms of income rather than admit to the impossibility of achieving this goal?

Moreover, at least two reasons support the desirability of taxing all forms of income neutrally. One is the basic tenet of income taxation that persons in like circumstances should be taxed equally. Thus, it may be argued that one taxpayer receiving B/5000 in profits has the same ability to pay an income tax as another person receiving a salary of the same amount, and that therefore both persons should pay the same amount of tax.

The other reason for objecting to Panamá's income tax discrimination against unearned income is that it is inconsistent with the government's policy of encouraging private investment. In effect, the heavier burden on unearned income in Panamá is tantamount to saying that entrepreneurial activity in general is to be discouraged as compared with non-entrepreneurial activity. This is hardly a desirable policy for a country aspiring to have higher levels of private investment.

If the discrimination in favor of labor income should be retained in Panamá, or if its removal should be viewed as more appropriate as a long-run goal, an improvement would result if the present system were made more consistent. The only type of unearned income presently exempt from the heavier surtax is rents. Since this exemption serves principally to stimulate investment in middle- and upper-income group rental housing, for which no positive incentive is necessary or desirable, it should be removed.

The Taxation of Capital Gains

Capital gains in Panamá are excluded from taxation if they do not constitute a regularly recurring source of income and they are realized on property or investment held for more than two years. Gains on property held for less than two years are taxed as other income. Little is known about the characteristics of capital gains in Panamá. There are no statistics on the amount of assets held and sold within a two-year period—taxable in full as compared with those held for more than two years which are thus rendered nontaxable. It seems reasonable, however, to assume that there would be an overwhelming tendency to hold assets for more than two years. There are no statistics, either, on the derivation of capital gains, though probably the bulk arise from the sale of real property. It seems reasonable to assume also that capital gains are principally a source of income for higher income groups.

Capital gains logically fall within the category of income. When gains are realized, the proceeds are available for consumption or investment just as surely as if the income had been received as wages or profits. As a result, if capital gains are partially taxed or exempt, persons receiving this form of income are favored as compared with those receiving other forms of income. On the other hand, when capital gains are not taxed, investment on which gains can be realized is made more attractive as compared with other forms of investment.

The principal problem with respect to taxing capital gains is that it is not feasible to tax them on an accrual basis, with the result that it is necessary to levy an income tax at the time of realization of the gain. But taxation on a realization basis, in turn, can be seriously discriminatory when an asset is held for a long period and all the gain is taxed in one year at progressive rates. This problem can be resolved by the averaging of income from capital gains, or by having a series of tax rates related inversely to the length of time the asset is held.

The special treatment of capital gains in Panamá, under which gains realized on assets held more than two years are exempt from the income tax, is much more generous than is necessary in order to tax capital gains equitably. Therefore, the provision detracts from the neutrality of the income tax by favoring a particular type of income, and it discriminates in favor of upper income groups. On the other hand, the liberal treatment of capital gains encourages investment. Consequently, the issue to be faced in Panamá is the need to weigh a tax provision

which detracts from equity, but one which is conducive to investment.

Placed in this light, it would seem that a controlling argument is the likelihood that the special treatment of capital gains is for the most part an incentive for encouraging relatively riskless investments in commerce and real estate and various forms of speculation. More than anything else, the liberal treatment of capital gains in Panamá probably favors investments in real property. An illustration is a parcel of property located near El Panamá Hilton Hotel, which was purchased in 1925 for B/5000 and is now assessed for property tax purposes at B/900,-000. Thus, there appears to be little justification for the favorable tax treatment of capital gains for investment purposes, while the present provisions are clearly undesirable from an equity point of view.

To place the same tax burden on capital gains as on other income would require a form of averaging. A simple device for this purpose is to divide the gain by the number of years the asset was held, calculate the tax on this fraction after it has been added to other income, and then multiply the tax by the number of years the asset was held. Capital losses should be deductible in the year of realization, and if not fully absorbed, carried forward to be offset against future income. If an averaging approach is not used, it would be necessary to have a formula which relates the level of tax rates in an inverse relationship to the period over which the asset is held.

Another important problem that seriously detracts from equity is the exemption from income taxation of capital gains on assets held until death. There is no justification for this exemption, since the estate tax applies whether or not the assets have been taxed previously under an income tax. Therefore, all capital gains on assets should be construed as realized at death and subject to the income tax.

Finally, reconsideration should be given to a proposal made by the income tax administration in 1961, but which was not adopted by the Assembly. The proposal was that a depreciated asset held more than two years should be taxed in full on the difference between the sales price and the depreciated value of the asset. This recommendation is both equitable and rational.

Personal Exemptions

Panamá uses the type of personal exemption in which any income in excess of the exempt amounts (B/900 for a single person and B/1800 for a couple) renders the totality of the income taxable. This procedure creates what is known as a "notch problem"— the incongruity whereby a taxpayer receiving a small increment of income in excess of the exemption level can be worse off than if his income had been lower and exempt. To illustrate, a married couple without children receiving B/1,825 in 1962 would have a tax liability of B/40.15, or an income after tax of B/1,784.85. On the other hand, if the income received had been B/1800, the couple would have been better off, for they would have had no tax liability. It is precisely because of this problem that many countries allow personal exemptions to be subtracted from gross income at every level of income before application of the tax.

Another criticism which may be made of personal exemptions in Panamá is that the use of the exemption of B/100 for each dependent child does not serve to render a taxable income exempt. For example, a married couple with an income of B/2000, and supporting ten children, would have a tax liability based on B/1000 (B/2000 minus ten exemptions of B/100 each). On the other hand, a couple without children with an income of B/1800 would have no tax liability. Thus, the Panamanian exemptions operate in such a way as to discriminate against couples with children.

The exemption of B/100 per dependent child also gives scant consideration to the cost of raising children. One of the advantages of a net income tax is that allowances may be made for the personal circumstances

of taxpayers through the use of exemptions and other deductions. And one of the factors which accounts for the greatest difference in tax capacity among income receivers is the number of dependents. In Panamá, however, the exemption of B/100 per child results in little differentiation among taxpayers. Consider the illustration below, in which the tax liabilities and income after tax have been calculated at 1962 rates for a gross income of B/3000 with different assumptions as to the number of dependent children. It may be noted that a couple with ten children would have a tax liability of B/44.00, only B/25.30 less in taxes than a couple without children. Under these circumstances, the government in effect is saying that a couple with ten children should live equally as well on B/2,956.00 as a childless couple can live on B/2,930.70.

Dependency Status	Tax Liability on B/3000	Income after Tax
Couple with no children	B/69.30	B/2,930.70
Couple with one child	B/66.55	B/2,933.45
Couple with two children	B/63.80	B/2,936.20
Couple with five children	B/55.55	B/2,944.45
Couple with ten children	B/44.00	B/2,956.00

To a considerable degree, however, the foregoing discussion is academic, because exemptions for married couples and children must be claimed and substantiated, and this process is so burdensome in practice that the exemptions for most taxpayers are meaningless. For example, a couple with an income of B/1700, which is below the exemption limit of B/1800, is required to initiate a formal request of exemption from the Ministry of Finance and the Treasury (at a cost in stamps of B/2.05), enclosing a marriage certificate (at an additional cost in stamps of B/2.05). Each petitioner is then visited by an auditor in order to insure that there is cohabitation and that the income of the couple is below the exemption limit. Similarly, a taxpayer wishing to claim an exemption for his children must petition the government and pay the relevant stamp taxes for the petition as well as for the birth certificates of each child. Each one of these cases is also investigated by an auditor before the exemption is granted.

Because of the cost and trouble involved in claiming the exemption for married couples, or out of ignorance, or simply because some taxpayers do not want to have an auditor pry into their affairs, most married persons in Panamá forego claiming exemptions. And since withholding of the income tax in the absence of an approved certification of entitlement to exemption begins with any income in excess of B/900, the *de facto* exemption in Panamá for most married couples is actually B/900 instead of B/1800. "Most" in this context means that possibly 90 per cent of the married couples in Panamá with an income between B/900 and B/1800, who are subject to withholding, are actually taxed under the income tax although they are legally eligible for exemption.

Similarly, because the exemption per child is only B/100, and the cost of applying for these exemptions is considerable both in money and in effort, it is to be expected that few taxpayers would bother to take advantage of the exemptions. In 1961, 535 taxpayers in the whole of the Republic claimed exemptions for children. Even many of the income tax auditors, who are, of course, very well informed of their best interests under the provisions of the income tax, do not claim exemptions for dependent children. Another factor encouraging taxpayers to forego the claiming of exemptions for children is that there is no limit on the time established for claiming a refund from the government for the overpayment of taxes. Thus, some taxpayers deliberately forego the claiming of exemptions for children, and overpay their taxes, with the intention in mind of filing a claim for a refund in the future, perhaps for as many as ten or fifteen years of overpayment. These are very serious faults. It is meaningless to have exemptions for couples and children that are in practice inoperative. Both of these exemptions are important for equity purposes and they should be freely available.

Despite these very conspicuous faults in the Panamanian system of personal exemptions, there is one important virtue to the system. This is the feature that renders any income in excess of the exempt amount taxable on the totality of the income. Ideally, an exemption should be regressive in its effect in the sense that it should be more important for those who are in the greatest need of it, and less important or even nonexistent for those who are in lesser need. The Panamanian system of exemptions accomplishes this goal by limiting exemptions to the group of persons who should not be taxed, and by denying the exemptions to all others. The present system also has the virtue of simplicity from a compliance and enforcement point of view, for a large percentage of taxpayers in effect are being taxed on their gross income. Finally, by taxing on the totality of income above the exemption limits, the effective rates of the tax are higher than they would be if all taxpayers were allowed to deduct personal exemptions from their gross income.

Under the Panamanian system of exemptions, there will always be a "notch problem," but its severity will depend on the level of the initial tax rate. Provided that the initial rate is kept moderate, the "notch problem" should not be an important liability.

In summary, the recommendations which appear to be appropriate for the Panamanian system of exemptions are: 1) Exemptions for couples and for children should be liberalized so that they are fully operative. 2) Exemptions should be available only to individuals and couples and not to legal entities like partnerships and corporations. 3) The income of a married couple should be exempt when the use of exemptions for children reduces the taxable income below the exemption limit for a couple. 4) Exemptions should be reduced to the following levels: B/600 for single persons, B/900 for couples, and B/100 for each dependent child.

Separate versus Joint Returns

Separate returns must be filed in the event that both a husband and wife receive income, with the husband being required to claim all of the exemptions for children. For a tax liability to arise in the filing of separate returns, the income of one return must exceed B/900, and the total income of the two returns must exceed B/1800. For example, if a husband files a return showing an income of B/1000, and his wife files a return with an income of B/600, both returns would be exempt because the total income is less than B/1800. If, however, the husband received B/1600 and the wife B/600, the husband's income only would be taxable because the total of the two incomes exceeds B/1800. Under these circumstances, Panamá formally is requiring separate returns but actually is combining incomes in order to determine tax liability.

But there is an unneutrality in the above procedure. If only the husband works and earns B/2400, the entire amount will be taxable, because it exceeds the exemption limit of B/1800. On the other hand, if the husband earns B/1600 and his wife B/800, the family income is again B/2400, but the taxable income is only B/1600, since the wife's earnings are below the exemption limit of B/900. Under these circumstances, there is also an incentive for wives to earn less than B/900.

An improvement in the law would result if joint rather than separate returns were required, with tax liability determined on the basis of the aggregate income of a husband and his spouse. This system has the advantage of determining income tax liability on the basis of family income, which is a better yardstick of ability to pay than the separate incomes of husbands and wives.

Income Tax Jurisdiction

Panamá's income tax is based on the territorial principle that it is the source of the income rather than the citizenship or residence of the taxpayer that determines income tax liability. Thus, the tax is applicable to all income arising in Panamá, but income arising outside the country is exempt. Under these circumstances, all income received from abroad by a Panamanian individual or corporation is exempt.

The territorial principle of taxation has been an incentive for the establishment of so-called base companies and holding companies, which have been attracted to Panamá in order to earn income construed to arise from abroad. These companies enjoy a permanent type of income tax exemption without benefit of contract, and merely on the basis of the definition of income tax jurisdiction. On the other hand, the contribution of these "paper companies" often is minimal in terms of investment and employment, since their operations do not involve the physical receipt or handling of goods. Their advantage to the economy may be summarized by the term "corporate tourism."

Panamá has the alternative of taxing its residents on all their income regardless of source, and there are two compelling reasons why this is desirable. Taxation based on residence encourages investment at home by eliminating any tax advantages of foreign investment. Also, equity among taxpayers is served by including all income regardless of source, for ability to pay an income tax obviously is based on all income received regardless of source.

Panamá has used the territorial principle of taxation as a deliberate lure for attracting foreign firms. This is evident from Article 694 of the Income Tax Act enacted on September 23, 1957, which reaffirms that all income arising from sales negotiated in Panamá is exempt, provided that the goods are not physically received in Panamá. Article 694 further affirms that the income is exempt even though a commission for the "handling" of the goods is charged in Panamá. As a result, a shift in this policy is not realistically to be expected. There is no reason, however, why it would not be possible to straddle the incentive effect of the territorial rule and equity considerations. This could be achieved by taxing individuals on the basis of all their income regardless of source and reserving the territorial principle for firms organized for the purpose of undertaking a business activity. If the foreign income of individual residents were taxed, however, it would be necessary to give these taxpayers a credit for foreign income taxes paid.

Depreciation

The Panamanian income tax has a relatively rigid depreciation policy. No asset can be depreciated in excess of 100 per cent of cost and unused depreciation allowed in one year cannot be carried forward to another year. In addition, a straight-line method is required. The depreciation schedules currently in use were adopted in 1947 and show a general tendency to depreciate assets over a longer period than is warranted. For example, automobiles used for business purposes must be depreciated at 10 per cent, cement-type buildings at 2 per cent, and most types of machinery at 5 per cent. These schedules are only suggestive, however, and a more liberal write-off is permitted when justified by taxpayers.

It is important in terms of equity to insure that firms will be allowed to recover all of their capital tax-free. Furthermore, unless capital can be recovered during the course of its actual deterioration, investment in new capital goods will be discouraged. It is also reasonable to permit an accelerated method of depreciation, in which a heavier proportion of the total depreciation is allowed in the earlier years, for in practice the actual decline in the value of assets is more rapid in the earlier years.

Several reforms should be introduced in order to rationalize and liberalize depreciation allowances in Panamá:

1) Depreciation should be based on the actual useful life of the assets. In the case of light machinery and equipment, an eight-to-ten-year life is suggested as reasonable, with fifteen to twenty years being appropriate for heavier equipment.

2) New depreciation schedules should be introduced, but in developing these, a relatively small number of categories should be used—perhaps only fifteen or twenty. More than this number complicates tax compliance and enforcement.

3) Faster depreciation should be provided for machinery and equipment through the adoption of the declining-balance method with a factor of two. This would reduce the value of assets more rapidly in early years in accordance with actual declines in market values. For example, with a machine that has a useful life of ten years, the application of the declining balance method with a factor of two would permit 48.8 per cent of the cost of the asset to be depreciated over the first three years.

4) In the event that an asset is sold at a price in excess of its depreciated value, the gain on the transaction should be taxable in full.

Business Deductions

Article 699 of the income tax law, outlined earlier in Chapter 1 in the section entitled "Statutory Provisions," lists seven categories of nondeductible business deductions. This article is in need of statutory revision, for three of the nondeductible expenses should be permitted, while the deduction of other expenses needs to be denied or clarified. The three business expenses which are currently denied but should be permitted are: 1) the cost of repairs made to real and personal property if depreciation is allowed on the same property; 2) contributions that are not directly related to the business activity of the firm; and 3) the payment of bonuses in excess of one month's salary. These three expenses are actually so reasonable and necessary that the income tax administration permits their deduction in practice.

Another section of Article 699 denies the establishment of reserve funds *except* those for depreciation and bad debts. As would be expected, permission to establish a reserve for bad debts, when discretionary, may be utilized as an avoidance device, and apparently this is often the case. To resolve this problem, it would not appear to be an undue hardship to eliminate the reserve for bad debts and to require firms to deduct the actual amount of bad debts during the year in which they are experienced.

Probably the most important and immediate statutory revision that is needed is to remove the possible threat posed by Law No. 63 of December 11, 1961. It is possible that this law merely affirms that all interest incurred as a business expense is deductible, but it is also possible that it legalizes the deductibility of interest charges incurred for personal expenditures. If the latter were the case, the income tax division would be overwhelmed with refund claims on 1962 tax liabilities, and would face a very burdensome enforcement problem in the future. Privileged personal deductions, like interest, complicate the income tax law, add to compliance and enforcement problems, and are of dubious value from an equity point of view.

Insurance companies receive a special deduction, which is very difficult to justify, of up to 40 per cent of their net income.[2] This deduction is rationalized on the grounds that it is necessary for reserve purposes, yet the income tax law already permits a deduction for necessary technical reserves based on actuarial principles before determination of net taxable income. A further problem is that the insurance companies may invest the proceeds of this special deduction in government bonds or corporate stock, both representing exempt income to the recipient. Accordingly, there arises the very irregular situation in which an insurance company may have a net income of B/1,000,000 after deduction of technically necessary reserves, but this income may be reduced by B/400,000 for an additional reserve, and again by nontaxable income of B/200,000, leaving only B/400,000 as an income tax base.

Loss Carry-over

One of the basic problems of an income tax is to obtain equality of treatment between fluctuating incomes and those which are relatively regular from year to year. This problem arises because a tax year is invariably regarded as a closed period for tax purposes, but in reality the division of a flow of income into annual segments is arbitrary and inequitable. If a taxpayer has a net income of B/10,000 one year and a net loss of B/10,000 the following year, there is actually no taxable income over the two-year period, and the ideal income tax would not exact a payment. Unfortunately, however, any fundamental solution of this problem requires a system of averaging incomes over a period of years, and this would be too demanding in Panamá for compliance and enforcement purposes.

Something can be done to ameliorate the problem with respect to fluctuating business income, however, through the introduction of a loss carry-back and carry-forward provision. Apart from equity considerations, this type of deduction appears to be particularly desirable in Panamá because of the need to stimulate and encourage private investment. In the United States, business firms are permitted to carry losses back three years and forward five years. In Panamá, a carry-back of two years and carry-forward of three years would probably suffice for equity and incentive purposes.

The Imputed Income of Owner-occupied Dwellings

There is justification in principle for taxing the imputed rent of owner-occupied dwellings under an income tax in order to provide equal treatment between owners and renters. The introduction of this reform, however, requires accurate valuations of real property. There-

---

[2] The law requires a deduction of 40 per cent until reserves have reached B/250,000; not less than 30 per cent when the reserves are greater than B/250,000 but not more than B/500,000; and not less than 20 per cent when the reserves are greater than B/500,000. Article 32 of Law No. 17 of August 22, 1956.

fore, the taxation of imputed rent under the income tax should be delayed until the current project for the reassessment of all properties in Panamá is completed.

ADMINISTRATION

Despite the emphasis that is given in this study to the functional and structural problems of the Panamanian income tax, it is recognized that an equitable and productive income tax requires high levels of compliance and enforcement. Some students of public finance are pessimistic concerning the role of an income tax in a relatively underdeveloped country because of the pervasive compliance and enforcement difficulties, while others are more sanguine. Be that as it may, it is indisputable that an income tax statute can be defeated in practice by slipshod administration, and if this is not to happen, a number of administrative techniques or tools of enforcement must be used efficiently. The use of these techniques are reviewed briefly below for the purpose of assessing the overall strength of income tax administration in Panamá.

Auditing

After the income tax returns are filed by taxpayers, they are given a "liquidation." This procedure is not auditing in any sense of the word, for it consists merely of calculating the tax on the basis of information provided by the taxpayer, or verification of the tax calculation. When the liquidation is completed, taxpayers are advised of their tax assessments by means of "receipts." These are mailed by April 30, well in advance of the due date for tax payments of June 30. Article 718 of the income tax law requires that each return must be given a liquidation, but the forwarding of receipts is a service provided by the income tax administration.

During January and February, when the flow of income tax returns is not heavy, the liquidation process is handled by a group of five persons in a "receipts and statistical section." In order to complete this process, however, it is necessary for all auditors, both office and field, to devote their full time to the operation for about one month. The liquidation process is considered necessary because the majority of taxpayers do not bother to calculate their tax. Moreover, it is reported that most taxpayers make errors in their tax calculations with a tendency toward overpayment.

Auditors glance through the tax returns during the liquidation process, and this affords the opportunity to select certain returns for audit. Other cases for audit are obtained by the chief auditor, who reviews all returns after the liquidation procedure has been completed. The principal criterion used in selecting returns for audit is to identify those taxpayers who report decreases in their tax liabilities. There is a positive disinclination to audit large firms on the argument that these assignments are too difficult and time-consuming. Merely to audit one large firm, it is maintained, might require as much as one-third of the total auditing resources for a two-month period. As a result, there are some large firms in Panamá that have never been audited during the past twenty years.

Office and field auditors are divided into five groups, each of which is assigned to a particular category of tax returns: 1) large businesses maintaining elaborate accounting records; 2) commercial establishments with installment sales; 3) small businesses; 4) wholesale firms; and 5) professionals and other individuals. Each of these groups has five auditors, including a supervisor, and each group also has a ratio of one office auditor to four field auditors. Thus, there is a total of five office auditors and twenty field auditors. Auditors are assigned to the five groups according to their ability and experience; i.e., the superior auditors are assigned to group 1 above, and so on down the list.

The historical auditing record shown in Table 3.1 reflects several serious inadequacies. The additional amount of tax assessed shows very capricious movements, from over B/1

TABLE 3.1

Number of Income Tax Audits, Additional Assessments, and Additional Tax

| Year | Doomage Assessments | | | Office and Field Audits | | | |
	Number of Assessments	Additional Assessments (Balboas)	Additional Tax (Balboas)	Number of Audits	Additional Assessments (Balboas)	Additional Tax (Balboas)	Total Additional Tax (Balboas)
1953	426	8,897,174	340,282	948	7,696,571	691,210	1,031,492
1954	608	¹	485,036	393	5,252,178	399,988	885,024
1955	82	2,593,394	99,892	74	7,655,361	289,119	389,011
1956	59	2,876,364	58,836	157	942,522	782,227	841,063
1957	214	3,153,341	95,112	231	2,900,533	305,474	400,586
1958	436	6,179,213	89,306	692	8,779,490	1,076,795	1,166,101
1959	197	6,431,971	33,547	424	1,454,014	87,592	121,139
1960	337	3,448,507	47,408	329	1,692,087	150,680	198,088
1961	288	2,208,883	69,790	568	2,916,380	250,944	320,734

¹ Data not available.   *Source:* Income Tax Office, Ministry of Finance and the Treasury.

million in 1953 and 1958 to only B/121,139 in 1959. In explanation of this variation, it is reported that income tax enforcement was practically non-existent until 1953, when a private consulting firm reorganized the income tax office. This reorganization, together with higher income tax rates, led to a high level of additional tax assessments in 1953 and 1954, only to be followed by a deterioration in enforcement activities in 1955 and 1956. The employment of new auditors in 1957 led to a higher level of assessments in 1958, but these assessments, in turn, resulted in a large number of appeals. Then, when the auditors were employed in the processing of appeals rather than in auditing, the additional assessments fell precipitously in 1959.

The record of additional assessments for 1961, although showing an improvement over 1959 and 1960, is far from impressive. In 1961, the total of additional tax assessments of B/320,734 was lower than for six of the eight years from 1953 to 1960. The additional tax assessed in 1961 also represented only about 3 per cent of total income tax collections of B/10,672,200. While the use of doomage assessments for taxpayers not filing tax returns is an exemplary practice, the frequency with which this device is used reflects a high level of non-compliance with the filing requirements of the income tax law. Further, the total number of 568 tax returns

audited in 1961 represents less than 8 per cent of all tax returns and only about 1 per cent of all taxpayers (including those subject to withholding who are not required to file tax returns).

No statistical breakdown is maintained for the auditing results that are attributable to office as compared to field auditing. In terms of the number of audits performed, it is reported that about 80 per cent of the investigations from 1953 to 1956 were office audits, but within recent years there were approximately the same number of office and field audits. However, field auditing is presently stressed in the sense that about 80 per cent of the auditors are engaged in this type of enforcement activity. It is also reported that field auditing is appreciably more productive of additional revenue than office auditing.

One of the principle faults in the auditing procedure in Panamá is this imbalance between office and field auditing. It could be corrected by requiring taxpayers to calculate their own tax liabilities, and on the basis of these calculations, to pay their final tax payments for the preceding year, as well as their first installments for the current year, by March 15. The liquidation process could then be converted into an office audit procedure with this type of auditing continuing throughout the course of the year. With these changes office auditing should be as productive of revenue as field auditing, and a much higher percentage of all income tax returns would be audited.

Net Worth Assessments

The net worth assessment should be an indispensable tool of income tax auditing in Panamá in those cases where it is suspected that two sets of books are maintained or where fraud appears likely. This procedure is used relatively little, however, because only about six auditors have sufficient technical ability to undertake a net worth assessment. In addition, two restrictions on investigatory powers constitute very severe limitations on the undertaking of a net worth assessment. One is that winnings from governmentally-sponsored games of chance (the casino, horse racing, and lottery) are not taxable, with the result that taxpayers are always able to account for non-business income by maintaining that they have been unusually lucky as gamblers. Second is the maintenance of numbered accounts in commercial banks, which are construed to be a matter of confidence between the banks and their clients and are thus not made available to auditors.

Penalties

Quite unbelievably, Panamá has never levied a penalty on an income tax evader for negligence or fraud, and only since 1961 have penalties been levied for non-filing and for the filing of late returns. Penalties for non-filing and late filing were levied in 1961 about 1500 times to the total amount of about B/20,000, while the comparable figures to July of 1962 were 687 penalties amounting to B/8630. Thus, in the whole history of income tax administration in Panamá, a total of about B/28,630 in penalties has been levied. Under these circumstances, it is impossible to administer an income tax effectively, for the government in effect is encouraging taxpayers to be dishonest by providing them with an incentive to evade.

To some degree, Panamá's weak record in applying penalties in the past is attributable to inadequate statutory authority in the form of a fraud penalty that required proof of *intent* to defraud the government. Now that this restriction of *intent* has been removed by legislation enacted in 1961, and it is now only necessary to prove the existence of certain infractions in order to levy penalties on tax evaders, some improvement in the application of penalties may result. This improvement was not possible until 1962 income tax returns were filed in 1963, however, for the amendment did not have retroactive effect for income years prior to 1962.

The Statute of Limitation

The length of the statute of limitations for the auditing of returns in Panamá is two years for ordinary cases and five years if no returns have been filed or if fraud is proven. These limits are unduly restrictive on the income tax administration. The length of time for the statute of limitations should be long enough in order to convenience the income tax administration in its enforcement activities, but also short enough to be fair to taxpayers. There is a consensus among income tax authorities that about four years is a desirable compromise to serve both of these objectives for ordinary cases, but there is no reason why the period for fraud should not be at least ten years.

Review and Appeals

Auditors are encouraged to obtain written acceptances of additional assessments from taxpayers in order to avoid appeals, but they are not permitted to negotiate a compromise settlement unilaterally with taxpayers. After the audits have been completed, and they are either accepted or rejected by the taxpayers, they are reviewed at three levels—by a group supervisor, by the head of the investigation section, and by the chief auditor. After this ritual, the taxpayers are formally notified of their additional assessments.

Appeals from the assessments are said to be more the rule than the exception, either in order to achieve a reduction in the original assessment or merely to delay the payment of the tax. Accurate statistics are not available to determine the total amount of revenue lost through the process of appeals, but the available data suggests that it may be significant. For example, in 1960 the total of original additional assessments amounted to B/198,087, but by the end of 1960, only B/50,882, or 26 per cent of the total of additional assessments, had been collected. There was some improvement in 1961, when a total of B/320,735 in additional assessments was levied, and B/154,301, or 48 per cent, was collected by the end of 1961. No doubt, additional collections were made of 1961 assessments during 1962, but these figures are not available.

The evidence suggests, however, that there is an excessive number of appeals, and this in turn suggests that it is relatively easy for taxpayers to reduce their liabilities. Excessive compromising with taxpayers is to be avoided because it detracts from equity, reduces the revenue productivity of the income tax, and is destructive of auditors' morale.

Information Returns

The use of information returns is one of the most important tools available to an income tax administration, for there is no better way of verifying the receipt of certain types of income received by taxpayers. Panamá's statutory authority in this respect errs in the direction of excessive coverage, for Article 716 requires information returns for every payment (without limit) of rent, interest, and personal service income. In practice, however, information returns are of negligible functional value, since the income tax administration has not found it possible to obtain the necessary personnel in order to match information returns with tax returns. This matching probably should be accomplished mechanically, since the necessary equipment

is available in the Ministry of Finance and the Treasury. But even if this matching is undertaken in the future, it should be noted that it will have limited value in the absence of tax returns from most of the taxpayers subject to withholding.

Withholding and Current Payment

Previous analysis in Chapter 1 indicates that the system of withholding the income tax from wages and salaries operates reasonably well with at least 90 per cent of all taxable workers being covered. Relatively little is done, however, to insure that the system operates at maximum effectiveness. An examination of the withholding procedure discloses at least three important shortcomings: 1) No attempt is made to develop a comprehensive list of employers liable for withholding. 2) The monthly and annual reports from employers are not matched for inconsistencies, and are not checked with the employer's tax returns except when audits are undertaken. 3) Since most employees subject to withholding are not required to file tax returns, it is not possible to compare withholding statements with the employees' tax returns. In view of these shortcomings, the withholding system for the income tax probably operates reasonably well only because there is more effective enforcement of withholding for social security purposes, and the policing of the latter compels employers also to withhold for income tax purposes.

The system of current payment for those taxpayers not subject to withholding also has certain weaknesses. Under the present system, the taxpayer is required to estimate his current year's income by March 15. There is no penalty for an underestimate provided that the estimated income is not less than the preceding year's actual income. The tax on the estimated income may be paid in full on or before June 30, or in three equal installments, on or before June 30, September 30, and December 31.

An improvement in this current payment procedure is related to the suggestions made previously in the section concerned with auditing. If the final tax payment on the previous year's income is moved ahead from June 30 to March 15, the first quarterly installment on the current year's estimated tax should also be due on March 15. The remaining three installments could then become due on or before June 30, September 30, and December 31.

Canvassing for Non-Filers

Experience in other countries demonstrates that a search for non-filers is warranted, for it can never be taken for granted in an income tax jurisdiction that all taxpayers fulfill their filing requirements. Evidence of the need for this search in Panamá is the frequent use of doomage assessments in those instances in which it is determined that taxpayers are delinquent in filing tax returns.

Panamá has undertaken some canvassing for delinquent returns, but the effort has been capricious and minimal. (For particulars, see the section in the previous chapter entitled "Evasion.") These efforts should be systematized by the training of a special group of employees which would undertake a search for nonfilers on a continuous and comprehensive basis throughout the whole of Panamá.

Doomage and Investigatory Powers

Panamá has the authority to levy a "doomage" assessment, which is the right to assess the tax on the basis of the auditor's best guess of the correct income whenever the taxpayer fails to file a tax return. As shown in Table 3.1, doomage assessments are used quite frequently. Panamá is also vested with the authority to obtain all the books, records, and documents in possession of the taxpayers, as well as with the right to obtain information from commercial banks. But despite these powers, one severe investigatory problem exists in the undertaking of field auditing. As mentioned previously, this arises from the

existence of numbered accounts maintained by commercial banks, which are construed by the banks to be confidential. The law permitting numbered accounts was enacted in 1959 on the argument that this provision would attract foreign capital. Even if this argument is defensible, there is no reason for extending the privilege to Panamanian citizens in view of the income tax enforcement problem these accounts create.

Taxpayer Assistance

Attention should be given in administering an income tax to the various ways in which taxpayers may be assisted in meeting their obligations. The reason for this is that the income tax will function well only in an environment in which there is a high degree of taxpayer knowledge of the law and voluntary cooperation with its requirements. In other words, most taxpayers cannot be *compelled* to comply; they must, instead, be *willing* to cooperate.

Taxpayer assistance involves several possible types of activities: 1) assisting the taxpayer at filing time; 2) adequate and readily available information in the form of publications, which should include the income tax law, regulations, court rulings, and tax guides; 3) the use of newspapers, radio, and television for instruction and publicity; 4) educational programs for accountants and lawyers; 5) instruction sheets accompanying the income tax return; and 6) publicity of gross violations.

Panamá scores relatively low on the use of these types of taxpayer assistance. Newspapers and radio are used from January to March for the purpose of instruction and publicity, and some auditors are assigned the responsibility to assist taxpayers prior to the March 15 filing date. But this is about as far as taxpayer assistance goes. The income tax law is available only in the *Fiscal Code*, which is a privately-published compendium of tax laws. About twenty income tax cases have been ruled upon by the Supreme Court, but these have not been assembled or published, and no single person in Panamá appears to have a complete collection of opinions. A program of instructing school children on the income tax was terminated soon after it was started, and instruction sheets accompanying the income tax returns have not been used since 1959. In the light of these circumstances, it is not surprising to find that most tax returns are prepared and filed by accountants and lawyers rather than by taxpayers.

Research

There are four types of research activities that may be undertaken by an income tax department: 1) the provision of statistics that have a public service value rather than merely data for administrative use; 2) tax policy research for purposes of proposing amendments to the income tax law; 3) administrative research concerning the organization of the tax department, the determination of workloads, the development of tax forms and instructions for taxpayers, etc.; and 4) research in auditing for the purpose of studying such problems as the selection of returns for audit and the allocation of auditing resources.

It must be admitted that few income tax jurisdictions in the world undertake all of these activities, but it is also evident that few income tax administrations could accomplish less of them than Panamá. There is no person or group, either in the income tax division or in the Ministry of Finance and the Treasury, that is concerned with research activities regularly and with professional competency. There is a small statistical section in the income tax division, but this group is concerned only with the numbering and classifying of returns. Since this group does not *develop* statistics, and it does not include a statistician *per se*, it is really a clerical unit. Because of these shortcomings, even the most elementary income tax statistics are not readily available in Panamá and must be developed by the use of auditing personnel on an *ad hoc* basis.

Auditing Personnel

Out of the present staff of twenty-five auditors, only six may be considered to be fully-qualified and experienced auditors, with the remainder being more bookkeepers than accountants. Eight of the twenty-five auditors are newly hired, and are presently undergoing elementary training in accounting and auditing. Only one of the eight new employees is a university graduate. The beginning salary for auditors of B/250 per month prevents the employment of accountants, since an experienced accountant can earn a salary in private business of from B/300 to B/500 per month.

Another serious problem with respect to auditing personnel is the administrative practice of shifting employees from office to office within the Ministry of Finance and the Treasury under circumstances in which the income tax division is short-changed in the transfers. For example, the budget of the income tax office in 1962 provided for a total of forty-six employees, but through a process of loaning staff and receiving other personnel in exchange, there were actually only twenty-eight employees available for income tax enforcement activities. This loss in personnel resources to other tax offices amounted in 1962 to B/47,520 out of a total budget of B/123,900.

Exchange of Information

There are several ways in which it is possible for the various departments of a government to cooperate so as to facilitate the enforcement of an income tax. Among these are the exchange of lists of taxpayers, audits, and certain information helpful for enforcement activities, such as social security lists, and recipients of pensions. Once again, the essential problem in utilizing this information is a shortage of income tax personnel rather than statutory authority. The income tax law requires all government departments to forward information helpful for audit purposes to the income tax division. This is not done, however, and little effort is made by the income tax administration to encourage this cooperation because of the press of other burdens.

There are only two instances in which an attempt was made by the income tax division to take advantage of information available from other government offices. It is possible to obtain information on the movement of agricultural products into the province of Panamá, which is helpful in the auditing of the growers and sellers of agricultural goods. This information was assembled, but personnel resources were lacking to associate these data with income tax returns. Second, the income tax division assigned two clerks to the Instituto de Fomento Económico and Instituto de Vivienda y Urbanismo for the purpose of collecting information on government contracts and other data helpful for auditing. These data also have not been utilized, and are unlikely to be unless additional personnel resources are made available to the income tax division.

Collection

Table 3.2 provides a summary of income tax collections in Panamá during the period from 1958 to 1961. These statistics demonstrate that there is a tendency for about 9 per cent of income tax assessments to become delinquent each year. The collection problem, however, is characterized by a reluctance to pay the tax when due rather than by a hard core of uncollectible accounts. This is evident from the fact that the total of delinquent income taxes as of December 31, 1961, was B/677,361, but only B/127,472 of this amount was attributable to years preceding 1961.

There is no lack of legal authority to enforce collections in Panamá. The collection division has the authority to attach bank accounts and to sell property without court order, and the only recourse available to taxpayers from these actions is appeal to the Supreme Court. But in practice, collection efforts stop short of such punitive measures, principally because of cumbersome procedures and a limited number of enforcement personnel. The collection division is staffed by only three lawyers and twelve other employees, and these persons are responsible for the collection of *all* delinquent taxes for the whole of the Republic. There is also a reluctance to enforce collection in particular instances where political pressure is likely to be exerted.

Another problem is that there is no effective penalty that may be applied to income tax delinquents. There is a penalty of 10 per cent if the tax is not paid when due, and an additional penalty of 10 per cent plus costs if prosecution is necessary in order to collect the tax, but there is no provision for the payment of interest on uncollected taxes. As a result, the same penalty is applied regardless of the duration of the delinquency. Thus, there is no incentive for the taxpayer

TABLE 3.2
Delinquent Income Tax Collections

Calendar Years (As of December 31)	Income Tax Due (Balboas)	Income Tax Collections (Balboas)	Delinquent Income Tax Collections (Balboas)	Percentage of Delinquent Taxes of Original Assessments
1958	8,566,035	7,582,031	984,004	11.5
1959	4,523,639	4,273,873	249,766	5.5
1960	5,336,597	4,836,353	500,244	9.4
1961	6,332,690	5,782,800	549,890[1]	8.7

[1] In addition to this delinquency attributable to 1961, there was B/127,472 in uncollected income taxes attributable to years preceding 1961. Therefore, the total income tax delinquency as of December, 1961, was B/677,361.

Source: Income Tax Office, Ministry of Finance and the Treasury.

to settle his account quickly after it has become delinquent.

Conclusion

It is apparent from the foregoing review that income tax administration in Panamá has suffered from a long period of neglect and that the present enforcement of the law is critically weak. In fact, if one compares the structural faults of the present tax with its enforcement shortcomings, it is probably true that the greater weakness is in administrative performance. Or stating this another way, if the hypothetical choice were to be made between a more refined and equitable law with present levels of administration, or the present law with improved administration, probably the second alternative would be the more prudent choice.

But this is not a desirable or necessary choice, for Panamá actually needs *both* better administration of the income tax as well as an improved income tax law, and both are possible. Panamá can have an improved administration of the income tax whenever this objective is established as a desirable goal and the necessary resources are allocated for its attainment. The caveat should be offered, also, that any improvement in the income tax law would be largely ineffectual in practice unless income tax enforcement is strengthened.

Appreciable and over-all improvement in income tax administration depends, in the final analysis, on the employment of more and better staff resources. The income tax administrators in Panamá are aware of many of the shortcomings noted in this study, and, in fact, often have initiated steps to improve administrative procedures. Invariably, however, their efforts have been frustrated by a lack of resources. To achieve an adequate level of income tax administration in Panamá will require at least a doubling of the present staff; and, in this respect, significant improvement would result at the present time if the income tax division were given its budgeted staff allotment. In addition, there is a need

to raise the professional qualifications of the present staff, especially in accounting and auditing capabilities. This could be accomplished by the use of technical assistance personnel.

SUMMARY OF RECOMMENDATIONS

The reform of the Panamanian income tax will take time and perserverance, for there are several deep and fundamental structural changes that need to be introduced as well as a wide number of desirable technical amendments. No attempt is made in this study to schedule these reforms by annual periods, for governments do not approach a problem of tax reform in this manner. For purposes of convenience, a checklist of all reforms proposed in this and the preceding chapter are noted below, and it is suggested that most of these could and should be accomplished within a period of five years. Some of these changes will be relatively easy to introduce from a technical point of view, but the more fundamental reforms will require a gradualistic approach. One of the more difficult problems along these lines is to rationalize the system of personal exemptions and at the same time make the income tax more progressive and productive of revenue. A specific proposal to accomplish these goals follows the summary of income tax reforms.

Summary of Income Tax Reforms

1) The Panamanian income tax is largely a levy on unearned rather than on earned income, and an undue amount of income tax revenue is obtained from a relatively small number of taxpayers. Therefore, if the tax is to become a more productive and dependable source of revenue, the base must be broadened, particularly by obtaining a greater share of collections from the lower end of the income scale. At the same time, although tax rates have been increased recently on the middle and upper income

groups, the effective tax rates for these tax-payers are still very moderate and may be increased further.

2) The principle of tax discrimination in favor of earned income should be abandoned and replaced by a system of taxing all income neutrally. This reform would require the elimination of the differential surtaxes on earned and unearned income.

3) Four reforms should be introduced to the system of exemptions: 1. Exemptions for couples and for children should be liberalized so that they are freely available. 2. Exemptions should be available only to natural persons and not to legal entities like partnerships and corporations. 3. The income of a married couple should be exempt when the use of exemptions for dependents reduces the taxable income below the exemption limit for a couple. 4. Exemptions should be reduced to the following levels: B/600 for single persons, B/900 for couples, and B/100 for each dependent child.

4) Panamá should abandon the system of subjecting partnerships and corporations to progressive income tax rates and excluding partnership shares and dividends from taxation at the individual level. Instead, the earnings of partnerships should be attributed to the owners for tax purposes. Corporations should be subject to a flat-rate tax, with dividends taxable at the individual level of taxation.

5) Capital gains should be taxed as other income, but an averaging device should be utilized to prevent a discriminatory burden of taxation upon realization of the gains. Also, all capital gains on assets held until death should be construed as realized at death, and all gains realized should be subject to the income tax.

6) Joint rather than separate returns should be required, with the income tax liability determined on the basis of the aggregate income of a husband and his spouse.

7) Panamá should tax individuals on the basis of all of their income regardless of source, reserving the territorial principle of taxation for firms organized for the purpose of undertaking a business activity.

8) New depreciation schedules should be adopted with generally faster write-off periods. In addition, the declining-balance method with a factor of two should be permitted for the depreciation of machinery and equipment.

9) Article 699 of the income tax law should be amended in order to permit three business deductions: 1. the cost of repairs on depreciable property; 2. contributions that are not directly related to the business activity of the firm; and 3. the payment of bonuses in excess of one month's salary.

10) The reserve fund allowed for bad debts should be replaced by a system of requiring firms to deduct the actual amount of bad debts incurred during the year in which they are experienced.

11) Law No. 63 of December 11, 1961, which threatens to permit the deduction of interest charges incurred for personal expenditures, should be repealed.

12) The special deduction allowed insurance companies, which is in addition to a deduction for necessary technical reserves, should be disallowed.

13) A loss carry-forward and carry-back provision should be introduced.

14) Withholding of the income tax should be introduced on all Panamanians employed in the Canal Zone, and all private business firms operating in the zone should be subject to Panamanian income taxes.

15) All of the several techniques for the enforcement of the income tax should be improved, but these improvements in the final analysis depend on the employment of additional staff resources of higher quality. The present income tax staff should be doubled, and technical assistance should be obtained to raise the productivity of the staff.

A Specific Proposal for the Rationalization of Exemptions and Tax Rates

It is proposed that the more basic structural reforms of the income tax system should be introduced in two stages. The first stage would be concerned with rationalizing personal exemptions, increasing the tax rates on individuals, and eliminating the surtaxes that place differential burdens on earned and unearned income. After these reforms have been accomplished, corporations should be subject to a flat-rate tax with dividends taxable at the individual level.

Under the proposed new system of exemptions, a bachelor would receive an exemption of B/600, a married couple B/900, and each dependent child B/100. These exemptions would be freely available, so that bachelors and married couples with incomes below the exemption limits would be exempt from taxation. On the other hand, bachelors and married couples with incomes above the exemption limits (after deductions for dependent children) would be taxable on the totality of their incomes. Exemptions would be denied business entities.

To eliminate the differential surtaxes, it is proposed that all taxpayers, individual, partnership, and corporate, should be subject to the same tax schedule shown in Table 3.3. The increases in tax burdens that would result by applying this tax schedule to married couples, bachelors, and corporations are shown in Table 3.4, 3.5, and 3.6. It may be noted from these tables that several objectives with respect to fundamental income tax reform have been accomplished: 1) The tax base has been broadened by increasing the tax liabilities at the lower end of the income scale, but at the same time, the tax liability

of the lowest taxable income group has been reduced. 2) The progressivity of the tax has been increased. 3) Higher percentage increases in tax liabilities have been placed on individuals than on partnerships and corporations, which could make possible the eventual substitution of a flat-rate tax on corporations. 4) It is estimated that the adoption of this tax schedule would result in approximately B/2 million in additional revenues.

TABLE 3.3

Proposed Income Tax Schedule

Income Brackets (Balboas)	Tax Rates (Per Cent)
0 to 1,000	2
1,000 to 2,000	3
2,000 to 3,000	4
3,000 to 4,000	5
4,000 to 5,000	6
5,000 to 6,000	7
6,000 to 8,000	9
8,000 to 10,000	11
10,000 to 15,000	13
15,000 to 20,000	15
20,000 to 30,000	17
30,000 to 40,000	20
40,000 to 50,000	23
50,000 to 60,000	26
60,000 to 70,000	29
70,000 to 80,000	32
80,000 to 90,000	35
90,000 to 100,000	38
100,000 to 200,000	41
200,000 to 300,000	44
300,000 to 400,000	47
400,000 to 500,000	50
500,000 to 750,000	53
750,000 to 1,000,000	56
Over 1,000,000	59

FISCAL SURVEY OF PANAMA

TABLE 3.4

Effect of the Proposed Tax Schedule on Married Couples[1]

Gross Income (Balboas)	Tax Liability in 1962 (Balboas)	Effective Tax Rates in 1962 (Per Cent)	Proposed Tax Liability (Balboas)	Proposed Effective Tax Rates (Per Cent)	Proposed Percentage Increase in Tax
1,000	20	2.00	0	—	—
1,500	30	2.00	35	2.33	16.67
2,000	44	2.20	50	2.50	13.64
2,500	56	2.24	70	2.80	25.00
3,000	69	2.30	90	3.00	30.43
4,000	99	2.48	140	3.50	41.41
5,000	136	2.72	200	4.00	47.06
6,000	191	3.18	270	4.50	41.36
7,000	257	3.67	360	5.14	40.08
8,000	323	4.04	450	5.63	39.31
9,000	396	4.40	560	6.22	41.41
10,000	473	4.73	670	6.70	41.65
15,000	924	6.16	1,320	8.80	42.86
20,000	1,419	7.10	2,070	10.35	45.88
30,000	2,629	8.76	3,770	12.57	43.40
40,000	3,839	9.60	5,770	14.43	50.30
50,000	5,489	10.98	8,070	16.14	47.02
60,000	7,139	11.90	10,670	17.78	49.46
70,000	9,119	13.03	13,570	19.39	48.81
80,000	11,099	13.87	16,770	20.96	51.10
90,000	13,409	14.90	20,270	22.52	51.17
100,000	15,719	15.72	24,070	24.07	53.13
200,000	43,769	21.88	65,070	32.54	48.67
300,000	73,469	24.49	109,070	36.36	48.46
400,000	106,469	26.62	156,070	39.02	46.59
500,000	139,469	27.89	206,070	41.21	47.75
750,000	230,219	30.70	338,570	45.14	47.06
1,000,000	326,469	32.65	478,570	47.86	46.59

[1] Calculations assume two dependent children.

TABLE 3.5

Effect of the Proposed Tax Schedule on Bachelors

Gross Income (Balboas)	Tax Liability in 1962 (Balboas)	Effective Tax Rates in 1962 (Per Cent)	Proposed Tax Liability[1] (Balboas)	Proposed Effective Tax Rates (Per Cent)	Proposed Percentage Increase in Tax
500	0	0	0	—	—
800	0	0	20	2.50	—
1,000	25	2.50	25	2.50	—
1,500	37	2.50	44	2.93	18.92
2,000	55	2.75	62	3.10	12.73
2,500	70	2.80	87	3.48	24.29
3,000	86	2.87	112	3.73	30.23
4,000	124	3.10	175	4.38	41.13
5,000	170	3.40	250	5.00	47.06
6,000	239	3.98	337	5.62	41.00
7,000	321	4.59	450	6.43	40.19
8,000	404	5.05	562	7.03	39.11
9,000	495	5.50	700	7.78	41.41
10,000	591	5.91	837	8.37	41.62
15,000	1,155	6.31	1,650	11.00	42.86
20,000	1,774	8.87	2,587	12.94	45.83
30,000	3,286	10.95	4,712	15.71	43.40
40,000	4,798	11.99	7,212	18.03	50.31
50,000	6,861	13.72	10,087	20.17	47.02
60,000	8,924	14.87	13,337	22.23	49.45
70,000	11,399	16.28	16,962	24.23	48.80
80,000	13,874	17.34	20,962	26.20	51.09
90,000	16,761	18.62	25,337	28.15	51.17
100,000	19,649	19.65	30,087	30.09	53.12
200,000	54,711	27.36	81,337	40.67	48.67
300,000	91,836	30.61	136,337	45.45	48.46
400,000	133,086	33.27	195,087	48.77	46.59
500,000	173,336	34.67	257,587	51.52	48.61
750,000	287,774	38.37	423,212	56.43	47.06
1,000,000	408,086	40.81	598,212	59.82	46.59

[1] Includes retention of the 25 per cent surtax on bachelors.

TABLE 3.6

Effect of the Proposed Tax Schedule on Partnerships and Corporations

Gross Income (Balboas)	Tax Liability in 1962 (Balboas)	Effective Tax Rates in 1962 (Per Cent)	Proposed Tax Liability (Balboas)	Proposed Effective Tax Rates (Per Cent)	Proposed Percentage Increase in Tax
2,000	56	2.80	50	2.50	−10.71
3,000	88	2.93	90	3.00	2.27
4,000	126	3.15	140	3.50	11.11
5,000	174	3.48	200	4.00	14.94
6,000	244	4.07	270	4.50	10.66
7,000	328	4.69	360	5.14	9.76
8,000	412	5.15	450	5.63	9.22
9,000	504	5.60	560	6.22	11.11
10,000	602	6.02	670	6.70	11.30
15,000	1,176	7.84	1,320	8.80	12.24
20,000	1,806	9.03	2,070	10.35	14.62
30,000	3,346	11.15	3,770	12.57	12.67
40,000	4,886	12.22	5,770	14.43	18.09
50,000	6,986	13.97	8,070	16.14	15.52
60,000	9,086	15.14	10,670	17.78	17.43
70,000	11,606	16.58	13,570	19.39	16.92
80,000	14,126	17.66	16,770	20.96	18.72
90,000	17,066	18.96	20,270	22.52	18.77
100,000	20,006	20.01	24,070	24.07	20.31
200,000	55,706	27.85	65,070	32.54	16.81
300,000	93,506	31.17	109,070	36.36	16.64
400,000	135,506	33.88	156,070	39.02	15.18
500,000	177,506	35.50	206,070	41.21	16.09
750,000	293,006	39.07	338,570	45.14	15.55
1,000,000	415,506	41.55	478,570	47.86	15.18
2,000,000	840,000	42.00	1,068,570	53.43	27.21
3,000,000	1,260,000	42.00	1,758,570	58.62	39.57

CHAPTER 4

The Property Tax

PROPERTY TAXES MAY INCLUDE as objects of taxation virtually all forms of wealth, or they may be relatively narrow in application and be confined to real property. In Panamá, the property tax is relatively narrow. All rural and urban land and buildings, unless exempted by law, are taxable. Elevators, fixed machinery, and other attachments to a building are included.[1] On the other hand, all personal property and intangibles are exempt.

EXEMPTIONS

The considerable number of exemptions may be classified as conventional and special.[2] The conventional exemptions include property of the national government, municipalities, and municipal corporations; that belonging to the autonomous institutions of the national government; property used for religious, social, public welfare, or other purposes of a nonprofit nature; property of private schools, provided that they enter a contract with the Ministry of Education to grant from five to twenty-five permanent scholarships to low-income Panamanian students; property of private hospitals, provided the owners enter a contract with the Ministry of Health to care for any sick person in the event of an emergency, and to give free hospitalization each year to twenty-five low-income Pana-

manians; property exempt in accordance with international treaties or agreements; property constituting the *Patrimonio Familiar;* and finally, property of a value not more than B/500.

The special exemptions include all personal property, whether tangible or intangible; all new construction during the period from January 1, 1960 to December 31, 1967;[3] the land and buildings of El Panamá Hilton Hotel; and frozen or fixed rates of property taxation for certain corporations.[4]

BASE AND RATES

The base for application of the property tax is the value of the property, as declared by the owner, or as assessed by the Comisión Catastral. The tax is national, and the rate established by law. There are no local property taxes.

Before 1947, the rate was one-half of one per cent. In 1947, it was increased to one per cent, except that on a house occupied by the owner, a rate of one-half of one per cent was applicable on assessments of less than B/15,000. In 1953, as part of the legislation establishing the Comisión Catastral and providing for a revaluation of all real estate

---

[1] Article 763 of the *Fiscal Code.*
[2] *Ibid.,* Article 764.

[3] New houses of a cadastral value of not more than B/5000 may be exempt for five years. This provision, unlike the other, does not have a terminal date.
[4] See the chapter in this study on The Use of Fiscal Incentives for Development Purposes.

in the Republic, the rate was reduced to one-half of one per cent. It may be inferred that this action was taken on the assumption that the over-all assessment level would be doubled. In 1956, the rate was again increased to one per cent, except that on houses occupied by their owners, a rate of one-half of one per cent was retained on assessments below B/25,000.[5]

Finally, the following graduated scale of rates was adopted in 1960:

Assessments	Rates
Up to B/5000	¾ per cent
B/5000 to B/20,000	1 per cent
B/20,000 to B/50,000	1¼ per cent
B/50,000 to B/75,000	1⅜ per cent
More than B/75,000	1½ per cent

PROBLEMS WITH RESPECT TO EXEMPTIONS

Conventional Exemptions

The conventional exemptions raise few questions. They are mostly of public property, or of private property used for purposes recognized as serving the welfare of the public. The other exemptions in this group represent modest relief measures to low income groups. The patrimonial exemption (*Patrimonio Familiar*) applies to land granted by the government to encourage colonization in a given area or to maintain a settlement. The area of the plot exempted is usually less than five hectares, though occasionally it is ten hectares or more. There are forty-four of these colonies in the Republic, including twenty-two in the Province of Panamá. Of the twenty-two, two are housing colonies and twenty are agricultural.

The exemption of property with a value of less than B/500 was clearly designed as a relief measure. Property owners with higher valuations are not permitted to deduct the B/500.

[5] Law 53 of November 30, 1956.

Special Exemptions

The principal special exemption is that of new construction. Beginning January 1, 1960, all new construction is exempt from taxation, and all future construction completed before December 31, 1967. In appraising the consequences of this policy, it is fitting to examine the results of the preceding period of exemption. From 1953 through 1959, all new construction was exempt. The aggregate exemption for these years in the municipalities of Panamá, Colón, Baré, David, Chitre, and La Chorrera was B/51,338,600, of which B/49,890,600 was in Panamá and Colón. But for the last four cities, the only data available are for 1959; and the new construction in the remaining cities in Panamá as well as in the entire rural area is not included.

Assuming, then, that B/51,338,600[7] as a minimum was the taxable value lost by the exemption in 1959, the next question that may be raised is the loss of tax revenue. This is a matter of determining the rate of taxation to be applied.[8] New houses occupied by their owners comprised less than one-half the value of all new construction. On these the tax rate was one-half of one per cent up to a valuation of B/25,000, but on other property the rate was one per cent. Assuming that the average rate of taxation was three-fourths of one per cent, a loss of revenue of B/385,039

[6] These and other data concerning the exemption of new construction were obtained from *Estadística de Panamá, Industrias: 1961*, Series "F" No. 1, pp. 16–29.
[7] It was assumed in calculating this total that additions and repairs in Panamá and Colón equalled depreciation. In Panamá, additions and repairs represented 11 per cent of the total of construction, repairs, and additions for the period 1953 to 1961. The total for additions and repairs does not necessarily equal depreciation, but the latter amount is an unknown quantity. The thought throughout this and other calculations is to arrive at so conservative an estimate of the tax loss that it could be defended as the very least amount that could have been sustained.
It was not possible to distinguish church, school, and other non-profit private construction in Baru, David, Chitre, and La Chorrera. But in Panamá and Colón, the separation could be made, and for the years indicated above, it was 7 per cent of total new construction in Panamá, and 10 per cent in Colón. It was necessary to exclude the value of this type of construction when known, because it was already exempt under another article of the *Fiscal Code*.
[8] The effect of the exemption on the volume of new construction will be considered later.

is indicated. This amount, the result of a deliberately conservative calculation, was 18 per cent of the B/2,189,000 collected in 1959 in the Republic from the property tax. The percentage loss for the other years was less because of the smaller aggregate value of the exemption.

It is not possible to calculate the tax loss during the period from 1960 to 1967 as it depends on the future rate of construction. Based on past experience, however, it is likely to be substantial.

An objection should now be recognized. It may be said that the volume of new construction, and therefore its value, has depended and will continue to depend on the availability of tax exemption. The tax rate, however, is low. Consequently, the value of the exemption to the individual property owner is small. Moreover, the proportion of exempt to taxable property was such in 1959 that had all the property been taxed, the rate could have been reduced 15 per cent, and yet the same amount of revenue would have been obtained.

The composition of the exempt construction gives further support to the contention that the exemption of such property has little incentive value. The aggregate exemption of B/5,140,000 in Panamá for 1961 is composed as follows: individual residences, B/1,881,-000; apartment houses, B/2,094,000; certain small houses, B/23,000; commercial properties, B/984,000; and industrial establishments, B/158,000. Clearly, the building of an individual residence is affected only slightly, as against the personal considerations involved, by a property tax of from three-fourths to one and one-half per cent. As for apartment houses, the scale of rents is such that the tax could have scarcely any influence on their construction. These two types of properties represent B/3,998,000 or 78 per cent of the aggregate exemption of B/5,140,000.

It is conceivable that the imposition of the tax would have more effect on the other types of construction that compose the remaining 22 per cent. But the maximum ad-

verse influence would be small. Other elements are undoubtedly much more important in making an investment decision than a property tax of from three-fourths to one and one-half per cent.

The exemption of El Panamá Hilton Hotel is a special extension of this form of relief from taxes. The assessed value of the land, B/2,000,000, and of the building, B/5,000,-000, is exempt from taxation. If this property had been taxed, the revenue received in 1961 would have been B/104,780. In addition, El Panamá Hilton obtains a share in the profits of the government-operated casino. It received B/47,885 from this source in 1961, or a total of B/207,781 since 1956.[9] In return for these benefits, the hotel has agreed to pay B/31,000 for public services over a period of ten years, or B/3100 per year. The net calculable gain from property tax exemption and gambling profits received by El Panamá Hilton in 1961 was B/152,665 less B/3100 or B/149,565. This amount does not include the indirect gain to the hotel from the presence of the gambling room. Naturally, the visitors to the casino also patronize the bar, the dining room, and use the other facilities of the hotel. As a result, the casino probably is the most profitable public room in the establishment.

The remaining special exemptions for nineteen corporations have been granted under the general Panamanian development law that was in effect from 1950 to 1957. These exemptions take the form of a freeze in the rate of the property tax at levels in effect during 1950 to 1957 for a period of twenty-five years. At the present time, the effect of these exemptions is to reduce the amount of the tax liabilities by approximately one-third.

The loss in revenue occasioned by the exemption of new construction, and the special exemptions of El Panamá Hilton and of certain industrial corporations, is not the only consequence of the exemption policy. In examining the further and deeper

[9] The amounts received in other years were B/23,496 in 1956, B/36,997 in 1957, B/34,932 in 1958, B/44,922 in 1959, and B/19,549 in 1960.

effects, emphasis will be given to the exemption of new construction, because this is by far the most important part of the general problem.

To exempt some properties, while taxing others, is to confer an advantage on the favored ones, and thereby to disturb competitive relationships. Why should the newer properties pay less than the older? What purpose does the difference serve? Presumably, the reason for the exemption is to encourage new construction in the interest of increasing employment and the demand for building materials. But relief from the payment of any tax leaves money in the hands of taxpayers that they may spend for personal goods or services, or for investment. All these uses of funds stimulate the economy. Except as it can be demonstrated that the saving resulting from the exemption of new construction stimulates the economy *more* than would an equal saving derived from the reduction of some other tax, this form of subsidy has no special justification. And this supporting demonstration cannot be made. On the contrary, it appears likely that the exemption of new construction, because the incentive is a minor consideration in investment decisions, has had little effect on the volume of new construction.

The issue may be reduced, therefore, to whether a tax reduction, equal in amount to that arising from the exemption of new construction but general in availability, should be substituted. Such a measure would avoid the discrimination inherent in limiting the exemption to new construction. If the budget of the government is balanced, and fiscal policy considerations do not indicate the need for an increase in revenue, there is much to be said for this course. If, however, more revenue should be needed, the simplest and least harmful method of obtaining it would be to repeal the exemption for new construction.

Another important result, though not yet actual, claims attention. Since 1953, all new construction has had one or more years of tax exemption. Under present legislation, this policy is to be continued through 1967. Thus the actual and contemplated years of exemption extend to fifteen. Governments everywhere find great difficulty in discontinuing a subsidy. The persons who benefit oppose strongly any measure to eliminate the advantages. The great majority of taxpayers, who are not directly affected or who do not see themselves to be, are indifferent to the outcome. In this situation, the vested interest groups are almost certain to prevail. Given fifteen years of exemption of new construction, the benefits will become increasingly entrenched. At the end of that period it may be impossible to dislodge them.

ASSESSMENTS

The original rule of assessment both in the city and in the rural areas was the owner's declared value. The owner of a house, an apartment, a building used for business purposes, or a farm, simply declared or registered its value on an official form. No one viewed his property and placed a valuation on it. The office of assessor, in fact, did not exist. The owner was not supposed to declare a value lower than cost, though he might declare a higher one if he wished. Thus, if he bought the property, the purchase price was legally the minimum. But in practice, many lower values were declared to save taxes. This was possible, for there was no administrative supervision. The only effective limitation was that the value could not be lower than that previously declared, whether by the current owner or by an earlier one.

After the establishment of the National Bank of Panamá, an external factor developed. The bank made loans on real estate, and limited their amount to 60 per cent of the assessed valuation. Anyone wishing to obtain a loan had to tailor the declared value of his property to the amount desired. Thus, in order to borrow B/9000, a value of B/15,000 had to be declared. This development was undoubtedly helpful in raising assessment levels.

Urban Assessments

In 1953, the Comisión Catastral was established to revalue, or more accurately, to assess for the first time, all real property in the Republic of Panamá. When the work was initiated in the City of Panamá, the first undertaking was the development of an elaborate map for the property tax and other purposes. Since it was believed that the laying of water and sewer lines and other similar projects required a map, the information needed for these purposes was combined with that needed for the assessment of property. The construction of this map, because of its complexity, took far more labor and time than is usually allotted to such an enterprise.

Although the work of revaluation was begun shortly after the creation of the Comisión Catastral in 1953, it proceeded slowly until 1959, when the map was completed. Then the rate of progress increased. As of September, 1962, approximately two-thirds of the city had been assessed. It was estimated by a member of the professional staff of assessors that the work would be finished within a year. On the other hand, no assessments had been undertaken in the other cities or in the rural areas.

In the assessment of improvements, the buildings are measured by floors, and cost factors are applied. The use of maximum and minimum values provides a range within which account can be taken of special features of the construction. If the property is old or has deteriorated, an allowance is made for depreciation.

The assessment of new buildings is facilitated by the requirement that in order to obtain a permit for the construction of a building, the plans and estimated cost must be submitted to the Department of Municipal Engineering. After the construction is completed, a report of the actual cost must be made to the same unit, and the amount must be registered in the Registro de la Propiedad.

The assessment of the land begins with the determination of the highest value per front foot of a lot of standard depth. For this purpose sales data are obtained, with emphasis on recent transactions. These data include the offering prices of lots. Real estate agents are consulted, and lists of the prices at which they are offering properties are obtained. The values of the other lots are then calculated with reference to that of the "ideal" lot. Depth rules are applied, and corner influence is recognized by a 5 per cent increase for residential lots and a 10 per cent increase for business properties. The actual reassessment, meaning the measurement of the property, the application of cost and depreciation factors, and the calculation of the value of the lot, is done by a professional staff of assessors. These employees were placed under Civil Service in 1962.

But the value as determined by the assessors is not necessarily the taxable value. Under the law, three appointed commissioners have the responsibility of determining the assessment on which the tax is levied. This board may alter any assessment, but for most properties the changes made are minor.

If a taxpayer wishes to have his assessment reconsidered, he may obtain a review simply by initiating a request within five days after the assessments are officially published. In the case of requests received after the five-day period, the taxpayer must bear the cost of a reappraisal. If the taxpayer is still dissatisfied after the reappraisal, he may appeal to the Minister of Finance and the Treasury. So many of these appeals have been submitted during the last three years, however, that the Minister cannot dispose of them expeditiously.

The tax maps that collectively form the map of the city of Panamá appear to be of sufficient elaboration and quality. The records of the individual properties are not kept on cards, but on sheets of paper properly marked off for the purpose. The description of the property is lengthy and therefore presumably adequate. These elements, and the basic valuation of the property by professionals under Civil Service, suggest that a good beginning

TABLE 4.1

Effects of Revaluation in the City of Panamá

Type of Property	Number of Properties	Declared Value (Balboas)	Revaluation (Balboas)	Difference (Balboas)	Percentage Increase or Decrease in Valuations
Upper-income residential					
Block 428	30	718,525	1,112,800	394,275	55
Block 421	27	1,022,634	1,432,500	409,866	40
Below middle-class, residential, mixed with business					
Block 60	17	716,500	1,068,700	352,200	49
Business and residential, small properties					
Block 61	23	313,400	616,000	302,600	97
Lower-income residential					
Block 177	13	164,600	231,100	66,500	40
Area being transformed, wood to concrete, mixed business and residential					
Block 240	9	410,900	568,900	158,000	38
Business, below middle-class					
Block 164	10	353,745	501,900	148,155	42
Low-income residential					
Block 210	73	363,700	185,235	178,465	−49
Middle-class residential and business, rapidly improving					
Block 220	11	569,122	753,300	184,178	32
Mixed business and below middle-class residential					
Block 68	11	359,000	437,000	78,800	22
Low-income residential					
Block 208	79	156,271	491,500	335,229	215
TOTAL	303	5,148,397	7,398,935	2,250,538	44

Number of increases: 244
Number of decreases: 59

Source: Comisión Catastral.

toward an adequate assessment system for the Republic of Panamá has been made.

The test of the quality of an assessment, however, is only to be found in the uniform treatment of taxpayers. That test cannot be made by an inspection of the valuations in the assessor's office. An outside standard, either appraisals by disinterested, qualified persons, or by sales ratios, is required. The sample under either method should be stratified and statistically significant. Moreover, the sales should be those in the open market between a willing buyer and a willing seller. Clearly, for purposes of this study, which is designed to examine the broad administrative, social, and economic problems of the tax system, such a survey would be impractical.

The data in Table 4.1, however, provide some insights into the effect of the revaluations. These statistics show the old and the new assessments for 303 properties from ten different areas in the city of Panamá. The over-all increase of 44 per cent in valuation implies, with a fixed rate of taxation, at least the same percentage gain in revenue.[10] Changes in the individual area valuations are substantial, ranging from –49 per cent, the sole decrease, to an increase of 215 per cent. Of the individual properties, the valuations of 244 parcels were increased, and of 59 decreased. This evidence, together with the modern procedures of assessment employed, suggests that the Comisión Catastral is making an effective effort to assess real property in Panamá.

The difficulties that are faced in making adequate progress in assessment are formidable. Until the Comisión initiated its operations, there had been no real assessment of property in Panamá—only the declarations of the interested owners. Thus there were no property records on file in a central office, no beginning on which to build. Moreover, with a fixed schedule of rates, the higher assessments at least result in proportionate increases in tax liability. These increases, in turn, are resisted by taxpayers, which is evident from the large number of appeals.

The Comisión also, in common with other agencies of the national government, pays low salaries to its professional staff. The more proficient employees, therefore, are subject to the temptation to leave the public service for more remunerative private employment. Such a policy asserts in effect, though not in words, that private business is more important than public. No general proposition could be more fallacious. The significance of property tax assessments is illustrative. An accurate assessment at once promotes equity among taxpayers, and also the maintenance at competitive levels of the property tax item in business costs. Thus both the end of justice and that of sound economic relationships is furthered. The competition with private enterprise for the services of assessors should be recognized by an upward adjustment of their salaries.

[10] Perhaps some of the additional tax due to higher assessments will not be collected, but offsetting this loss is the graduation in the rate structure.

THE TAXATION OF AGRICULTURAL LAND

Land Tenure and Use

The agricultural industry in Panamá presents two extremes in terms of land tenure and use. On the one hand, there are the modern, productive dairy and poultry farms near the city of Panamá, the cattle ranches scattered through several provinces, and the mechanized rice farms, coffee plantations, orange groves, and vegetable farms of Chiriquí Province. The products of these enterprises are marketed and earn profits, but the actual number of persons operating these farms is small. At the other extreme are the small farmers, the campesinos. According to the census of 1960, there are 95,237 farm operators in Panamá. Data on their distribution by size of farm, and on the percentage of squatters, are presented in summary form below.

Area	Percentage of All Operators	Percentage of All Lands in Farms	Percentage of Operators Who Are Squatters
Less than 3 hectares	31.0	2.4	65
Less than 5 hectares	46.1	5.2	66
5 to 20 hectares	33.2	16.1	66
Less than 20 hectares	79.3	21.3	66
20 hectares or more	20.7	78.7	51
Entire country			63

Certain facts stand out in this tabulation: 1) the large percentage of operators who farm small areas; 2) the small proportion of the agricultural land used by them; 3) the correspondingly small percentage who farm the large areas and the large proportion of agricultural land in their possession; and 4) the predominance of squatter operators.

Panamá has a serious problem of unequal distribution of land. This is illustrated in Table 4.2, in which, unlike the above summary, the emphasis is placed on large holdings. According to Table 4.2, thirty-eight individuals or companies own 28.2 per cent of all the agricultural land in the Republic. Their holdings range from 3000 to 157,000 hectares. Sixty-two persons or companies with farms of from 208 to 2,880 hectares own 5.2 per cent of the land. Thus, one hundred individuals or companies own one-third of the agricultural land, and 34,936 operate the remaining two-thirds. The word "operate" is used, because not all these persons own the land they work. If the exact area *owned* were known, the proportion in the possession of the one hundred owners of extensive holdings would probably be even larger than that shown.

Panamá also has a serious problem of squatter occupancy. Sixty-three per cent of all farm operators are squatters. And the proportion of squatters is 51 per cent even on holdings in excess of twenty hectares. Among the small farmers, squatters are predominant in Panamanian agriculture. Nearly one-half of all farmers (46.1 per cent) operate five hectares or less, and two-thirds of them are squatters. Four-fifths of all farmers (79.3 per cent) operate holdings of twenty hectares or less. Again, two-thirds of this group are squatters.

Clearly the prerequisite for a substantial improvement in the economic status of agriculture in Panamá is an upgrading of the lot of the small farmer, particularly of the squatter. The prosperous farmers can be trusted to look after themselves. What is the lot of the small farmer? In ways of living, they are like pioneers of the early eighteenth century. They are almost self-sufficient, consuming their own products and buying little. To them, the figures that are prices, and the paper that is money, matter little. Quite literally, they live outside of the pale of what is called civilization.

Agricultural Taxation

There is no assessment of rural property in the formal meaning of the word. No assessor views or places a valuation on property. Instead, the owner simply reports the declared value of his property, with the only effective limitation that it must not be lower than the preceding declared value. No

TABLE 4.2
Distribution of Ownership of Rural Land in Panamá

Number of Owners[1]	Size of Property (Hectares)	Number of Hectares Owned	Percentage of Hectares[3] Owned of Total Agricultural Land in the Country
6	20,000 to 157,000	293,217	15.8
6	10,119 to 18,666	81,486	4.4
13	5,000 to 9,525	80,463	4.3
13	3,000 to 4,825	49,656	2.7
Subtotals 38		504,822	27.2
Subtotals 62	208 to 2,880	92,640	5.2
Totals in group 100		597,462	32.4
Remaining operators 34,936[2]		1,189,635	67.6

[1] Source for the distribution among the 100 owners is a release by the Minister of Finance and the Treasury dated June 29, 1962. The data in the release contain ten owners from each of eight provinces and twenty from the province of Panamá. Each province shows the owners in order of size of holdings. Thus, the minimum holdings in hectares among provinces varies. They are as follows: Herrera, 355; Veraguas, 2,255; Chiriquí, 890; Panamá, 3,000; Colón, 2,293; Darién, 1,000; Los Santos, 208; Bocas del Toro, 383; and Coclé, 1,087.

[2] According to the census of 1960, which includes owner-operated, patrimonial, rented, and mixed farms. Squatters (60,301) are not included.

[3] The total number of hectares in agriculture was 1,845,700 in 1960. This total, less the Chiriquí Land Company (United Fruit Company) holdings of 58,603 hectares, leaves an aggregate of 1,787,097 hectares.

doubt, except when a loan is needed, this value is as low as the former owner dared to make it. And the former owner had small cause to restrict himself. There was no administrative check, supervision, or even inquiry. The declared value, whatever it happened to be, was accepted for purposes of computing the property tax liability.

Furthermore, the special measures that have been taken for the taxation of agricultural land have been inadequate. Since 1952, there has been an annual tax of B/1.50 per hectare levied on idle lands in excess of five hundred hectares.[11] The purpose to be inferred from the language of this law was to compel the owners to make economic use of their land. It may be assumed that the members of the National Assembly in enacting this legislation thought that the existence of large tracts of unused land contributing nothing to the economy was detrimental to the nation, and that there were enough of such lands to warrant the passage of a punitive tax law.

In only four years since 1952 has any revenue been collected from this tax. In two years, B/100 was collected, in one, B/200, and in another B/2800. A reading of the legislation will immediately disclose a number of reasons for the low collections. The definition of idle land is loose, in fact, a sieve of loopholes. The tax applies only to land in excess of five hundred hectares. But in a country in which many property boundaries are not known, and hence the areas included are uncertain, this provision offers a means of escape. Land in the process of preparation for cattle grazing is also exempt. But nowhere does the law state *how much* preparation is required, or for what length of time the preparation gives relief from the tax. Moreover, for each cultivated hectare, five are exempt. In administering the tax, dependence is placed on the declaration of the owners; no provision is made for an annual inspection of the land by an agricultural expert.

Further, the tax is extremely high as compared to the regular property tax. The amount is equivalent to 1 per cent of a valuation of B/150 per hectare.

Such was and continues to be the nature of rural real property taxation except as affected by legislation so recent that the results are not yet fully known. Under a law passed late in 1961, *titled* land must have a *minimum* cadastral value for taxation of B/30 per hectare. Under a companion measure, a tax of 50 cents per hectare is levied on the *possession* or occupancy of *untitled* land in excess of ten hectares.[12]

The National Assembly considered the two measures together, because it wished to attain the proper relationship between them, as well as to obtain more property tax revenue from agricultural land. The initial proposal was for a tax of 30 cents per hectare on *both* titled and untitled land.[13] Then another element entered the discussion, the desirability of providing a value base for loans. This led to the proposal of a minimum assessment of B/30 per hectare for titled land. The tax of 50 cents per hectare on untitled land, on the other hand, was intended to provide an incentive for settlers on the public lands to obtain titles. This they can do by purchasing their holdings from the government, or if sufficiently fortunate, by acquiring them by gift from the government. A family with an income of not more than B/600 annually may be given ten hectares of land for the father and five hectares for each child.

The price of public land is variable, depending on the length of occupancy. For lands not previously worked, it is B/6 per hectare; for lands worked less than three years, it is B/2; for lands worked from three

---

[11] Article 798 of the *Fiscal Code*. The Spanish word in the law, *las incultas* means "uncultivated" but the usage in the text is that of "idle."

[12] Law 73 of December 27, 1961.

[13] Untitled land is that settled by squatters. By far the greater proportion is in the public domain, but some is privately owned. An example of the latter is the occupancy of a hill near Panamá City. This land is valuable for residential purposes, but squatters have covered nearly all of its accessible slopes with houses, some of concrete. There is even a church. Certain of the more enterprising persons have built houses for rental purposes. But neither they, nor the other squatters, pay any tax on the property. Nor do they pay a rent to the owner. They refuse to move, and the government does not compel them to leave the area.

TABLE 4.3

Effect of the B/30 Minimum Assessment on the Property Taxes of One Hundred Owners
of Large Holdings of Rural Land

Province	Number of Owners	Number of Hectares	Property Taxes Paid (Balboas)	Property Taxes Under New Minimum Assessments (Balboas)	Increase in Taxes (Balboas)	Percentage Increase in Taxes
Herrera	10	9,698	625	3,231	2,606	417
Veraguas	10	214,062	2,131	94,293	92,162	4,325
Chiriquí	10	25,642	1,871	9,473	7,602	406
Panamá	20	176,274	19,769	69,887	50,118	254
Colón	10	54,419	3,751	22,449	18,698	498
Darién	10	78,403	3,251	33,287	30,036	924
Los Santos	10	3,277	465	864	399	86
Bocas del Toro	10	8,092	645	2,575	1,930	299
Coclé	10	27,595	5,712	10,910	5,198	91
TOTAL	100	597,462	38,220	246,969	208,749	546

Source: An official but unpublished document of the Ministry of Finance and the Treasury.

to ten years, it is B/1.50; and for lands worked more than ten years, it is B/1 per hectare. From the data appearing below on land purchases during the period from July 7, 1960 to June 30, 1961, it is apparent from a comparison of total payments with the number of hectares bought that very little unworked land was purchased.

Number of Persons		Number of Hectares	Total Payments
Purchasing land	421	18,286	B/30,875
Obtaining land by gift	59	4,346	
	480	22,632	

All persons who have possession rights to more than twenty-five hectares of land are required to file a request for recognition of their titles.[14] The document certifying this recognition had to be presented to the Public Register before March 1, 1963. The penalty for not fulfilling this requirement is an increase of 20 per cent to the property tax for the first two years after the listing of the title. Apparently, this provision was designed to force the owners of all holdings of more

than twenty-five hectares to obtain titles to their land, and thereby to be taxed under the B/30 minimum assessment.

The budget estimate of the revenue to be obtained from taxing the occupancy of untitled land is B/25,000, the amount from 50,000 hectares. But the total of such land is 599,875 hectares.[15] Thus the official expectation is that only one hectare in twelve will be taxed. Assuming that the tax will be collected, this partial implementation will introduce an additional discrimination into a system already loaded with discriminations.

The effect of the new minimum valuations on the taxes paid by one hundred owners of large areas of rural land is shown by provinces and as a total in Table 4.3. Assuming full collection of the taxes, the percentage increases to be paid range from 86 in Los Santos to 4,325 in Veraguas. All provinces will bear heavier tax burdens. Moreover, an inspection of the data underlying the table discloses that each of the individual property owners will pay higher taxes. These increases range from substantial to great, and the total taxes to be paid will increase from B/38,220 to B/246,969, or by 564 per cent. The pres-

[14] Law 73 of December 27, 1961.

[15] *Segundo Censo Nacional Agropecuario, 16 de Abril de 1961,* Cifras Preliminares, Panamá, Febrero de 1962, Cuadro No. 3B.

ent taxes are unbelievably low, however, which is demonstrated for the twenty-seven owners shown in Table 4.4.

While the minimum assessment of B/30 per hectare of titled land, and the B/.50 tax per hectare for the possession of more than ten hectares of untitled land promise some short-run improvements, the faults inherent in both measures outweigh their virtues. With respect to the minimum assessment of B/30 per hectare, the tax on some properties of average productivity will be much too high, and therefore repressive on agricultural operations. Further down the scale with land

TABLE 4.4

Property Taxes Paid by Owners
of Large Areas of Rural Land
(Three Owners in Each Province)

Province	Number of Hectares Owned	Taxes Paid (Balboas)	Taxes in Cents per Hectare
Herrera	3,950	87.50	2.2
	1,000	47.50	4.8
	774	21.90	2.8
Veraguas	157,000	1,281.50	0.8
	13,630	107.50	0.8
	5,150	87.50	1.7
Chiriquí	7,377	375.00	5.1
	5,279	312.50	5.9
	2,700	56.46	2.1
Panamá	31,402	389.57	1.2
	20,000	562.50	2.8
	12,702	230.70	1.8
Colón	18,616	684.20	3.7
	4,825	77.50	1.6
	4,399	147.50	3.4
Darién	34,815	1,357.25	3.9
	15,171	500.00	3.3
	7,301	185.50	2.5
Los Santos	700	127.50	18.2
	425	70.50	16.6
	392	62.60	16.0
Bocas del Toro	3,137	187.50	6.0
	601	47.50	7.9
	600	15.00	2.5
Coclé	3,434	42.50	1.2
	2,831	212.50	7.5
	1,819	77.50	4.3

Source: An official but unpublished document of the Ministry of Finance and the Treasury.

of poor quality owned by low income groups, the burden will be harsh. On the other hand, the tax will not be high enough for the best land, though it will make the owners pay much more than most of them now pay.

At the same time, the B/.50 tax per hectare on the possession of untitled land, deliberately made higher than the other tax, will be a harsh penalty on extremely poor persons. The underlying idea of forcing these persons to buy public land, when they are without the means to do so, is fundamentally inequitable and inoperable.

If neither of these measures is suitable for the taxation of agricultural land, what kind of an impost may be suggested? The tax should do two things. First, it should discourage the holding of land out of use. The way of the speculator, ignorant of farming and indifferent to the results, and aware only of economic trends likely to increase the value of the land, should be made hard. Even if he receives no income from the land, he should be required to pay as much as the owner of cultivated land that is equal in economic opportunity and that is being used. Thus, the speculator would have to pay the tax on his agricultural land from other income. As a result, he would be placed under economic pressure to use the land in order to realize income from it.

Second, the tax should encourage the most efficient use of the land. The indifferent farmer who does not realize the potential of his land should be taxed as if he did. The owners of large areas of land devoted to cattle grazing would either pay for the privilege, or would shift their hectares to a more economic use. The virtue of this type of tax pressure is that it is not intermittent, but continuous. Assuming no reduction or repeal of the tax, the pressure never lets up. It is, therefore, always in the calculation of the taxpayer. Accordingly, the cumulative effect of the tax is great.

To bring the problem to the concrete, exactly what tax or taxes would have these desired effects? Only two taxes would accomplish the results desired: a tax on the net economic rent of the land, or one on its capital value. By net economic rent is meant the return, free of all expenses, that could be obtained by offering the land for rent in an open market. It is not the actual sum earned, because that amount depends on the competence and work of the operator, and accordingly may be more or less than the economic rent. By the capital value is meant the price that the land would bring in an open market sale between a willing buyer and a willing seller.

It will be noted that under a perfect administration of either tax, the market governs the base. And this is exactly what should happen, for the market is impersonal. It rewards intelligence and effort; it penalizes ignorance and slackness. Thus it is an efficient regulator, and the effect of its functioning is to make for efficiency in economic operations. If applied with substantial impact to the agricultural land of Panamá, there would be a significant increase in productivity.

Which of these two taxes should be imposed? In theory, there is no difference between the results. Assuming an interest rate of 6 per cent, a property worth B/50,000 should yield a net rent of B/3000. If so, a tax of 1 per cent on the capital value, or one of 16.66 per cent on the net rent, would yield the same amount, B/500.

The existing practice, however, is to assess property on its capital value. The Comisión Catastral has followed that procedure in the revaluation of two-thirds of the city of Panamá. And even the previous procedure based on declared value was an attempt to obtain the capital value for purposes of taxation. Since the public as well as the tax administrators are accustomed to the use of a capital value base, there is no value in changing to another.

But how about the *campesinos,* who are to be settled by gifts of public land on viable economic units? Are they to pay the tax? Most certainly, and exactly like all other owners of land. Only by making them subject to this impost could the tax act as a spur to efficiency. The single concession warranted

is that the tax should not be applied until the close of the second year of occupancy. If the *campesinos* are settled on public lands as owners, the Republic will begin to receive revenue from this source, and a continually increasing amount. Moreover, the gift of these lands to *campesinos* would also be highly desirable socially and would be productive of large gains to the national economy.

The Revenue Productivity of the Rural Property Tax

The statistics for property tax payments are not maintained by classes of property but by districts. Consequently, there are no data on the total taxes paid on agricultural land. However, it is possible from the data in Table 4.3, used in connection with statistics from the 1960 Census of Agriculture, to establish a highly probable upper limit to the amount of taxes paid on agricultural land.

The analysis begins with the total area of agricultural land, 1,845,700 hectares. From this total should be deducted the 58,603 hectares owned by the Chiriquí Land Company (United Fruit Company).[16] Although the property of this firm yields agricultural products, this is only the formal result of the company's operations. The Chiriquí Land Company is a large corporation doing business on an international scale, employing scientific methods in the production and marketing of agricultural products, principally bananas. The land on which the crops are grown might almost be regarded as the site of a factory in which biological controls are used instead of machines. Certainly, the results of an operation of this kind have little application to Panamanian agriculture in general. Moreover, the inclusion of the Chiriquí Land Company would distort a calculation of taxes paid on agricultural land. In 1961, this firm paid B/99,124 in property taxes on its

[16] Converted to hectares from acreage figures presented in *United States Business Performance Abroad, the Case Study of The United Fruit Company in Latin America* by Stacy May and Galo Plaza, National Planning Association, 1958, table on p. 80. An adjustment was also made for the sale of 6,250 acres of land in 1962.

58,603 hectares, but it has already been shown that 100 large owners of 597,462 hectares paid only B/38,220.

Subtracting the 58,603 hectares owned by the Chiriquí Land Company from the census total of 1,845,700 hectares leaves 1,787,097 hectares. This area is distributed as follows: 725,443 hectares owned and operated privately; 87,047 hectares owned privately but rented; 24,276 hectares owned in *Patrimonio Familiar;* and 950,331 hectares occupied without title.

The next step in the calculation of property taxes paid on agricultural land is to determine the maximum area in private ownership that is subject to taxation. The 725,443 hectares occupied by owners falls into this class. Similarly, the 87,647 hectares of rented land is all, or at least practically all, privately-owned, and so is taxable. Thus, the definitely indicated taxable area becomes 812,490 hectares.

The remaining area (excluding 24,276 hectares exempt from tax and held in *Patrimonio Familiar*) includes 950,331 hectares operated without title. By far the major part of all land occupied without title is in the public domain, for this is the only area recognized by universal acceptance, if not by policy, as open to settlement. Public land is not taxed. There are, however, some squatters on private land. The amount of land that they occupy is not known, but it is assumed for present purposes to be 150,000 hectares.

The result indicated by this line of reasoning is that the total amount of agricultural land in private ownership is 812,490 plus 150,000 hectares, or 962,490 hectares. It is known, however, from Table 4.2 that 100 owners of 597,462 hectares paid B/38,220 in property taxes. These persons owned 62 per cent of the private land. If the owners of the remaining 38 per cent paid taxes in the same proportion, the amount of taxes paid would be B/23,408, and the total of property taxes paid on agricultural land would be B/61,628.

Suppose, on the other hand, that 200,000 hectares of the land occupied without title is owned privately. On this assumption, the area in private ownership would be 1,012,490 hectares. The 597,462 hectares owned by 100 persons would represent 59 per cent of the total of taxable agricultural land. And using the same procedure as before, the total taxes on agricultural land would be B/64,788.

Several qualifications should now be introduced, the effect of which is to reduce both totals. The property tax exemption on holdings of less than B/500 would decrease only very slightly the property taxes paid by the one hundred large owners of 597,462 hectares, but it would reduce greatly the taxes on the small holdings. The quantitative effect, however, depends on the size of holding that would be exempt. Thus there are 79,344 hectares in farms of less than 20 hectares in size, and 184,918 hectares in farms of less than 50 hectares.[17] These amounts, particularly the latter, are significant proportions of the total under consideration of 365,028 hectares.[18]

A second qualification concerns comparative values. On this issue little information exists. It is to be expected, however, that the lands in possession of the large owners are, generally speaking, the more valuable. But without assessments, and with only a declared value basis for taxation, the full effect of variable land values is not reflected in its taxation.

A third qualification arises from the comparative payment of the taxes levied. The one hundred large landowners paid their taxes, but it is unlikely that all of the others did. This is known from the statistics on collection. The Republic has a serious problem of tax delinquency which will be examined later in this chapter.

Now arises the problem of combining three indefinite considerations, each tending to re-

[17] These data refer only to the areas privately owned.
[18] The total of 962,490 less 597,462 owned by one hundred persons or companies. If the second calculation is accepted, the total becomes 1,012,490, and the area other than that owned by the one hundred owners is 415,028 hectares.

duce the amount of taxes already assigned to landowners other than the one hundred owners, into a quantitative figure so that it may be subtracted from the two possible maxima of rural property taxes of B/61,628 and B/64,788 previously determined. If B/5000 is subtracted, the amount becomes B/56,628 or B/59,788. If B/10,000 is deducted, the amount becomes B/51,628 or B/54,788. The range then of B/51,628 to B/59,788 is indicated as the highly probable maximum total of property taxes paid on agricultural land.

How significant are these amounts? This can be determined best by a comparison. The Chiriquí Land Company paid B/99,124 in property taxes on 58,603 hectares. All the remaining agricultural land in private ownership paid from B/51,628 to B/59,788. In 1961, agriculture, less the Chiriquí Land Company, contributed B/83,200,000 or 19 per cent of the gross national product of B/457,000,000. In that year, the aggregate revenue of the Republic from taxes on real property was B/3,256,800. If B/51,628 in property taxes was paid on farm land, the percentage of agricultural taxes to total property taxes was 1.6; if B/59,788, the percentage becomes 1.8. Thus the percentage contribution of farm land to the total of property taxes paid was one-tenth to one-twelfth of the percentage contribution of agriculture to the gross national product.

Such is the status of rural property tax assessment and of legislation affecting it in the Republic. A significant change, however, is in the making. It will be recalled that the Comisión Catastral is charged with the task of revaluing all real property in the country, rural as well as urban. Present plans for rural assessment include photographing the agricultural land from the air. Tax maps are to be prepared from these photographs. The information for the determination of property boundaries, much of which is vague and uncertain, will have to be obtained by a ground survey in which agreements are sought from the owners. Once this information is obtained, boundary lines can be marked on the photographs and then trans-

ferred to a map. The use of a planimeter will yield the approximate areas of holdings adequate for tax purposes. With the location, area, and shape of each property known, the Comisión Catastral can begin the work of assessment, opening offices for this purpose in various parts of the country.

But the enormity of the task raises the question whether the Comisión Catastral has the necessary resources. The Comisión was established a decade ago, and while the progress made has been solid, it has also been slow. Not only are the inequalities continuing between the declared value parcels and those revalued, but other inequalities are emerging between the earlier revalued properties and the later ones. The work of the Comisión needs to be accelerated.

COLLECTION

The assessment of taxable real property provides a base, the multiplication of which by the rate gives the tax liability. This calculation of the amount owed by each taxpayer is made by the Department of Accounting in the Ministry of Finance and the Treasury. The roll of tax liabilities is then sent to the Receptoría in the city of Panamá, and to the special collectors in the provinces. The collectors in the city of Panamá are salaried personnel, but the special collectors in the provinces are paid by fees according to the following scale:

Each Payment	Fees in Percentage of Payment
Up to B/50	10
B/50 to B/100	8
B/100 to B/200	6
B/200 to B/1000	4
More than B/1000	3

When the tax does not exceed B/10,000, the payment is on an annual basis; but on assessments exceeding this amount, taxes are payable on an installment basis, with a payment due every four months. Property owners who pay within thirty days of notice of the amount due receive a discount of 10 per cent.

Taxpayers have 30 additional days in which to pay the amount owed, but they receive no discount during this second period. Sixty days following the receipt of a notice, a penalty of 10 per cent is imposed on unpaid taxes. There is, however, no interest charge. As a result, once a taxpayer becomes delinquent, he has no financial incentive to pay until legal proceedings to collect are instituted. When legal proceedings are initiated, a 20 per cent penalty is added, except that sometimes a prompt settlement leads to a demand for only the 10 per cent penalty.

The collection of the tax is difficult. An official in the Department of Collection estimates that only 60 per cent of the taxpayers meet their obligations on time. A formidable difficulty in the city of Panamá is the determination of the taxpayer's address. In registering his property, the taxpayer provides only his name and area address, which is not sufficient for purposes of sending him a tax notice. Sometimes undelivered notices accumulate in the post office, and telephone calls must be made to banks making loans on real estate to obtain information on addresses.

Many taxpayers, however, do not pay even when they receive notices. Each day a messenger from the Department of Collection leaves the office with a thick packet of notices. He hands these out individually to delinquent taxpayers, obtaining their signatures acknowledging receipt. But then he must return time after time to remind the persons of their obligations. The delinquents cover a wide economic and social spectrum. Some persons of

unstable income are delinquent. Areas where people are buying houses on the installment plan are centers of delinquency, but the delinquents also include persons who have completed payments on their houses. Some wealthy and politically prominent persons are also delinquent in their tax payments. In this group, are individuals who owe thousands of balboas. Clearly, property tax morale in Panamá is low.

Legal proceedings to collect the tax by the sale of the property depend on administrative discretion. Property is not sold unless the amount of the delinquency exceeds B/350 or B/400. The reason for this, according to the officials, is the time and trouble involved. This is another way of saying that administrative resources are in such short supply that they must be allocated first to their more profitable uses.

Not all the efforts to collect the tax by the sale of the property are effective. Sometimes legal action to collect is inhibited because of political pressure, the taxpayer knowing an important official who intervenes on his behalf.

When land is sold for taxes, the bidding is regulated. By legal requirement, the first bid must be at least 80 per cent of the assessed value. If no such bid is received, a second offering of the property is made after a specified period. The first bid must then be at least 50 per cent. If the land is offered a third time, the government bids the exact amount of the delinquent taxes. In this case, a bid by an individual of only one cent more

TABLE 4.5
Property Tax Collections, 1955 to 1961

(All in Balboas)

	Balance Owed on January 1	Taxes Levied during Year	Total Taxes Due	Total Collected during Year	Balance Owed on December 31
1955	2,833,227	2,472,330	5,305,560	2,099,013	3,206,547
1956	3,076,267	2,529,624	5,605,891	1,835,040	3,770,851
1957	3,403,618	2,663,729	6,067,339	2,563,731	3,503,608
1958	3,067,354	2,720,944	5,788,298	2,326,839	3,461,459
1959	3,276,049	2,483,519	5,759,559	2,387,601	3,371,958
1960	3,322,362	3,613,299	6,935,661	2,933,900	4,001,761
1961	3,573,839	4,122,523	7,696,362	3,458,134	4,238,228

TABLE 4.6

Property Taxes Levied during 1962, Amounts Paid within Thirty Days, and Balances Due[1]

Provinces and Municipalities	Taxes Levied (Balboas)	Amounts Paid When Due (Balboas)	Balances Due (Balboas)	Percentages Collected of Amounts Levied
Bocas del Toro				
Almirante	4,791	799	3,992	16.7
Bocas del Toro	13,022	966	12,056	7.4
Changuinola	3,058	16	3,042	0.5
Guabito	4,059	2,360	1,699	58.1
Chiriquí Grande	1,849	—	1,849	0.0
TOTALS	26,779	4,141	22,638	15.5
Coclé				
Cust. de Rec. Penonomé	18,684	4,199	14,485	22.5
Aguadulce	20,177	6,380	13,797	31.6
Antón	31,679	10,566	21,113	33.4
La Pintada	1,809	264	1,545	14.6
Natá y Olá	18,010	14,294	3,716	79.4
TOTALS	90,359	35,703	54,656	39.5
Colón				
Cust. de Rec. Colón	158,530	106,883	51,647	67.4
Chagres y Donoso	7,515	2,471	5,044	32.9
El Porvenir	—	—	—	—
Piña	—	—	—	—
Portobelo	—	—	—	—
Puerto Obaldía	189	68	121	36.0
TOTALS	166,234	109,422	56,812	65.8
Chiriquí				
Cust. de Rec. Chiriquí	98,030	29,444	68,586	30.0
Alanje	11,961	4,813	7,148	40.2
Barú	5,046	1,818	3,228	36.0
Boquerón	2,331	239	2,092	10.3
Boquete	26,846	11,766	15,080	43.8
Bugaba	31,560	4,282	27,278	13.6
Dolega	3,795	1,368	2,427	36.0
Gualaca	3,237	532	2,705	16.4
Remedio	4,059	2,549	1,510	62.8
San Félix	4,234	2,343	1,891	55.3
San Lorenzo	5,523	1,693	3,830	30.7
Tolé	2,508	716	1,792	28.5
TOTALS	199,130	61,563	137,567	30.9
Darién				
Chepigana-La Policía	7,749	677	7,072	8.7
El Real-Pinogana	11,313	143	11,169	1.3
Jaque	—	—	—	0.0
TOTALS	19,061	820	18,241	4.3

(Continued)

will be accepted, and the property transferred. Any amount received in excess of the sum of the delinquent tax and penalty is paid to the delinquent owner of the property.

The various difficulties of collection are evident from the data in Table 4.5. The first and last columns of the table show the totals of property tax delinquency in the Republic at the beginning and end of each year from 1955 to 1961. The earlier years include some delinquent amounts dating back for long periods. In 1961, however, a special

TABLE 4.6 (*Continued*)
Property Taxes Levied during 1962, Amounts Paid within Thirty Days, and Balances Due[1]

Provinces and Municipalities	Taxes Levied (Balboas)	Amounts Paid When Due (Balboas)	Balances Due (Balboas)	Percentages Collected of Amounts Levied
Herrera				
Cust. de Rec. Chitré	33,876	3,616	30,260	10.7
Las Minas	510	103	407	20.2
Los Pozos	679	25	654	3.7
Parita	5,161	1,102	4,059	21.4
Pesé	3,653	435	3,218	11.9
Ocú	4,504	873	3,631	19.4
Santa María	5,547	1,670	3,877	30.1
TOTALS	53,930	7,824	46,106	14.5
Los Santos				
Cust. de Rec. Las Tablas	15,052	2,020	13,032	13.4
Guararé	2,493	821	1,672	32.9
Los Santos	5,795	599	5,196	10.3
Macaracas	2,195	74	2,121	3.4
Pedasí	5,273	1,849	3,424	35.1
Pocrí	3,136	842	2,294	26.8
Tonosí	2,107	353	1,754	16.8
TOTALS	36,051	6,558	29,493	18.2
Panamá				
Cust. de Rec. Panamá	1,205,846	866,204	339,643	71.8
Arraiján	16,567	2,584	13,983	15.6
Capira	12,699	1,603	11,096	12.6
Chame	6,922	756	6,166	10.9
Chepo	45,691	7,344	38,347	16.1
La Chorrera	25,774	5,242	20,532	20.3
San Carlos	6,900	1,482	5,418	21.5
Taboga	2,568	558	2,010	21.7
Balboa	3,334	131	3,202	3.9
TOTALS	1,326,301	885,904	440,397	66.8
Veraguas				
Cust. de Rec. Santiago	47,934	7,575	40,359	15.8
Atalaya	1,491	91	1,400	6.1
Calobre	1,264	80	1,184	6.3
Cañazas	603	92	511	15.3
La Mesa	2,540	113	2,427	4.4
Las Palma	2,551	774	1,777	30.3
Montijo	72,404	219	72,185	0.3
Río de Jesús	1,145	190	955	16.6
Santa Fé	4,912	20	4,892	0.4
San Francisco	1,355	561	794	41.4
Soná	13,709	3,515	10,194	25.6
TOTALS	149,908	13,230	136,678	8.8
GRAND TOTALS	2,067,753	1,125,165	942,588	54.4

[1] For the cities of Panamá and Colón, the data refer only to a four-month period.

Source: Department of Accounting, Ministry of Finance and the Treasury. Totals may not be exact because of elimination of cents.

effort was made to exclude all delinquencies of more than ten years.

In 1961, the accumulated total of tax delinquency for the period in which the amounts can be collected by legal action, namely ten years, was about equal to the annual revenue from the property tax. This amount of delinquency is much too large. When collections lag, the state is denied revenue permanently as the earlier obligations recede past the period in which collections can be enforced. Further, the very presence of a large tax delinquency encourages taxpayers to postpone payment, and thus to add to the delinquency problem. The matter indeed becomes a kind of lottery in which the prize is to be delinquent for more than ten years, and thereby to be legally free of the obligation for payment.

Table 4.6 presents data on the levy and collection of the property tax for 1962. In the cities of Panamá and Colón, the amounts shown are for four months, while they refer to the entire year in the remainder of the country. Of the aggregate assessment of B/2,067,753, only B/1,125,165, or 54.4 per cent, was paid promptly. These taxpayers received the 10 per cent discount. Payments were most nearly on time in the cities of Panamá and Colón, and in the small municipality Natá y Olá, where the percentages collected on time were 71.8, 67.4, and 79.4 respectively. Payments lagged most in Chiriquí Grande, where no collections were made on time. But the record is nearly as poor in Montijo with 0.3 per cent collected on time, in Santa Fe with 0.4 per cent, and in Changuinola with 0.5 per cent.

There are also large differences in the collection record among municipalities in the same province. Thus the range in the percentage of taxes paid on time in Bocas del Toro is from 0.5 to 58.1 per cent, and in Chiriquí from 10.3 to 62.8 per cent. And the provinces also differ greatly among themselves in the proportion of the levy paid promptly. In Darién, the percentage of early payments was 4.3; in Veraguas, 8.8; and in Herrera, 14.5; but in Chiriquí it was 30.9, and in Coclé, 39.5.

Not all of the uncollected balances can be said to be delinquent. After the expiration of the first thirty-day period in which the 10 per cent discount is allowed, the taxpayer has a second thirty days in which he receives no discount. Only after this second thirty-day period does the tax become delinquent. How much delinquency will emerge from the balances shown in Table 4.5 is not known. But these data, nevertheless, indicate a serious collection problem. It is obvious that property tax morale in Panamá is low, and that many persons seek an escape from the tax by postponement of the payment.

A tax must be collected. No proposition is more fundamental in taxation than this. To levy a tax, but not to collect the amounts owed, creates inequities among taxpayers. It also disturbs competitive relationships, for when a businessman does not pay his taxes, he gains an unwarranted and wholly uneconomic advantage. Further, the reward of being relieved from taxation is for an anti-social action, the refusal to meet an obligation imposed by the law. And the greater the amount of the tax that is evaded, the greater is the anti-social action.

Property Tax Rates

As it has been shown, the tax on real property is graduated. Five rates are levied. The lowest rate, three-fourths of one per cent, is on property with a taxable valuation up to B/5000, the highest, one and one-half per cent, is on property valued at more than B/75,000.

Admittedly, there are good reasons for not having a progressive property tax. In the first place, the only distinction that may be made among taxpayers is in the comparative values of their real properties. Many other differences would have to be recognized in a true comparison of the capacities or abilities of individuals to pay. Second, the difference in value is between or among things and not persons. Thus, debts are not subtracted under a property tax, which results in unneutralities if the tax is related to the ability to pay of the owners. And finally, the progressivity of the tax may be avoided by subdividing and distributing the ownership of real property among members of a family.

Despite these arguments, there are even more compelling reasons in favor of progressive property tax rates. A basic characteristic of the tax system in Panamá is the comparatively light burden borne by the owners of land and buildings. There is also a tendency toward speculation in land, conspicuous consumption in the form of residential housing, and investment in upper-income rental housing. There is, too, the need to effect a redistribution of income and wealth through the tax system. To resolve these problems, it may be argued that the ideal instrument is the income tax. This is true in principle, but the income tax is so weak in terms of progressivity and administration that it needs supplementation through other taxes. Among these other taxes, the property tax is probably the best supplement available. Thus, if there is a fault with the progressive rate of the property tax, it is with the mildness of the progressivity.

THE NET WEALTH TAX

When one reflects on broad fiscal reform in Panamá, the tax that immediately comes to mind is a levy on the net worth or net wealth of individuals and business firms. This tax has three principal arguments in its favor. First, it has a beneficial effect on the redistribution of wealth, and as a result, promotes a more equitable distribution of income. Second, it serves as a penalty that activates existing wealth into more productive use. And third, the tax facilitates the administration of an income tax. Despite the advantages to be derived from the use of a net wealth tax, however, its adoption should be deferred until there are adequate cadastral values of land and improvements in Panamá.

SUMMARY OF RECOMMENDATIONS

1) The exemption of new construction should be repealed. There should be no legal obstacles to this reform, for the exemption is not a contract, but only the implementation of a policy. If one National Assembly could grant the exemption, it would appear that another could deny it. However, if it should prove legally impossible to deny the exemption to existing construction, it could be denied to all future construction.

2) No additional contracts should be made with corporations that freeze the rate of the property tax. (For more particulars, see the chapter entitled "The Use of Fiscal Incentives for Development Purposes.")

3) The revaluation of property should be accelerated through a contract with a foreign firm. This firm should revalue all real estate in the Republic except for the city of Panamá.

4) When sufficient progress has been made on the revaluation of rural land, the B/30 per hectare minimum assessment of titled land and the B/.50 per hectare tax on the possession of untitled land should be repealed, and the property tax should be based on market value assessments.

5) Public land should be distributed to the campesinos by gift rather than by sale, with a property tax exemption provided until the close of the second year.

6) The 10 per cent discount for paying the property tax within 30 days should be eliminated.

7) An interest charge of 1 per cent per month should be added to the amount of delinquent taxes.

8) The property of delinquent taxpayers should be sold promptly when the period of grace has expired.

9) The names of delinquents should be published, listing those owing the largest amounts first.

10) The progressivity of the property tax should be increased by the adoption of the following schedule:

Valuation	Rate
Up to B/10,000	1 per cent
B/10,000 to B/25,000	1¼ per cent
B/25,000 to B/50,000	1½ per cent
B/50,000 to B/75,000	1¾ per cent
Over B/75,000	2 per cent

CHAPTER 5

Inheritance and Gift Taxes

PANAMÁ LEVIES TAXES on the inheritance and gift of property.[1] There is no tax on the estate. Thus in death taxation, what is received is taxed, not what is left.

THE INHERITANCE TAX

The shares received by the heirs of an estate are of the net amount. Consequently, in the application of the tax, the value of the gross estate must first be determined, and second, it must be adjusted for the amount of exclusions, exemptions, and deductions.

The gross estate comprises only the value of real estate and other property, tangible and intangible, located in Panamá. The securities of corporations, bank deposits, and other intangible assets outside Panamá, are *not* included. Thus Panamá taxes according to source. The value of the assets is computed as of the date of death.[2]

The exemptions include gifts to the government and its institutions, and to educational, religious, charitable, and similar organizations; the patrimonial exemption;[3] an exemption of B/1000 if the inherited share does not exceed B/3000;[4] indemnities paid on account of the death of the deceased; the

entire amount of life insurance; payments by mutual companies because of the death of the deceased;[5] allowances or gifts to persons mentally or physically handicapped, if the amount does not exceed B/5000;[6] and finally, any community property of the surviving spouse.[7] When government bonds are issued, they are made tax exempt. But provision for this treatment is not in the *Fiscal Code*.

The deductions include all debts clearly justified by the death of the deceased, funeral expenses up to B/500, and subsistence pensions. The latter arise when the deceased was compelled by law to maintain some person or persons. Certain debts, however, are not deductible. In this category are those in favor of the family; debts of the deceased that are uncollectible; debts recognized only in the will; and any other debts payable only because of the death of the deceased.

Process of Valuation

The property of the deceased is valued by two persons. One represents the heirs, and the other the government.[8] The representative of the government is not employed regularly, but is engaged only for this special task.

---

[1] Articles 813, 814, and 815 of the *Fiscal Code*.
[2] Article 833 of the *Fiscal Code*.
[3] This refers to the small area of public land that is sometimes given to individuals. This exemption is discussed in Chapter 4, dealing with the property tax.
[4] If it exceeds B/3000, there is no exemption.

[5] Benefits from lodges, cooperatives, burial societies, and similar organizations.
[6] If it exceeds B/5000, there is no exemption.
[7] Community property ownership in Panamá is voluntary, and there is little. A couple on being married either chooses to have community or individual property.
[8] Article 831 of the *Fiscal Code*.

According to the law the Executive must prepare lists of from ten to fifty eligible persons every two years.[9] A list is made for the city of Panamá and one for each province. The names of these persons are published in the *Official Gazette,* and the list may not be changed during the two-year period. The representative of the government for the valuation of *each* estate is selected by lot from the appropriate list. The formal appointment in the city of Panamá is then made by the General Administrator of Internal Taxation, and in the provinces by the local administrator.

The persons chosen must not be related to the decedent or to one of the heirs. He must not have been convicted of perjury, and he must not on three previous services of this kind have submitted values determined to be too low.

Each appraiser is paid a fee according to the schedule appearing below. As it may be seen, the amounts of the fees are modest, and the graduations are mild.

Value of Property (Balboas)	Fee in Percentage of Value
301 to 5,000	1.0
5,000 to 10,000	.9
10,000 to 15,000	.8
15,000 to 20,000	.7
20,000 to 25,000	.6
25,000 to 30,000	.5
30,000 to 40,000	.4
40,000 to 50,000	.3
50,000 to 100,000	.2
100,000 or more	.1

Such is the law. Actually, however, it is not enforced in its entirety. The lists are not prepared. In practice, the administrators mentioned above, each in his respective division of government, make the appointment. Despite the law, the rule of long custom antedating the legislation prevails.

The appraisers are required to value the property of the deceased or the amount of any taxable gift at its commercial value or cost, whichever is higher.[10] If the two appraisers disagree on the valuation, the judge of the probate court appoints a third member. But disagreement leading to this step is rare.

If movable properties have been transferred, the heirs are supposed to provide the necessary data for valuation. If they do not cooperate in this respect, the properties are to be appraised at the highest commercial value within their class, and in the light of other known circumstances.[11]

Upon completing their work, the appraisers send the report on the valuation of the estate to the General Administrator of Internal Taxation. The General Administrator then turns the report over to his auditors in order that they may check the accuracy of the valuation. After the audit, the document is submitted to the judge of the probate court.

Outside the city of Panamá, the report of the two appraisers is submitted to the administrator of the province. An audit is discretionary.

The representative of the estate may object to the increases made by the audit. Formerly, when such a protest was lodged, the judge was required to take into consideration the assessed valuation of any real property included in the estate. In practice, this provision meant that the assessed valuation governed, and that, as a consequence, any undervaluation for purposes of property taxation served also as a reduction of the inheritance tax. As for the other important component of the value of property, that of securities, the judge was given no guidance.

Under a recent amendment to Article 833, the judge is required, in the event of an appeal by the tax administration, to take into account the appraisals of the Comisión Catastral, the registered or declared value of the property, and the commercial value. The first two considerations apply exclusively to real estate, and the third to all other property. The first consideration gives recognition to

---

[9] Article 832 of the *Fiscal Code.*

[10] There is no formal definition of value in the *Fiscal Code.*

[11] Article 833 of the *Fiscal Code* as amended, January 18, 1962.

the important changes brought about by the recent revaluations. The second admits the evidence of the owner's declaration for those properties that have not been revalued by the Comisión. The third is presumably the objective that the first and second serve, though for the record, the qualification "in theory" should be introduced. But perhaps of greater importance, the third defines the goal sought to be reached by the administration.

The new legislation is too recent for the application of the test of experience. But the General Administrator has on his side the weight of the valuation data from tax sources. The representative who protests is unlikely to have an equally firm basis for his arguments. On the other hand, it is to be recognized that judges in the past have not always decided in favor of the administration.

An inheritance tax case is not a formal trial with testimony by witnesses testifying and argument by lawyers. The government and the opposing estate representative submit briefs. The proceeding is entirely a matter of examining and then of passing judgment on written material.

Tax Rates

The rates of the inheritance tax are shown in Table 5.1. Six classes of heirs are recognized, and each is taxed at rates graduated according to the amount of the inheritance. The lowest rate, applicable to blood descendants and the most favored class of heirs, is 4 per cent on shares up to B/5000, while the highest, 32.25 per cent, is on inherited shares of more than B/400,000. On the same amounts of inherited shares, the lowest rate for the least favored heirs is 5.50 per cent, and the highest, 33.75 per cent. The differences, of course, are less between the groups within these two extremes. However, it can readily be concluded from the table as a whole that the differences in rates for classes of heirs are small. Much complication has been introduced into the administration of the inheritance tax for the purpose of making distinctions of only slight importance.

In Table 5.2, another difference is introduced which depends on the age of the heir. This application is for heirs with a life use of properties and no power of appointing their successors. The scale of age from twenty

TABLE 5.1

Inheritance Tax Rates

Amount of Inheritance (Balboas)	A Blood Descendants, Adopted Child, Wife or Husband (Per Cent)	B Blood Ascendants (Per Cent)	C Brothers, Brothers- and Sisters-in-Law (Per Cent)	D Collateral Relatives to the Third Degree (Per Cent)	E Collateral Relatives to the Fourth Degree (Per Cent)	F Other Relatives and Strangers (Per Cent)
Up to 5,000	4.00	4.25	4.50	4.75	5.00	5.50
5,000 to 10,000	5.00	5.25	5.50	5.75	6.00	6.50
10,000 to 15,000	6.25	6.50	6.75	7.00	7.25	7.75
15,000 to 20,000	7.50	7.75	8.00	8.25	8.50	9.00
20,000 to 30,000	9.50	9.75	10.00	10.25	10.50	10.75
30,000 to 50,000	11.75	12.00	12.25	12.50	12.75	13.25
50,000 to 75,000	14.00	14.25	14.50	14.75	15.00	15.50
75,000 to 100,000	16.25	16.50	16.75	17.00	17.25	17.75
100,000 to 150,000	19.00	19.25	19.50	19.75	20.00	20.50
150,000 to 200,000	21.75	22.00	22.25	22.50	22.75	23.25
200,000 to 300,000	25.25	25.50	25.75	26.00	26.25	26.75
300,000 to 400,000	28.75	29.00	29.25	29.50	29.75	30.25
More than 400,000	32.25	32.50	32.75	33.00	33.25	33.75

years or fewer to seventy years or more is translated into life expectancy by means of a reverse scale of the percentage of full value taxed. Property given to a man of twenty years is taxed on 70 per cent of its full value, but that given to a man of more than seventy years of age is taxed only on 10 per cent of its value.

All inheritance tax rates are subject to a 30 per cent discount dating from 1954. This discount, it is reported, was enacted in response to protests and in fear of a flight of capital after the rates were increased in 1955.

Unduly Rapid Succession

If an heir dies within a specified period after receiving an inheritance on which the tax has been paid, his estate receives a variable credit depending on the number of years the property was owned by him. The credit is 90 per cent for one year, 80 per cent for two years, 70 per cent for three years, and so on, until finally, after ten years, no credit is given.

THE GIFT TAX

The exemptions and the tax rates for the gift tax are the same as those for the inheritance tax. This means that gifts of property outside Panamá (real estate and securities of foreign companies) are not taxable. The 30 per cent reduction in the tax is also applicable.

TABLE 5.2

Value of Life Use of Property

Age of Heir	Percentage of Full Value
20 years or less	70
20 to 30 years	60
30 to 40 years	50
40 to 50 years	40
50 to 60 years	30
60 to 70 years	20
More than 70 years	10

Source: Article 817 of the *Fiscal Code.*

Each taxable gift is treated without regard to the amounts of other taxable gifts, except that gifts made within five years of death are cumulated for the application of the rates. A credit, however, is given for the sum of the previous tax payments.

Two appraisers, one representing the government and the other the donor, value the gift, and the auditors of the General Administrator of Internal Taxation check the valuation. But unlike in the instance of the inheritance tax, the procedure is wholly administrative and there is no report to a judge. Appeals may be made to the Minister of Finance and the Treasury.

COLLECTION OF INHERITANCE
AND GIFT TAXES

The payment of the inheritance tax is due within one year after death. The administration is strict in demanding the money owed. No excuse for non-payment is accepted.[12] A surcharge of 25 per cent is added if the collection is made during the second year, and one of 5 per cent for each succeeding year of delinquency.

The executor of the estate pays the tax, and then deducts the proper amount from the share of each heir. Owing to the relationship differentiation, and the graduation of the rates, the amounts deducted vary.

The payment of the gift tax is the obligation of the donee. The tax is due immediately upon acceptance of the gift. In practice, the tax is collected only on gifts of real property, for the latter cannot be transferred legally without payment of the tax.

The application of the gift tax is for "gifts" only. Suppose that instead of giving a parcel of real estate to his son, a father transfers it for a consideration. Then there has been no "gift" in the legal sense, and no tax is due. The question whether the consideration was but the financial guise for a gift cannot be

[12] The judge may, if liquid assets are lacking, and the payment can be made only at a sacrifice, grant an extension of one year (Article 835 of the *Fiscal Code*).

raised until five years have passed—assuming that the donor is still living.[13] And even then the tax administration does not act, because of the difficulty of obtaining the necessary proof. Instead, reliance is placed on the "law of public action" whereby a citizen may act in the public interest. A citizen who suspects that the transaction was a fraud may present evidence to this effect to the inheritance tax administration. If the evidence is sustained, he is paid 25 per cent of the tax and 50 per cent of any fine imposed. Some persons specialize in uncovering such evasions. Two actual instances of fraud, and their outcome to the defrauders and to the Treasury are shown below. As it may be seen, the fines imposed are steep.

Amount of Gift Not Reported	Tax Paid	Fine Paid	Total Paid
B/10,000	B/809.91	B/1,619.82	B/2,429.73
5,000	359.96	719.92	1,079.88

Securities can also be transferred by the same device of a fraudulent consideration. Transfers of this kind, and their consequences, are not obvious either to the revenue officials, or to citizens motivated by patriotism or selfish gain to discover and disclose the circumstances. And gifts of jewelry, cash, and other such items are even more easily concealed.

THE YIELD OF THE INHERITANCE AND GIFT TAXES

The revenue received from the inheritance and gift taxes is indicated annually for the preceding five years in Table 5.3. The distribution between the province of Panamá and the total from the other provinces is also shown. Two observations may be made with respect to the data. First, the revenue has

[13] If he dies within that period, the gift is included in his estate.

increased greatly, yet the rate schedule has not been changed. This statement, however, is subject to the qualification that the period included is short, and that the yield from taxes of this kind is subject to wide variations caused by the unusual concentration or dispersion of the deaths of wealthy persons. The second observation is that the amounts collected in Panamá greatly exceed those obtained in the other provinces. The single exception to this was in 1959.

Table 5.4 shows the total value of all estates from B/10,000 to more than B/1,000,000, the total deductions including community property, the total net value, the total collection from the inheritance and gift taxes, and finally, the percentage of taxes to net value classified by size of estate. But in interpreting the gross and net valuations of the estates in Table 5.4, it should be understood that only the *taxable* value is included. Because of the exemption of government bonds in Panamá, and of the securities of foreign corporations, bonds, bank accounts, or other property located abroad, the actual full value of the estates may be much larger than that shown in the table.

The aggregate of taxes on inheritances and gifts for the five-year period was slightly less than 10 per cent of the net value of the estates. The range was from an effective rate of 3.4 per cent for estates of B/10,000 to B/25,000 to one of 18.8 per cent for the single estate with a net value of more than B/1,000,000. The progression of effective rates was gradual up to the classification of

TABLE 5.3
Revenue Collected from Inheritance and Gift Taxes

Year	Panamá	Other Provinces	Total
1957	B/ 211,874	B/ 67,881	B/ 279,755
1958	262,454	26,727	289,181
1959	166,024	149,045	315,069
1960	464,679	87,866	552,545
1961	621,380	52,602	673,982
TOTALS	1,726,411	384,121	2,110,532

Source: Inheritance Tax Administration, Ministry of Finance and The Treasury.

TABLE 5.4

Statistics for Inheritance and Gift Taxes, 1957 to 1961

Classification of Gross Estates (Balboas)	Total Value of All Estates (Balboas)	Total Deductions (Balboas)	Total Net Value (Balboas)	Total Taxes on Inheritances and Gifts (Balboas)	Total Taxes as a Percentage of Net Value
10,000– 25,000	2,417,590	228,123	2,189,466	74,093	3.4
25,000– 50,000	2,810,260	322,342	2,487,917	118,381	4.8
50,000– 100,000	3,112,236	315,201	2,797,035	147,442	5.3
100,000– 200,000	4,178,581	363,169	3,815,411	270,207	7.1
200,000– 300,000	1,066,809	79,552	987,257	72,292	7.3
300,000– 500,000	3,828,740	111,199	3,717,541	288,339	7.8
500,000– 1,000,000	6,172,116	1,033,907	5,138,209	855,118	16.6
Over 1,000,000	1,520,651	4,675	1,515,976	284,660	18.8
TOTALS	25,106,983	2,458,168	22,648,812	2,110,532	9.3

Source: Inheritance Tax Administration, Ministry of Finance and the Treasury.

B/300,000 to B/500,000, but for the next bracket the effective rate more than doubled.

The greater concentrations of total net value were in the classes from B/100,000 to B/1,000,000. Here, perhaps, the lone exception of B/987,257 for the classification of B/200,000 to B/300,000 should be disregarded, because of the narrowness of the classes, or possibly because of some variation in the distribution of property by amount.

A comparison of the rates in the last column of Table 5.4 with the graduated schedules of rates in Table 5.1 shows the significant reduction under an inheritance tax from statutory to effective rates. The reason is clear. Since a sizable estate is rarely left to one heir, the portions into which it is usually divided are much smaller than the whole. Consequently, the lower rates of the graduation apply.

ANALYSIS OF PROBLEMS

Procedure of Valuation

The provision for valuation by a representative of the estate and by a non-professional person is surely a singular arrangement. The result is to treat an administrative function of the State as a matter of compromise or arbitration.

The interest of the representative of the estate is in reducing to a minimum the amount of taxes paid, and he constitutes one-half of the number of appraisers. The interest of the other one-half, the representative of the government, may not be described with such certainty, but it cannot be said that he is motivated only by the public interest. This representative is not a public employee and not a professional appraiser. Moreover, his appointment is temporary, for he is concerned only with the valuation of one estate. Thus, in this small committee, private interest and casual performance are combined in the determination of a valuation that is basic to the levy of the inheritance tax.

Doubtless, the audit by the office of the General Administrator of Internal Taxation provides a valuable check of the results, but the original discovery and listing of the property is made by the special committee. Besides, the review by professional auditors is recognized practice only in the city of Panamá. The local administrator in the provinces is not required to follow this procedure.

It would appear that the valuation of estates and gifts throughout the Republic of Panamá for purposes of taxation should be made by professional experts in the Internal Revenue Department. They should be qualified for their positions by training, and they should also learn by experience. This is the procedure for the valuation of estate and inheritance taxes in the United States, Canada, Great Britain, and many other countries. The adoption of this practice by Panamá would prevent some of the gift tax evasion, and would result also in a general improvement in the administration of the inheritance tax.

Definition of Value

The absence of a clear and adequate definition of value in the *Fiscal Code* undoubtedly results in the undervaluation of many properties, particularly real estate. Why, for example, should the judge of the probate court be required to take into account for real estate the declared value and the appraisal of the Comisión Catastral? Doubtless these provide evidence, which may be strong or weak, of the actual or market value, but they do not necessarily represent the market value.

Exemption of Life Insurance

There is justification for the exemption of a certain amount of life insurance. Other investments, it is true, may be made for the benefit of beneficiaries, but they do not have the same close personal linkage. More important, life insurance is the only method open to an insurer of providing protection to a beneficiary *in advance* of the accumulation of savings or property. A person may take out an insurance policy one month or even one day before death and leave dependents financially protected.

The exemption of the entire amount of life insurance, however, would seem to carry a sound principle too far. To exempt all insurance is to provide wealthy persons an important avoidance device. The use of this means of escape depends on many factors, among which are the comparative rates of return on insurance and other investments and the prospective tax on the inherited shares. Nevertheless, the fact that it is legally available is important.

Bearer Shares

Bearer shares may be issued by certain Panamá corporations.[14] These shares offer an ideal means of escape from the inheritance and gift taxes. Bearer shares have all the rights to dividends or other distributions to stockholders, but being payable to bearer, they are practically equivalent to money. Consequently, they may be sold or transferred without any record being made. The heirs may know where the shares owned by their father are kept, and therefore they may be able to obtain them as his death approaches. Or the father may, while living, divide his bearer shares among his beneficiaries.

It is difficult, though, to draw a firm conclusion as to the importance of this source of evasion. One prominent administrator believes that bearer shares are of small importance; another that they are very important. No study has been made of the problem.

Exemption of Government Bonds

The exemption of government bonds provides an easy opportunity for the avoidance of the inheritance and gift taxes, and it is one that has been made available deliberately by the government. The purpose of the exemption is to provide an additional incentive for the purchase of government bonds, and thereby to increase their sale. The advantage of the exemption, however, accrues to the upper income groups, and the larger the income or wealth of the purchaser the greater is the advantage. Moreover, the interest rate paid, or the price at which the bonds are offered, as compared with issues of taxable bonds, are indeterminate. Therefore, by issuing tax-exempt bonds, a certain loss is traded for a doubtful advantage.

---

[14] Whenever the activities listed in the charter of incorporation are exclusively for the benefit of Panamanian citizens, bearer shares may *not* be issued. The chief examples are corporations engaged in retail business.

Exemption Limits

The B/1000 exemption is limited to inherited shares of not more than B/3000. A similar limitation, but of B/5000, applies to gifts made to persons mentally or physically handicapped. The application of these restrictions is illogical. Why should an inheritance of B/3000 be taxed on B/2000, yet one of B/3,001 be taxed on the full amount? And the same question may be asked of the other exemption.

Taxation According to Source

The inheritance tax law was designed to provide consistent treatment of resident and nonresident heirs. Resident heirs are taxed on their shares in property located within Panamá, but their shares in property located outside Panamá are exempt from the levy. Nonresident heirs are subject to the same rule.

This arrangement presents several difficulties. Perhaps the most obvious is the discrimination between resident heirs, depending on whether one inherits property in Panamá, or property located outside. With progressive rates, the difference between payments on inheritances of the same amount could be substantial, depending on the proportion of the inheritance located outside of Panamá. But even if the value of the property in Panamá were the same proportion of the total received by all heirs, another difficulty would be evident. The effect of the progressive rates would be made less by the exemption of the property situated outside.

A third difficulty is a possible disproportion or inequality between the amounts of outside property exempted to resident heirs, and of inside property taxed to nonresidents. There is nothing inherent in the arrangement to make for such equality. Moreover, several considerations support the view that it places Panamá at a disadvantage, and therefore costs the Treasury revenue. Presumably, only a limited number of foreigners would invest in Panamá, for investment opportunities are limited, and so is the necessary financial information. On the other hand, the wealthy Panamanian investor has the entire investment world open to the employment of his funds, with abundant financial information. It would appear, therefore, that investment abroad by Panamanian residents is greater than that in Panamá by persons living in other countries.

All in all, a better rule would be to tax resident heirs on their shares in real estate and tangible personal property located within Panamá, and on their shares in intangible property, irrespective of the location of the underlying physical assets. Nonresidents could then be taxed on their shares in real estate and tangible property located within Panamá, but could be exempted from taxation on the securities of Panamanian corporations.

Inheritance versus Estate Taxation

An inheritance tax is on what is received from the decedent, while an estate tax is on what is left by him. Panamá levies an inheritance tax, but several countries use estate taxes. This diversity of practice raises the issue of the comparative advantages of inheritance versus estate taxation.

An inheritance tax permits a distinction among heirs, especially with respect to relationship differentiation. The means by which this is done are variations in the exemptions and in the scale of rates. Thus, the exemptions for sons and daughters may be higher than for the other heirs, and the scale of rates lower. Elaborate distinctions are possible, particularly through the recognition of numerous classes of heirs, each with a different exemption and scale of rates. In Panamá, only rate distinctions are made, each of the six classes of heirs being assigned a different graduation of rates.

The principal assumption underlying the application of graduated rates of taxation to the shares of *all* classes of heirs is that the heirs receiving the larger amounts have more ability or capacity to pay. Hence, an increasing or progressive scale of rates is levied on such bequests. In addition, shares of the same amount are taxed at different schedules of rates depending on the relationship (or lack of it) of the heirs to the decedent. Apparently this is done on the theory that the variations in the tax obligation correspond to what the decedent would have wished, that they give recognition to any assumed contribution to the accumulation of the property, or that they serve the alleged public purpose of encouraging, by lower taxation, bequests within the immediate family of the deceased.

An estate tax, without an intermixture of inheritance tax features, results in no distinctions among heirs. Once the amount of the gross estate is determined, the exclusions recognized, and the exemptions and deductions subtracted, the remaining or taxable estate is subject to taxation at progressive rates. Thus, all estates of the same taxable size pay the same amount. One wealthy man may leave all his property to a son, while another may bequeath an equal amount to dozens of persons, no one of whom receives a major part. Under these differing assumptions, the amounts of the estate tax will be identical.

The estate tax is based, in part, on the principle that the deceased owes a debt to the society in which he made his fortune. That debt exists regardless of the number and size of the shares into which his estate is divided. The tax levied by the government on the total estate may then be thought of as a means of discharging that obligation. There is also in this tax, as in the one on inheritances, additional justification on the principle of ability to pay, and on the grounds that death taxation promotes a more equal distribution of wealth.

Finally, for both taxes there is the important question of revenue. In this respect, both forms of death taxation have peculiar and very special advantages. The decedent owned the property during life, but now it is to be passed on to one or more persons. The transfer is not by natural right, but by a legal procedure, for the state confirms that the heirs have title to the property. In succeeding to the wealth of the deceased, the heirs are thus the beneficiaries of a privilege, which is to some degree an unearned increase. No one feels sorry for them, least of all the large number of persons who pay taxes on wages, profits, or other earned income. Here, then, is a series of circumstances that provides an ideal opportunity for taxation.

Which form of death taxation, inheritance or estate, is to be preferred? That depends on the emphasis attached to the problem of administration, and on the comparative effects of the two imposts. For purposes of inheritance taxation, not only must the taxable value of the estate be determined, but also that of each share. Since the distribution of property, depending on the terms of the will of the deceased, may be complicated, the valuation of the shares may be difficult. On the other hand, under an estate tax, only the taxable value of the estate need be determined, for the shares into which the property is divided are not relevant for the calculation of the amount of the tax. On that score, the estate tax has an advantage.

If distinctions among heirs by relationship, amount inherited, or both are considered to be essential, the inheritance tax is the better levy. But if the governing purpose of the tax is to obtain revenue, and to reduce inequalities in the distribution of wealth, the estate tax is superior. An estate tax levied at steeply graduated rates absorbs increasing proportions of the value of the property. And, depending on the scale of rates and the amounts subjected to them, the proportions absorbed by the tax may be very large. Moreover, though the decedent, while living, may reduce the taxable value of his estate by certain exclusions and deductions, his actions in that respect may be limited by careful drafting of the law. Thus, under adequate estate law legislation, the tax will be based on substantially all of the property that has been accumulated.

An inheritance tax, on the other hand, involves a differentiation among heirs. With the heirs distributed into several classes, and with property divided into parts, under the same average schedule of graduated rates the sum of the taxes on these portions is less than the amount of the tax on the whole. Further, by increasing the number of bequests and limiting the amounts, the aggregate tax paid to the government can be decreased greatly. This holds for all sizes of estates. And the distribution of the estate, as well as the minimization of the tax, is completely at the discretion of the decedent while still living. He has only to make the proper dispositions in his will.

On this possibility, an argument can be made to the effect that an inheritance tax, by offering an incentive to make a wider distribution of property, actually furthers the general objective of promoting a more equal distribution of wealth. The difficulty with this position is the fact that, irrespective of the form of death taxation, the overwhelming proportion of large taxable estates is distributed to family members of the decedent, particularly to the immediate family. The share of friends and employees in the total is small. Thus, the distribution of large properties is predominantly to upper income groups.

An estate tax imposed at steeply graduated rates not only yields more revenue than an inheritance tax levied at corresponding rates, but through the expenditure of the revenue received, effects a broader distribution of the resulting benefits. The shares of individuals in the public services so financed are on the whole not far from equal, though the low income groups probably receive somewhat more than the average.

As against the distributional effects of estate taxation, the advantages, actual or alleged, of inheritance taxation are of small moment. The estate tax, as judged by the comparative effects on the society in which it finds application—the only relevant test— is much the better form of death taxation.

Nevertheless, despite this bias in favor of estate taxation, it probably would be a mistake to shift from an inheritance to an estate tax in Panamá. Any shift of this magnitude is disturbing both to taxpayers and tax administrators.

The Scale of Rates

The inheritance and gift taxes apply distinctions based on the relationship to the decedent or donor and the size of the bequest or gift. A glance at Table 5.1 will show the complications of the differentiation employed. Yet the results, in terms of variations in the effective rates, and consequently in the revenue obtained, are small, and especially for the larger estates, are very small. The question arises, therefore, whether the complications are worth the cost of the resulting administrative difficulties.

Reference to the scale of inheritance and gift tax rates in Table 5.1 as reduced 30 per cent, and to the effective rates in Table 5.4, shows the mild nature of the progression. The effective rates, in particular, are very modest. The average effective rate for all estates is only 9.3 per cent. And on estates of B/300,000 to B/500,000, the effective rate is only 7.6 per cent. True, on estates of B/500,000 to B/1,000,000, and on the single estate of more than B/1,000,000, the effective rates were 16.6 and 18.8 per cent respectively. But even these rates are low in comparison with those levied in the United States, Canada, Great Britain, and the Western European countries.

Clearly, then, when additional revenues are needed in Panamá, higher inheritance taxes should be considered. Several aspects may be worthy of attention in this regard; there is one, however, which bears special examination and that is the type of society that is desired. The characteristics of a society may be determined by the action of unguided and unfettered human and natural forces, or by thought, deliberation, and plan. The differences in the social structures shaped by these approaches are immense. And taxation, particularly of inheritances or estates, is an instrument of prime importance for the alteration of society from what it would otherwise be.

A presentation of the extremes may serve to sharpen the issues raised. The taxation of inheritances may be light or even nonexistent on property inherited by children, thus favoring the further accumulation of wealth by the richer families, and thereby greater inequality in the distribution of wealth and income. On the other hand, a policy of heavy taxation of inheritances interposes a substantial barrier to additional accumulation, and if sufficiently heavy, would decrease the holdings of the richer families. This policy, together with public expenditures made possible from the revenue, would result in a greater equality in the distribution of wealth.

Which policy is to be preferred? Several approaches press for consideration. Thus, the economic effects on investment, consumption, employment, and the gross national product might be held to form a sound basis for a policy of more equal distribution of wealth. Or the comparative consequences to society of a maldistribution of wealth might be stressed, with attention to such matters as the need to remove poverty and suffering. Still a third approach is that of Henry Simons, highly regarded scholar of Public Finance. To him a society characterized by extreme inequality of wealth was unlovely—it lacked esthetic appeal.

All these ways of moving toward a solution of the problem are beset by difficulties of one kind or another. The economic approach deals with matters of importance, but because of the many unknowns involved, and consequently the numerous assumptions made, it does not arrive at a goal, but only at an uncertain and speculative outcome, lacking the substance required to instill conviction. The social approach, the way of ethics, depends for implementation on the acceptance of certain social values or goals. But these standards or attitudes are formed and shaped slowly. As of any given time, either they are accepted or they are not. The difficulty with the esthetic test is that its subjective emotive content is impossible to demonstrate as valid.

There is, however, another and more pragmatic approach in which the answer may be sought. This is the emergence of the common man, the unpossessed, the nameless, who forms the mass and does nearly all the work of any society. The movement to recognize his needs, and to shape the society in his interest, started many years ago in Europe and spread to North America. As a result, there has been a tremendous increase in the volume of social services, including old age pensions, unemployment insurance, the care of dependents, public education, public health, medical assistance, and many other services. And the total expended for such purposes continues to grow at a rate not limited to the growth of the national product.

These and other costs of government, including the ever-mounting military expenditures, had to be financed, and taxes were increased. At first, the taxes were almost entirely on commodities entering or leaving the country, or sold within it. Thus they burdened the masses, while the rich largely escaped. But gradually another conception of the proper source of revenue took form: income and wealth were to contribute. The underlying theoretical work, however, had not been done. The new ideas were crudely expressed, and their implications only faintly realized. At first, the taxes levied on income and wealth contributed little, for the exemptions or allowances were large and the rates were low.

But the seed had been planted in the minds of the people, and it germinated. Scholars developed the underlying theoretical justifications. The theory of taxation according to ability to pay was developed and popularized. As a result of the growing acceptance of the new ideas, the need for additional revenue was supplied in part by the taxation of the upper income groups at higher rates than were paid by the mass of the population. Income and death taxes became the media by which larger relative contributions were exacted from the wealthy.

The outcome of this development over a long period is the very high income and death taxes in Western Europe, England, Canada, and the United States. The acceptance in these countries of such levies is now practically universal. No politician who opposed them could win an election. The reasons advanced for this general position usually center in the idea that those who have greater ability should pay the greater amount as determined by the application of steeply graduated rates.

But the large effect—and this is the important matter—is that such taxes result in less inequality of wealth and income. They diminish the wealth and accumulation of the rich, and through the expenditure of the revenue in the form of public services, add to the real incomes of the low income groups. In this way, these taxes further political stability. Envy of the rich and successful is reduced. The opportunity of the person with low income to advance in economic position is increased. The level of living for most persons rises. Change comes by evolution and consent, instead of by revolution and bloodshed.

SUMMARY OF RECOMMENDATIONS

1) The valuation of estates, inherited shares, and gifts should be the exclusive responsibility of professional experts in the Ministry of Finance and the Treasury.

2) A report should be required from the administrator of the estate or the donor, but the government should assess the tax without accounting to the probate judge. If the ad-ministrator of the estate does not agree with the assessment, he should be allowed a hearing. If he is still dissatisfied after the hearing, he should be given the right of legal action.

3) The differentiation among heirs should be simplified by having only three groups: (a) wife, husband, children, and parents; (b) brothers and sisters, and (c) all others.

4) The 30 per cent tax reduction in the amount of the tax should be eliminated and the tax rates on all inherited shares of more than B/25,000 should be increased by 50 per cent.

5) The B/1000 exemption should apply to all inheritances. Similarly, an exemption of B/5000 should be given to all persons physically or mentally handicapped even though the amount received exceeds B/5000.

6) The exemption of life insurance should be reduced to B/10,000.

7) The issuance of tax-exempt government bonds should be terminated.

8) Value for tax purposes should be defined as market value, or that value which would be realized in an open market sale by a willing seller to a willing buyer.

9) The rule of tax jurisdiction should be changed from the source or location of the property to the residence of the heirs. Resident heirs should be taxed on their shares of the decedent's real estate and tangible personal property located in Panamá, and on intangibles wherever located. Non-resident heirs should be taxed only on their shares of real estate and tangible personal property located in Panamá.

CHAPTER 6

Taxes on Foreign Commerce — Basic Characteristics, Incidence, and Administration

INTRODUCTION

CUSTOM DUTIES ARE NOT ONLY Panamá's principal source of revenue but are relied on extensively as a means of promoting economic development. Import duties accounted for B/20.9 million or 43.5 per cent of total tax revenues in 1961. At the same time, heavy, often prohibitive duties are levied on many products to protect domestic producers of the same or substitute products from foreign competition, and to provide an inducement to firms willing to undertake their production. Similarly, such firms are often "exonerated" [1] from the burden of duties on imports necessary to their productive activities, such as capital goods, raw materials, and semi-manufactures.

Panamá has unusual problems of administering the customs. The Canal Zone is a strip of Panamanian territory approximately ten miles wide administered by the United States government. Physically contiguous, it is not separated by any barriers, natural or artificial, control posts or any other impediments to egress and ingress. Panamá's two main ports are located within the zone. Many Panamanians work, reside, and purchase within the zone. Administration is further complicated by an unusually irregular coast line, the absence of a coast guard, and a lack of vigorous and persistent policy to avoid smuggling activities.

The relatively heavy taxation of consumer goods combined with protectionist tariffs creates problems of distributing the tax burden equitably. The revenue tariffs fall nearly entirely on consumers. However, it is not clear that they are therefore regressive throughout the income scale. The protective tariffs, while yielding little revenue, raise prices, placing on consumers of the protected products a substantial part of the burden of economic development. Most of these appear to be regressive. These and other problems are the concern of this and the following chapter.

Basic Characteristics of Taxes on Foreign Commerce

While taxes on foreign commerce were Panamá's most important source of tax revenues in 1961, amounting to nearly one-half

[1] The terms exonerated and exempted are used interchangeably.

of the total tax collections, they have been declining in relative importance since the period preceding World War II, when they were approximately two-thirds of the total (see Table 6.1). Nevertheless, while they have been declining in relative importance, they rose substantially in absolute terms from B/4,346,000 in 1938 to B/23,099,000 in 1961. After allowing for an increase in the price level of roughly 100 per cent, this would still represent an increase of nearly 200 per cent. Moreover, as Table 6.1 indicates, very little change in the relative im-

TABLE 6.1

Taxes on Foreign Commerce and
Total Tax Revenues,
1937 to 1961

(Thousands of Balboas)

	Total Tax Revenues	Revenues from Foreign Commerce	Percentage of Revenues from Foreign Commerce to Total Tax Revenues
1937	6,524	4,346	66.6
1938	6,482	4,225	65.2
1939	6,934	4,332	62.5
1940	9,330	5,799	62.2
1941	11,963	7,338	61.3
1942	14,712	8,262	56.2
1943	16,714	7,902	47.3
1944	16,249	7,442	45.8
1945	18,300	8,700	47.5
1946	22,100	11,800	53.4
1947	24,700	13,700	55.5
1948	24,000	12,500	52.1
1949	23,900	12,700	53.1
1950	24,000	13,000	54.2
1951	24,800	13,200	53.2
1952	26,980	14,895	55.2
1953	31,044	15,701	50.6
1954	33,031	16,792	50.8
1955	35,571	16,822	47.1
1956	36,816	18,203	49.4
1957	37,911	21,201	55.9
1958	39,961	18,176	45.5
1959	37,994	19,014	50.0
1960	44,325	21,429	48.3
1961	47,630	23,099	48.5

Sources: Data for the years 1937 to 1944 from David Lynch, *Report on the Tariff Policy of Panamá* (Washington: Inter-American Development Commission, 1946); for the years 1945 to 1951, Romeo Dalla Chieza, *Public Finance of Panamá* (Washington: International Bank for Reconstruction and Development, May 6, 1957), App. A–11; for the years 1952 to 1961, Contraloría General, *Hacienda Pública y Finanzas*, 4° trimestre y Año 1961 (Panamá, 1962).

portance of the taxes on foreign commerce to total tax revenues has occurred since 1953. The sudden decrease in importance from 1952 to 1953 was due mainly to the increase in direct taxes of nearly B/3.4 million effected in the latter year.

The most important items in the taxes on foreign commerce are import duties and consular fees. Of lesser importance are the taxes on exports, consular receipts, taxes on re-exports, and storage charges. To some extent during most of the period shown in Table 6.1, consular fees were an additional *ad valorem* levy, being a charge of 5 per cent *ad valorem* on all dutiable imports and 8 per cent on imports on the so-called "free list." The bulk of these were eliminated by the reform law of 1957, Decree Law No. 25 of 23 September, 1957, which also adopted a standard nomenclature according to the Nomenclatura Arancelaría Uniforme Centroamericana (NAUCA). In Table 6.2, the importance of the taxes on foreign commerce, of import duties and of consular fees is shown for the period from 1951 to 1961.

Consular fees continued to be imposed on those firms that have contracts with the government exempting them from import duties but which do not provide for exoneration from consular fees, or which expressly make them liable to such fees (Article 490 of the *Código Fiscal*). Consular fees of 5 per cent also continued to be imposed on merchandise consigned to official warehouses (i.e., in bond), and of 1 per cent on merchandise re-exported before withdrawal from customs. Revenue from consular fees decreased from B/4,700,900 in 1957 to B/-211,400 in 1959, increasing thereafter to B/1,352,700 in 1961.

Since the consular fees on imports were in effect customs duties, and since they were altered substantially in 1957, it is more meaningful when making intertemporal comparisons to include total taxes on foreign commerce rather than merely "import duties."

Re-exports from official warehouses (*Almacenes Oficiales de Depósito*) are subject

TABLE 6.2

Taxes on Foreign Commerce, 1951 to 1961

(Thousands of Balboas)

	Total Taxes on Foreign Commerce	Taxes on Imports[1] (Excluding "Fees")	Consular Fees	Other Consular Receipts	Taxes on Exports and Re-exports	Other Receipts[2]
1951	13,376.7	9,341.8	3,488.0	355.9	146.0	45.0
1952	14,895.2	10,417.4	3,874.8	488.8	113.8	40.4
1953	15,700.6	10,984.8	3,805.7	689.8	186.4	33.9
1954	16,792.0	11,527.5	3,841.6	1,197.6	199.5	25.8
1955	16,822.2	11,883.5	3,656.2	1,059.6	200.4	22.5
1956	18,202.5	13,271.1	3,900.1	813.6	193.1	24.6
1957	21,201.1	15,280.0	4,700.9	960.9	233.2	26.1
1958	18,176.4	16,710.3	412.7	796.6	230.5	26.3
1959	19,014.0	17,762.4	211.4	740.6	277.3	22.3
1960	21,428.6	19,383.8	1,072.6	715.2	222.0	35.0
1961	23,098.7	20,738.1	1,352.7	737.5	218.8	51.6

[1] Includes an anti-tuberculosis tax on liquors, stamp taxes, and a charge of two cents per package.

[2] Includes warehousing charges and a surcharge on exemptions.

Source: Ministry of Finance and the Treasury.

to a tax equal to 5 per cent of the import duties to which they would have been liable on their importation into Panamá. Similarly, 95 per cent of import duties levied on goods worth more than B/50 are refunded upon re-exportation.

Export duties are imposed on minerals, scrap iron and other metals, and bananas. Precious metals are subject to a tax of one per cent, bananas to two cents per cluster (racimo), scrap iron to B/4.00 per metric ton, and scrap bronze to B/24.00 per metric ton. No metals were exported in 1961. Of B/21.6 million in exports in 1961, B/13.4 million were bananas and B/5.9 million were shrimp. Of B/219,000 collected in export and re-export duties, bananas accounted for B/174,000, other exports, B/9,000, and re-exports, B/35,000.

Beginning in 1960, each request for an "exonerated" import became subject to a B/10 surcharge. This surcharge on exonerations yielded B/12,300 in 1960 and B/26,700 in 1961. Exonerations will be discussed in detail in the following chapter.

Taxes of B/0.20 per liter or fraction thereof of champagne, sparkling wines, and liquors, and one of B/0.15 on wine and B/0.05 on beer are imposed in addition to

other duties for an anti-tuberculosis fund (Law No. 53 of 1928). These taxes produced B/153,500 in revenue in 1961.

Other taxes include a charge of B/0.02 per bundle or package, and stamp taxes. The former raised B/106,500 in 1961 and the latter B/269,900.

Character of the Duties

The most important class of imports is that of *Manufactured Articles Classed According to Material,* which includes rubber products, textiles, iron and steel, glass products, paper and cardboard, and some metal manufactures. These amounted in 1961 to B/34.3 million or 27.6 per cent of total imports. Following closely were *Machinery and Transport Material,* which includes autos, buses and tractors, and totaled B/30.3 million or 24.3 per cent. So far as duties paid are concerned, the chief category was *Fuels and Mineral Lubricants,* chiefly petroleum products, which accounted for B/11.0 million of imports or 8.9 per cent, but paid B/4.3 million in duties or 21.5 per cent. *Beverages and Tobacco,* chiefly alcoholic beverages, while only B/2.8 million in value of imports, or 2.3 per cent, accounted for B/3.4 million of duties or 17.0 per cent (see Table 6.3).

The *ad valorem* rate on imports is indicated by the ratio of total duties collected to total imports. In 1961, B/20.1 million was collected on imports of B/124.4 million, indicating an average duty of 16.2 per cent. Some B/28.9 million of imports normally

subject to duties were totally exonerated, i.e., imported free of duty by privileged firms and government agencies, and an additional B/0.83 million were partially exonerated. As a result, B/6.4 million in duties were exonerated. The indicated nominal rate of duty, that is, assuming that all imports had paid the applicable duties, is 21.3 per cent. In addition, consular fees and other charges

TABLE 6.3

Value of Imports, F.O.B., and Duties Paid by Major Category and for a Selected List of Sub-Categories, 1961

Description	Value (thousands)	Percentage of Total Value	Duty Paid (thousands)	Percentage of Total Duties
Major Tariff Categories　　　　　TOTALS	B/124,414	100.0	B/20,112	100.0
Food products	14,528	11.7	2,790	13.9
Raw materials, excluding combustibles and foodstuffs	1,469	1.2	311	1.5
Fuels, mineral lubricants, and related products	11,041	8.9	4,319	21.5
Oils and fats of animal and vegetable origin	424	0.3	144	0.7
Chemical products	13,251	10.7	1,255	6.2
Manufactured articles classified principally according to their material	34,295	27.6	2,616	13.0
Machinery and transport material	30,274	24.3	2,677	13.3
Diverse manufactures	15,826	12.7	2,574	12.8
Transactions	501	0.4	2	0.0
Tariff Sub-Categories				
Canned meats and meat preparations	1,203	0.97	312	1.55
Wheat	2,387	1.92	328	1.63
Preparations of cereals	1,133	0.91	239	1.19
Fresh and dried vegetables except those artificially dehydrated	1,097	0.88	227	1.13
Alcoholic beverages	11,699	9.40	2,659	13.22
Petroleum products	10,974	8.82	4,313	21.44
Inorganic chemicals	1,070	0.86	24	0.12
Medicinal and pharmaceutical products	3,632	2.92	450	2.24
Perfumes, cosmetics, soaps, and cleaning preparations	2,725	2.19	394	1.96
Fertilizers	1,425	1.15	0	0.0
Insecticides, etc. for agriculture	1,082	0.87	9	0.04
Automobile tires	1,263	1.02	185	0.92
Paper and cardboard	3,223	2.59	137	0.68
Articles of paper, pulp, and cardboard				
Cotton fabrics of common type	3,705	2.98	284	1.41
Other fabrics of textile fibers, common type	2,605	2.09	234	1.16
Ready-made articles totally or principally of textile materials (blankets, sheets, etc.)	1,750	1.41	135	0.67
Manufactures of glass	1,111	0.89	58	0.29
Iron and steel products	5,076	4.08	359	1.79
Metal manufactures n.s.e.[1]	7,328	5.89	445	2.21
Power-generating machinery	1,393	1.12	50	0.25
Highway and agricultural tractors except steam-operated	1,228	0.99	97	0.48
Machinery for mining, construction, and industrial uses	9,386	7.54	368	1.83
Electrical machinery, apparatus, and utensils	7,936	6.38	614	3.05
Automotive vehicles	8,286	6.66	1,381	6.87
Clothing	4,852	3.90	899	4.47
Shoes	1,006	0.81	431	2.14
Professional and scientific instruments	1,378	1.11	129	0.64
Manufactured articles n.s.e.[1] including domestic refrigerators	3,884	3.12	488	2.43

[1] n.s.e.: not specified elsewhere.　　　　　*Source: Comercio Exterior, 1961.*

amounted to an additional 1.51 per cent, making a total indicated *ad valorem* rate of 22.8 per cent. The duties are based on the value of imports F.O.B., i.e., on the manufacturer's or distributor's prices on shipboard, not retail prices. As a percentage of retail prices, they would of course be smaller (see Table 6.4).

Subject to heavy duties are *Beverages and Tobacco*, indicated average rate, 122.7 per cent; *Fuel and Lubricants*, mostly gasoline, 48.5 per cent; *Oils and Fats*, 34.9 per cent; and *Food Products*, 30.9 per cent. Relatively low duties apply to *Manufactures Classed*

According to Materials, 13.0 per cent; *Machinery and Transport Materials* (excluding automobiles), 10.6 per cent; *Diverse Manufactures*, 18.0 per cent; and *Chemical Products*, 14.2 per cent. Within these general classes are some important exceptions (see Table 6.4).

Among the sub-categories, very high rates may be noted for *Milk Products, Eggs, and Honey*, 77.4 per cent; *Sugar and Sweets*, 31.1 per cent; *Other Food Preparations*, 52 per cent; *Margarine*, 64 per cent; *Lard*, 104 per cent; *Whiskey*, 163 per cent (now B/3.50 per liter); *Cigarettes*, 237 per cent; *Natural Ferti-*

TABLE 6.4

Ad Valorem Rates of Customs Duties, F.O.B., by Classes of Imports, 1961

(Thousands of Balboas)

	Value of Imports	Duties Paid	Duties Exonerated	Duties Paid and Duties Exonerated	Indicated Ad Valorem Rate in Percentage Col. 4÷1
Major Tariff Categories					
Food products	14,527.5	2,790.1	1,693.4	4,483.5	30.9
Beverages and tobacco	2,804.2	3,424.1[1]	16.8	3,440.8	122.7[1]
Raw materials, inedible, non-fuels	1,469.2	311.0	95.2	406.2	27.6
Fuels and lubricants, minerals	11,040.9	4,319.1	1,032.7	5,351.7	48.5
Oils and fats, animal and vegetable	424.4	144.4	3.3	147.7	34.8
Chemicals	13,251.4	1,255.0	624.1	1,879.1	14.2
Manufactures, classified according to material	34,295.4	2,616.0	1,756.0	4,372.0	12.7
Machinery and transport materials	30,273.5	2,676.9	872.2	3,549.1	11.7
Diverse manufactures	15,826.1	2,574.0	270.7	2,844.7	18.0
Transactions and miscellaneous	501.0	1.6	3.2	4.8	1.0
Consular fees,[1] etc.	—	1,882.6	—	1,882.6	—
TOTALS	124,413.6	21,994.8	6,367.6	28,362.2	22.8
Tariff Sub-Categories					
Live animals	6.2	1.6	—	1.6	25.8
Meat and meat products	1,634.3	436.1	10.4	446.5	27.3
Milk products, eggs, honey	2,048.5	139.2	1,446.1	1,585.3	77.4
Fish, seafood, and fish products	873.9	89.4	—	89.4	10.2
Cereals and cereal products	4,011.0	693.0	47.3	740.3	18.5
Fruit and vegetables	3,460.5	634.6	167.9	802.5	23.2
Sugar and sweets	370.3	114.1	1.0	115.1	31.1
Coffee, tea, cocoa, spices	576.1	77.6	4.0	81.6	14.2
Animal feed	387.3	15.6	—	15.6	4.0
Other food preparations	1,135.2	584.2	16.5	600.7	52.9
Beverages	1,700.4	2,659.1	15.9	2,675.0	157.3
Tobacco products	1,103.9	765.0	0.9	765.9	69.4
Seeds and nuts	838.5	179.2	—	179.2	21.4
Wood and cork	221.4	108.1	0.3	108.4	49.0
Textile fibers (not manufactures)	92.0	2.4	6.4	8.8	9.6
Unprocessed fertilizers	139.7	11.1	52.2	63.3	45.3
Minerals, metallic and scrap	16.9	0.5	0.0	0.5	3.0

lizers, 45.3 per cent; *Furniture and Accessories*, 25.4 per cent; and *Shoes*, 43 per cent (see Table 6.4).

Low rates may be noted for *Fish, Seafood, and Their Products,* 10.2 per cent; *Animal Feed,* 4.0 per cent; *Essences of Perfume, Lotions, and Cosmetics,* 15.1 per cent; *Medicinal and Pharmaceutical Products,* 16.2 per cent; *Textiles,* 9.8 per cent; and *Professional and Scientific Instruments,* 11.5 per cent (see Table 6.4).

A few examples from the duty list may give a better idea of the nature of the duties. Fresh meats are subject to duties of B/0.50 per kilo;[2] processed hams, B/0.08 per kilo;

prepared beef, B/0.50 per kilo; butter, B/0.05 per kilo; wheat, B/0.015 per kilo; conserved fruits, B/0.05 to B/0.25 per kilo; strawberries, B/0.50 to B/1.00 per kilo; sugar B/0.25 per kilo; coffee, B/0.60 to B/1.20 per kilo; margarine and lard, B/0.20 to B/0.30 per kilo; lumber, B/0.05 to B/0.07 per square foot; gasoline, B/0.12 per gallon; vegetable oils, B/0.30 per kilo; portland cement, B/0.01 per kilo; automobiles, 20 to 40 per cent; mattresses, 35 per cent; wood furniture, 35 per cent; ready-made mens' and boys' suits, 40 per cent; shoes, B/3.00 to B/30.00 per

[2] Per gross kilo, including the weight of the packaging materials.

TABLE 6.4 (Continued)
Ad Valorem Rates of Customs Duties, F.O.B., by Classes of Imports, 1961

(Thousands of Balboas)

	Value of Imports	Duties Paid	Duties Exonerated	Duties Paid and Duties Exonerated	Indicated *Ad Valorem* Rate in Percentage Col. 4÷1
Curde animal and vegetable products, inedible	118.9	8.3	35.6	43.9	36.9
Fuels and lubricants	11,040.9	4,319.1	1,032.6	5,341.7	48.4
Oils and fats, animal or vegetable origin	309.0	138.7	3.3	142.0	46.0
Chemical compounds and elements	13,007.6	38.4	281.1	319.5	24.6
Tars, etc., extracted from carbon and petroleum	—	—	5.4	5.4	81.8
Tanning and dyes	996.6	187.8	21.6	209.4	21.0
Medicinal and pharmaceutical products	3,632.4	449.5	140.5	590.0	16.2
Essences and soaps	3,031.6	445.3	13.5	458.8	15.1
Fertilizers, manufactured	1,425.1	—	—	—	—
Explosives and other similar products	2,794.8	133.1	162.0	295.1	10.6
Leather and leather products	236.0	14.8	0.3	18.7	7.9
Rubber products	2,941.2	279.1	18.7	297.8	10.1
Wood and cork products	404.0	60.6	42.5	103.1	25.5
Paper and cardboard products	5,101.7	300.3	386.7	687.0	13.5
Thread and textiles	9,842.2	755.8	205.9	960.7	9.8
Non-metallic minerals	2,322.2	170.3	86.4	256.7	11.1
Silver, platinum, gems	1,096.9	154.0	5.3	159.3	14.5
Common metals	5,726.1	416.7	277.7	694.4	12.1
Metal manufacturers, n.s.e.[2]	7,347.4	448.6	732.6	1,181.2	16.1
Machinery (not electrical)	13,156.6	633.7	512.9	1,146.6	8.7
Machinery and appliances, electrical	7,936.0	614.3	225.6	839.9	10.6
Transport equipment	8,867.1	1,426.6	133.7	1,560.3	17.6
Pre-fabricated building products	600.6	84.4	30.7	115.1	19.2
Furniture and accessories	821.3	162.6	46.6	209.0	25.4
Travel articles	402.3	80.5	0.0	80.5	20.0
Clothes	4,852.1	899.0	1.8	900.8	18.6
Shoes	1,006.0	431.4	1.1	432.5	43.0
Professional and scientific instruments	2,780.5	238.3	50.3	318.6	11.5
Other manufactures	5,363.2	647.6	140.5	788.1	14.7

[1] Includes consular fees, B/1,352,700; tax to fight tuberculosis imposed on liquors, B/153,500; the 2 cents tax per package imported, B/106,500; and stamp taxes, B/269,900. These amounted to 1.51 per cent of total imports.

[2] n.s.e.: not specified elsewhere.
Source: Comercio Exterior, 1961, and Dirección de Estadística y Censo.

dozen; watches, 10 per cent; phonographs, 15 to 25 per cent; radios and television sets, 5 to 30 per cent; air-conditioners, 12 per cent; agricultural machinery, zero to 5 per cent; sewing machines, 15 per cent; dishwashers, 20 per cent; buses, 20 per cent; and trucks, 15 per cent.[3]

Purposes of the Tariff

The preamble to the tariff reform law of 1957 recites that "the tariff cannot be an instrument which concerns itself exclusively with commercial policy nor, much less, which has as its objective only to produce revenue for the public treasury. The necessity of economic development requires that the tariff serve as a guide to economic development of the country and which enables us to take better advantage of our geographical situation and our natural and human resources" (paragraph 3).

The characteristics of the tariff reform according to the preamble were:

1) adoption of a standard classification and nomenclature;
2) achievement of greater uniformity and simplicity;
3) consolidation of the import duties and consular fees;
4) reduction in tariffs on raw and semi-processed materials to encourage domestic production;
5) generalization of the incentives given to contract firms in the form of exemptions by reducing tariffs on machinery, parts and equipment;
6) protection and stimulation of domestic production by protective tariffs; and
7) encouragement of tourism by low duties on tourist articles.

The steps taken in terms of tariff reform in 1957 conformed with the objectives as thus stated. However, vigilance is required to prevent retrogression, additional progress needs to be made, and some of the steps need to be reconsidered.

[3] Source: *Arancel de Importaciones.*

Uniformity and Simplicity

The present tariffs consist of both *ad valorem* and specific duties. In general, foodstuffs are taxed by specific duties of so much per bulk kilo. Most manufactured products are taxed *ad valorem,* but there are exceptions.

Specific duties are not harmful in their economic effects as long as the object of the tax is a homogeneous commodity, and as long as the tax is based on net weight. When the goods are not homogeneous and vary in value, specific duties discriminate against the less expensive items in the class. Specific duties in such cases are defective in two respects: they result in changes in relative prices which distort the allocation of resources; and they tend to be regressive.

For example, consider the tax on liquors of B/3.50 per liter. Suppose one type of liquor is priced at B/1.00 F.O.B. per liter, and another at B/2.00 F.O.B. Their relative prices are in the ratio of 1:2. After imposition of the duty, their prices become B/4.50 and B/5.00 per liter respectively, or in the ratio of 9:11. Thus such duties lack neutrality since they tend to favor consumption of the more expensive items relative to the less expensive. They tend also to be regressive, the consumer of the more expensive product paying exactly the same tax as the consumer of the less expensive, and the former may be presumed to be wealthier.

Secondly, the specific duties are levied on bulk weight, including the packaging. The tax tends to favor the light-weight, often more expensive packaging, and penalizes the bulkier but less expensive containers. Since neutrality among alternative choices is a desirable characteristic of a tax system, the taxes should be based on net weight to avoid such discrimination. Among the products that are presently characterized by unneutral specific duties are: alcoholic beverages, tobacco, wood, leather, textiles, rubber, glassware, bottles, gasoline, lubricants, lotions and hair tonics, margarine, fish, meats, paper products, cereal preparations, preserved fruits and vegetables, construction materials, towels, and household products.

Consolidation of the Duties

Notwithstanding the previous attempts to consolidate duties and consular fees, the latter have become increasingly important once again. They are paid by companies whose contract of exoneration (exemption) does not specifically exempt them from such fees. There is also the tax of B/0.02 per package (which incidentally discriminates against small packages), stamp taxes, and a tax on liquors to provide an anti-tuberculosis fund.

There is no reason why all of the above taxes, with the exception of the consular fees, should not be eliminated. The Minister of Finance and the Treasury and the Finance Committee of the National Assembly should resist attempts to use imports as an easy way of raising revenues. If it is found necessary and desirable to increase revenues from the customs, increasing the tariffs rather than imposing supplementary taxes is preferable in the interest of simplicity and uniformity.

Reduction in Tariffs on Raw and Semi-processed Materials, Machinery and Equipment, and Protective Tariffs

While at first glance exemptions of raw and semi-processed materials appear desirable as a stimulus to domestic production, they must be considered in the broader framework of tax policy. If the tariff is employed not simply as a revenue device, but as a corrective for balance-of-payments and relative price disequilibria, exemptions ought to be granted only to the extent that the firm is engaged in export trade, or when it adds value or otherwise provides a benefit sufficient to compensate for the loss of taxes involved. By and large, this is the policy of the industrial development laws under which exemptions are granted.

Closely related are protective tariffs, which similarly are designed to stimulate domestic industry, and often are granted by the same

contract that provides exemptions. If it is desirable to assist an infant industry, as a general rule the assistance should not be in the form of a protective tariff. In the first place, the burden of subsidizing these industries should not fall exclusively on the consumers of the protected products. Second, protection encourages inefficiency by removing foreign competition. Third, the possibilities of abuse by monopolistic pricing and output practices are enormous.

Subsidies to infant industries should be direct, preferably in the form of government participation in the risk of the enterprise. The government may also provide technical assistance and adequate provision for loss-offsets. Moreover, subsidized firms should not be permitted to realize excess profits. These issues will be discussed at greater length in the following chapter dealing with exonerations and protective tariffs.

INCIDENCE OF THE CUSTOMS DUTIES

Any consideration of the incidence of the tariffs must include an analysis of the burden of those tariffs that are productive of revenue as well as those that effectively bar imports. Protective duties, while they do not yield significant revenue as a rule, frequently impose a burden on consumers by causing a rise in the prices of protected products, especially in the short run.

Incidence of the Revenue Tariffs

The assumption is made in the following analysis that the burden of the Panamanian import duties is shifted forward to the consumers of the imported products and not backward to producers. The possibility of backward shifting is ruled out because of Panamá's small size relative to the world market.

Like all excises, customs duties lack interpersonal equity. A very rich person who neither drinks nor smokes, neither owns nor drives an automobile, will escape the very heavy duties on imported beverages, tobacco, autos, and gasoline. The incidence of customs duties therefore is somewhat haphazard, in contrast to the income tax in which the utmost in interpersonal equity is attainable.

It is possible, nevertheless, to evaluate the customs from the standpoint of broad equity among income classes. One can do this by examining in as much detail as possible the duties paid on imported goods and the proportion of income which the various income classes spend on them. Limitations of the available data make an exact determination impossible, but some general conclusions can be drawn.

The Burden of Specific Duties

In 1961, of total import duties of B/20.1 million, duties on gasoline totaled B/3,772 million; duties on passenger automobiles and accessories, B/933,000; on tires, B/184,000; and on spare parts, B/132,000. Of some 27,890 vehicles registered in Panamá in 1961, 73 per cent were passenger automobiles, 6 per cent were buses, and 21 per cent were trucks and miscellaneous. Distribution of these duties among the various income groups was based on studies of consumers' behavior and of income distribution.

The ownership and operation of passenger automobiles is narrowly confined on the average to a small proportion of the population constituting the highest income groups, there being but one automobile to every fifty-six persons in the population. Some of these duties are shifted upon resale of automobiles, but even the ownership of second-hand vehicles is restricted to relatively high income groups on the average. Moreover, due to the rapid depreciation of automobiles, most of the tax burden must be borne by the original owners. According to one estimate of the distribution of income, only 23 per cent of the families have incomes of over B/3000 per year.[4] According to the Ministry of Fi-

---

[4] Departamento de Planificación y Administración, *Informe Económico*, 1962, p. 32, Table 3.

---

nance and the Treasury, less than 20,000 taxpayers, including corporations, reported incomes of over B/1800 in 1961. Of course, there is often more than one taxpayer in the wealthier families. Accepting the former, somewhat more optimistic estimates, automobile ownership must be restricted generally to the 23 per cent of families with incomes of over B/3000 per year. Although somewhat out-of-date, studies of consumer behavior in the city of Panamá for 1952 and 1953, and in David for 1956, confirm that automobile ownership and operating expenses are limited to above median income groups and correlate positively with income (see Tables 6.5 and 6.6).

Although automobiles constitute 73 per cent of total vehicles, and buses and trucks only 27 per cent, the latter consume much more gasoline per vehicle. Oddly enough, the category of "Other Transport Expenses" in the Panamá consumer study remains a fairly constant percentage of family income at nearly all income levels, while in David the consumer study shows no correlation. This is probably due to the fact that it is customary to use buses to transport children back and forth to private schools. In smaller communities, also, public transportation is used less frequently for purposes of traveling to work than is the case in the larger cities. Taxes on gasoline consumed by trucks may be assumed to be shifted to consumers in proportion to consumption expenditures. Tables 6.5 and 6.6 show a remarkably high average propensity to consume among all income classes up to B/7500, with only a slight decrease from the level of B/1500. Allocated on the basis of average consumption expenditures, the tax on gasoline used by trucks is slightly regressive. However, the total effect of the gasoline taxes must be considered progressive with respect to income except for the highest percentile of income.

Although the proportion of income spent on food decreases as income increases (see Tables 6.5 and 6.6), the relatively high prices of imported foods necessarily place them in the luxury category and restrict their con-

TABLE 6.5

Family Income and Expenditures for Selected Consumption Categories in the City of Panamá,
1952 and 1953

| | Income Categories (Balboas) | | | | | | | | | |
	500 to 999	1,000 to 1,499	1,500 to 1,999	2,000 to 2,499	2,500 to 2,999	3,000 to 3,999	4,000 to 4,999	5,000 to 5,999	6,000 to 7,499	All Groups
Number of families	62	92	83	51	50	45	26	15	9	499
Average income	B/789	1,253	1,732	2,245	2,705	3,465	4,427	5,405	6,618	2,324
Average consumption expenditures	B/869	1,351	1,806	2,329	2,915	3,600	4,417	5,335	6,791	2,432
Foodstuffs (%)	46.0	41.6	39.8	39.1	34.0	31.6	29.4	31.0	27.8	34.5
Utilities (%)	5.1	4.3	4.0	3.4	3.2	3.2	3.3	2.8	3.8	3.5
Furniture (%)	2.7	4.1	4.4	5.1	5.6	3.6	5.8	6.5	7.0	4.9
Clothing (%)	8.8	11.9	12.1	13.3	13.2	13.2	12.6	13.5	10.7	12.7
Automobiles (%)	0.0	0.0	0.2	0.5	2.2	3.4	4.4	0.3	9.2	2.7
Other transport (%)	2.6	3.5	2.9	2.7	2.7	2.7	2.2	3.9	2.2	2.8
Tobacco and alcohol (%)	2.0	3.0	3.5	2.8	3.6	2.8	2.5	3.5	0.8	2.7
Consumption to Income (%)	110.1	107.8	104.2	103.7	107.8	103.9	99.8	98.7	102.6	104.6

Source: Contraloría General de la República, Dirección de
Estadística y Censo, *Estudio de los Ingresos, Gastos y Costo de la
Vida*, 1952 and 1953 (Panamá, 1955).

TABLE 6.6

Family Income and Expenditures for Selected Consumption Categories in the City of David, 1956

| | Income Categories (Balboas) | | | | | | | | |
	750 to 999	1,000 to 1,499	1,500 to 1,999	2,000 to 2,499	2,500 to 2,999	3,000 to 3,999	4,000 to 4,999	Over 5,000	All Groups
Number of families	B/55	85	46	21	24	17	7	10	349
Average income	B/859	1,236	1,737	2,235	2,782	3,426	4,447	6,987	1,571
Average consumption expenditures	B/987	1,270	1,813	2,253	2,834	3,160	4,460	6,805	1,608
Foodstuffs (%)	48.3	46.4	41.7	39.0	34.0	27.2	31.0	21.6	38.6
Utilities (%)	4.4	4.9	4.2	4.1	4.3	4.7	2.8	3.7	4.3
Furniture (%)	4.6	6.1	5.4	4.5	6.2	5.5	5.7	4.6	5.3
Clothing (%)	10.7	11.2	11.4	11.9	10.4	15.7	13.7	9.2	11.3
Automobiles (%)	0.6	0.5	4.6	1.3	4.7	5.2	4.6	14.5	4.0
Other transport (%)	0.5	0.8	1.1	1.3	1.8	1.6	2.6	1.0	1.1
Tobacco and alcohol (%)	3.4	3.6	4.0	4.3	4.1	2.8	2.5	3.9	3.5
Consumption to Income (%)	114.9	102.8	104.4	100.8	101.9	92.2	100.3	97.4	102.4

Source: Contraloría General de la República, Dirección de
Estadística y Censo, *Precios y Costo de la Vida* (Panamá, May,
1956), pp. 78–79.

sumption by families of below median income. The median family income is estimated at about B/1,870,[5] and this estimate probably errs on the high side.[6] Nearly all of the consumption of cereals (except wheat), meats, fruits, and vegetables is satisfied from

the lower-priced domestic supply. The principal exceptions are wheat, with duties collected of B/327,000 in 1961, and lard with duties of B/441,000. The latter two amount to 27.5 per cent of the duties on foodstuffs. Because of the declining percentage of income spent on foodstuffs as income increases, the duties are probably regressive over the range of incomes above the median.

[5] Departamento de Planificación, *Informe Económico*, 1962, p. 39, Table 3.
[6] About 60 per cent of the population is rural, with all but a few of these persons having very low incomes.

Alcoholic beverages is another important category of customs revenues which is progressive in its impact as between less than median and above median income families. The duties on alcoholic beverages amounted to B/2,658,620 in 1961. Because domestic products are taxed at much lower rates and are very good substitutes for the imported ones, at least where conspicuous consumption is not involved, nearly all of the duties fall on upper income groups. Nearly 78 per cent of the consumption of alcoholic beverages is satisfied from domestic sources. The same can be said for the duties on imported cigarettes and cigars, amounting to B/196,000 in 1961.

Another group of duties that is probably progressive in its impact as between less than median and above median income families are those on jewelry, B/154,000; furniture, B/163,000; travel accessories, B/80,000; clothing, B/899,000; shoes, B/431,000; watches, B/74,000; musical instruments, including phonographs, B/86,000; refrigerators, B/91,000; domestic appliances, B/40,000, and television sets, B/52,000. Justification for this conclusion is the fact that in the case of furniture, shoes, and clothing, domestic production accounts for 66 per cent, 82 per cent, and 66 per cent respectively of total consumption. Moreover, clothing purchases are an increasing proportion of income as family income increases to B/2000, rising from 8.8 per cent at incomes of about B/800 per annum to 13.3 per cent at an income of about B/2,250.[7] Similarly, purchases of furniture and household goods rise faster than income for most of the population. Purchases of other luxury goods like cameras, perfumes, and cosmetics similarly may be presumed to increase faster than income. Deducting 50 per cent of the gasoline duties which may be ascribed to buses and truck use, the duties on the foregoing products amounted to B/10.4 million in 1961, or about 52 per cent of total import duties.

[7] See Table 6.5.

The remaining duties may be allocated among the various income groups in accordance with their propensities to consume, on the assumption that the duties enter into the prices of all goods sold in Panamá proportionally. Tables 6.5 and 6.6 show a high average propensity to consume at all income levels, but a slightly lower propensity in the higher income categories. About 48 per cent of the duties are therefore probably slightly regressive.

On balance, the burden of the import duties appears to be borne somewhat more heavily by middle and high income groups, say between B/2000 and B/6000, than by either the lowest groups, i.e., below B/2000, and the highest, above B/6000.

THE TARIFFS AS A TAX ON CONSUMPTION

It will be noticed that the objectives for the tariff reform law of 1957 referred to previously did not include mention of an intent to use the tariffs as a means of levying

TABLE 6.7

Import Duties Distributed Progressively among Income Groups, 1961

	Duties Paid
Gasoline (50 per cent of total)	B/1,886,000
Automobiles	933,000
Tires	184,000
Automobile parts	132,000
Foodstuffs	1,795,000
Alcoholic beverages	2,659,000
Cigarettes and cigars	196,000
Jewelry	154,000
Furniture	163,000
Travel accessories	80,000
Shoes	431,000
Watches	74,000
Clothing	899,000
Musical instruments	86,000
Refrigerators and domestic appliances	131,000
Combination radio-phonographs	51,000
Television sets	52,000
Photographic equipment and supplies	114,000
Perfumes, cosmetics, and soaps	394,000
TOTAL	B/10,414,000

Source: Table 6.3.

TABLE 6.8

Duties on a Selected List of Luxury Imports, 1962

Description	Rate (per cent)[1]
Perfumes	10
Lotions	10
Cosmetics	10
Jewelry and precious metals	10
Costume jewelry	15
Precious stones	10
Stoves, gas	20
Stoves, electric	20
Electric washers and dryers	20
Radios, up to B/30 F.O.B.	5
Radios, B/30 to B/60 F.O.B.	15
Radios, B/60 to B/80 F.O.B.	20
Radios, over B/80 F.O.B.	25
Fans, electric	10
Air conditioners	12
Electric shavers	20
Combination radio-phonographs	30
Battery radios	15
Televisions, up to B/150	5
Televisions, B/150 to B/250	10
Televisions, over B/250	15
Cameras, still	10
Cameras, movies, 8mm.	10
Watches	10
Refrigerators, electric	15
Marine motors	5
Automobiles, less than B/1500	22.5
Automobiles, B/1500 to B/2200	27.5
Automobiles, B/2201 to B/2500	30
Automobiles, B/2501 to B/3000	50
Automobiles, B/3001 to B/3500	60
Automobiles, over B/3500	65
Boats, launches, and yachts, less than 250 tons, wood	50
Boats, launches, and yachts, less than 250 tons, metal	25

[1] Based on F.O.B. prices.
Source: Arancel de Importaciones.

a progressive tax on consumption. The possibility of utilizing the tax in this manner was considered by a commission appointed by the President in 1960.[8] The commission recommended increases in the duties on stoves and domestic electrical appliances, refrigerators, air conditioners, radios, television sets, phonographs, marine motors and boats, automobiles and other vehicles, and furniture. Notable by their omission were goods that are considered to be important to the tourist trade, a strategic factor in the Panamanian economy.

[8] Comisión de Asuntos Económicos. *Reporte* (Panamá, 1960).

The taxation of imported luxury goods is complicated in Panamá by the importance of the tourist industry and the problem of contraband. Taxes on watches, perfumes, cameras, jewelry, transistor radios, and other luxury items would seriously restrict the tourist trade unless some way were devised to administer exemptions to tourists.

At the present time, only a few luxury items are heavily taxed, notably automobiles, with duties from 22.5 to 65 per cent, and radio-phonograph combinations, with a duty of 30 per cent. Even non-tourist goods like household appliances are taxed at relatively low rates of 10 to 20 per cent. Table 6.8 shows the level of duties for a selected list of luxury-type imports.

It should not be too difficult to devise a means by which genuine tourists could be exempted from import duties. It would appear that duties could be refunded on the basis of a procedure which clearly identifies the purchaser as a tourist, or which shows delivery to ships or planes. Such a system would enable prices to be attractive to tourists, continuing Panamá's reputation as a tourist center, without extending the privileges of duty-free purchases to Panamá's upper income groups.

Somewhat more difficult would be the problem raised by the existence of the Canal Zone, because of the area's duty-free status and the problem of contraband. Residents of the Canal Zone may import merchandise from the United States free of duties. For this reason, they could not be induced to purchase the same merchandise in Panamá at higher prices. At present, many persons from the zone purchase tourist items in Panamá because of the variety of goods available at prices that are attractive because duties are so low. They may also purchase items in Panamá to be delivered to the Canal Zone free of Panamanian duties. Moreover, high duties in Panamá on goods that can be purchased duty-free in the zone would result in merchandise being purchased in the Canal Zone for Panamanian friends and relatives.

At present, low duties on luxury goods are the most effective means of preventing their illegal introduction into the country. High duties would create a temptation to smuggle merchandise from the Canal Zone, from the Colón Free Zone, and from other sources.

On bulky items like refrigerators, freezers, and television sets, the duties might be raised without creating a serious contraband problem. At least, vigilance in the case of these goods is more likely to be effective. For automobiles, the high taxes are easily administered, since their owners must show proof of legal entry and payment of the duty when they apply for registration.

Whether or not Panamá should increase the duty on luxury items depends on the administrative burden that would result from exempting tourists and residents of the Canal Zone, and the cost of the increased vigilance which would be required. It would be easy to exaggerate the increase in revenues that would result from increased taxes on the smaller luxury items, and the progressive effect on the tax system of the resulting increases. In the first place, the sales to tourists will produce no additional revenues. Second, many Panamanians are in a position to avoid the import duties by buying luxury items during their foreign travels and introducing them duty-free. Third, contraband activities undoubtedly would increase.

CONTRABAND AND ADMINISTRATION

Administration of the customs is complicated by Panamá's unusual geographical situation. A long isthmus with many miles of coast line is difficult to patrol against smuggling. In addition, there is the Canal Zone, a strip of territory on either side of the canal under United States jurisdiction, with no barriers either natural or artificial between the zone and Panamá. For good measure, mix in the Free Zone of Colón, and the lack of a vigorous and persistent policy to avoid smuggling activities, and there is a contraband potential of large proportions.

Smuggling

Small ships are believed to ply an extensive smuggling trade. Some of these operate from Panamanian ports, taking on a cargo of cigarettes, liquors, or coffee from the Free Zone of Colón ostensibly bound for some foreign port. There have been many instances of small boats that return to port within two days after embarking on a voyage that should require eight or ten days. Presumably the cargo is unloaded on some isolated beach and transported inland, or unloaded on some fishing vessel to be smuggled into Panamá. Or, of course, the cargo may be smuggled into nearby countries.

To combat this type of smuggling, the government has required that no goods may be shipped on vessels of less than one hundred tons without prior authorization of the customs officials. No doubt this control is effective to some extent, and it could be made more effective if the arrival of shipments in foreign ports were to be confirmed by requiring a landing certificate, either by the Panamanian consular official resident there or by the port or customs authority. In this connection, some action by the Organization of American States to create reciprocal arrangements of this type would be desirable.

Some shipments from the Free Zone of Colón are reported to be diverted into Panamá while ostensibly en route to Tocumen airport in the Republic, or Albrook Field, Cristóbal, and Balboa in the Canal Zone. Fictitious amounts are entered on the shipping papers, with only part of the shipment actually intended for export. At least one case involving a leading Free Zone firm has been fully documented. Since customs personnel accompany these shipments, the fault must lie with the low pay of customs personnel, the political appointment of employees, or the political protection of violators.

No doubt smuggling from neighboring countries into Panamá occurs, and vice versa. During the latter part of 1962, extensive publicity was given to gun-running from Panamá into Colombia, and of coffee into

Panamá. Reciprocal arrangements of the type mentioned above would be helpful to all the countries concerned in controlling this traffic.

Extensive reliance must be placed also on identifying contraband after it has entered Panamá. Combatting contraband requires effective police work. Since the smuggled goods must be moved, stored, and sold in Panamá, there should be some way of identifying contraband, especially liquors and cigarettes. Imported cigarettes and liquors should be appropriately identified with a numbered stamp on entry, not merely with the smaller domestic stamps as they are at present. Once identified by police or customs officials, the sources of contraband could be uncovered by appropriate investigation. A few successful prosecutions would also curtail contraband activities.

The Canal Zone

The Canal Zone creates problems of contraband that are more difficult to solve. Canal Zone authorities and residents may import goods into the zone from the United States free of Panamanian duties. Since movement of persons and vehicles between the zone and Panamá is completely unhindered, goods may pass freely into the Republic of Panamá. Although the Panamá Canal Company, a wholly-owned United States government corporation, has a monopoly of all retail stores selling to civilians, it is possible to control only the blatant instances of contrabanding into Panamá.

By the terms of the General Treaty of Friendship and Cooperation concluded in 1936 between Panamá and the United States, the latter agreed to restrict sales in the zone to employees and their families. Employees of contractors and private firms working in the zone received purchase privileges only when they actually resided in the zone. In 1955, these provisions were modified by the Treaty of Mutual Understanding and Cooperation so as to exclude "from the privilege of making purchases as well as the privilege of making importations into the Canal Zone all those persons who are not citizens of the

United States of America . . . *and who do not actually reside* in the Canal Zone . . . it being understood nevertheless that all personnel of the agencies of the United States of America will be permitted under adequate controls to purchase small articles, such as meals, sweets, chewing gum, tobacco, and similar articles near the sites of their jobs" (Article XII).

Thus, only employees of the U.S. government and its agencies who actually reside in the zone currently remain eligible to purchase in the zone. A large but indeterminate number of domestic servants reside in the zone, while about 14,200 Panamanians work in the zone but reside in Panamá, not including domestic servants. In the aggregate, up to 25,000 Panamanians work in the zone. But starting in 1957, only those persons employed by the U.S. government and residing in the zone (about 2,400 employees) retained full purchase privileges. Other employees of U.S. government agencies lost their purchase privileges except for cigarettes, candy, and other food items intended for immediate consumption.

The effect of this order was to reduce annual retail sales of goods by the Panamá Canal Company by $8 to $10 million. In 1955, sales of goods amounted to $24.4 million. These increased to $26.4 million in 1956 in anticipation of the new regulations, but then declined to $21.0 million in 1957 and to $16.1 million in 1958 (see Table 6.9).

Since nearly all of the Panamanians who reside in the zone have relatives in Panamá, it is highly probable that most of them introduce a small amount of contraband into Panamá regularly, without necessarily having a personal commercial motive. But the small amount of goods introduced by each employee on the average results in a considerable amount of contraband when the total number of employees is taken into consideration. Even those who work in the zone but do not reside there may purchase a considerable quantity of tax-free tobacco and edibles in the aggregate when consideration is given to the number of employees involved.

TABLE 6.9

Retail Sales and Services, Panamá Canal Company, 1955 to 1961

(Thousands of U.S. Dollars)

	1955	1956	1957	1958	1959	1960	1961
Commissary sales of goods	21,919	23,332	18,163	13,231	13,332	12,850	13,935
Commissary sales of services	195	186	157	169	144	159	177
Service Center, goods	2,907	3,068	2,860	2,903	3,374	3,605	4,017
Service Center, services	367	353	285	265	246	248	257
TOTALS	25,388	26,939	21,465	16,568	17,096	16,862	18,386
TOTALS, GOODS ONLY	24,826	26,400	21,023	16,134	16,706	16,455	17,952

Source: Panamá Canal Company.

To prevent flagrant abuses, the Canal Zone authorities require each purchaser at its commissaries to have in his possession an appropriate identification card, and they limit total purchases of certain classes of goods by non-citizens of the United States to a fixed proportion of their salaries. This rationing system is administered by marking the amount of purchases on cards issued to employees. Inspectors are also employed to police these activities, and it is estimated that the zone authorities spend about $75,000 annually to restrict contraband activities.

But contraband activities persist because of the sizable price differentials between Panamá and the Canal Zone. An appreciation of these differentials may be gained from a comparative food-price study by economists of the Panamá Canal Company. Based upon the buying patterns of non-citizens of the United States, a weighted average of food prices showed that prices in Panamá were 50 per cent higher than those in the Canal Zone.[9] Some of the individual price differences are shown in Table 6.10. The tendency to engage in what may be termed petty contraband is aggravated by a Panamanian preference for American over domestic products even where there is a price differential favorable to the Panamanian brand. This type of contraband, which in the aggregate may be of significant proportions, could not be completely controlled short of denying purchase privileges to Panamanian residents of the

zone, or subjecting American non-military residents of the zone to Panamanian customs duties. As an alternative, consideration should be given to the operation of Panamanian-controlled commissaries in the Canal Zone to serve Panamanian citizens residing there.

Although manufactured goods may be smuggled into Panamá from the Canal Zone, this problem is not acute. For these goods, prices in Panamá and Colón are generally competitive with those in the zone. Thus commercial outlets in the Republic of Panamá have little if anything to gain by contraband activities. The small amount of smuggling of manufactured goods is done by residents of the zone for the benefit of their relatives and friends in Panamá on a more or less non-commercial basis.

Alcoholic Beverages and Tobacco Products

Of greater concern is the illegal traffic in cigarettes and alcoholic beverages. Cigarettes sell in the Canal Zone retail stores for as low as 15 cents per package, and they are only 10 cents per package in the military exchanges and commissaries. In Panamá, domestic brands sell for 15 cents per package, and imported brands for 45 to 50 cents per package. Contraband imported cigarettes are peddled almost without hinderance in the Republic. They are widely believed to have their source in the Canal Zone and the Colón Free Zone.

Executive Order No. 6997 of March 25, 1935, ordered U.S. government agencies in

[9] *Food Price Comparison, Panamá Canal Retail Store— Panamá City,* July 17, 1962.

TABLE 6.10

Prices of Selected Products in the Canal Zone and in Panamá, July to September, 1962

Item	Price in Canal Zone (U.S. product)	Price in Canal Zone (Panamá product)	Price in Panamá (U.S. product)	Price in Panamá (Panamá product)	Panamá Price Index[1] (Canal Zone)
Rice, 3 lbs.	B/ .33	B/	B/ .79	B/ .45	144
Beef, chicken, lb.		.32		.45	141
Round steak, lb.	1.08	.60		.45	75
Codfish, dry, lb.		.31		.55	177
Butter, lb.	.45[2]		.67	.55	78
Tomato soup, 10½ oz.	.14	.22	.38	.22	157
Corn, U.S. No. 303 can	.21	.12	.32		152
Tomatoes, lb.		.18		.29	132
Cabbage, lb.				.15	125
Carrots, lb.				.28	156
Lettuce, lb.	.18			.48	267
Tomato ketchup, 14 oz.	.28		.73	.45	161
Margarine, lb.	.25		.49	.40	160
Vegetable shortening, 3 lbs.	1.10		1.78		162
Peanut butter, 12 oz.	.47		.75		160
Sugar, 5 lbs.		.40		.44	110
Eggs, doz.	.55			.60	111
Ice cream, pint		.25		.30	120
Frankfurters, lb.	.68			.60	88
Fresh milk, qt.	.20[3]	.25		.29	116
Tomato paste, 6 oz.	.13		.35	.18	138
Coffee, lb.	.62			.70	112
Powdered whole milk, 5 lbs.	3.55			3.95	111
Salt, 26 oz.	.13			.12	92
Shoes, dress, men's	11.95			7.50	63
Shoes, work, men's	9.75			6.25	64

[1] Based on minimum prices shown.
[2] U.S. surplus.
[3] Reconstituted milk.

Source: Food Price Comparison, Panamá Canal Retail Store—Panamá City, July 17, 1962.

the Canal Zone to import their requirements of alcoholic beverages from the Republic of Panamá. Panamá agreed in 1955 to grant a reduction of 75 per cent of the import duty on alcoholic beverages which are sold in Panamá for importation into the Canal Zone.[10] The duty currently applicable to liquors imported into Panamá is B/42.00 per case of 12 liters, or B/3.50 per liter. This amounts to B/2.77 per "fifth." Making allowance for the 75 per cent reduction in the duty for Canal Zone sales, the duty applicable to Canal Zone imports is B/0.69 per "fifth." In addition, there is a tax of 20 cents per "fifth" for an anti-tuberculosis fund, and a stamp tax of B/1.00 per "fifth." Pan-

[10] *Memorandum of Understanding Reached, Treaty of 1955.*

amá thus collects B/1.89 on each "fifth" sold for consumption in the zone.

Liquor is not sold in retail stores in the Canal Zone, but sales by the bottle are made by private clubs operating in the zone. Only Canal Zone residents are eligible to purchase liquors by the bottle at these clubs, but Panamanian residents are eligible for membership in most of them. Individual residents of the zone, military and civilian, who wish to purchase bottled liquors, may obtain a certificate of exemption. Upon presentation of this certificate at a retail liquor store in Panamá, bottled liquors may be purchased at Panamanian prices less 75 per cent of the import duty. Abuse of these exemption certificates was quite general. To establish more effective controls, a single Panamanian outlet in each of the cities of Panamá and Colón was designated to handle all transactions. Some appreciation of the magnitude of contraband activities that existed prior to this change may be gained from the fact that the number of exemptions issued declined from an average of about 650 per month to about one-half this number after the central outlets were opened in the fall of 1961.

Despite the controls, a large traffic in contraband liquors is still believed to exist. It is alleged that private clubs in the zone abuse their exemption privileges by selling bottled liquors directly or by subterfuge to ineligible persons and to Panamanian retail outlets. No attempt has been made apparently to compare the amount of exemption certificates issued with the liquor sales of clubs, which might reveal abuses. In this connection, the application of statistical samples might be used to detect discrepancies and to deter offenders. The Canal Zone authorities inspect records of sales, and on more than one occasion have compelled clubs to alter their practices. They have also suspended liquor licenses to enforce the treaty provisions.

Beer and wines are of lesser importance in the contraband picture. The duties on beer are not intended to be productive of revenue, but are designed mainly to protect the domestic industry. The introduction of contraband beer is thus not significant in terms of a loss of customs duties. However, the contraband that does exist could be eliminated by reducing the duty to a more reasonable level. The present duty of B/1.01 per liter is an invitation to contraband a product, which by reason of its bulk relative to its usual price, would seldom be contrabanded. It is possible that a reduction of the duty to a moderate protective level, say 20 cents per liter, would actually increase revenues, while it would still provide the local industry all of the protection it needs.

The duty on table wines is B/0.46 per liter. The level of the duty relative to the bulk of the product makes wine an unattractive item to contraband, for the saving is too small to justify the risks to all parties concerned. On the other hand, champagnes and other sparkling wines are subject to heavy duties of B/2.28 per liter. They are probably contrabanded, and the remarks above with respect to liquors are equally applicable to these products.

The Free Zone of Colón

There is always the danger when a free zone is created that the duty-free merchandise behind the fence will sift out. The only effective means of preventing this is adequate policing. The use of statistical controls and sampling would bring contrabanding to light and prevent the Free Zone from being a source of contraband. Devices such as rotation of customs personnel and random assignments of customs personnel to particular vehicles suggest themselves. Effective inventory control, inventory reporting, and spot-checking on consignees of dutiable merchandise should be routine practices.

From 1958 to 1961, the weight of imports of certain classes of goods into the Colón Free Zone exceeded shipments. As would be expected, the category of greatest concern is *Beverages and Tobacco,* which showed an excess of imports over exports of 1,191,000 kilograms during the period. *Manufactured Articles Classed According to Material* showed an excess of 1,844,000 kilos, *Diverse Manufactures,* one of 3,840,000 kilos, and *Food Products,* one of 496,000 kilos (see Table 6.11).

These discrepancies could be accounted for by increases in inventories, but there is no reporting of inventories by importers to the Director of Customs, and no auditing of inventory reports for customs purposes. Aside from increased inventories as an explanation of the discrepancies, it was suggested by the Free Zone authorities that the articles are repacked for airplane flights, and therefore weigh less after repacking. But this explanation does not apply to cigarettes and liquors, and in most cases, repacking involves placing bulk shipments into smaller containers, which increases the weight of shipments rather than

TABLE 6.11

Imports and Shipments from the Free Zone of Colón, by Weight, 1958 to 1961

(Thousands of Kilograms)

Description	1958	1959	1960	1961	Total 1959 to 1961
Foodstuffs					
Imports	2,691	2,242	2,959	3,520	11,412
Shipments	2,520	2,198	2,678	3,635	11,031
Difference	171	44	281	−115	381
Beverages and tobacco					
Imports	2,146	2,306	2,879	3,461	10,792
Shipments	1,976	1,948	2,503	3,174	9,601
Difference	170	358	376	287	1,191
Raw materials, excluding edibles and combustibles					
Imports	201	821	528	688	2,238
Shipments	280	807	786	674	2,547
Difference	−79	14	−258	14	−309
Fuel and lubricants					
Imports	1,025	889	17	110	2,041
Shipments	1,154	903	73	83	2,213
Difference	−129	−14	−56	27	−172
Oils and greases of animal and vegetable origin					
Imports	47	39	40	32	158
Shipments	35	43	37	26	141
Difference	12	−4	3	6	17
Chemical products					
Imports	1,502	1,739	2,712	3,149	9,102
Shipments	1,333	1,538	2,211	2,602	7,684
Difference	169	201	501	547	1,418
Manufactured articles classed according to materials					
Imports	5,432	3,834	4,250	4,405	17,921
Shipments	4,659	3,532	3,482	3,762	15,435
Difference	773	302	768	643	2,486
Machinery and transport materials					
Imports	1,156	1,450	2,451	2,416	7,473
Shipments	1,001	1,232	1,969	2,186	6,388
Difference	155	218	482	230	1,085
Manufactured articles					
Imports	1,903	1,630	2,208	2,735	8,476
Shipments	724	551	626	2,620	4,521
Difference	1,179	1,079	1,582	115	3,955
Other					
Imports	10	10	9	17	46
Shipments	6	10	42	14	102
Difference	4		−33	3	−56

Source: Adapted from information provided by the Colón Free Zone.

the reverse. Inventory control may remove a potential source of contraband, or at least insure against any misrepresentation of facts. Also, the inability of firms to account for differences between receipts and shipments should render them liable to duties on the discrepancies.

During the latter part of 1962, many allegations were made of coffee contrabanding through the Free Zone. To the degree that this product is smuggled into Panamá, the explanation lies in the high protective tariffs that invite contrabanding. A moderate protective duty would provide ample protection unless the industry is grossly inefficient, in which case it should not be protected. Much of the contrabanding of food items is traceable to excessive protective tariffs and unduly high domestic prices, as was noted above in the section dealing with protective tariffs.

News items in 1962 also contained allegations from Colombia that smuggled arms were originating in Panamanian territory. In return, charges have been made that liquor and coffee have been entering Panamá from her neighbors. It would appear that all of the governments involved have an interest in removing this illegal trade. Negotiations should take place for mutual cooperation. It would facilitate control if each country offered to reveal the destination of all cargoes and each checked on the receipts, at least on a sampling basis.

Administration

The total budget of the Administration of Customs and related divisions amounted to B/391,780 in 1961. Of this amount, B/324,030 was spent on items directly related to customs collection and vigilance. The latter amount represents 1.42 per cent of total customs revenues, excluding consular receipts (see Table 6.12).

Salaries of customs personnel are quite low. The General Administrator of Customs has a salary of about B/6000 per year, while chief assessors receive B/3000 to B/3600. Customs inspectors are paid as little as B/1600, with most of them receiving about B/1800. The head of the Department of Vigilance receives less than B/4000 annually, and his inspectors receive only B/1200. To develop the efficiency, integrity, and morale of the customs personnel will require additional resources to be made available for planning, training, and enforcement purposes. At present the service is seriously handicapped by inadequate resources.

Personal relationships between customs personnel and importers should be discouraged by such means as frequent rotation of assignments among personnel. In addition, statistical sampling of shipments should be utilized as a routine measure by the Department of Vigilance. The employment of a statistician for the purpose of developing sampling techniques should prove worthwhile. Technical assistance from other countries for the establishment of examination and training programs would contribute to the development of the customs service.

TABLE 6.12
Budget of the Customs Administration, 1962

	Estimated Expenditures
General Administration of Customs	B/ 44,590
Customs Division	234,480
Parcel Post Division	19,460
Department of Vigilance	25,500
SUB-TOTAL	B/324,030
Related Activities	
Tariff Commission	8,000
Division of Consuls and Ships	21,750
Inspection of Ports	38,000
TOTAL, Customs and Related Activities	B/391,780

Note: Does not include Panamá's contribution to the International Iceberg Patrols.
Source: Ministry of Finance and the Treasury.

CHAPTER 7

Taxes on Foreign Commerce — Tariff Policies

THE PROTECTIVE TARIFFS

RELYING HEAVILY on customs duties for financing government expenditures, Panamá nevertheless employs protective tariffs extensively as a means of promoting economic development. There is a general disposition within the country to levy a protective duty whenever a domestic industry shows it is capable of supplying part of the market. A wide variety of products are subject to imposts whose prime purpose is protective. Among the products with protective duties are: fresh meats and poultry, milk and milk products (except butter and nutritive preparations for children), eggs, honey, citrus fruits, tomatoes, sugar, coffee, margarine, lard, salt, beer, soft drinks, liquors, tobacco products, leather, inexpensive perfumes, vegetable oils, some soaps, shoes, some clothing (especially work clothing), wood and wood products, and printed materials except books and periodicals. (A selected list of protected goods and the applicable duties are shown in Table 7.1.)

In a few cases, the protective duties result in incongruities. Thus, butter has a very low duty of B/0.05 per kilo, while margarine is subject to a high levy of B/0.20 per kilo. Cheap perfumes are subject to a prohibitive

levy of B/25 per liter, while expensive perfumes are subject to a modest 10 per cent duty. Fresh meat and sausages are heavily taxed at B/0.50 per kilo, but canned and smoked hams are taxed at the very modest rate of B/0.08 per kilo.

Duties on alcoholic beverages are both revenue-producing and protective in that domestically-produced alcoholic beverages are subject to very modest internal excises compared to the duties on imported products. The same is true of tobacco products.

THE ECONOMICS OF PROTECTION

Loss of Revenue

The very nature of a protective tariff results in the substitution of domestic products for foreign, and in a decline in imports of the protected product. Imports of margarine and lard decreased 57 per cent from 1953 to 1961; tobacco products, 63 per cent; shoes, 9 per cent; milk, eggs, and honey, 15 per cent; oil and fats, 17 per cent. In many other protected categories, imports rose less than the average. This was true of fruits and vegetables, sugar and sweets, alcoholic beverages, soaps, and clothing.

111

In the absence of a rise in the tariff sufficient to offset the decline in imports, revenue from the customs will decline. As a case in point, revenues from imports of tobacco products in 1950 were B/714,000, and tobacco in bulk produced an additional B/40,000, for total revenues of B/754,000. The effective

TABLE 7.1

Tariffs Applicable to a Selected List of
Protected Goods, 1961

	(*per gross kilo*)
Fresh beef	B/ .50
Fresh pork	.50
Poultry	.50
Sausages	.40
Powdered milk	1.25
Rice	.20
Strawberries	.50 to 1.00
Tomatoes	.85
Tomato soup	.47
Sugar	.25
Sweets	.20 to .40
Coffee, unroasted	.60
Coffee, roasted	1.20
Cocoa	.30
Margarine	.20
Lard	.30
Cigars	1.25
Cigarettes	7.00
Animal fats	.30
Vegetable fats	.30
Printed matter, except books and periodicals	1.00 to 3.00
Paper, wax	.20
Vinegar, artificial	1.00
Leather	3.00
Soles, not cut according to size	2.00
Soles, cut according to size	6.00
Paper products	.50
Cement, Portland	.01
Cardboard paper, cut to size	.30
	(*per liter*)
Beer	1.01
Whiskey, rum, gin	3.50
Rectified alcohol	3.00
Perfume, F.O.B. less than B/20 per liter	25.00
	(*per cent*)
Manufactures of wood	.50 to .75
Mattresses	.35
Work clothes	.50
Ready-made suits	.40
	(*per dozen*)
Shoes	3.00 to 30.00
Eggs	1.00
	(*per square foot*)
Lumber	.05 to .07
	(*per bar*)
Soap	.15

Source: Arancel de Importación.

duty on imported cigarettes was 45 per cent of the F.O.B. price in 1950. In 1961, revenues from cigarette duties were B/178,709 on imports of only B/75,429, the duty having been increased to 237 per cent. But tobacco imports in bulk had increased from 1950 to 1961, which resulted in a slight rise in revenue from tobacco and its products from B/754,000 in 1950 to B/765,000 in 1961.

Economic Development

On the basis of production data, agricultural products subject to protective duties have behaved in a manner which is consistent with the goals of a protective tariff. As Table 7.2 shows, sugar production nearly doubled from 1950 to 1961, salt production increased 70 per cent, cattle and pig slaughtering advanced while the stock of cattle and pigs also increased, canned milk production increased 400 per cent, and tomato production increased from the relatively insignificant amount of 345 thousand pounds to over 12 million pounds.

Similarly, the protected industries appeared to be doing well on the whole with respect to the amount of value-added, which increased in all the industries shown in Table 7.3 except alcoholic beverages and leather and leather products. However, the gross national product increased 31.9 per cent during the same period, and several of the industries recorded increases of less than this amount. Among them were perfumes, cosmetics and soaps, chemicals and paints, and clay, glass and cement. Included also in this group is non-alcoholic beverages, but the latter is singular in that it produced 100 per cent of domestic consumption.

For the same industries shown in Table 7.3, total employment from 1956 to 1960 actually decreased by about 1 per cent. But substantial increases in employment resulted in paper products, 130 per cent; sawmills, planing, and woodworking, 89 per cent; tobacco products, 78 per cent; shoes, 25 per cent; and milk, 30 per cent. During the period, the total labor force increased by 14 per cent,

TABLE 7.2
Production of Selected Farm Products, 1950 to 1961

	1950	1955	1960	1961
Sugar (000's of quintals)	287	328	498	560
Salt (quintals)	100	207	144	170
Cattle slaughtered (000's)	73	78	93	106
Pigs slaughtered (000's)	49	61	70	70
Production of condensed, evaporated, and powdered milk (000's of kilos)	1,221	2,750	6,561	6,351
Tomatoes purchased for tomato products (000's of pounds)	345	2,956	8,186	12,099
Rice (000's of quintals)	1,849	2,126	2,114	2,401
Corn (000's of quintals)	1,376	1,757	1,327	1,631
Cattle (000's)	570	578	666	765
Hogs (000's)	182	215	248	237
Coffee plants (000's)	15,839	19,391	26,365	—
Honey (latas)	—	8,285	12,795	—

Source: Dirección de Estadística y Censo.

TABLE 7.3
Level of Employment and Value-Added in Selected Industries, 1956 to 1960

	1960			1956				
	Number of Firms	Number of Employees	Value-Added (000's)	Number of Firms	Number of Employees	Value-Added (000's)	Employment Index	Value-Added Index
Preparation and canning of meats and food products, and coffee roasting	17	698	B/ 3,007	17	504	B/ 1,728	138	174
Milk products	5	580	2,694	7	447	1,751	130	154
Mills and refiners of sugar, and manufacturers of cocoa, chocolates, and candy	4	624	2,222	10	2,135	1,585	29	140
Bakeries	28	625	1,171	16	356	683	176	171
Alcoholic beverages	11	719	4,538	16	1,117	4,680	64	97
Non-alcoholic beverages	8	273	881	8	197	714	139	123
Tobacco products	3	246	972	3	138	714	178	136
Men's clothing and tailoring	22	820	1,326	21	732	804	112	164
Production and repairing of mattresses and other textile manufactures	3	48	139	4	41	79	117	176
Sawmills, planing, and other wood working	15	618	717	13	327	664	189	108
Wood products for the construction industry	5	84	485					
Shoes	13	424	1,435	9	343	455	124	315
Paper products	5	152	555	5	66	202	230	275
Leather and leather products	5	94	201	5	161	378	58	53
Perfumes, cosmetics, and soaps	4	69	143	6	68	119	101	120
Chemicals and paints	5	87	272	6	70	246	124	111
Clay, glass, and cement products	15	855	3,226	16	685	2,526	125	128
Power and gas	8	1,243	7,177	8	947	5,132	131	140
TOTALS	176	8,259	B/31,161	170	8,334	B/22,460	99	139

Source: Estadística Panameña, Industrias: Encuestas de 1957 y 1961.

and most of the industries shown in Table 7.3 realized increases greater than this. Exceptions were sugar and sweets, alcoholic beverages, men's clothing, leather, and perfumes and cosmetics.

Since value-added is affected by prices, the increases in employment should be given somewhat greater weight in interpreting the effects of protective policies. This is especially so since protection implies some degree of price increase in the domestic market. While increases were recorded in employment in most of the industries shown, the numbers involved were quite small. After subtracting the employment increases in sugar and sweets, the total increase in employment in the other industries was only 1,436. It is also worth noting that manufacturing employment increased by only 4,500 from 1950 to 1961, or by 24.5 per cent, while the labor force increased by nearly 77,000, or by 28.5 per cent. But since there is a variation in the number of firms from which the foregoing data were taken, the data shown should be interpreted carefully. However, there is little reason to doubt that the orders of magnitude indicated are more or less reliable.

Additional evidence that the protective tariffs are furthering the development of the protected industries may be obtained by a temporal comparison of the proportion of total consumption of various goods which is satisfied from domestic sources. From 1950 to 1959, the percentage of total private consumption satisfied by domestic production increased from 67.9 to 73.5 per cent, while the same percentage for foodstuffs rose from 78.5 to 84.6 per cent. Among the foodstuffs, domestic production of meat increased from 91.5 per cent of consumption in 1950 to 95.8 per cent in 1959; of milk, cheese, and eggs, 73.9 to 87 per cent; of oils and fats, 18.4 to 39.6 per cent; and of coffee, cocoa, and tea, 77.19 to 97.1 per cent. Non-alcoholic beverages, subject to a prohibitive impost, are produced entirely within the country. For alcoholic beverages, the percentage of consumption domestically produced increased from 73.2 to 78.0 per cent, while the domestic production of tobacco products increased from 8.9 to 90.4 per cent, clothing and personal effects from 48.5 to 61.0 per cent, and shoes from 38.4 to 81.6 per cent (see Table 7.4).

Incidence of the Protective Tariffs

While there is little doubt that protective tariffs will encourage domestic production,

it is usually done at the expense of a rise in prices for the protected good, at least in the short run. If the choice of an industry to be protected is sound, and protection results in the development of a healthy industry able to take advantage of economies of scale, prices in the long run should fall below the pre-existing prices, or at least should return to

TABLE 7.4

Domestic Production and Imports as Compared to Domestic Production of Consumption Goods, 1950, 1955, and 1959

(Millions of Balboas)

	1950	1955	1959
Total production and imports	243.17	283.24	344.99
Domestic production	165.07	198.73	253.40
Per Cent	67.9	70.2	73.5
Foodstuffs	87.35	99.41	117.57
Domestic production	68.54	80.55	99.42
Per Cent	78.5	81.0	84.6
Bread and cereals	19.28	24.32	27.65
Domestic production	18.11	22.54	26.53
Per Cent	93.9	92.7	95.9
Meat	19.18	22.20	24.45
Domestic production	17.55	20.07	23.43
Per Cent	91.5	90.4	95.8
Seafood	1.36	2.00	3.16
Domestic production	0.43	0.78	1.66
Per Cent	31.6	39.0	52.5
Milk, cheese, and eggs	9.93	10.70	12.78
Domestic production	7.34	8.85	11.12
Per Cent	73.9	82.7	87.0
Oils and fats	4.03	3.16	6.37
Domestic production	0.74	0.90	2.52
Per Cent	18.4	28.5	39.6
Fruits and vegetables	22.70	24.64	28.29
Domestic production	16.69	18.59	21.42
Per Cent	73.5	75.4	75.7
Sugar and sweets	4.10	5.89	7.95
Domestic production	3.56	5.02	7.23
Per Cent	86.8	85.2	90.9
Coffee, tea, cocoa	4.69	3.00	4.83
Domestic production	3.62	2.88	4.69
Per Cent	77.2	96.0	97.1
Other foodstuffs	2.09	3 51	2.09
Domestic production	0.50	0.92	0.84
Per Cent	23.9	26.2	40.2
Alcoholic beverages	12.31	14.25	16.01
Domestic production	9.01	10.72	12.52
Per Cent	73.2	75.2	78.2

TABLE 7.4 (Continued)

(Millions of Balboas)

	1950	1955	1959
Non-alcoholic beverages	2.43	3.06	3.98
Domestic production	2.42	3.06	3.98
Per Cent	100.0	100.0	100.0
Tobacco	4.36	4.71	4.48
Domestic production	0.39	1.79	4.05
Per Cent	8.9	38.0	90.4
Clothing and other personal			
effects	30.61	34.97	42.71
Domestic production	14.85	17.76	26.05
Per Cent	48.5	50.8	61.0
Shoes	3.62	5.25	9.75
Domestic production	1.39	2.26	7.96
Per Cent	38.4	43.0	81.6
Clothing	22.28	24.97	26.96
Domestic production	13.30	15.31	17.87
Per Cent	59.7	61.3	66.3
Furniture, accessories, and			
household goods	12.56	12.72	14.60
Domestic production	1.83	2.23	1.99
Per Cent	14.6	17.5	13.6
Furniture and accessories			
(durable)	3.18	3.26	2.99
Domestic production	1.83	2.23	1.99
Per Cent	57.5	68.4	66.6
Non-durable household goods	5.18	4.10	7.2
Domestic production	—	—	—
Per Cent	0.0	0.0	0.0
Durable household goods	4.11	5.30	4.36
Domestic production	—	—	—
Per Cent	0.0	0.0	0.0
Transportation and commu-			
nication	23.99	29.51	39.37
Domestic production	14.52	17.98	22.83
Per Cent	60.5	60.9	58.0
Personal transport equipment	5.41	4.73	5.14
Domestic production	—	—	—
Per Cent	0.0	0.0	0.0

Source: Dirección de Estadística y Censo, Ingresos Nacionales, various years.

about the former levels. To the extent that the protective tariffs prevent the importation of goods, they are not revenue-producing; but there is a presumption nevertheless that prices will be higher for the articles in question, at least in the short run. Consumers will in that case bear a burden without there being any direct compensating increase in government revenues.

A protective policy may be justified if, in the long run, the protected industries survive without requiring a continuation of the subsidy exacted from consumers. In this respect it should be kept in mind that if a subsidy is considered desirable for employment and income effects regardless of the price effects, there is no justification for placing the burden of the subsidy exclusively on the consumers of the protected product. A subsidy from general tax revenues would be more equitable. Should the choice of protection be unwise, or should the protected industry fail to achieve a "satisfactory" rate of growth, or level of output and employment, the government would incur a loss of customs revenue, consumers would pay higher prices, and the protected industry would enjoy higher profits without any advantage to the country. In effect, the consumers would be paying a "tax" to the owners of firms in the tariff-protected industry.

There is demonstrated evidence of growth in the protected industries, but at the same time, what has been the corresponding price behavior? Have prices shown the decreases that one would expect if the protected industries had been prudently selected and had behaved in accordance with anticipations?

For some products there is evidence that prices have behaved satisfactorily in accordance with the foregoing criteria. In general, the duties on fresh and processed meats (except smoked ham and bacon) have not resulted in higher prices to the consumer than if similar products had been imported. Panamanian beef undersells imported untaxed beef in the Canal Zone.[1] For meat products not produced in Panamá, such as bacon, the price in Panamá is of course higher as a result of the duties. The duties on these products are less concerned with protecting an existing domestic product than with encouraging the substitution of fresh meat and of frankfurters.

On the other hand, it is difficult to find other products that have lower domestic prices as compared to possible imports. Do-

[1] See the preceding chapter, Table 6.10.

mestic salt, of inferior quality and packaging, costs more in Panamá than high-quality salt in the Canal Zone. Rice, tomatoes and tomato products, shortening, salad oils, peanut butter, beer, milk, powdered milk, margarine, coffee, strawberries, and sugar are all priced above the level at which they could be imported and sold.[2] Other products such as shoes, wood furniture, and mattresses appear to be priced competitively, but it is difficult to draw any definite conclusions because of differences in quality and style.

Unfortunately, those duties that have resulted in higher prices are also those that weigh heavily on low income groups. The protective tariffs on sugar, coffee, margarine, shortening, salad oils, milk, and even beer are highly regressive in their effects.

Many of the protective tariffs have been employed for an extended period. In 1946, the tariffs on the following were considered to be protective: meat, poultry, meat products, fats and oils, milk, cheese, fish, eggs, rice, corn flour, spaghetti, macaroni, tomatoes, fresh vegetables, beans, potatoes, lemons, coffee, cocoa, sugar, salt, jellies, marmalades, candy, biscuits, beer, fruit juices, laundry soap, lotions, toilet waters, perfumes, tobacco, shoes, leather articles, straw hats, cotton dresses, children's suits, linen suits, pillows, mattresses, furniture, wooden manufactures, blinds, printed materials (except books and periodicals), tile and clay products, boxes, filing cabinets, other wood items, and steel furniture.[3] Since 1946, this list has not changed much. Consumers are still paying relatively high prices for eggs, oils, milk, tomatoes, coffee, sugar, jellies, and marmalades, not to mention the manufactured items on which price data are not available.

The prices of some of the products that receive protection have fallen somewhat in recent years. Price comparisons are available for thirty-six products shown in Table 7.5 for the interval from 1952 to 1959. Twenty-

five products declined in price, twelve by more than 10 per cent. Eleven products rose in price, four by more than 10 per cent. Most of these items are food products, however, and it should be borne in mind that food prices on the average still remain considerably higher than comparable import prices.

One agricultural specialist in a study prepared for the government of the Republic of Panamá concluded that the prices in some protected industries are unduly high:

The general level of prices for agricultural products in Panamá is high in relation to world markets and the local wage rates and purchasing power. . . .

The high price structure is mainly the result of governmental price policies which are basically designed toward national self-sufficiency. . . .

Pricing policies have been one of the major measures taken toward this end. These have covered the fields of tariffs, import quotas, import prohibition, agricultural price supports, and maximum price regulation. . . .

There is a very wide margin between the prices to farmers and maximum prices to consumers for some agricultural products. For example, farmers receive 6 cents per lb. for first quality rice . . . while the wholesale price for milled rice is 13.5 cents, more than twice the price at which it could be imported. The retail price is 15 cents.

Farmers are paid for sugar cane on the basis of a little over 3 cents per lb. refined sugar, while the wholesale price is 11 cents and the retail price is 12.5 cents. Only two companies benefit from this processing margin. Again with milk, suppliers to the processing factories are able to produce at 8 cents per liter. The four or five large-scale suppliers of whole milk to Panamá City receive 15 cents and the same interests sell pasteurized bottled milk at 29 cents. . . .

Largely as a result of this high price structure, self-sufficiency has now been achieved for many products previously imported, including beef, milk and some milk products, sugar, rice and most fresh fruits and vegetables.

While artificially high prices may have been justified during a period of expansion, this will no longer be valid once domestic

[2] *Ibid.*
[3] David Lynch, *Report on the Tariff Policy of Panamá* (Washington: Inter-American Development Commission, May, 1946), p. 39.

TABLE 7.5

Index of Consumer Prices of Selected Articles
Produced in Panamá, 1959

Articles	Index 1952 = 100
Beef, fresh	96.5
Pork, fresh	97.5
Poultry, fresh	88.2
Prepared meats	99.5
Fish (Corvina)	109.3
Shrimp	70.2
Rice	104.2
Cornflour	71.5
Macaroni	87.3
Fresh vegetables	88.8
Tomato paste	78.9
Tomato sauce	108.2
Eggs	74.5
Oil, vegetable	87.0
Sugar	90.4
Coffee	99.0
Salt	99.8
Vinegar	77.5
Soap, bar, five ounces	102.1
Soap, powder, two ounces	97.4
Starch, per pound	96.0
Shirts, men's	105.2
Pants, work, men's	74.5
Shoes, men's	111.6
Shoes, women's	
Type A	92.6
Type B	89.0
Shirts, children's	83.3
Pants, children's	96.0
Shoes, children's	111.3
Soap, toilet	104.0
Mattresses, cotton	92.6
Cigarettes	118.2
Beer	116.7
Milk, powdered	98.6
Milk, pasteurized, fresh	96.0
Cheese, white	100.1

Source: Dirección de Estadística y Censo, *Precios y Costo de la Vida*, 1959.

TABLE 7.6

Prices and Consumption of Milk in
Central America and Panamá

Country	Annual Per Capita Consumption (Liters)	Retail Price per Liter (Balboas)	Price at the Farm per Liter (Balboas)
Costa Rica	136.0	0.18	0.13
Nicaragua	70.7	0.17	0.07
El Salvador	58.0	0.25	0.16
Honduras	57.4	0.20	0.15
Guatemala	56.5	0.20	0.15
Panamá	40.0	0.29	0.18

Source: Comisión de Asuntos Económicos, *Reporte Económico*, Panamá, 1960.

to curtail production to the high cost market, rather than to expand demand (and in some cases, open up export opportunities) through lower prices.[4]

The need for lower prices of some products in order to satisfy the nutritional needs of the population is a policy issue that should be emphasized. In a study of the nutritional requirements of Panamanians made in 1950, Dr. Menalco Solís noted that the Panamanian diet was deficient in calcium, and that a much greater consumption of milk was needed.[5] The per capita consumption of milk in Panamá is less than in any Central American country, and the price is also higher (see Table 7.6). Moreover, some milk products such as powdered milk are not available in domestic markets (except imported high-taxed varieties), although these products would provide the greatest nutritive value (minus fat) per unit of expenditure.

Subsidies for products nutritionally important in the Panamanian diet should be financed from general tax revenues rather than by high prices. It is not clear, however, that some of these products, like milk and margarine, need to be subsidized at all. Domestic supplies of milk obviously have a great advantage from the standpoint of trans-

[4] P. A. Reid, *Agricultural Development in Panamá* (Washington: International Bank for Reconstruction and Development, June, 1957), pp. 17–19.
[5] *Demanda Alimenticia de la Póblacion de la República de Panamá en 1950* (Panamá: SICAP y Ministerio de Agricultura, Comercio, e Industrias, 1955), p. 21.

requirements are met. The high prices severely curtail domestic demand and particularly so because of the low purchasing power of the bulk of the population.

Although greatly increased consumption of meat, milk and protective foods is necessary for even minimum standards of adequate nutrition, most of the people simply cannot afford to purchase more. In addition, most prices are so far above world levels that exports offer little prospects for wider markets.

Now that production is catching up with demand, the general attitude of farmers is

port over the imported product. Furthermore, it should be shown that the rates of return are not excessive before a subsidy is justified. Since the latter information has never been made available, there is little justification for the subsidy.

An appropriate policy with respect to an industry like the milk industry would be to take advantage of surpluses in other countries, which are often translated into "bargain" prices for powdered and canned milk, and butter. The processing of fresh milk hardly needs protection because of the marketing advantages enjoyed by domestic producers and processors. But assuming that it does, it does not appear desirable to protect the domestic industry when the effect is to raise prices and to deny consumers the advantage of a key nutritional product.

Margarine presents another questionable case of protection, for the protection afforded the domestic industry is at the expense of the lowest income group in the population. Margarine is a substitute for butter, but it is cheaper and of equal nutritive value. It is thus a desirable item in the diet of low-income families. Accordingly, the industry should be given a direct subsidy rather than tariff protection so that it may offer the product at the world price. Efforts to this end ought to be taken immediately before vested interests become so entrenched that the present policy could not be changed. As it is now, the "tax" is a glaring inequity.

The combined impact of protective and revenue tariffs on food prices may be appreciated from the fact that food costs in Panamá are nearly 50 per cent higher than those in the Canal Zone.[6] While not all of this difference can be attributed to tariffs, most of it can. Although the comparison applies to the buying pattern of Panamanians with higher than average incomes, the data also suggest the regressive burden of tariffs, both revenue and protective.

The conclusion appears warranted that if the financial sacrifice on the part of con-

sumers could be calculated and capitalized, it would total in some cases more than the contribution of the industries being protected. The high prices in these cases have been simply a private "tax" protecting monopolists and redistributing income from low to upper income groups.

A protective tariff is justified if it brings into being or accelerates the development of a healthy industry, whose costs of production and prices become competitive with levels elsewhere. If it protects a sick industry, far from being a gain to the economy, it actually reduces the standard of living, and nearly always the standard of living of the low income groups. Since protective tariffs are often granted in connection with contracts for customs exemptions, the means of preventing abuses is discussed in the following section on exemptions.

EXEMPTIONS

Closely related to the issue of imposing protective tariffs is the policy of granting relief from the burden of customs duties to new or expanding enterprises. These exemptions or exonerations are granted through contractual arrangements with the government. The contracts may also provide government loans, technical assistance, protective tariffs and quotas, and guarantees with respect to the burden of other taxes.

Many of the contracts were entered into under Decree Law No. 2 of May 10, 1950, under which exemptions from customs duties could be, and usually were, granted for a period of twenty-five years. The 1950 law was superseded by the current statute, Law No. 25 of February 7, 1957, which limits benefits to a maximum of fifteen years. In recent years, grants of exemption have been given for varying terms of up to fifteen years. Moreover, the current law does not provide for the exemption of taxes on income and real property, or social security and local taxes.

---

[6] See Table 6.10 in the preceding chapter.

The procedure for obtaining a contract requires the applicant to file a petition showing the current prices of the articles he intends to produce; his financial capacity; his methods of production, patents, and licenses; the period required to complete the investment; his experience in the business; "detailed technical information" regarding costs, total investment, and materials he will employ; the required numbers of skilled and unskilled laborers; and whether there are similar firms in existence.

The petition is filed initially with the appropriate ministry, usually the Ministry of Agriculture, Commerce and Industry. After a preliminary review, the ministry forwards the petition to the National Economic Council for its opinion. The Council may recommend approval, approval with modifications, or disapproval. The final decision on the application is made by the cabinet, which designates the appropriate minister to sign the contract if it is approved. Approved contracts are published in the *Gaceta Oficial.*

Competitive firms are entitled to identical privileges, provided that they undertake similar commitments. A Supreme Court ruling on the 1957 law even upheld the claim of a petitioner for privileges identical to those which his competitor received under the earlier 1950 law.

To import an item duty-free or partially-exempted under a contract, a firm files a request with the Vice-Minister of Finance and pays a fee of B/10 for each category of imports in which exemption is requested, a so-called *gravamen sobre exoneraciones.* This charge levied on exemptions yielded B/26,700 in 1961. The burden is in the nature of a "fee" to help finance the administration of exemptions as well as to discourage petty requests.

The contracts usually provide that the grantee will purchase materials and supplies in Panamá when these are available. To insure this, an application to introduce an exempted import must be accompanied by an official certification that the items to be imported are not produced in Panamá.

The 1957 law provides that qualifying enterprises could be exempted from the payment of taxes on: 1) the importation of machinery, equipment, and instruments to be used in manufacturing plants and laboratories, and for the construction of buildings to be used for manufacturing, maintenance, or storage activities; 2) the imports of fuels and lubricants used in manufacturing, excepting gasoline and alcohol; 3) the imports of packages and packaging materials not produced in Panamá or produced in insufficient quantities to satisfy the total demand; 4) the capital of the enterprise, its installations, operations, production, distribution, and sale of its products; 5) the earnings from sales effected exclusively outside of the country, except in the case of extractive industries and those exploiting natural resources; and 6) the export of the products of the enterprise and re-export of raw materials and equipment which should prove to be unnecessary to its activities.

Amount of the Exemptions

In 1961, B/29.7 million of imports were exempted from import duties, including the imports of government agencies and charitable and educational institutions. Private firms, excluding aviation companies, were permitted to import free of duties [7] B/23.1 million of goods on which the duties exonerated were B/3.6 million. Aviation companies were exempted of an additional B/1.8 million of imports and B/0.48 million of duties. Partially exempt were some B/0.83 million of imports resulting in some B/0.09 million of duties exonerated. The fully exempted imports of the private firms, including aviation companies, amounted to 20 per cent of total imports. The duties exonerated for these firms, including partial exemptions, represented 28.5 per cent of total import duties and fees (see Table 7.7).

The amount of exemptions has been growing steadily as can be seen from Table 7.8.

---

[7] Part of the merchandise imported remained subject to a 2 per cent consular fee.

TABLE 7.7

Summary of Import Exemptions, 1961

(Thousands of Balboas)

Category of Importer	Value of Imports	Duties Exempted
Aviation companies	1,770.7	478.4
Diplomatic and consular corps	98.4	35.3
Government agencies	3,640.2	2,045.7
Private firms	23,133.9	3,609.3
Charitable and educational institutions	213.2	42.6
Total full exemptions	28,856.4	6,211.3
Partial exemptions (private firms)	830.5	92.9
TOTALS	29,686.9	6,304.2

Source: Departamento Consular Comercial, Contraloría General.

TABLE 7.8

Duties Exempted, Selected Years from 1950 to 1961

(Thousands of Balboas)

	Duties Saved on Fully Exempted Imports (Private Companies)	Duties Saved on Partly Exempted Imports (Private Companies)	Duties Exempt, Government and other Public Use	Total[1]
1950	—	841.3	808.3	1,649.6
1952	498.6	879.5	565.3	1,943.3
1954	522.7	360.4	351.9	1,235.0
1956	648.9	206.5	1,480.4	2,335.8
1957	1,094.9	158.0	1,253.7	2,506.6
1959[3]	1,955.1	154.0[2]	2,088.9	4,198.0
1960[3]	2,636.0	111.5	951.4	3,698.9
1961[3]	4,087.7	92.9	2,123.5	6,304.1

[1] Totals may not add due to rounding.
[2] Estimated.
[3] Partially exonerated imports were liable to an 8 per cent consular fee after 1957. This amount has been deducted from the duties exonerated. The data shown are the actual savings in taxes.

Source: Contraloría General.

Private Companies saved B/841,300 in import duties in 1950 and B/4,180,600 in 1961. Exempted duties more than doubled between 1959 and 1961. The amount of imports exonerated, fully or partially, increased from B/6,728,200 in 1950, or 10 per cent of total imports, to B/29,686,900 in 1961, or 23.8 per cent.

The government and its agencies accounted for B/3.6 million of the B/28.9 million of total exonerations in 1961. The principal categories of government imports exonerated and their values were as follows:

Pharmaceuticals	B/ 722,950
Foodstuffs	342,387
Fuels and lubricants	274,758
Common metals	326,106
Machinery	763,982
Electrical equipment	393,467
Transport	211,470
Furniture	115,915
Other	489,176
TOTAL	B/3,640,211

Particular government agencies charged with insuring an adequate domestic supply of certain highly-protected goods may import the necessary quantities of those goods free of duties. For example, government agencies imported B/260,387 of milk, eggs, and honey in 1961, on which the scheduled duties would have been B/1.4 million. These agencies often sell the imported products at market prices, making a profit on the transactions. Some food imports, of course, like CARE parcels and foods distributed under aid programs, are distributed free. Except for these instances, and Social Security purchases of pharmaceuticals, government imports reflect consumption expenditures by the government.

Nature of the Imports Exempted

Over 30 per cent of the imports in the following categories were exempted in 1961: manufactured goods classified according to materials, machinery and transport equipment, and fuel and lubricants and related products. Nearly 29 per cent of the chemical products category was exempted. When the categories are classified into narrower groups, relatively high percentages of certain imports were exonerated, the more important being: inorganic chemicals, 76 per cent; agricultural insecticides, 84 per cent; and mining, construction, and industrial machinery, 60 per cent. Other groups are shown in Table 7.9 together with the value of imports in each category, the duties paid, and the duties exempted.

Rate of Exempted Duties

The full exemptions for private firms (excluding aviation companies) amounted to B/23.1 million of goods in 1961, on which the duty exempted was B/3.6 million, indicating average duties of 15.6 per cent *ad valorem*. In many categories of imports in which there are substantial exonerations, the duties are a relatively modest percentage of value. For power-generating machinery, the *ad valorem* rate averaged 7 per cent; for common metal products (bars, shapes, tubing, etc.), the average was 11.1 per cent; for electrical machinery, 10.1 per cent; and for chemical products, and chemical elements and compounds, 9.1 and 7.3 per cent respectively.

In some categories the duties are relatively heavy, and their exemption, therefore, is inconsistent with a policy of protection. For

TABLE 7.9

Value of Imports and Amounts Exempted for a Selected List of Goods, 1961

(Thousands of Balboas)

Description	(1) Value of Imports	(2) Duties Paid	(3) Value of Imports Exempted	(4) Col. 1 Less Col. 3	(5) Col. 2 as a Percentage of Col. 4	(6) Percentage of Imports Exempted
Chemical products, inorganic	1,070	24.4	810	260	9.4	76
Chemical products, organic	230	14.0	105	125	11.2	46
Dyeing, tanning	127	7.0	57	70	10.0	45
Aromatic oils, etc.	306	51.4	94	212	24.2	31
Cellophane, without printing	129	2.7	76	53	5.1	59
Other plastic materials, not woven or manufactures	389	9.2	296	93	9.9	76
Insecticides, agricultural	1,082	8.6	909	173	5.0	84
Insecticides, domestic	147	12.1	26	121	10.0	18
Resin or rosin	59	1.6	26	33	4.8	44
Other chemicals	357	25.0	230	127	19.7	64
Manufactures of cork	45	1.5	26	19	7.9	58
Paper and cardboard	3,223	137.1	1,636	1,587	8.6	51
Articles of paper and cardboard pulp	1,879	163.2	836	1,043	15.6	44
Yarns and threads	345	16.3	37	308	5.3	11
Cotton fabrics	3,705	284.4	1,093	2,612	10.9	30
Special fabrics	854	37.6	312	542	6.9	37
Glass	392	17.3	158	234	7.4	40
Bolts, nuts, etc.	234	6.0	59	175	3.4	25
Hand tools	452	17.9	96	356	5.0	21
Cases, boxes of common metals	346	1.3	333	13	10.0	96
Hardware	460	34.3	114	346	9.9	25
Machinery, power generating	1,393	50.2	393	1,000	5.0	28
Machinery and mechanical apparatus for agriculture	300	1.4	49	251	0.6	16
Machinery for mining, construction and industrial uses	9,386	367.6	5,636	3,750	9.8	60
Generators and dynamos	635	9.3	499	136	6.8	79
Motors	147	4.6	101	46	10.0	69
Transformers, alternators	213	8.0	55	158	5.1	26
Mechanisms for circuit breakers, etc.	166	3.4	127	39	8.7	77
X-ray equipment	107	0.5	101	6	8.3	94
Cranes, irrigating equipment, etc.	226	17.5	158	68	25.7	70
Textiles, cloth (not cotton)	2,605	234.0	330	2,275	10.3	13
TOTALS	31,009	1,569.4	14,778	16,231	9.7	

Source: Contraloría General, Dirección de Estadística y Censo.

the category of preserved and prepared fruits, the duties exempted were 68.5 per cent of the value of the imported goods. Such an exemption would not be inconsistent if the industry re-exported its products, but in this case, exports were only B/143 as compared to imports of B/168,000. Other categories with exemptions of relatively high import duties were fuels and lubricants (mostly diesel oil, fuel oil, and aviation fuels), paper and cardboard, and diverse manufactures.

Economic Effects of the Exemptions

Private firms, excluding aviation companies, were relieved of nearly B/3.7 million in customs duties in 1961 through the exemptions. This represented saving in the costs of both capital and production materials. Over B/10 million of the exempted imports were in what may be considered the capital goods category, namely, the imports in the categories of machinery and transport equipment and metal manufactures. The duties exempted in these categories amounted to about B/1.6 million, an amount representing a saving of fixed capital required to finance those enterprises. Most of the remaining exemptions, about B/2 million, were in categories of raw materials and semi-manufactures which are processed or fabricated into finished products. For the latter two categories, the B/2.0 million of duties exempted saved working capital as well as lowered costs of materials. The amount of working capital saved would depend on the frequency of inventory turnover.

The saving of capital costs to the enterprises does not represent a saving in foreign exchange, and it does not change the amount of capital available in the economy, but it enables a greater use to be made of private capital. It increases the capacity of private firms to invest, but it does not determine the level of investment. It increases the marginal and average net product of capital, and therefore acts as a stimulant to investment.

In addition to representing a reduction in the amount of capital required, the exemption of raw materials and semi-manufactures lowers costs of production by the amount of the exemption. Reduced costs make it possible for the firms to sell their products at lower prices, or perhaps to increase their profits if the savings in cost are not passed on to consumers.

To the extent that the saving in duties results in lower prices to consumers, the exemption from duties is a saving for consumers. Of course, there is no assurance that all of the saving will be passed on to consumers. If, for example, the exempted firm is a monopolist in the Panamanian market, only part of the reduction in average cost will be passed on to the consumer.[8]

The degree to which the exemption is passed on to consumers depends on the price that is eventually established in Panamá compared to the "international" price. If the exemption makes it possible for the Panamanian firm to meet foreign competition, the exemption is neither a gift to the exempted firm nor to the consumer. If it enables the Panamanian firm to undersell its foreign competitor in Panamá, then the consumer has been "exonerated" to the extent of the relative reduction in price. If, however, the exemption is associated with a protective tariff, and the price becomes higher than before, then there are two possibilities: 1) the firm may charge a monopoly price and make excessive profits, with the consumer contributing to the profits in addition to all or part of the exemption; and 2) the firm may not make excessive profits, in which case the government through decreased revenues and the consumer through higher prices subsidizes the factors of production in the protected industry.

To sum up the preceding arguments, the exemptions reduce the capital requirements for a given production facility in Panamá. They also lower the cost of raw materials and semi-manufactures, but the saving to the firm in this respect is principally in the

---

[8] The reason for this is that the monopolist's price is not equal to marginal cost. He operates where marginal revenue equals marginal cost. Marginal revenue is more inelastic than price; therefore, with a decline in costs, price declines less than the reduction in cost.

requirement for working capital; the saving is the interest on the amount of duty exempted. Yet the advantage that the firm acquires if it is a monopolist probably exceeds the interest saved on the working capital. The exemptions of imported raw materials and semi-manufactures represent a transfer of the substantial part of the duties exempted to the firm when foreign competition is excluded.

Since foreign competition is in fact usually excluded, a substantial part of the approximately B/2.0 million in exonerated duties on raw materials and semi-manufactures in 1961 represented a direct subsidy to the exonerated firms. But the total of the "direct" subsidies (exemptions) and indirect subsidies (protective tariffs) greatly exceed B/2.0 million, although the amount is indeterminate. Thus, an important disadvantage of a subsidy in the form of protective tariffs is that the amount of the subsidy is never fully known. Like an iceberg, only part of the subsidy is visible. This is utilizing the state to advance private special interests in a particularly undesirable way.

A recent case is illustrative. Contracts had been given to certain Panamanian manufacturers of paper products, which accorded them protective tariffs on their finished products. Then a new manufacturer of paper products decided to apply for a contract and to enter into production in Panamá. Under the law the new firm was entitled to the same privileges that had been accorded its predecessors. While the contract could not be denied, its sphere of activity was restricted by an informal understanding between the government and the firm which was designed to insure that it would not compete with the existing firms with respect to certain products. No wonder that there is a widespread belief in Panamá that the government has been too generous with its contracts. The over 200 firms that have contracts are often sarcastically referred to as the "Exonerations Club" (*Club de los Exonerados*).

THE POLICY OF GRANTING EXEMPTIONS

Equity or Non-Discrimination

One should distinguish between legislation which requires negotiation between an authority or agency of the government before privileges or exemptions will be granted, and legislation which exempts whole classes of goods or persons from taxation. In the former case the benefits depend on how well the investor presents his case, who presents the case for him, and his general bargaining power. In the latter case, the benefits are available to all on equal terms and require no prior negotiations to become effective. They are self-operating and self-implementing. In the perspective of a development law, the problem is to extend the benefits to all enterprises which actually increase production or employment and at the same time to avoid excessive subsidies, both direct and indirect.

As long as a law exists in which special exemptions and privileges can be obtained, nearly all prospective investors will try to obtain excessive direct and indirect subsidies, whether or not their investment would have taken place without the rewards. Thus, the legislation becomes a boon to lawyers and influence-peddlers.

Most of the exemptions apply to machinery, equipment, and materials used in the production of goods. Such a policy is a good one, but why restrict it to contract firms? The exemption of capital goods should not be a subject of negotiation between a firm and the government. It is difficult, if not impossible, to discriminate among different entrepreneurs on the basis that one is making a constructive contribution to the economy and the other is not. It would be the better part of wisdom to assume that all manufacturing activities are equally valuable and to remove the import duties on all capital goods. If the government adopted a policy of exempting all machinery and equipment (but not raw materials and intermediate goods),

TABLE 7.10

Loss in Revenue from Placing Machinery and
Equipment on the Free List

(Thousands of Balboas)

Description	Duties Exempted, 1961	Duties Paid, 1961
Machinery, power, generating	19.5	50.2
Machinery and mechanical equipment for agriculture	.3	1.4
Machinery, mining, construction and industrial	551.4	367.6
Generators	35.0	9.3
Motors	10.2	4.6
Transformers, alternators	2.8	8.0
Mechanisms for circuit-breakers	11.4	3.4
X-ray equipment	40.8	17.5
	671.4	462.0

the items in Table 7.10 could be totally exempted with an indicated loss of revenue of B/462,500.

The rates applicable to the imports on which duties were paid in the categories of chemicals, manufactures classed according to materials, and machinery and equipment were shown in Table 7.9. With the exceptions of aromatic oils, other chemicals, and articles of paper and cardboard, the rates are quite low, indicating that they are not protected products and that their use in manufacturing is intended to be encouraged. If all but the few categories mentioned above were exempted from duties, the loss of revenue would total B/1,329,900. As a result, all firms using these products, both the contract firms and those which do not have contracts, would receive equal treatment. In other words, the intent of the reform law of 1957 to provide "generalization of incentives to firms and individuals which do not have contracts" could be implemented further by placing these categories on the free list.[9]

What Goods Should Be Exempted?

The preceding description of the exemptions shows that most of the goods exempted are either capital goods, including materials

[9] (Par. 43), *Prólogo a Decreto Ley No. 25.*

for buildings and other facilities, or raw materials and semi-finished goods that are processed into finished products. The question arises as to whether or not all these goods should be exempted. In order to answer this question, it is necessary to consider the possible economic functions of tariffs.

The first and the most likely function of tariffs is simply to raise revenues. Indirect taxes have long been a favorite of politicians, who may lack an understanding of "functional finance," but know only too well the art of politics. From an economic point of view, customs duties distort relative prices and lack interpersonal equity. When the level of revenues from customs is maintained, exemptions simply shift the burden of taxes from some taxpayers to others.

Second, is the use of specific customs duties to stimulate domestic production in industries where a comparative advantage is anticipated in the long run. This is the justification for protective tariffs. In this case, exonerations apply to protected items only to the extent that domestic producers are unable to supply the quantity or quality demanded.

Third, is the imposition of a general level of customs duties with the intent to redirect resources by changing the relative general price levels of imported goods compared to goods produced domestically. This policy may be employed as a substitute for currency depreciation. Indeed, given the U.S. dollar as the circulating currency in Panamá and the absence of a central bank, raising and lowering the general level of tariffs may perform an equilibrating function. The policy may not be as efficient as currency depreciation and appreciation, since it does not stimulate exports or affect invisible transactions like tourism. In fact, with respect to the latter, it has negative effects, for a high price level at home encourages foreign travel and reduces the attractiveness of Panamá to foreign tourists.

Fourth, is the employment of specific customs duties as a redistributive mechanism. By taxing so-called luxury imports such as automobiles, a rough sort of progressivity in the distribution of the burden of taxation is obtained. Duties used for this purpose fall on finished products and are seldom exempted.

With respect to these four functions of tariffs, the first and third are of greatest importance for determining the appropriate policy with respect to exemptions. In the long run, the first function of revenue should diminish in importance as a greater reliance is placed on direct taxes. When duties are levied generally, as in the case of Panamá which has practically no free list of imports, they have the characteristics of the third function or general import duty. Furthermore, given fairly extensive unemployment and under-employment in Panamá, the tariff performs the function of an equilibrating general import duty.

General Duties

The effect of a general or "across-the-board" tariff differs in several respects from a duty on a single imported product. It changes the relative prices of all imports vis-à-vis domestic goods and services. If it is assumed that world prices will be unaffected, all imports will rise in price proportionately, and the relative attractiveness of domestic products will be increased causing substitution of domestic for foreign products.

The rise in prices of all imported goods will affect the amount of each which will be imported differently. This results, first, because of different income elasticities even though relative prices remain unchanged. Second, it results because some products have better domestic substitutes than others. The prices of those products that are produced domestically will not rise in proportion to the increase in the general level of the tariff. In fact, whether they rise or not, especially in the long run, cannot be determined *a priori*. If excess capacity and unemployment exist, prices need not rise, even in the short run. In the long run, the possibility of achieving productive efficiency and effecting economies of scale may likewise operate to prevent price increases.

With respect to the utilization of general customs duties to promote full employment, the general contempt for a beggar-one's-neighbor policy is justified. But when unemployment exists under circumstances in which "balance of payments" difficulties are encountered in spite of a common currency, a country or region may be a victim of such policies. In the case of Panamá, its factor prices may simply be too high in the light of existing foreign exchange rates. By imposing a general tariff under such conditions, relative factor prices are brought closer to a full-employment equilibrium.

But a general tariff would not stimulate exports. On the contrary, there would be a tendency for export resources to be redirected to production for the domestic market. Just as imports are priced too low relatively to domestic prices, export costs are too high relatively, and export subsidies would be in order. To the extent that resources are mobile between the export industries and those producing for the domestic market, and to the extent that they are fully-employed (capital, technical abilities, and labor), they would be bid away from the export market. In Panamá's actual condition, there is probably very little elasticity of substitution of resources between the agricultural and seafood sectors, which dominate Panamá's exports, and the manufacturing sector. Nevertheless, import duties do not provide the encouragement to export that currency depreciation would. Furthermore, investment for the domestic market is stimulated by the increased relative attractiveness of the domestic market.

Whether or not capital goods and semi-manufactures should be exempted from import duties depends on the role to be assigned to import duties. To the extent that the function assigned to the tariffs is that of equilibrating relative international prices, exemptions extended to companies producing for internal consumption is actually inconsistent.

The Choice of Subsidies

Among the types of incentives offered by the government to stimulate economic development are exemptions, technical assistance, loans, assurances against tax increases, and protective tariffs. In all of these except protective tariffs, it is possible to calculate the amount of the subsidy with some accuracy. The cost consists either of prospective taxes foregone or government expenditures. Only in the case of protective tariffs is the amount of the subsidy unknown.

Moreover, only in the case of protective tariffs is there an actual encouragement to monopolistic practices. Businessmen do not need such encouragement; they have a quite natural tendency to wish to eliminate competition. By eliminating foreign competition, protective tariffs deprive the economy of the most important mechanism assuring fair play to consumers.

Not all tariffs are protective. Those that alter the relative prices of imported versus domestic goods, in effect making the terms of exchange more realistic, are not protective. In general, duties at the level of the average *ad valorem* rate cannot be considered protective.

As long as protection is offered, many unnecessary claims for the subsidy will be made. In all such requests, one may assume anticipated profits to be understated. It is too much to expect any commission, no matter how conscientious its members, to be able to discriminate among all claimants, rejecting those that are spurious. Moreover, the opportunities for exerting influence cannot be ignored.

The possibility of abusing the privileges granted by contracts was recognized and anticipated by the current law in Panamá. For example, the appropriate ministries are given the right to inspect the grantees for the purpose of determining whether they are complying with their contractual obligations and maintaining the appropriate quantity and quality of their products. The ministries may call upon other agencies for assistance, in-cluding the Office of Price Regulation, which is required "to see that wholesale prices are such as to avoid conflicts and disarrangements in the distribution of the product and repercussions prejudicial to the economy." [10] The grantees are also obliged to provide the information and data required for this supervision.

Policing of this nature is clearly difficult to accomplish. The exemption law restricts the policing power to the obligations of the contract, and supervision is circumscribed by ambiguity: there is reference to prices which might "upset" the orderly distribution of the product, or which are "prejudicial" to the national economy.

Any firm requesting a protective tariff should be willing to agree to a progressive diminution of the level of protection. This progressive reduction in the level of protection would place the firm under constant pressure to become more efficient.

THE FUTURE OF CUSTOMS REVENUES

As noted at the beginning of this chapter, customs duties are Panamá's most important source of revenue. Although it may be hoped that direct taxes will play a more important relative role in the future than they do at present, customs duties will continue to be *quantitatively* as important as they are at present, and will probably increase in absolute importance.

In recent years imports have been increasing more rapidly than the national income. From 1953 to 1961, total imports increased by 76 per cent, from B/71.4 million to B/124.4 million. During the same period, the national income increased from B/296.1 million to B/425.4 million, or by 59 per cent.

Import duties, however, have been declining relative to the national income, and even more so with respect to imports. Import duties, including consular fees, increased

[10] Article 9, Law No. 25, 1957.

from B/14.8 million in 1953 to B/22.1 million in 1961, or by 49 per cent, as compared with a 59 per cent increase in the national income and a 76 per cent increase in imports.

Imports of beverages and tobacco, and of animal and vegetable oils, decreased by 8.6 per cent and by 17.3 per cent respectively. On the other hand, foodstuffs increased by 20.6 per cent. The most significant increases in both absolute and relative terms were the categories of machinery and transport material by 173.1 per cent, and manufacturers classed according to material by 90.7 per cent. Chemical products also increased substantially by 79 per cent.

Exports increased from B/15.1 million in 1953 to B/21.6 million [11] in 1961 or by 42.8 per cent, which was less than the growth in the national income. Nearly all of the increase was in foodstuffs: bananas, an increase of B/5.2 million or 63 per cent; seafood, an increase of B/3.8 million or 180 per cent; and sugar, an increase of B/0.4 million or 105 per cent. Coffee and cocoa exports decreased. The exports of raw materials declined greatly: hides and skins from B/156,000 to B/8100; wood, B/398,000 to B/130,000; textile fibers, B/1,030,000 to zero; fertilizer, B/34,500 to zero; and other animal and vegetable products, B/184,000 to B/64,000. Wood manufactures and cement likewise declined to minute quantities, the former from B/422,600 and the latter from B/679,600 (see Table 7.11).

It is probable that the demand for imports will continue to increase more rapidly than the national income for several reasons. First, in some categories of goods the possibilities of substituting domestic production for imports are approaching their limits. Eighty-six per cent of the foodstuffs consumed are produced domestically already. In 1959, 82 per cent of shoes, 66 per cent of clothing, and 67 per cent of furniture were produced domestically. While the total consumption of these products tends to be a smaller propor-

tion of income as income increases, the luxury characteristics of the imported items within these groups will probably result in an increase in demand as income rises. Second, the import trends in all other categories, as will be demonstrated below, continue to increase more than the national income.

Based upon annual imports and national income data for the years from 1952 to 1961, linear functions calculated by the least squares method were obtained for each major class of imports. These are shown in Table 7.12 together with the 1961 ratios of imports to the national income. Column 1 in Table 7.12 shows imports as a percentage of the national income in 1961: $100 \frac{(a + bx)}{(x)}$. Column 2 shows the percentage of national income to which the function tends: $\frac{Lim}{x \to \infty} \frac{a + bx}{x} = b$. When the values in Column 2 are less than those in Column 1, it indicates that imports are tending to become a smaller proportion of the national income as the national income increases, and *vice versa*.

Since recent changes in customs duties and other factors may have affected the results, the elasticity of imports with respect to the national income was calculated for the period from 1956 to 1961. These calculations are shown in Column 5 of Table 7.12. An elasticity of less than one indicates that imports in the class increased less rapidly than the national income, while more than one means more rapidly. These elasticities confirm the trends in all classes except oils and fats and transactions.

Comparing the changes in elasticity of food imports with respect to the national income, there is a negative correlation from 1953 to 1956 (—.56), but a positive correlation (+.65) from 1956 to 1961. There is a similar relationship for clothing (—1.37 and +1.02), and for shoes, (—2.37 and +.47). This means that there is an upward trend in the elasticity of imports in these products with respect to the national income.

[11] Excluding re-exports.

The import demand for nearly all classes of goods other than foodstuffs, beverages and tobacco, raw materials, and diverse manufactures has shown a tendency to increase faster than the national income. From 1956 to 1961, the imports of beverages and tobacco decreased, while foodstuffs, diverse manufactures, and raw materials increased, but at a slower rate than the national income. All the other classes increased more rapidly than the national income (Table 7.12, Column 5).

The results of these calculations may be summarized as follows: imports are likely to increase more rapidly than the national income, but import duties, assuming the 1961 ratio of exonerations and 1961 *ad valorem* rates, are likely to increase at a slower rate than the national income. The estimated percentages are as follows:

Linear regression method:	*Per cent*
Increase in imports, 1961 to 1967	42.9
Increase in import duties, 1961 to 1967	33.9
Assumed increase in the national income	37.9

Elasticity method:	
Increase in imports, 1961 to 1967	48.2
Increase in import duties, 1961 to 1967	37.0
Assumed increase in the national income	37.9

TABLE 7.11

Changes in the Value of Exports, 1953 to 1961

Groups	Value of Exports (Thousands of Balboas)		Percentage Change
	1953	1961	
Foodstuffs	12,153	21,263	75
Beverages and tobacco	8	1	−88
Raw materials, not edible	1,825	246	−87
Chemical products	1	2	100
Manufactures classed according to material	1,105	11	−99
Diverse manufactures	40	72	80
Other	1	—	−200
TOTAL	15,133	21,595	43
Sub-Groups			
Meat and meat preparations	2	58	2,800
Milk products, eggs, honey	—	24	—
Seafood	2,127	5,952	180
Fruits and vegetables	8,340	13,448	61
Sugar	381	780	105
Coffee	287	258	−10
Cocoa	1,016	507	−50
Hides and skins	156	8	−95
Rubber	23	61	165
Wood and lumber	398	130	−67
Textile fibers	1,030	—	−100
Fertilizer	34	—	−100
Other animal and vegetable products	184	64	−65
Leather and leather products	4	9	125
Wood products (not furniture)	423	—	−100
Cement and clay products	680	1	−99
Clothing	35	—	−100
Brooms	4	—	−100
Handbags	—	64	—

Source: Anuario de Comercio Exterior.

SUMMARY OF RECOMMENDATIONS

1) Specific duties—those expressed as a fixed sum per unit—should be converted to an *ad valorem* basis in each category of imports whenever the products vary considerably in value.

2) Proposals to levy consular fees or to impose across-the-board tariff increases should be resisted for three reasons: (1) they increase the complexity of the customs duties; (2) they raise the tax burden on non-exempted producers through their application to capital goods, raw materials, and intermediate goods; and (3) they are regressive with respect to their application to goods consumed by low income groups.

3) Existing duties should be consolidated. Miscellaneous duties like the tax per package, stamp taxes, and the anti-tuberculosis tax should be eliminated and incorporated into the regular duty list.

4) Firms that export products produced in Panamá should be exempt from duties on capital goods, intermediate goods, and raw materials in proportion to the ratio of their exports to their domestic sales. No contract with the government should be required to give effect to this exemption.

5) Protective tariffs should have limited and diminishing application. In general, they should not exceed the average rate of duties (excluding imports and duties in the categories of liquor, gasoline, and automobiles). Tariffs in excess of this average should be reduced gradually to the average level or below.

6) When it is necessary to protect a product which is nutritionally important and is consumed extensively by low income groups, or whose consumption should be encouraged as a matter of public policy, a low domestic price should be maintained by government subsidies. Consumers of the protected products should not be required to subsidize the industry. Among these items are powdered skimmed milk, salt, margarine, tomato products, vegetable oils, lard, rice, wheat, sausages and frankfurters, sugar, and coffee.

7) The Minister of Agriculture, Commerce and Industry, in cooperation with the Minister of Finance and the Treasury, should

TABLE 7.12

Functional Relationship between Major Classes of Imports and the National Income, 1952 to 1961

Classes	(1) 1961 Imports as a Percentage of the National Income	(2) Slope of the Regression Function "b" Values (percentage)	(3) "a" Values[1] (millions of Balboas)	(4) Coefficient of Correlation	(5) Elasticity with Respect to the National Income[2] (1956 to 1961)
Foodstuffs	3.57	1.76	7.53	63.7	0.65
Beverages and tobacco	0.69	−0.32	3.89	29.1	−0.32
Raw materials	0.36	0.31	0.19	48.1	0.66
Fuels and lubricants	2.71	3.61	−2.81	96.1	1.38
Oils and fats	0.10	−0.07	0.59	23.8	2.47
Chemical and chemical products	3.25	3.86	−2.49	19.7	1.20
Manufactures classified according to materials	8.42	9.88	−7.49	97.2	1.38
Machinery and transport	7.43	11.90	−19.05	98.5	1.80
Diverse manufactures	3.89	3.35	2.96	97.2	0.79
Transactions	0.12	0.09	0.66	10.1	4.31
TOTAL IMPORTS	30.54	34.37	−16.02	98.2	1.20

[1] The slope of the regression function is the "b" value in the relationship y = a + bx, where "y" equals imports and "x" equals the national income.

[2] Elasticity is the percentage change in imports divided by the percentage change in the national income.

publish annually the profits, ratios of profits to sales, and ratios of profits to investment of all companies having contracts with the government, or which manufacture products protected by tariffs.

8) When a domestically-produced luxury item is protected by tariffs, a domestic excise tax should be imposed on its production.

9) Only capital goods, raw materials, and intermediate goods should be subject to exemptions. Office equipment and furniture, transport equipment, and construction materials should not be exonerated. The duties on capital goods should be reduced or eliminated.

10) Luxury goods not important to the tourist trade should be subject to higher duties than at present in order to make the duties more progressive in their impact. For luxury goods that are important to the tourist trade,

duties should be raised, but a system should be introduced whereby tax-free purchases are available to *bona fide* tourists.

11) Salaries of employees in the customs service should be increased in accordance with responsibility, and only qualified personnel should be employed and retained. Consideration should be given to the creation of a bonus fund, which would be shared among all customs employees. The bonus fund could be created from the collection of undeclared duties, confiscated contraband, and fines and penalties.

12) Reports of inventories maintained in the Colón Free Zone should be submitted periodically to the Director of Customs. Failure to account for the difference between imports into the zone and re-exports should make the firms liable for the customs duty on the difference.

CHAPTER 8

Other Indirect Taxes

INTRODUCTION

IN GENERAL, indirect taxes are an inequitable way of raising revenues. Since they do not as a rule accord with ability to pay, they are regressive. Moreover, they fall capriciously on individuals with the same tax capacity. Each separate tax requires its own administrative staff, resulting in a proliferation of tax agencies. They are a boon to politicians, however, since their burden is concealed in prices or they are paid in trifles with the cumulative burden usually ignored by the taxpayer.

Some indirect taxes may be justified on the grounds that the taxpayer consuming certain taxed goods or services receives a benefit from the government or imposes a burden on society roughly proportional to the amount of the tax. There is also an increasing disposition among economists to take into account the deficiencies of direct taxes as they are currently administered in less developed countries, and the supposed economic defects of income taxes with respect to incentives. As a result, many economists have become reconciled with the defects of indirect taxes, and advocate their development as a means of taxing wealthier taxpayers and inhibiting luxury consumption. In any case, until taxes on wealth and income in the less developed countries become more significant and their administration improved, reliance on indirect taxes as a revenue device appears inevitable.

Indirect taxes, excluding revenues from foreign commerce, amounted to B/9.9 million in 1961. They increased 75.6 per cent from 1950 to 1961, although they declined in relative importance from 23.4 per cent of total tax revenues in 1950 to 20.8 per cent in 1961. Together with taxes on foreign commerce, indirect taxes accounted for 69.2 per cent of total tax revenues in 1961.[1]

The excise taxes on the domestic production of alcoholic beverages were by far the most important. They accounted for B/3.87 million in 1961 or 39.1 per cent of collections from indirect taxes. Together with taxes on retail and wholesale liquor dealers amounting to an additional B/0.91 million, liquor taxes accounted for 48.4 per cent of indirect taxes. In addition, beginning in 1961 with Law 81, a stamp tax of B/1.00 was levied on each bottle of imported liquor and sparkling wine, and a Soldado de la Independencia stamp of B/0.02 per bottle. Because of their revenue importance, the taxes on alcoholic beverages are reviewed in a subsequent chapter.

Excluding customs duties and taxes on the production and distribution of alcoholic beverages, the remaining indirect taxes may be

---

[1] This chapter deals only with the indirect taxes levied by the national government. Local government taxes are discussed in Chapter 13, on Municipal Finance. Not included also are the social security contributions of employers of B/3.1 million, which might be considered as an indirect tax.

131

conveniently grouped into four categories: production and consumption taxes, business license taxes, registration and filing fees, and stamp taxes. These taxes increased from B/2.14 million in 1950 to B/5.11 million in 1961, an increase of 138.4 per cent. By

TABLE 8.1

Indirect Taxes Excluding Taxes on
Foreign Commerce, 1950 and 1961

(Thousands of Balboas)

	1950	1961	Percent-age Change, 1950 to 1961
Production and consumption taxes	606	2,149	254.6
Cigarettes	—	928	—
Slaughtering of livestock	399	666	66.9
Theater admissions	95	164	72.6
Insurance premiums	50	198	296.0
Foreign travel	—	192	—
Production of perfumes	1	1	0
Production of sugar	61	—	−100.0
License taxes	788	1,028	30.5
Commercial and industrial licenses	163	193	18.4
Banks and currency exchanges	9	37	311.0
Tax to promote tourism	1	262	26,100.0
Tax on games or wagers	7	103	93.2
Ship registry	605	422	−30.2
Private markets	3	11	266.7
Registration and service fees	437	417	−4.8
Property registration	370	360	−2.7
Civil registers	43	7	−83.7
Patents and trade-marks	24	42	75.0
Wharfage	—	8	—
Stamp Taxes[1]	371	1,512	307.5
Various national stamps	219	790	260.7
Soldiers of Independence stamps	—	373	—
Stamped paper	152	349	130.0
SUB-TOTAL	2,202	5,106	131.9
Production and distribution of alcoholic beverages	3,491	4,833	38.4
Beers	753	1,724	129.0
Liquors	1,892	2,188	15.6
Wines	9	7	−22.2
Retail liquor outlets	817	892	9.2
Wholesale liquor outlets	20	22	10.0
TOTAL	5,693	9,939	74.6

[1] Does not include stamp taxes on imports amounting to B/269,900 in 1961 and B/150,100 in 1950 which are included under import duties.

1961, these four categories of indirect taxes represented 10 per cent of tax revenues. The bulk of the revenue increase from 1950 to 1961 was due to the development of cigarette manufacturing in Panamá and the introduction of a higher levy on cigarettes, increases in the stamp taxes, and the introduction of a levy on travel abroad. Table 8.1 shows the revenues obtained from the various indirect taxes in 1950 and 1961.

STAMP TAXES

Stamp taxes of various types and stamped paper yielded B/1.51 million in 1961. The term stamp tax is, of course, a misnomer. It refers to the method of collecting a tax and does not tell anything about the base of the tax. Some of the stamp taxes are in reality fees for services rendered. Others are in part fees and in part taxes, where the charge bears little relation to the service rendered. Still others are taxes pure and simple.

Official Stamped Paper (Papel Sellado)

The sale of official stamped paper yielded B/349,000 in revenue in 1961. Official stamped paper of the first class (B/1.00 per sheet) is required to be used in all actions at civil law and all criminal actions initiated by private persons. Second-class stamped paper (B/0.10 per sheet) is required for use in memorials and petitions to official authorities; evidentiary documents, accounts, receipts, copies and certificates for judicial or official uses, or documents that private parties present for action by government authorities; notarized documents and copies of certificates; and sealed testaments. There are certain documents that are exempt from the requirement to use official stamped paper: suits involving constitutional rights, holographic wills, suits involving sums less than B/100.00, marriage licenses, and so forth.

The bases for these taxes ought to be the benefit received by the taxpayer. Court costs and the costs of maintaining legal records should be borne by the litigants and beneficiaries. There is obviously no relation between the number of pages of a document and the benefits received.

Court costs, filing and recording fees, and certified copies of documents should be charged on the basis of an evaluation of the actual annual cost of these services apportioned among those who annually use them. In other words, the charges should be related to the costs of the services rendered.

The right to petition the government and to express grievances to the authorities should not be impeded by making the procedures expensive. Requiring petitions to be written on stamped paper will discourage them, which the officials may consider desirable, but which reflects an attitude that people exist for the government rather than the government for the people. It is presumed that government officials are servants of the people and expressions from the public ought not to be discouraged.

Other Stamp Taxes

Stamp taxes, other than stamped paper, consist of various national stamps and the Soldiers of Independence stamp, the total yield of which was B/1,163,000 in 1961. This total does not include stamp taxes on imports collected by the customs officials, which in 1961 amounted to B/269,900. Following are the amounts of the stamps and the documents to which they must be affixed:

B/0.01   Sight drafts drawn or payable in the country; sight drafts drawn or payable outside the country and negotiated in Panamá, for each B/100 or fraction; receipts for professional services not exceeding B/50; and all other receipts for each B/10 or fraction.

B/0.02   Receipts for house rent exceeding B/50; receipts for professional services exceeding B/50; pawnshop receipts; each sheet of books of account; and each bottle of domestic or imported liquor.[2]

B/0.05   Each carton of imported cigarettes; each flask of imported perfume; tickets of admission to public entertainment of more than B/0.35; checks; short-term drafts; foreign checks and short-term drafts, for each B/100 or fraction; and all public instruments, certificates, copies, registered documents, tax payments, bills and invoices at wholesale, export documents, and commercial licenses.[3]

B/0.10   Short-term drafts drawn and paid in Panamá for each B/100 or fraction; and all contracts for more than B/10, for each B/100 or fraction.

B/0.50   Each use of a bill of lading, consular invoice, and customs declaration prepared in Panamá for foreign ports and airports, B/100 or fraction thereof; and each cablegram and radiogram to the exterior.

B/1.00   Each declaration and payment of customs duties of more than B/10; and each container of cognac, whiskey, sparkling wines, and liquor of foreign origin.

B/2.00   Each sheet of a manifest, list of crew members and provisions of ships, guys, requests to discharge cargo, certificate of sanitation and other documents that must be presented in the ports of the Republic by ships engaged in foreign commerce exceeding five tons; diplomas; certificates executed by consular officials abroad; first authentication of signatures of Panamanian officials and documents of foreign officials; copyrights; and requests for exemption of more than B/20 in taxes.

B/10.00   Passports; certificates of professional qualifications; concessions to exploit national properties; and authentication of resolutions granting exemptions for each class of merchandise on the import list.

---

[2] Soldiers of Independence stamp.

[3] *Ibid.*

B/25.00   Provisional naturalization.
B/50.00   Final naturalization.

Among the stamp taxes that are in the nature of charges or fees for services are the following: the filing and registration of legal documents, court costs, certified copies of legal documents, records of court actions and decrees, export and import declarations, copyrights, certificates of professional qualifications, and naturalization fees. In each of the above cases some action is required by a government official, and therefore a service is rendered. Of course, only that part of the tax which more or less accords with the cost of the service can be considered justified by the so-called benefit principle. Any excess is in the nature of a tax.

The stamp taxes on the following are in the nature of taxes: checks and drafts, rental receipts, receipts for professional services, contracts, pawnship receipts, each sheet of books of account, liquors, wines, cigarettes, perfumes, theater tickets, public entertainment, bills and invoices at wholesale, cablegrams, and radiograms. In none of the foregoing is any direct service by the government involved. The stamp taxes on liquors and on public entertainment may involve social costs (policing, etc.), and therefore some part of the tax may be justified on the grounds that the prices of these products should reflect these costs.

Indirect taxes can be justified when they bear a relation to particular benefits received by the taxpayer or to social costs. They also can be justified when the government intends to reduce the consumption of the item taxed (where demand is elastic), or intends to penalize consumers of the item taxed (where demand is inelastic). As a device merely for raising revenue, these taxes are usually deficient in three respects: 1) they fall arbitrarily on consumers of particular products; 2) they are usually regressive; and 3) they lack neutrality with regard to resource utilization.

The taxes on personal checks are probably progressive as between lower than median and above-median incomes, simply because the lower income groups do not utilize this type of payment. Taxes on business checks, bills of exchange, and drafts increase the cost of doing business. In theory, these taxes would be shifted to customers, at least in the long run. In practice, they may not enter into the calculation of marginal costs, and therefore are probably not shifted.

While time drafts drawn outside the country are taxed at B/0.05 per B/100 or fraction, all checks are taxed at B/0.05 regardless of the amount. The latter tax thus has a built-in regressivity, penalizing more heavily the drawers of smaller amounts and those firms that must make many small payments.

The tax on rental receipts must be considered a tax on rent and is probably borne by the landlord at least in the short run. The tax is insignificant, B/0.01 to B/0.02, depending on whether the rent is less than or more than B/50. The law does not indicate the rental period. Rather, it is each rental receipt that is taxed. There is no reason why stamps of a certain percentage of the rent should not be assessed instead of a fixed amount per receipt. The tax would thus become proportional to the rental payment.

The taxes on receipts for professional services, contracts, and pawnshop receipts add to the marginal cost of the good or service, and in theory would be passed on to consumers. However, the practice is for the seller to affix the stamp, and it is unlikely that they are shifted because of their insignificance. If they were larger in amount, they probably would be taken into account and shifted. The taxes on sheets of books of account, and probably those also on wholesale bills and invoices, do not add to marginal cost and are not shifted in the short run. As in the case of the tax on rental receipts, there appears to be no reason why the stamp taxes should not be *ad valorem* instead of a fixed amount per receipt. The latter results in a built-in regressivity with respect to payments made. An *ad valorem* tax on bills and invoices at wholesale would, of course, be in the nature of a sales tax, and would therefore affect marginal cost and tend to be shifted.

FEES AND CHARGES

Public Registry Fees

Closely related to the stamp taxes are the fees for registering transfers of property, incorporations, changes of legal status, trademarks, and the like.

Registrations of property yielded B/360,000 in 1961, and civil registrations an additional B/7000. The recording of documents involving the transfer of property or of rights to property are subject to the following fees:

1) *Transfers of real property.* B/0.40 for each B/100 value up to a value of B/1000, and B/2.00 for each subsequent B/1000 of value. If the value expressed in the document is less than the assessed value for real estate tax purposes, the latter is used as the base.

2) *Rental agreements.* B/0.10 for each B/100 or fraction thereof of annual rent or the rent for the term of the contract.

3) *Mortgages and pledges of real estate.* B/0.20 for each B/100 or fraction thereof of value.

4) *Other property rights.* Fees ranging from B/1.00 to B/5.00 are charged for the creation or elimination of certain other rights to property such as easements, rights-of-way, and rights to mine.

5) *Forms of business organization.* B/15.00 for registering a partnership, B/3.00 for documents confirming the legal status of individuals, and B/14.00 for documents not specifically enumerated.

For recording the establishment of a corporation, the fees vary with the amount of capital stock stated according to the following schedule: Up to B/10,000, the fee is B/10; each additional B/1000 of capital up to B/100,000, B/0.75; each additional B/1000 of capital up to B/1,000,000, B/0.50; each additional B/1000 of capital over B/1,000,-000, B/0.10. Stock without par value is valued at B/20 per share. Fees of B/5.00

are charged for each recording of minutes and for each commercial or industrial license filed, and B/4.00 for any other recorded document of the corporation.

6) *Miscellaneous.* There is a B/1.00 fee for certified copies of public documents. Fees for filing documents of naturalization or emancipation range from B/10 to B/15, changes of names are charged B/5.00, and the fee for establishing the residence of foreigners is B/2.00.

Fees for registering changes in titles to property are customary and have a usefulness beyond the revenues they produce. They provide a basis for the taxation of capital gains, for assessing property for real estate tax purposes, and for auditing income tax returns.

The provision that the basis of the tax on property transfers is the declared value in the contract *or the assessed value for real estate tax purposes,* whichever is higher, lends itself to tax avoidance, since the assessed value often is a small fraction of market value. The basis for the fee should be fair market value. If a provision taxing capital gains as other income is enacted, the income tax on capital gains should be liquidated by the seller at the time of sale. A *Paz y Salvo* from the Department of Internal Revenue certifying payment of the tax on capital gains should accompany the registration of the property.

With respect to the incorporation fee, there does not appear to be justification for the regressive rates. If the rate is .001 for a corporation with an authorized capital stock of B/10,000, why should it be .0001 for a much larger corporation? Most of the other public registry fees can be justified as a charge for registering the documents and for the privileges granted.

Trade-marks, Trade-names, and Patents

A fee of B/25.00 is levied for registering a trade-mark and B/10.00 for a trade-name. These fees are paid only once during the period of protection. Patents, on the other hand, are subject to a fee of B/5.00 annually over the entire life of the patent. In 1961, these fees produced a revenue of B/42,000. They may be justified as a charge for the grant of the privilege and for its registration. The fees are probably not shifted.

Wharfage

Charges are made for loading and unloading vessels at public wharves. The rates are established by the executive branch, as no special law exists specifying the rates. Merchandise left on the wharves more than twenty-four hours is subject to a 25 per cent surcharge of the unloading fee. The charges produced a revenue of B/8000 in 1961. They are justified as a charge for a direct service rendered to the taxpayer.

PRODUCTION AND CONSUMPTION TAXES

Cigarettes

A tax on the production of cigarettes of B/0.025 per package of twenty cigarettes yielded B/928,000 in 1961. Tobacco products yielded an additional B/765,000 from customs duties, B/44,076 from consular fees, and B/78,478 from Soldiers of Independence stamps. In the aggregate, B/1,819,000 in duties, stamps, and other indirect taxes were paid into the national treasury by the producers and consumers of tobacco products.

The manufacture of cigarettes began in Panamá in 1954, and the history of the industry since then is a perfect example of the successful use of exemptions and protective tariffs. While the subsidies encouraged domestic investment and employment, at the same time they resulted in lower prices to the consumer and increased revenues to the government.

In 1953, a package of imported cigarettes was subject to a duty of B/1.65 per gross kilo, or about B/0.047 per package of twenty cigarettes. In addition, there was a 5 per cent *ad valorem* consular fee that added less than one-half cent per package in duty. The duty was raised to B/4.00 per gross kilo in 1954 in accordance with contracts entered into with the tobacco companies, and again to B/7.00 per gross kilo in 1958. A Soldiers of Independence stamp of B/0.05 per carton of imported cigarettes was added in 1961. At the present time, the total amount of taxes per package of imported cigarettes is B/0.2275. At the same time, the duties on bulk tobacco were increased in stages from B/0.75 per gross kilo in 1954 to B/1.25 per gross kilo in October, 1962.

In November, 1958, a tax of B/0.025 per package was imposed on the production of cigarettes. The only additional levy is a stamp tax of B/0.02 per carton of domestically-produced cigarettes. Cigarettes made predominantly from imported tobacco are taxed at B/1.25 per kilo, or approximately B/0.05 per package.

As part of their contracts, the cigarette manufacturers agreed to develop the production of tobacco in Panamá. In 1949, 485 hectares were devoted to the cultivation of tobacco, producing 7,190 quintals, while in 1961, 764 hectares were used in the cultivation of tobacco, producing 14,725 quintals. Since a quintal equals 45.45 kilos, the 1961 production amounted to 669,318 kilos compared with 536,154 kilos imported in 1961. Domestic tobacco is not taxed. Therefore, revenues from taxes on imported bulk tobacco will tend to fall with the continued development of domestic production.

Table 8.2 shows the taxes collected from the tobacco industry in duties, stamps, and other excises from 1953 to 1961. Total revenues increased from B/1,088,284 in 1953 to B/1,816,023 in 1961. The shift from imported to domestically-produced cigarettes is shown in Table 8.3.

In 1953, domestic cigarettes were selling for B/0.20 per package, but in 1958 each company in Panamá introduced a brand to sell for B/0.15 per package. This action had two noteworthy effects. It resulted in a very rapid substitution of domestic for imported

TABLE 8.2

Revenues from Taxes on Tobacco Products, 1953 to 1961

(In Balboas)

	Import Duties	Consular Fees	Tax of B/0.02 per Package	Soldiers of Independence Stamps	Production Tax on Cigarettes	Total
1953	941,763	98,616	114	47,791	—	1,088,284
1954	862,263	80,659	127	47,342	—	990,391
1955	815,809	82,311	127	51,372	—	949,619
1956	764,083	83,196	125	54,418	—	901,822
1957	851,765	93,659	137	65,761	—	1,011,322
1958	671,290	54,102	133	61,012	27,452	813,989
1959	571,629	30,366	94	59,863	707,868	1,369,820
1960	838,776	52,121	184	71,266	861,876	1,824,223
1961	765,004	44,076	176	78,478	928,289	1,816,023

Source: Tabacalera Istmeña, S. A. and Dirección General de Estadística y Censo.

cigarettes, and it reduced the contrabanding of cigarettes from the Canal Zone and elsewhere to less significant proportions. The latter effect illustrates the importance of relative prices in curtailing contraband activities. The moral seems to be that competitive prices are the best insurance against contraband, at least as far as products produced domestically are concerned.

Livestock Slaughtering

A total of B/666,000 in 1961 was obtained from the tax on livestock slaughtering. The tax varies in accordance with the species of the animal and the location of the slaughterhouse. In Panamá and Colón, the taxes range from B/1.00 for a hog weighing less than twenty pounds to B/4.00 for a steer and

TABLE 8.3

Consumption of Imported and Domestic Cigarettes, 1953 to 1961

(Net Kilos)

	Imported Cigarettes	Domestic Cigarettes
1953	477,912	—
1954	353,424	120,000
1955	293,722	220,000
1956	247,827	296,361
1957	258,478	399,136
1958	33,202	576,927
1959	14,552	584,805
1960	23,168	689,500
1961	18,790	742,700

Source: Tabacalera Istmeña, S. A.

B/5.00 for a cow. Elsewhere in Panamá, the tax range is B/0.50 to B/4.00. The tax is undoubtedly regressive, at least as far as the urban population is concerned. Since the animals within a class vary in weight and quality, the tax falls with the greatest weight on animals of lower values. To the extent that the tax recovers costs of inspection, it might be justified on the basis of the benefit principle, but it is inadequate for this purpose in its present form. If the tax is not eliminated, it should be replaced by a levy based on the total value of the meat processed rather than a fixed amount for each class of animal.

Entertainment Tax

Theater admissions and admissions to public entertainment are subject to taxes ranging from B/0.005 on admissions of B/0.20 or less to B/0.05 on admissions of over B/0.60. Revenues amounted to B/164,000 in 1961. The tax is regressive and is made more so by its upper limit of B/0.05 per admission. Since the tax rate is 12.5 per cent on an admission of B/0.60, there seems no reason why this rate should not extend to all admission prices above B/0.60.

Insurance Premiums

Gross premiums on all types of insurance except for fire are subject to a tax of 2 per cent. A tax of 7 per cent is levied on fire insurance premiums, of which 5 of the 7 per cent is allocated to the support of the fire department and the purchase of fire-fighting equipment. On premiums paid to Panamanian companies on risks assumed in the Canal Zone, only the 2 per cent rate applies. These taxes produced a revenue of B/198,000 in 1961. They are probably shifted to the policy-holders.

The additional 5 per cent tax on fire in-surance premiums can be justified on the grounds that in maintaining a fire department the government confers a benefit roughly corresponding to the taxes paid. The taxes on life insurance premiums are progressive in their impact, since the premiums tend to increase in relation to income.[4] Taxes on automobile insurance would be similarly pro-gressive over most of the range of incomes.

Fire insurance premiums tend to be shifted in the long run to tenants. In the short run, they may fall on the landlord, since demand is the determining factor in rents, given the existing supply of dwellings. With respect to owner-occupied dwellings, the burden is not shifted, and the incidence appears to be slightly regressive.[5] On the assumption that tenants pay the tax, the levy on fire insurance premiums would on balance tend to be slightly regressive. On the assumption that landlords pay the tax, the tax would be roughly progressive, since a large number of rural dwellers and squatters are not cov-ered by the tax. With respect to that portion of the tax which is allocated for maintenance of the fire department, the tax is in the nature of a charge for services.

Foreign Travel

Transportation tickets for trips from Pan-amá to any foreign destination or for return to Panamá are subject to a 5 per cent tax. Residents of the Canal Zone, employees of the United States government or its agencies, and diplomatic and consular officials are

exempt from the tax. The yield of the levy was B/191,000 in 1961. The tax is probably progressive since foreign travel is likely to have a high degree of positive correlation with income.

LICENSE FEES

Business License Fees

A business license (*patente*) is required be-fore engaging in any commercial or indus-trial activity, excepting only Panamanian citizens, or corporations wholly-owned by Panamanians, engaging in the purchase and sale of animals or products produced in Panamá, or in various agricultural or stock-raising activities. These licenses produced a revenue in 1961 of B/193,000.

The licenses are of three classes. A first class license of B/100 per annum is required of wholesalers, banks, public utilities, restau-rants (with capital above B/2500), hotels (with capital above B/2500), manufacturing, mining and similar enterprises, and laundries and dry cleaners (except hand laundries) in cities with over 35,000 inhabitants.

General licenses (*patentes generales*) are issued only to Panamanians and to corpora-tions wholly-owned by Panamanians. These permit the licensee to engage in any com-mercial or industrial activity, and to conduct any number of activities under one roof. The fee is B/125 per annum.

Licenses of the second class are required for retail enterprises of all types. The amount of the tax per annum varies in accordance with the capital of the enterprise as follows:

Capital	Tax
B/ 500 or less	B/ 4.00
B/ 501 to B/ 1500	B/10.00
B/1,501 to B/ 3000	B/15.00
B/3,001 to B/ 5000	B/20.00
B/5,001 to B/10,000	B/30.00
Over B/10,000	B/40.00

In communities of less than 35,000 in-habitants, the fees are reduced by 50 per cent.

---

[4] *Estudio de los Ingresos, Gastos y Costo de la Vida, 1952, 1953* (Panamá, 1955), p. 67.
[5] *Ibid.*, p. 55, line 11.

There seems to be no valid reason for the existence of three types of licenses. A single *ad valorem* license fee based on the total assets of the enterprise, or total assets less current liabilities, should replace the existing licenses. In the case of retail stores, the base of the tax could be the value of inventories. As it is at present, the first class license fee remains fixed at B/100 regardless of the size of the enterprise. The general license is subject to the same criticism. The second class license is regressive in its impact up to B/10,000 of capital, even though the rates are progressive, and beyond B/10,000 of capital the tax remains fixed at B/40.00. Moreover, the present schedule is subject to fluctuations in rates within and between brackets. These shortcomings are shown in Table 8.4.

License fees are generally presumed to be shifted to consumers in the long run on the theory that enterprises in the long run must cover fully all their costs. However, in the short run, only those costs that relate directly to the additional unit sold, i.e., marginal

TABLE 8.4

Effective Rates of Second Class Licenses at Selected Levels of Capital

Capital (Balboas)	Tax (Balboas)	Effective Rates (Per Cent)
100	4	4.00
200	4	2.00
300	4	1.33
400	4	1.00
500	4	.80
600	10	1.67
1,000	10	1.00
1,500	10	.67
1,600	15	.94
2,000	15	.75
3,000	15	.50
3,100	20	.65
4,000	20	.50
5,000	20	.40
5,100	30	.59
6,000	30	.50
8,000	30	.38
10,000	30	.30
10,100	40	.40
20,000	40	.20
100,000	40	.04
1,000,000	40	.004

costs, can affect price. Since license fees are in the nature of fixed costs, they do not affect marginal costs, and therefore do not affect prices. Unless prices are affected, the tax cannot be shifted.

Even in the long run, license fees may not be shifted forward, but may be shifted backward to landowners or borne by the owners of the enterprise. In order to be shifted forward, the tax must affect the marginal or non-profit firm in the industry. The marginal firm may shift the tax to landowners if every alternative equally profitable use of the building site is similarly taxed. The tax is likely to be borne by entrepreneurs in its entirety if the industry is monopolistic. License fees, it may be concluded, are probably not shifted forward to consumers, and in terms of incidence and economic effects they are probably good taxes if properly designed.

Tax to Promote Tourism

This tax is similar to the business license fees, but the receipts are used to support the activities of the National Tourist Council. The tax is levied on commercial and industrial enterprises likely to benefit from an increased number of tourists in Panamá. Assessments vary from B/1.00 to B/100.00 per month. Commercial enterprises with a circulating capital of less than B/1,000.00 are exempt. The amount of the assessment is determined by the National Tourist Council. Outside the cities of Panamá and Colón, the tax ranges from B/1.00 to B/50.00, and it can be imposed only on enterprises with a circulating capital greater than B/5000. This tax produced a revenue of B/262,000 in 1961.

Since the tourism tax is levied on those enterprises that benefit from the efforts of the Tourist Council to promote tourism, it can be justified on the benefit principle. Like license fees, the tax probably is not passed on to the consumers since it does not enter directly into the costs of additional units of products or services sold.

Other Business Taxes

Banks and currency exchanges are subject to a monthly assessment ranging from B/20 to B/300 according to their classification into one of four groups. The classification is undertaken by a council consisting of the Minister of Finance and the Treasury, the Comptroller General, and one businessman appointed by the President. The tax produced a revenue of B/37,000 in 1961.

Public markets operated by private persons or firms in cities or towns where the government operates a public market are subject to a monthly tax of 10 per cent of the rentals received.

Ships registered in Panamá and engaged in international traffic are assessed B/0.10 annually for each net ton. Ships not engaged in international traffic are subject to an annual tax of one-half of one per cent of their value, which is assessed by the Port Inspector in consultation with official experts. Ships with a value of less than B/1000 are exempt. The tax produced a revenue of B/422,000 in 1961.

These taxes, like license fees in general, are probably not passed on to consumers, since they do not enter into the costs of additional units of service sold. The tax on rents from public markets is probably borne by the landlord. What he can charge as a rental is based on the profitability of the stalls, but the latter is not affected by the tax on rent, but rather determines it.

Tax on Gambling

In addition to its proprietary interests in the casino at El Panamá Hilton Hotel, the National Hippodrome, the Atlas Bingo, and the National Lottery, the government collects a tax on other forms of gambling and games which lend themselves to gambling. In charge of all gambling is a board (*Junta de Control de Juegos*) headed by the Minister of Finance and the Treasury, which promulgates the rules concerning games of chance subject to the approval of the executive branch of the government.

Taxes are levied on cock-fights, bowling, a local form of bowling called *boliche,* raffles, billiards, so-called merchandise "clubs," and other sports. These taxes produced a revenue of B/103,000 in 1961, in addition to the more than B/6 million raised from government-operated gambling activities. Government-operated gambling activities are considered in the chapter on autonomous and semi-autonomous institutions. It may be mentioned that an illegal "numbers" game is operating in Panamá, which is another source of potential revenue that presently escapes taxation. It is popularly known as the *"bolita"* or little ball.

Possible Additional Excises

Aside from automobiles, gasoline, imported alcoholic beverages, and radio-phonograph combinations, few luxury products are subject to heavy import duties or domestic excises. It was noted in the chapter on customs duties that the importance of the tourist trade, the "competition" from the Canal Zone, and the problem of contraband have contributed to a policy of deliberately low duties on most portable luxury items.

Since nearly all luxury goods are imported, it is easier to collect sumptuary taxes at the port of entry than by levying taxes at the retail level. Domestic excises, therefore, afford few opportunities for luxury taxation in Panamá. Taxes on durable consumer goods are more economical to collect from the importers. Annual registration fees on automobiles are considered in the chapter on Municipal Finance.

The principal opportunities for genuine sumptuary taxation in Panamá, aside from customs duties, would be taxes on residential real estate and on tangible personal property. Experience with the latter tax in most countries does not recommend it for adoption in Panamá. Therefore, taxes on real estate remain the principal opportunity for a progressive sumptuary tax.

SUMMARY OF RECOMMENDATIONS

Aside from taxes on alcoholic beverages, municipal taxes, and the customs duties, the principal indirect taxes are the excises on cigarettes, slaughter taxes, taxes on insurance premiums, business license fees, registry fees, and the stamp taxes. Under the theory that old taxes are good taxes, few of the existing indirect taxes should be eliminated. Improvements in the existing taxes, however, can and should be made:

1) Stamped paper, except where the tax is a charge for a service rendered by the government, should be eliminated. In some instances, revenue could be increased by relating the tax to the costs of the service for which the stamped paper is required (e.g., in the case of documents used in judicial proceedings). The tax requirements should be eliminated as far as petitions to the government and bids for government contracts are concerned.

2) The stamp taxes should be based on the value of the check, draft, contract, or receipt to which they are affixed. For example, a check for B/5.00 should not bear the same tax as a check for B/5,000,000.

3) The existing tax on cigarettes may have to be increased in order to offset the decline in import duties on imported tobacco, which is being displaced by domestic tobacco production.

4) The tax on livestock slaughtering is regressive, and if it is not eliminated, it should be converted to an *ad valorem* tax based on the value of the animal rather than a fixed amount per head.

5) The tax on theater admissions should be made proportional to the price of admissions.

6) The present categories of business license fees should be replaced by a single *ad valorem* levy based on net assets or in the case of retail stores, on merchandise inventories.

7) The basis of the fee for registering transfers of real estate should be the sales price, or the fair market value, whichever is higher. In this connection, a capital gains tax, if enacted, should be assessed and liquidated at the time that property is sold or transferred.

8) The fee for registering corporations should be revised. For particulars, see Chapter 11 on the use of tax incentives for development purposes.

9) The possibility of using internal excise taxes as a means of penalizing the consumption of luxury goods is restricted to customs duties and property taxes. The reasons are that nearly all luxury goods are imported, and these taxes are most economically collected at the port of entry. Unfortunately, the importance of the tourist trade, Canal Zone customers, and contraband operate to limit the possibilities of taxing portable luxury consumer goods. Apart from annual taxes on automobiles, the only important progressive consumption tax that could be levied is one on luxury-type residential housing.

CHAPTER 9

The Taxation of Alcoholic Beverages

LIQUORS OF HIGHER alcoholic content, such as rum and whiskey, can be made in two different ways. First, they can be produced from the distillation and natural aging of various fermented food products. For example, rum is the result of the distillation of fermented cane sugar, and whiskey can be produced from various fermented grains. When liquor is made in this way, it is customary to use charred wooden casks, tanks, or vats for aging. The aging process eliminates impurities through a process of oxidization.

Panamá uses this method of liquor manufacture only for the production of rum. The rum is stored in government-owned or government-controlled tanks. By legal requirement, the rum must be stored for a minimum of three years, a period considered necessary for the removal of impurities. No tax is paid until the liquor is released for bottling. In order to extend the period of aging, and thus to raise the quality of the rum, the government allows certain discounts of the tax if the rum is stored for more than three years.

A second way in which liquor may be produced is the manufacture of "rectified alcohol" or "distilled neutral spirits." In this method, the alcohol is "rectified" or made potable by an additional distilling operation. Whether the actual source of the alcohol is rye, corn, sugar, or some other product, the end result is the same—rectified alcohol or distilled neutral spirits. In Panamá, the major source of rectified alcohol is cane sugar.

Rectified alcohol has the advantage that no aging is necessary before the alcohol is processed into various types of liquors. Most of the rectified alcohol in Panamá is placed in storage tanks that are government-owned or controlled and is released to the manufacturers of liquor as needed. Rectified alcohol contains a minimum of 94.6 per cent alcohol, while most of the Panamanian liquors contain between 40 and 45 per cent alcohol (80 to 90 per cent proof). To manufacture the marketable blended products (rum, brandy, whiskey, etc.), distilled water is added to the rectified alcohol to decrease the alcoholic content to acceptable levels. Then, depending on the product to be manufactured, various extracts, flavors, or even other liquors are added in predetermined proportions.

The relevance of the foregoing explanation is that rectified alcohol is the principal basic ingredient of Panamanian liquors, whether the end product is "Scotch" whiskey, "Canadian" rye, or "Jamaica" rum. It is estimated that about 80 per cent of the liquors produced in Panamá are blends produced from rectified alcohol. About 85 per cent of Panamanian wines are also produced from rectified alcohol.

The liquor industry in Panamá is closely regulated by the government. Not only does the government own or control the storage facilities, but it also approves the equipment used, supervises production, controls the flow of alcohol, collects the taxes due on the production of alcohol, and inspects wholesale and retail establishments.

The Structure of the Liquor Industry

There are seven distilleries in Panamá, including those producing rectified alcohol as well as firms manufacturing rum from the distillation and aging of sugar cane. In addition, there are thirteen manufacturing plants that convert the rectified alcohol into the various blends, such as rum, brandy, and whiskey. Three firms are both distilleries and liquor manufacturing plants.

The distribution of alcoholic beverages is effected through wholesalers, retail package liquor stores, and "cantinas" or bars. Each level of distribution undertakes a specialized service. Wholesalers distribute goods to package liquor stores and bars, accepting minimum orders of one case. As of July, 1962, there were 48 wholesalers in Panamá, about 75 per cent of them located in the cities of Panamá and Colón (see Table 9.1). Retail package liquor stores (*bodegas*) sell only bottled goods, and 80 per cent of these 169 stores are in Panamá City. Finally, the 1,015 bars may sell drinks for consumption on the premises or bottled liquor for home consumption. About 36 per cent of the bars are located in Panamá City, while the two cities of Panamá and Colón account for 55 per cent of these retail outlets.

The Taxation of the Liquor Industry

Panamá has two types of liquor taxes. One is a tax on the manufacture of alcohol, beer, and wine. All liquors of higher alcoholic content are taxed through a levy on alcoholic content, while beer and wine bear a volumetric tax on the finished products. The second tax is a levy on wholesale and retail establishments selling alcoholic beverages.

The tax on alcohol has experienced two increases within recent years. On March 9,

1958, the tax rate was raised from B/0.020 to B/0.025 for each grade or degree of alcohol in a liter, while on April 9, 1962, the rate was increased from B/0.025 to B/0.0267 per degree of alcohol in a liter.

Rum produced from the distillation of fermented cane sugar must be stored for three years, but a discount of the tax is permitted for storage in excess of this period. A discount of 10 per cent is allowed if the rum is stored for four years, while a discount of 5 per cent per annum is allowed for each year after the fourth year up to a maximum discount of 40 per cent. Thus, the tax on rum is subject to a cumulative discount up to a maximum storage period of ten years.

The tax rate on beer has also been increased recently on two occasions. On March 18, 1958, the rate was raised from B/0.060 to B/0.075 per liter, and on April 9, 1962, from B/0.075 to B/0.080 per liter.

Most of the wine produced in Panamá is subject to two taxes. Since about 85 per cent of all wine is produced from rectified alcohol rather than through the fermentation of fruits, wine bears the tax on alcoholic content. There is also a tax of B/0.05 per liter on the manufacture of wine, a rate that has remained unchanged since 1946.

The tax on liquor, beer, and wine is refunded in its entirety when these products are exported from Panamá, while shipments to the Canal Zone are subject to a refund of 75 per cent of the tax. In the case of liquors of higher alcoholic content, this discount of 75 per cent was introduced on August 23, 1955. For beer, the discount was 50 per cent until it was raised to 75 per cent in 1958.

The specific excise taxes on the manufacturing of alcohol have a capricious impact on the various liquors of higher alcoholic content. Table 9.2 shows the results obtained by expressing the tax per bottle as a percentage of the retail price for a sample of liquor brands. For Herrerano Seco, the tax is 44.4 per cent of the retail price, while it is only 22.6 per cent in the case of Kentucky Cream Bourbon. According to the evidence in Table 9.2, the tax on alcohol

TABLE 9.1

Number of Distilleries, Manufacturing Plants, and Wholesale and Retail Establishments,
by Province, as of July 1, 1962

Province	Distilleries	Manufacturing Plants	Wholesale Establishments	Retail Establishments Package Liquor Stores	Bars
Panamá	2	7	23	139	366
Coclé	2	0	2	4	59
Chiriquí	1	1	8	6	178
Colón	0	2	10	14	103
Los Santos	1	1	2	1	88
Herrera	1	1	2	1	45
Veraguas	0	1	1	2	102
Darién	0	0	0	1	33
Bocas del Toro	0	0	0	1	41
TOTAL	7	13	48	169	1,015

Source: Ministry of Finance and the Treasury.

tends to be regressive as related to price: the higher the price of the product, the lower the tax burden as a percentage of retail price. The tax is probably also regressive with respect to the income of consumers, since Seco is the traditional drink of lower-income workers. It may be noted also in Table 9.2 that the tax on beer as a percentage of retail price is considerably less than that in the case of liquors of higher alcoholic content.

TABLE 9.2

Excise Taxes as a Percentage of Retail Prices
for a Sample of Domestic Liquors

Brand	Retail Price (Balboas)	Tax Per Bottle (Balboas)	Percentage of Tax to Retail Price
Agewood Bourbon	3.25	.86	26.5
Campaña Gin	2.10	.80	38.1
Carta Vieja Rum	2.75	.82	29.8
Herrerano Seco	1.80	.80	44.4
Royal Mounted Whiskey	3.50	.86	24.6
Kentucky Cream Bourbon	3.50	.86	24.6
Imperial Vodka	3.35	.86	25.7
Balboa Beer	.20	.03	15.0
Panamá Beer	.20	.03	15.0
Málaga Wine	1.00	.03	3.0

Source: Sample of liquor prices in the city of Panamá.

The unneutralities with respect to the tax burdens on various liquors of higher alcoholic content could be eliminated by shifting from a specific to an *ad valorem* tax. In other words, the tax could be levied as a certain percentage, say 25 per cent, of the manufacturer's price. This type of levy should be no more difficult to administer than a tax on alcohol, since it would only be a matter of levying the impost on the gross sales of the manufacturer.

The second major tax on the liquor industry is levied on wholesale and retail establishments. These establishments are taxed on the basis of geographic location apparently on the assumption that the latter reflects tax capacity. For wholesale establishments, there are three different annual flat fees: B/600 for firms located in Panamá and Colón; B/450 for firms in David and Barú; and B/300 for firms in all other localities. Wholesale establishments owned by manufacturers are exempt from the tax provided that they sell only liquors produced by their parent firms.

Retail establishments pay a monthly rather than an annual tax, and the tax schedules are different for package liquor stores and bars. The tax rates for package liquor stores vary from B/200 to B/50 monthly according to the following geographic locations:

Location	Tax Rate
Panamá and Colón	B/200
Las Sabanas, Pueblo Nuevo, Río Abajo, San Francisco de la Caleta, and Juan Díaz	B/ 75
Capital cities of provinces	B/ 75
All other locations	B/ 50

The monthly tax on bars also varies by geographic location from rates of B/175 to B/15:

Location	Tax Rate
Panamá and Colón	B/175
Las Sabanas, Pueblo Nuevo, Río Abajo, San Francisco de la Caleta, and Juan Díaz	B/ 60
Capital cities of provinces and the cities of Aguadulce, Soná, Puerto Armuelles, Almirante, Las Tablas, and La Chorrera	B/ 50
Capital cities of districts, villages of more than 300 persons, and bars situated along the highway between Panamá and Colón	B/ 25
All other locations	B/ 15

Administration

All taxes on alcoholic beverages are administered by the General Administrator of Internal Revenue, whose central office is located in the city of Panamá. There are also nine provincial offices corresponding to the nine provinces.

Fiscal control and tax collection are accomplished through two types of employees— inspectors and tax collectors. There are seventy-six inspectors, thirty-six of them employed in Panamá City and the remainder throughout the Republic. Their function is to enforce the alcoholic beverage tax laws and to prosecute violators. For this purpose, it is necessary for them to supervise the manufacture and storage of liquors, as well as to inspect wholesale and retail establishments. All of the inspectors are under civil service.

The tax collectors, on the other hand, are concerned only with the collection of taxes on alcoholic beverages. There are sixty-nine tax collectors, and at least one is assigned to each of the sixty-two collection districts in the Republic. Tax collectors are paid a commission based on collections and are not covered by civil service. While this arrangement for remuneration is an advantage in rural areas where the volume of collections is too small to warrant full-time salaried employees, there are also disadvantages. In a few instances, where districts are adjacent to provincial capitals, the yield of the commissions is considerable, amounting to as much as B/1000 per month. These particular assignments are valuable as "political plums" and encourage a practice of using government positions for political pay-offs.

Revenues

Internal excises from the manufacture and sale of alcoholic beverages amounted to B/4,832,600 in 1961. This total represented 9.91 per cent of total tax revenues and approximately 80 per cent of internally-levied excise taxes. From a revenue point of view, internally-levied taxes on the manufacture and sale of liquors were even more productive than the B/3,256,800 raised from property taxes in 1961.

The taxes on the manufacture of alcohol and beer were the principal producers of revenue, accounting for 45.3 and 35.7 per cent respectively of total revenues derived from alcoholic beverages in 1961. Next in importance was the tax on retail establishments, resulting in 18.5 per cent of revenues from alcoholic beverages. Thus, the two remaining taxes on wine and on wholesale establishments amounted to only .05 per cent of the revenues derived from alcoholic beverages in 1961.

TABLE 9.3

Revenues Derived from Internal Excises on
Alcoholic Beverages in 1961

Source	Revenues (Balboas)	Revenues as a Percentage of Total Tax Revenues
Alcohol	2,187,600	4.49
Beer	1,723,900	3.54
Wine	7,300	.01
Retail establishments	891,700	1.83
Wholesale establishments	22,100	.04
TOTALS	4,832,600	9.91

Source: Ministry of Finance and the Treasury.

Alcohol

Revenues resulting from the tax on the manufacture of alcohol have increased from B/1,880,500 in 1952 to B/2,187,600 in 1961, an average annual rate of increase of only 1.7 per cent. By comparison, total tax revenues have increased from B/26,980,400 in 1952 to B/48,652,000 in 1961, an average annual rate of increase of 8.9 per cent. Revenues from alcohol expressed as a percentage of total tax revenues have decreased from 7.0 per cent in 1952 to 4.5 per cent in 1961.

Table 9.4 shows that the total production of alcoholic beverages (excluding beer) has

decreased slightly during the twelve-year period from 1950 to 1961, falling from 2,424,613 liters in 1950 to 2,362,257 liters in 1961. Further, there has been a significant shift in production from higher to lower-priced products. In 1950, rum accounted for 33.2 per cent of total production, while Seco, a lower-priced product made entirely from rectified alcohol, was second in importance, representing 24.9 per cent of total production. By 1961, however, Seco had risen to first importance with 41.1 per cent of total production, while rum had fallen to 26.8 per cent of total output.

The tax discount on rum stored in excess of three years appears to have had little effect on increasing the length of the storage period. Table 9.5 shows the quantities of rum in aging tanks as of June 30, 1962. As of this date, only rum produced and stored before 1958 was eligible for a tax discount. Thus, according to Table 9.5, 31.15 per cent of all rum in storage on June 30, 1962 was eligible for a tax discount. Only 3.44 per cent of the rum was eligible for a discount of 25 per cent or more of the tax, and none of the rum was eligible for the maximum discount of 40 per cent. Furthermore, the rum presently in storage in excess of three years is often blended with rectified alcohol or with rum stored for the minimum re-

TABLE 9.4

Total Production of Alcoholic Beverages (Excluding Beer) with Percentages of Different Types Produced

Calendar Years	Total Production (Liters)	Percentage of Total Production							
		Anisette	Cognac	Gin	Rum	Seco	Wine	Whiskey	Misc.
1950	2,424,613	4.0	7.5	17.1	33.2	24.9	6.1	5.3	1.9
1951	2,305,848	3.7	5.3	16.0	32.8	27.1	5.8	7.3	2.0
1952	2,389,577	3.8	4.2	13.0	34.4	28.5	6.1	7.9	2.1
1953	2,152,640	3.3	4.6	15.2	29.9	29.0	6.0	10.2	1.8
1954	2,186,049	3.1	5.9	17.6	30.8	26.6	6.3	8.1	1.6
1955	2,155,919	2.9	7.6	20.3	30.6	25.0	5.6	6.9	1.1
1956	2,491,612	2.7	5.9	21.4	29.7	28.5	5.8	5.5	0.5
1957	2,430,988	2.2	4.4	20.1	26.1	36.1	4.9	5.8	0.4
1958	2,046,390	2.4	4.2	20.8	29.3	31.1	5.4	6.4	0.4
1959	2,045,409	2.1	3.1	19.9	24.9	38.5	5.2	5.9	0.4
1960	2,308,805	1.8	2.6	16.5	24.2	40.9	6.8	6.8	0.4
1961	2,362,257	2.1	3.1	14.2	26.8	41.1	6.0	5.8	0.9

Source: Ministry of Finance and the Treasury.

quired period of three years. It follows from this evidence that the tendency in Panamá is to produce a lower-priced product with minimum aging.

Beer

The production of beer has increased by nearly 60 per cent from 1951 to 1961, rising from 14,695,960 liters to 23,310,139 liters.

TABLE 9.5

Rum in Storage as of June 30, 1962

Date of Distillation	Amount in Storage (Liters)	Percentage of Total Amount in Storage	Applicable Percentage Tax Discount
1953	4,063	0.35	35
1954	2,015	0.17	30
1955	22,189	1.92	25
1956	67,517	5.85	20
1957	130,869	11.34	15
1958	121,406	10.52	10
1959	215,266	18.65	—
1960	170,990	14.82	—
1961	198,350	17.19	—
1962	221,470	19.19	—
TOTALS	1,154,135	100.00	

Source: Ministry of Finance and the Treasury.

TABLE 9.6

Beer Production and Tax Revenues from Beer, 1951 to 1961

Calendar Year	Production (Liters)	Tax Revenues (Balboas)	Tax Revenues from Beer as a Percentage of Total Tax Revenues
1951	14,695,960	817,000	3.3
1952	16,853,600	956,000	3.5
1953	16,359,350	947,300	3.1
1954	15,419,230	895,500	2.7
1955	14,850,276	867,400	2.4
1956	15,267,729	888,500	2.4
1957	18,152,218	1,046,300	2.8
1958	18,362,653	1,305,600	3.3
1959	18,943,085	1,411,800	3.7
1960	20,891,485	1,566,500	3.5
1961	23,310,139	1,723,900	3.6

Source: Ministry of Finance and the Treasury.

Most of this increase has occurred since 1956. The increase in the production of beer together with higher beer taxes in 1958 and 1962 have resulted in an increase in revenues from beer taxes by more than 100 per cent during the period from 1951 to 1961. Revenues derived from beer expressed as a percentage of total tax revenues have risen from 3.3 per cent in 1951 to 3.6 per cent in 1961.

Wholesale and Retail Establishments

Revenues from wholesale and retail establishments have increased only slightly within the past decade, and are of declining relative importance as a source of revenue. Tax revenues from wholesale establishments have increased from B/21,200 in 1951 to B/22,100 in 1961, while collections from retail establishments during the same period rose from B/813,500 to B/891,700. In combination, the two taxes decreased from 3.38 per cent of total tax revenues in 1951 to 1.95 per cent in 1961. Probably one reason for the lack of revenue productivity of these taxes, especially in the case of bars, is the tendency to locate these businesses outside the city limits of Panamá and Colón in order to avoid the higher tax rates in these cities.

The flat-rate taxes on wholesale and retail establishments are unrelated to ability to pay as measured by the net income of the firms. This may be demonstrated by comparing the taxable income (as reported for income tax purposes) of a small random sample of firms. Table 9.8 shows that eight wholesalers, all subject to an annual tax of B/600, varied widely in profitability, from one firm with a taxable income of B/89,900 to another firm with a loss of B/17,808. Similarly, eight retail package liquor stores, each subject to a monthly tax of B/200, varied from one with a loss of B/746 to another with a taxable income of B/9,087. Each of the eight bars in the sample paid a monthly tax of B/175, but their taxable income varied from B/902 to B/11,293. It is apparent, also, that these flat-rate liquor taxes on business establishments are relatively more burdensome on retail as compared to wholesale establishments. While the eight wholesalers in Table 9.8 each pay a flat-rate annual tax of B/600, the comparable *annual* tax for the package liquor stores is B/2,400, and for the bars, B/2,100. On the other hand, Table 9.8 shows a tendency for the wholesalers to have more tax capacity as measured by net income than either the package liquor stores or the bars.

IMPORT DUTIES AND SHIPMENTS TO THE CANAL ZONE

Import Duties

Integrally related to the internal excises on alcoholic beverages is the level of import taxes on foreign liquors. An issue bearing on both of these levies, in turn, is the shipment of domestic and foreign liquors from Panamá to the Canal Zone, for the zone currently obtains all of its liquors of higher alcoholic content from the Republic.

Panamá has followed a long-run policy of protecting the domestic beer industry against foreign competition. From 1934 to 1958, customs duties on beer were B/0.48 per liter or approximately B/0.16 per bottle of about 12 ounces. Customs duties were raised to B/0.78 per liter (B/0.26 per bottle) in 1958 and to B/1.01 per liter (B/0.33 per bottle) in 1962. By comparison, the domestic excise tax on a bottle of beer in 1962 was only B/0.03. The customs duties have been sufficient to exclude foreign beer almost completely from the domestic market, which un-

TABLE 9.7

Tax Revenues from Wholesale and Retail Establishments, 1951 to 1961

Calendar Year	Tax Revenues from Wholesale Establishments (Balboas)	Tax Revenues from Wholesale Establishments as a Percentage of Total Tax Revenues	Tax Revenues from Retail Establishments (Balboas)	Tax Revenues from Retail Establishments as a Percentage of Total Tax Revenues
1951	21,200	0.08	813,500	3.3
1952	19,400	0.07	847,400	3.1
1953	22,700	0.07	838,500	2.7
1954	22,500	0.07	837,300	2.5
1955	23,800	0.07	841,300	2.4
1956	17,600	0.05	834,900	2.3
1957	26,900	0.07	872,300	2.3
1958	25,600	0.06	855,200	2.1
1959	32,000	0.08	850,900	2.2
1960	26,300	0.06	907,100	2.0
1961	22,100	0.05	891,700	1.9

Source: Ministry of Finance and the Treasury.

TABLE 9.8

Taxable Income of a Sample of Wholesale and Retail Liquor Establishments, 1961

Wholesalers Firm Number	Taxable Income (Balboas)	Package Liquor Stores Firm Number	Taxable Income (Balboas)	Bars Firm Number	Taxable Income (Balboas)
1	1,232	1	8,587	1	2,881
2	14,696	2	8,234	2	9,141
3	89,900	3	746	3	6,089
4	36,594	4	4,363	4	1,145
5	17,808 (loss)	5	3,057	5	1,799
6	11,615	6	1,175	6	11,293
7	45,239	7	5,649	7	1,488
8	30,162	8	9,087	8	902

Source: Sample of income tax returns drawn from the files of the Ministry of Finance and the Treasury.

doubtedly has been a contributing factor in the robust growth of the domestic beer industry.

Import policy with respect to liquors of higher alcoholic content has been quite different historically, with a shift in policy from relatively low import taxes and relative ease of entry to one of high duties for revenue-producing purposes. For Scotch whiskey, customs duties were B/1.10 per liter (B/0.83 per "fifth") from 1934 to 1947, B/1.90 per liter (B/1.43 per "fifth") from 1947 to 1958, B/2.50 per liter (B/1.84 per "fifth") from 1958 to 1962, and were raised once more to B/3.50 per liter (B/2.64 per "fifth") in 1962. Despite these increases in duties, the volume of imported liquors rose from 1,106,668 liters in 1950 to 1,333,001 liters in 1961. Meanwhile, the domestic production of alcohol, as noted previously, remained relatively stable from 1950 to 1961.

The combination of heavier import duties on liquors of higher alcoholic content, combined with rising levels of imports, has resulted in a sharp increase in revenues derived from imported liquors. Tax revenues from imported liquors have risen from B/921,100 in 1951 to B/2,682,900 in 1961. This represents an increase of from 3.7 per cent of total tax revenues in 1951 to 5.7 per cent in 1961. The high level of imports shown in Table 9.9 for 1957, and the lower levels in 1958 and 1959, were caused by inventory speculation in anticipation of a tax increase.

The Canal Zone

In the early history of the Canal Zone, all liquors purchased by Canal Zone employees, whether by Panamanian or United States citizens, were exempt from tax. This led to the smuggling of liquor into the Republic, and to allay this difficulty Executive Order No. 6997 of March 25, 1935, required all U.S. government agencies in the Canal Zone to import their requirements of alcoholic beverages from the Republic of Panamá. Thus, all liquor entering the zone from Panamá

after 1935 was subject to the full amount of Panamanian taxes, whether these were levied in the form of internal excises or import duties. The only exception to this rule was liquor of less than 3.2 per cent in alcoholic content (principally beer), which could continue to be introduced to the zone directly from foreign countries and exempt from Panamanian taxes.

Two important changes were introduced to this procedure as a result of the 1955 Treaty of Mutual Understanding and Cooperation between Panamá and the United States. First, the Republic of Panamá agreed to grant a reduction of 75 per cent in the import duty on alcoholic beverages that are sold in Panamá for importation into the Canal Zone. Second, it was agreed that only employees of the U.S. government and its agencies who were actually *residing* in the zone would be given purchase privileges for this tax-discounted liquor. As of November, 1962, this means that about 2,400 Panamanian employees (1,800 families and 600 bachelors) out of a total Panamanian employment of about 13,500 persons, are accorded Canal Zone purchase privileges. But as previously, liquor of less than 3.2 per cent in alcoholic content could continue to be introduced into

TABLE 9.9

Liquor Imports and Duties, 1951 to 1961

Calendar Year	Imports (Liters)	Customs Duties (Balboas)	Customs Duties as a Percentage of Total Tax Revenues
1951	1,106,668	921,677	3.7
1952	1,257,061	1,086,104	5.0
1953	1,211,562	1,146,525	3.7
1954	1,095,847	1,040,554	3.1
1955	1,194,233	1,276,363	3.5
1956	1,301,317	1,671,378	4.5
1957	1,684,206	2,530,936	5.7
1958	705,077	1,398,673	3.6
1959	986,395	2,011,024	5.3
1960	1,221,380	2,572,892	5.8
1961	1,333,001	2,657,789	5.7

Source: Ministry of Finance and the Treasury.

the zone directly from foreign countries and exempt from Panamanian taxes.

The method of affecting sales to the Canal Zone has also undergone changes. As mentioned previously, Canal Zone agencies before 1955 were required to purchase all of their liquor of higher alcoholic content from distributors in Panamá, the sales being subject to the full amount of Panamanian taxes. During this period, therefore, there was no ostensible reason for the movement of contraband liquors of higher alcoholic content from the Canal Zone to the Republic, since all liquors sold in the zone and Panamá bore the same tax levies. In practice, however, it is reported that there was some smuggling of liquor. It is alleged by informed sources that certain military establishments in the Canal Zone imported tax-free liquor by air from such places as Jamaica, Cuba, and the Virgin Islands. This liquor was, in turn, sold to civilian employees in the Canal Zone, and was also in part smuggled into Panamá. Whether these allegations are in fact true cannot be substantiated.

But while no substantial reason for the existence of large-scale contraband liquor sales existed before 1955, one was created in this year by the provision of a refund of 75 per cent of liquor taxes on all sales of imported liquors made to the Canal Zone. This provision was first implemented by a system whereby liquor distributors in Panamá claimed a refund of 75 per cent of the taxes levied on shipments of imported liquor to the zone. But this system led to abuses and was superseded in September of 1961 by a system of central liquor stores, one each in Panamá and Colón, created for the sole purpose of making deliveries to the Canal Zone. Together with the creation of the central stores, the system of refunding 75 per cent of the tax to the distributors was replaced by one in which the distributors paid only 25 per cent of the tax on all liquors consigned to the central stores.

These central liquor stores are simply a device for channeling all of the orders for liquor from the Canal Zone into two physical locations for the purpose of facilitating customs surveillance. The stores function under the vigilance of the Administrator of Customs, who has established controls over the movement of merchandise, the level of inventories, and the amounts of liquor purchased by each person. In theory, this procedure should restrict contraband sales within tolerable limits, but it is alleged, and it is widely believed, that it has not.

The obvious reason why liquor probably is purchased in sizable amounts by unauthorized persons is the price differential caused by the 75 per cent tax discount on Canal Zone sales. As shown in Table 9.10, this price differential is currently very substantial for a case of Scotch whiskey. Since April 8, 1962, when customs duties and other taxes were raised, the price *before distributor's mark-up* of a case of twelve bottles ("fifths") of Scotch whiskey sold to the Canal Zone was B/35.88, while it was B/59.36 or 66 per cent higher when sold for Panamanian con-

TABLE 9.10

Taxes on a Case of Scotch Whiskey Sold in Panamá and in the Canal Zone[1]

Before April 8, 1962	Panamá	Canal Zone
C.I.F. cost	B/14.36	B/14.50
Customs duties	22.50	5.62
Anti-tuberculosis tax	.90	.90
Package tax	.02	.02
Independence Soldiers stamp	.24	.24
Stamp tax	2.40	2.40
1½ per cent tax on F.O.B. cost	.18	.18
TOTALS	B/40.60	B/23.86

After April 8, 1962	Panamá	Canal Zone
C.I.F. cost	B/14.36	B/14.50
Customs duties	31.50	7.88
Anti-tuberculosis tax	.99	.99
Package tax	.02	.02
Independence Soldiers stamp	.24	.24
Stamp tax	12.00	12.00
2 per cent tax on F.O.B. cost	.25	.25
TOTALS	B/59.36	B/35.88

[1] Prices shown are before distributor's mark-up for a case of twelve bottles. The bottles are "fifths" containing 25.6 ounces.

sumption. This is a difference of B/2.99 per bottle in the Canal Zone as compared to B/4.95 in Panamá, or very close to B/2.00 per bottle.

It is apparent, also, that the Republic of Panamá is deriving substantial revenues from the sales of imported liquors to the Canal Zone despite the tax discount of 75 per cent. At the present time, Panamá collects B/1.82 in tax revenue on each bottle ("fifth") of Scotch whiskey exported to the zone. It is estimated that Panamá collected approximately B/300,000 from the sales of imported liquors to the Canal Zone in 1961.

An interesting irregularity appears in Table 9.10. Among the six taxes levied on imported liquors, it may be noted that only the customs duty is subject to the 75 per cent discount on sales made to the Canal Zone. This conforms to a very literal construction of the Memorandum of Understanding Reached of 1955 which provides that ". . . the Republic of Panamá will grant a reduction of 75 per cent in the import duty on alcoholic beverages which are sold in Panamá for importation into the Canal Zone pursuant to such Executive Order." [1] But in the case of imported foreign liquors, is it not more logical to construe any tax levied in the nature of an import duty, and thus subject to the 75 per cent discount? If only *customs duties* are to be subject to the 75 per cent discount, what is to prevent the Panamanian government from utilizing taxes other than customs duties in order to avoid granting the 75 per cent discount? This, in fact, has been done. When the Panamanian government raised several taxes on imported liquors on April 8, 1962, it may be seen in Table 9.10 that proportionately more emphasis was given to raising the stamp tax, for which the 75 per cent discount was not applicable, than to raising the customs duty.

Another irregularity exists in the comparable retail prices being charged (during

November, 1962) for foreign liquors in the Panamanian market as compared to prices being charged Canal Zone purchasers. Table 9.11 shows that the central liquor stores are charging Canal Zone purchasers B/4.15 for a bottle ("fifth") of Scotch whiskey while similar products are selling in the Panamanian market for as low as B/5.25 per bottle. On the other hand, if the full amount of the tax differential were reflected, the price of a bottle of Scotch whiskey in Panamá would be at least B/2.00 higher than it would be for Canal Zone purchasers. The reason for this irregularity is that the liquor distributors

[1] *Report on United States Relations with Panamá.* Subcommittee on Inter-American Affairs of the Committee on Foreign Affairs (United States Government Printing Office, Washington, 1960), Article *XIII*, Sub-section 3, p. 70.

TABLE 9.11

Comparison of Liquor Prices in Panamá, the Central Liquor Stores, and the Canal Zone

Brand	Panamá	Central Liquor Stores	Canal Zone Clubs[1]
Imported Liquors			
Johnny Walker Red Label Scotch	B/5.50	B/4.15	B/4.98
Vat 69 Scotch	6.00	4.15	4.98
White Horse Scotch	5.25	4.15	4.98
White Label Scotch	5.25	4.15	4.98
Old Smuggler Scotch	6.00	3.75	4.50
Gordon's Gin	4.95	3.40	4.08
Bacardi Rum	5.50	3.90	4.68
Hennessy Cognac	6.25	5.00	6.00
Old Taylor Bourbon	7.25	4.90	5.88
Old Grand-Dad Bourbon	7.25	4.90	5.88
Italian Swiss Colony Wine	2.00	1.40	1.68
Dry Sack Sherry	3.25	2.40	2.88
Anis del Mono—Special	5.25	3.60	4.32
Seagrams V.O.	5.50	4.00	4.80
Canadian Club	5.50	4.00	4.80
Smirnoff Vodka	4.95	3.75	4.50
H. Munn Champagne	6.75	5.00	6.00
Schlitz Beer	—	.14[2]	.20
Budweiser Beer	—	.14[2]	.20
Domestic Liquors			
Agewood Bourbon	3.25	2.50	3.00
Campaña Gin	2.10	1.75	2.10
Carta Vieja Rum	2.75	1.60	1.92
Herrerano Seco	1.80	1.50	1.80
Royal Mounted Whiskey	3.50	2.60	3.12
Kentucky Cream Bourbon	3.50	2.05	2.46
Imperial Vodka	3.35	2.50	3.00
Málaga Wine	1.00	—	—
Balboa Beer	.20	.14[2]	.20
Panamá Beer	.20	.14[2]	.20

[1] Prices in the clubs are assumed to be 20 per cent higher than those in the central liquor stores.

[2] Prices charged in the Panamá Canal Company commissaries.

apparently are depleting their inventories, which were raised to very high levels before the tax increase in 1962, and they are doing so by offering price reductions only in the Panamanian market.

At a superficial glance, the present controls on contraband liquor sales appear adequate to restrict the smuggling of liquor from the zone to Panamá within tolerable limits. Permits for the purchase of liquor in Panamá are issued in the Canal Zone, and these must be signed by the intended purchasers. These signatures are then checked at the time that the liquor is purchased in the central stores. In addition, the permits specify the type and amount of liquor to be purchased. Customs officials are present in the central stores to control the movement of liquor into and out of the stores. The only liquors of higher alcoholic content not being sold through the central stores are Panamanian-produced products, which are shipped directly by the breweries and distilleries to the zone. No liquor sales are made in the zone except by civilian and military clubs, which sell individual drinks as well as bottled spirits.

In the light of these controls, what explanations may be offered for the general belief that illegal liquors (those subject to the 75 per cent tax discount) enter the Panamanian market in considerable quantity? One source of contraband is the approximately 2,400 Panamanian workers residing in the zone, each of whom probably has an extensive number of friends and relatives living in Panamá. Another source is probably the clubs, many of which accept Panamanian residents as members. Then there is always the likelihood of a number of professionals, who practice smuggling as a business operation, and have no difficulty recruiting accomplices among the large number of unemployed. And finally, there is the physical relationship of Panamá and the Canal Zone, with miles of open border, without fences or control points, which makes the movement of goods from one area to the other all but impossible to control. The smuggling is probably confined for the most part to liquors of higher alcoholic content. Beer and wine of good quality and without a marked price differential are available in Panamá, and products of low value to bulk are not susceptible to contraband.

POLICY CONCLUSIONS

On the basis of the foregoing evidence, certain basic characteristics of the system of taxing alcoholic beverages emerge that are important for tax policy purposes. These may be summarized as follows:

1) The system of internal excises on alcoholic liquors is unduly complicated, with taxes at the manufacturing, wholesale, and retail levels. In addition, the taxes at the wholesale and retail levels are essentially illogical and arbitrary in application and effect.

2) Very substantial amounts of revenues are derived from the production, importation, and sale of alcoholic beverages. In 1961, nearly 10 per cent of total tax revenues was derived from internal liquor excises, while another 5.7 per cent was obtained from customs duties on imported liquors. But some of the internal excises, especially the taxes on wholesale establishments and on the manufacture of wine, are relatively unimportant from a revenue point of view.

3) The domestic production of liquor of higher alcoholic content has remained relatively stable, while imports of foreign liquors have increased significantly. Thus, the level of customs duties on liquors of higher alcoholic content has not served to protect and foster the development of domestic production. But the beer industry under a policy of customs duty protection has experienced a very healthy growth.

4) The manufacture of liquors of higher alcoholic content has been characterized by a shift from higher-priced rum made from the natural fermentation of sugar to lower-priced Seco made from rectified alcohol. In this respect, the policy of permitting a tax discount for the purpose of encouraging the aging of rum has not been effective.

5) The existence since 1955 of a tax reduction of 75 per cent applicable to liquors imported into the Canal Zone has created a chronic and severe problem of contraband. In view of the free movement of people and goods between Panamá and the Canal Zone, it is doubtful if any degree of vigilance would be adequate to control the smuggling of liquors as long as a marked price differential in liquors exists between the two areas. Under the circumstances, it is also fruitless to indulge in speculation as to whether Canal Zone or Panamanian authorities are more responsible for the existence of smuggling.

From these basic characteristics of the alcoholic beverage tax system in Panamá, it would appear that no fundamental improvement can be brought about without a resolution of the contraband problem.[2] This large-scale bootlegging operation is undersirable on several counts: 1) it results in a loss of revenue to the Panamanian government; 2) it is inequitable, since it provides persons with shady ethics the opportunity to avoid tax liabilities; 3) it is destructive of taxpaying morale and serves to break down respect for the law and civil institutions; 4) it provides employment for Panamanians in an illegal business; and 5) the attempt to control smuggling, though in large part unsuccessful, is costly.

And if these arguments are not enough to constitute an overwhelming case in favor of equal tax burdens on liquors sold in Panamá and the Canal Zone, there is still one more that is probably more important than the others. During the period of time in which the Canal Zone has been leased from the Panamanian government, the United States has enjoyed certain privileges that constitute a high degree of sovereignty. Some of these privileges are necessary and justifiable for the operation and defense of the canal, but others like the present tax policy on liquor are in the nature of extraterritorial impositions that promote political frictions and distrust between Panamá and the United States. It would appear that the provision of low-cost liquor to civilian and military personnel in the Canal Zone is an excessive cost to pay for unfriendly and uncooperative relationships between the two countries.

If a policy of equal taxation of liquor between Panamá and the Canal Zone is not adopted, there are two lesser reforms that would provide some improvement over the present system. The first of these would be the denial of purchase privileges to Panamanians residing in the zone, while the second would be to prohibit the sales of all bottled liquors in Canal Zone clubs. If these two reforms were introduced, all purchases of bottled goods at a tax discount would be limited to United States citizens, and all bottled goods would be available only through the central liquor stores. Club sales would then be limited to liquor by the glass and beer. It is reforms of this substantive degree that are needed in order to control the illegal sale of liquors rather than additional customs inspectors or a reorganization of administrative procedures.

It is recognized that if all liquors of higher alcoholic content consumed in the Canal Zone were to be subject to the full amount of Panamanian taxes, then Panamá, in effect, would have the right to impose taxes on United States citizens. There is nothing unusual in this situation, however, for this was the case before 1955. The objection may be raised that the Panamanian government could continue to raise taxes on liquors in order to exact higher burdens from Canal Zone residents, but the fact that Panamanian citizens would also be subject to these taxes should be a deterrent to this possibility.

With the elimination of smuggling, or at least its control within tolerable limits, it would then be possible to turn to the problem of rationalizing the system of taxing alcoholic beverages. One issue in this respect is the amount of revenue that should be obtained from liquor taxes. At the present time, Panamá derives about 15.5 per cent of its

---

[2] There are other but probably less important sources of contraband liquor in Panamá and these should also be controlled more effectively. See chapters 7 and 12 dealing with taxes on foreign commerce and the Colón Free Zone, respectively.

total tax revenues from levies on alcoholic beverages. This is an excessive amount of revenue to be obtained from the taxation of one product, and in the future the relative degree of reliance on alcoholic beverages as a source of revenue should be decreased.

In principle, high taxes on alcoholic beverages are not desirable, since they tend to be regressive in their incidence and they prevent consumers from allocating their expenditures freely. The principal virtue of liquor taxes is that they are productive of revenue, but this in itself is a mixed blessing, for it prevents a country from facing the difficult problems involved in developing an equitable and rational tax system.

In terms of economic policy, both beer and liquors of higher alcoholic content have received all the customs protection that they need for the encouragement of domestic production. Neither are produced by infant industries, and the fact that domestic rum or gin is not more competitive with foreign imports must be attributed to the industry's shortcomings and consumer tastes rather than to a lack of customs protection. In fact, the prohibitive customs duty on beer is probably undesirable; a lowering of the tariff and some foreign competition would probably have a salutary effect on the industry's efficiency.

The present method of taxing domestically-produced liquors on the basis of their alcoholic content has been shown to be regressive, since the tax represents a greater percentage of the price in the case of lower-priced brands. Since the number of domestic manufacturers is limited in Panamá, it would be feasible and desirable to shift from the present system of specific excises to an *ad valorem* excise based on the manufacturer's selling price. It would also be desirable to eliminate the tax discount for storing rum more than three years, as this feature of the law has been ineffective in extending the storage period.

SUMMARY OF RECOMMENDATIONS

1) For the internal excise tax on beer and liquors of higher alcoholic content, an *ad valorem* rather than a specific excise tax should be utilized.

2) The civil service system should be extended to include tax collectors.

3) The tax discount for storing rum for more than three years should be eliminated.

4) The customs duty on imported beer should be reduced.

5) The smuggling of liquor from the Canal Zone to Panamá should be eliminated by subjecting all liquors of higher alcoholic content consumed in the zone to the full amount of Panamanian taxes.

CHAPTER 10

The Autonomous Agencies

INTRODUCTION

PANAMÁ HAS TWENTY autonomous and semi-autonomous institutions or authorities which were created by the National Assembly to conduct activities of a proprietary nature, and which vary in the degree to which they are independent of the executive power. Nearly all of them were initiated with government grants, most of them continue to receive government subsidies, but some rely to a great extent on their own revenues. The difference between the autonomous and semi-autonomous institutions does not depend on their financial characteristics. By and large, autonomous institutions are more independent of the executive, having been created by and made responsible to the Assembly. They usually include among their directors one or more government ministers or their representatives, and are required to account to the Comptroller General.

It is beyond the scope of this study to undertake a detailed analysis of all the specialized agencies of the government. The analysis, instead, is confined to the total impact of these institutions on government revenues and expenditures, with a detailed consideration reserved to the Social Security System and to a lesser extent to the finances of the Institute for Economic Development, the Institute for Housing and Urban Development, the National Lottery, several gov-ernment banks, and the Gambling Control Board.

IMPACT ON GOVERNMENT REVENUES AND EXPENDITURES

Among the *autonomous* agencies are the Social Security System, the Institute for Economic Development, the Institute for Housing and Urban Development, several banks, the Colón Free Zone, the National Institute of Sewage and Aqueducts, the University of Panamá, and agencies for the development of cattle and coffee exports, and tourism.

Nearly all of these institutions receive subsidies from the government. The Social Security System receives part of the tax on beer production, as well as a direct subsidy for the administration of the System. In addition, the government makes an employers' contribution to the System. Similarly, in 1961 grants of B/1.05 million were made to the Institute for Economic Development, B/1.0 million (including part of the tax on beer production) to the Institute for Housing and Urban Development, and B/100,000 to the Colón Free Zone. In 1962, an initial contribution of capital was made to the Popular Bank of B/400,000, to the Institute of Water Resources and Electrification of B/800,000, and to the Coffee Institute of B/100,000.

Among the *semi-autonomous* agencies are the National Lottery, the Gambling Control Board, the National Railroad of Chiriquí, and the Utilities Commission. The National Lottery and the other gambling activities produce revenue for the government. There are several other governmental agencies that perform proprietary functions and realize revenues. Among them may be included the Post Office and Telegraph, the provision of water (now part of a new autonomous institution), and the operation of wharves, airports, hospitals, and public markets.

According to the data assembled in Table 10.1, the autonomous institutions and other specialized agencies had total expenditures of B/29.4 million in 1961, excluding the savings of the Social Security System and the price-support payments by the Institute for Economic Development. If the latter two items were included, the total would be nearly B/9 million higher.

The sum of B/29.4 million also excludes agencies whose expenditures were reported among departmental expenditures of the government, such as the Post Office and Telegraph and the University of Panamá. The magnitude of this spending may be appreciated better by noting that the expenditures of the regular government departments amounted to B/72.28 million in 1961, while the revenues produced for the government by all specialized agencies amounted to B/11.64 million.

While the usual criticisms that may be leveled against governmental agencies apply to the autonomous agencies, there are some which apply specifically to the latter. Autonomy means self-government, and in the case of autonomous government agencies, it means independence of the executive. In theory such agencies are responsible to the Assembly which created them, but in practice the Assembly is not in a position to exercise proper supervision and control.

The annual reports made by these agencies to the Assembly, especially when the latter is in plenary session, are a very unsatisfactory substitute for the usual periodic reviews and investigations of the executive. The annual reports usually present glowing accounts of activities, without benefit of detail, and often conceal the facts needed for control and correction. Moreover, periodic supervision by legislative committees is not an adequate substitute for continuous control.

The principal advantage of the autonomous agency is its specialized administrative machinery for undertaking a particular activity. It is a sound administrative device to create a specialized agency to carry out a proprietary activity—one that provides a service and finances its own activities much like a private business. It is a sound principle not to mix the revenues and expenditures of these agencies with those of the regular government. But it is one thing to set up a distinct entity; it is quite another to deprive the executive of responsibility for its administration. It is one thing to require Assembly approval of key appointments; it is quite another to establish a government within a government. It is one thing to preserve the right of the Assembly to investigate and correct; it is quite another to deny the executive that right.

The executive power is responsible for implementing legislative policies, for coordinating complex and interwoven activities. In brief, the executive is responsible for administering. The creation of autonomous institutions is a way for the legislative branch to encroach on the executive power, to invade the executive domain. And it is also a way to perform the executive function badly because a legislative body cannot be organized for an administrative responsibility.

There is also a tendency in Panamá for the Assembly to allow the directors of the autonomous agencies to determine their own personnel policies, to prescribe what records should be maintained, and in general to establish the policies of the agencies within the general statements of responsibilities and powers in the law. In creating the autonomous institutions, the Assembly does not prevent them from becoming objects of political patronage. No rules of civil service apply.

TABLE 10.1

Expenditures of Specialized Agencies, and Their Impact on Government Revenues and Expenditures, 1961

(Millions of Balboas)

	Total Expenditures	Expenditures on Goods and Services	Government Subsidies Received	Contribution to Government Revenues
Autonomous Institutions				
Social Security System	7.6[4]	4.5[6]	1.4	—
Institute for Economic Development	4.1[5]	2.0	1.05	—
Institute for Housing and Urban Development	8.4	1.2	1.0	—
Colón Free Zone[1]	0.5	0.4	0.1	—
National Bank of Panamá	2.3	2.2	—	0.28
Savings Bank	0.7	0.7	—	—
Popular Credit Bank	—[2]	—[2]	(0.4)[2]	—
Cattle and Agricultural Credit Bank	—[2]	—[2]	—[2]	—
University of Panamá	(1.4)[3]	(1.4)[3]	(1.2)[3]	—
Cattle Institute	0.09	0.09	0.09	—
Coffee Institute	—[2]	—[2]	(0.1)[2]	—
Institute for Water Resources and Electrification	—[2]	—[2]	(0.8)[2]	—
Tourism Institute	(.26)[3]	(.26)[3]	(.26)[3]	—
Institute for Sewers and Aqueducts[2]	(n.a.)[3]	—	—	2.35
Semi-Autonomous Institutions				
National Lottery	3.3	3.30	—	5.8
Office of Price Regulation	(0.9)[3]	(0.9)[3]	(0.9)[3]	—
Gambling Control Board	2.1	2.1	—	.28
National Railroad of Chiriquí	0.2	0.2	—	—
Utilities Commission	(0.2)[3]	(0.2)[3]	(0.2)[3]	—
Red Cross	0.1	0.1	0.1	—
Other Specialized Agencies				
Post Office and Telegraph	(1.58)[3]	(n.a.)	(0.53)[3]	1.05
Wharves and Airports	(n.a.)[3]	(n.a.)	—	.73
Hospitals	(.99)[3]	(n.a.)	—	.64
Public Markets	(n.a.)[3]	(n.a.)	—	.14
Other	(n.a.)[3]	(n.a.)	—	.37
TOTALS	29.39	16.79	3.74	11.64

[1] The Colón Free Zone is analyzed in Chapter 12.
[2] Did not start operations in 1961. Data shown are budgeted figures for 1962.
[3] These amounts are not included in the totals, because they are carried in the regular government budget.
[4] Does not include "savings" of the Social Security System, i.e., additions to reserves. Total receipts were B/13.2 million.

[5] Excludes purchases of farm products because these were offset by sales, and therefore may be considered in the nature of a "wash" transaction.
[6] Does not include Social Security construction activity, for which data are not available.
n.a.—not available
Source: Adapted from a table developed by the Department of Planning and Administration.

Employees obtain and hold office on the whim of the directors. With a change in administration, wholesale changes in personnel occur, sometimes with highly qualified technicians being replaced by incompetent political appointments.

The autonomous and semi-autonomous institutions employed nearly 5,000 persons in August, 1960.[1] To mention a few, Social Security employed 828; the Institute for

[1] *Informe del Contralor General,* October, 1962, p. 109.

Economic Development, 366; the Institute for Housing, 135; the National Bank, 373; the racetrack, 144; and the lottery, 240. To become a director of one of these agencies in the absence of civil service restrictions is an important political attainment. It is more highly prized than to become a minister of a regular government department.

Autonomous agencies should be required to account for funds with the same degree of responsibility that is required of all fiscal agencies of the government. It is a serious omission on the part of the Assembly not to require this. Supervision of fiscal agents is a responsibility of the Executive and the Comptroller General. Therefore, the Executive and the Comptroller General should be required to audit and certify the accounts of autonomous agencies and to prescribe their accounting procedures.

THE SOCIAL SECURITY SYSTEM
(Caja de Seguro Social)

The Social Security System was created in 1941 as an autonomous entity with its own legal capacity and its own funds separate and independent from those of the national government. The administration of the system is vested in a general director and a board of directors, the latter composed of the following members: The Minister of Labor, Social Welfare, and Public Health (who is the presiding officer), three workers' representatives, three employers' representatives, the manager of the National Bank, and a physician not employed by the Social Security System.

Revenues

To cover the costs of the several risks and benefits included, the System has nine sources of revenue:

1) contributions of the compulsorily insured employees at the rate of 4.5 per cent of their salaries (5.0 per cent starting in 1963);

2) contributions of employers at the rate of 4.5 per cent of salaries (5.5 per cent starting in 1963 and 7.0 per cent in 1964);

3) contributions of the System's pensioners at the rate of 4.5 per cent of their pensions (5.0 per cent starting in 1963);

4) contributions of government pensioners at the rate of 4.5 per cent of their pensions (5.0 per cent starting in 1963);

5) a share of the tax levied on liquor, wine, and beer;

6) contributions of the government at the rate of 0.8 per cent of both the compulsorily insured employees' salaries and the voluntarily insured workers' basic salaries and incomes;

7) fines and charges levied on overdue contributions;

8) investment profits; and

9) inheritances, legacies, and donations.

From 1951 to 1961, the revenues of the Social Security System more than doubled, rising from B/5.8 million to B/13.2 million. Of the latter amount, B/10.4 million was derived from contributions, B/2.4 million from investment profits, and B/0.4 million from other sources. Although each of these three sources of revenue has increased since 1951, contributions have experienced the highest percentage increase. Within the category of contributions, those made by employers show the greatest gain (see Table 10.2).

Allocation of Revenues

The Social Security law established certain percentage allocations for broad expenditure categories. Out of the revenues arising from employers' and employees' contributions, an amount equal to 5.5 per cent of the salaries upon which contributions have been received in a given year must be spent to cover the services provided because of illness and maternity. Proceeds from pensioners' contributions are also to be used for these services.

TABLE 10.2
Social Security Revenues, 1951 and 1961
(Millions of Balboas)

Source of Revenues	Revenues		Percentage Increase, 1951 to 1961
	1951	1961	
Contributions			
Employees	2.0	4.9	145
Employers	1.1	3.1	182
Government	1.3	2.4	185
Investment profits	1.2	2.4	100
Other	0.2	0.4	100
TOTALS	5.8	13.2	128

Source: Dirección de Finanzas y Asesoría Administrativa de la Caja de Seguro Social.

To cover the risks of disability, old age, and death, two types of reserves are formed. The first reserve is sufficient to finance the current amount of pensions annually paid, while the second includes all other resources which may be used to finance future obligations.

The law provides that the administrative expenses for illness, maternity, disability, old age, and death must not exceed 1.2 per cent of the salaries on which the contributions have been received during the same year. If they exceed this percentage for three successive months, the board of directors must order adjustments to be made. The expenses related exclusively to the administration of the System cannot be imputed to the cost of providing the services.

Total expenditures of the Social Security System increased from B/2.3 million in 1951 to B/7.6 million in 1961 (Table 10.3). Since revenues also increased appreciably, savings increased from B/3.5 million in 1951 to B/5.6 million in 1961. Administrative expenses from 1951 to 1961 increased less than the cost of the services. While benefits in the form of services increased by 219 per cent during this period, and benefits in payments by 329 per cent, administrative expenditures rose by only 150 per cent. During this period, however, the Social Security System was experiencing a significant expansion due to the inclusion of additional geographic districts as well as the broadening of risks. If administrative expenses between 1951 and 1961 are compared on a per capita basis

TABLE 10.3
Social Security Expenditures, 1951 and 1961

(Millions of Balboas)

	1951	1961
Benefits		
Services	1.1	3.5
Payments	0.7	3.0
Administrative expenses	0.4	1.0
Other	0.1	0.1
TOTALS	2.3	7.6
Savings	3.5	5.6

Source: Dirección de Finanzas y Asesoría Administrativa de la Caja de Seguro Social.

for those insured, there was an increase from B/9.4 per insured person in 1951 to B/10.4 per capita in 1960 and to B/12.0 per capita in 1961.

Administrative expenses, as it has been mentioned, cannot exceed an annual rate of 1.2 per cent of the salaries on which the contributions have been received during the year. A rigid rule such as this one does not assure administrative efficiency, although it may serve to prevent flagrant abuses. Occasional inspections and studies by disinterested and qualified experts in administrative procedures would be a more effective way to promote efficiency.

Investments

The Social Security System is authorized to invest its funds in nine different ways:

1) real property, such as buildings, offices, hospitals, and other medical facilities needed to fulfill its functions;

2) buildings for commercial but not for residential purposes;

3) loans to those insured who provide mortgage collateral in order to buy or construct their own residences;

4) loans with first mortgage collateral upon improved real estate up to 60 per cent of the estimated value, provided the loans do not exceed the assessed values of the properties;

5) instruments of internal and external public debt and bonds of autonomous government institutions, provided that these are guaranteed by the government and the loans do not exceed 60 per cent of the reserves;

6) loans to finance the construction of buildings up to 80 per cent of the value of the land and its improvements;

7) fixed-term bank deposits yielding interest;

8) loans guaranteed by internal and external public debt instruments up to 80 per cent of their nominal value; and

9) loans to industrial, agricultural, and public utility firms up to 60 per cent of their paid-in capital.

As shown in Table 10.4, the investment portfolio of the Social Security System presently resembles that of a private insurance company, with the only difference being that the bulk of the funds is represented by public securities and by investments in social projects. There is a price to be paid for this investment in public securities, for most of the public bonds held by the System bear a rate of interest of 4.0 to 5.5 per cent, while the rate of interest on the private market is 7.0 to 8.0 per cent. The contributors of the System bear this cost in terms of foregone revenue.

If the funds of the Social Security System were invested in private securities, a greater return would be possible. At the same time, however, the risk of incurring losses would also be increased. Moreover, there are several other reasons in favor of investing Social Security funds in government bonds. One is that the efforts and resources needed to develop a diversified and profitable portfolio distract administrators of the Social Security System from their main task, which is to administer the benefits. Second, the government guarantees the solvency of the System *de facto,* if not by legal requirement. And finally, it is undesirable in principle to have an agency of the government making investments when it is autonomous and not subject to the coordinated economic policies of the government. For these reasons, it would be more desirable if the funds of the Social Security System were invested entirely in government bonds.

It should be borne in mind, also, that Panamá has had a remarkable degree of monetary stability, due principally to the use of the United States dollar as legal tender. If there were the same inflationary pressures in Panamá so typical of many other Latin American countries, there would be less of an argument in favor of fixed-interest securities. During inflation, these securities tend to lose their value, while pressures mount to increase pensions in order to maintain their real value. There are currently no potential inflationary pressures in Panamá, but should these develop, it would be advisable for government bonds to have a special clause guaranteeing the maintenance of their real value.

Another problem is the determination of the interest rate on government bonds purchased by the Social Security System in order to avoid subsidizing government spending at the expense of the contributors to the Social Security System. This problem may be resolved by providing that government bonds sold to the System should bear the market rate of interest.

Coverage

Workers covered by the Social Security System are classified into compulsorily and voluntarily insured. The first group comprises all public and private employees whose legal domicile is within eleven geographic districts incorporated under the compulsory system. The compulsory group also includes all employees working for enterprises engaged in constructing and maintaining public works, and all domestic workers. It is discretionary on the part of the directors to decide whether to incorporate other districts, activities, or enterprises under the compulsory system.

The voluntary group includes self-employed workers, employees previously insured under

TABLE 10.4
Assets of the Social Security System,
December 31, 1961

(Millions of Balboas)

Assets	Amount
Cash and bank deposits	0.7
Real property	8.3
Securities	
Public bonds	37.0
Debentures and other private bonds	0.4
Corporate shares	0.2
Loans	
Private mortgages	19.8
Public institutions	1.9
Other	6.3
Other assets	6.0
TOTAL	80.6

Source: Dirección de Finanzas y Asesoría Administrativa de la Caja de Seguro Social.

the compulsory system, workers domiciled in Panamá and employed by international institutions, Panamanians employed by diplomatic and consular missions, and employees working for persons or private institutions whose legal domicile is outside of the districts included under the compulsory system.

The law also enumerates those workers who cannot become insured: male workers over sixty years of age and women over fifty-five years of age; the spouse, parents, and children of less than sixteen years of age of the employer; occasional and seasonal workers; foreigners hired abroad to work in Panamá for a period of less than two years; and workers in non-permanent agricultural enterprises.

There were 80,416 workers insured in 1961. This total is nearly twice the number of 46,636 insured in 1942. Although the total insured has increased at a faster rate than that of the labor force, more than two-thirds of the labor force is still not covered. Of the total insured population in 1961, 79,396 were under the compulsory system and 1,020 under the voluntary one. Of the total covered under the compulsory system, 47,418 were private employees, 23,949 were employees of the national government, and 8,029 worked for autonomous agencies.

Risks Covered

The Social Security System covers the risks of illness, maternity, disability, old age, and death. Both services and monetary payments are provided. The following paragraphs contain a brief description of the general features of the various risks covered and the benefits provided.

Illness. There are two benefits that the System may provide because of illness: 1) medical, surgical, pharmaceutical, dental, and hospital assistance; and 2) monetary subsidies, when the illness results in temporary disability.

To be entitled to medical and hospital services, an insured must be contributing cur-

rently to the System and have made at least two monthly contributions during the four months prior to an application for assistance. There are two exceptions, however, to this general rule: 1) an insured who is at least fifty years of age and who has paid at least 240 monthly contributions (twenty years) is entitled to the benefits without making any additional contributions; and 2) an insured who stops paying his contributions because of involuntary unemployment remains covered by the System for three months. These benefits can also be extended, depending on the financial condition of the Social Security System, to the spouse and to the children of less than six years of age of the insured.

A person whose illness has resulted in temporary disability also may claim a daily monetary payment if at least six monthly contributions have been made during the nine months previous to disability. The subsidy is equal to 60 per cent of the daily average wage upon which a person has made contributions during the preceding two months. The payments are made for a period not exceeding twenty-six weeks for the same illness, but this period may be extended up to a year for special cases.

Maternity. Women are entitled to two types of pregnancy benefits: 1) prenatal and obstetrical care; and 2) a subsidy equal to 100 per cent of the average weekly salary upon which contributions have been paid during the last nine months. To receive the first benefit, it is necessary for the insured to be making current contributions, and to have made at least four monthly contributions during the eight months previous to an application. The insured is entitled to receive a weekly subsidy if at least nine monthly contributions have been made during the twelve months prior to the seventh month of pregnancy. This subsidy, which is paid for six weeks before and eight weeks after childbirth, is equal to the average weekly salary upon which contributions were made during the last nine months of payments.

Disability. A disabled worker is entitled to receive a pension equal to 50 per cent of his monthly basic salary [2] plus 1 per cent of his average salary for each year over ten that he has contributed.[3] To be eligible, a worker must meet the following requirements: 1) to have been declared disabled; 2) to have made at least thirty-six monthly contributions; 3) to have made payments one-half of the time during the last three calendar years prior to the disability, or during the period of enrollment if his registration had occurred within those three years; and 4) to be less than fifty-five years of age at the beginning of the disability in the case of women, and less than sixty years of age in the case of men.

Old Age. The old age benefits consist of life-time pensions, the amounts of which are determined in the same manner as the disability pensions. To be entitled to this benefit a person must meet the following requirements: 1) to be fifty-five years of age in the case of women and sixty years of age in the case of men; 2) to have made at least 180 monthly contributions; and 3) to prove to the Social Security administration that a salary is not being earned.

Survivors' Pensions. The widow or common-law wife of the insured or pensioner is entitled to a survivor's pension. A disabled widower has the same rights as a widow, provided he was dependent economically on his wife. The pension is equivalent to 50 per cent of the pension paid to the deceased on account of disability or old age, or of that pension to which he would have been entitled on the date of his death (excluding family allowances and supplements). The pension

is paid for three years, but is available for a longer period if minor children are supported.

Economic Effects of Social Security

The provision of medical, disability, old-age, and other social security benefits in lesser developed countries has often been condemned because it results in excessive burdens and expenditures, it denies resources to higher priority uses, and it places domestic industry at a disadvantage by adding to labor costs. On none of these grounds can the Social Security System in Panamá be criticized.

First, in terms of the actual amount of resources utilized, the System "consumes" only B/4.5 million in services and administration plus an additional B/3.0 million in transfer payments. The former represents only 1.1 per cent of the national income, and most of this amount would be a necessary expenditure even without a Social Security System. Second, while employers, too, must make contributions, incidence theory holds that the tax burden is shifted either forward in higher prices or backward in lower wages. Third, the Social Security System is one of the most effective ways of promoting savings. In a relatively short period of time, the System has accumulated B/80.6 million in assets, which it has invested in bonds, securities, and real estate. In this way, it has made possible many of the development projects of the government, stimulated construction, and made funds available to industry.

Finally, no formal system of relief payments exists in Panamá. The unemployed, the aged, and the disabled must provide for themselves, have their relatives do so, or throw themselves on the mercy of private charity. A program of insurance against such risks cannot be said to be a luxury. If any criticism can be leveled against the Social Security System, it is that an insufficient number of workers qualify for its benefits.

---

[2] The monthly basic salary is the higher average obtained from averaging the last 120 or 180 monthly contributions (ten or fifteen years). In the case of disability, if the period of contributions is shorter than those mentioned, the average would be estimated upon the contributions paid.

[3] Law Decree No. 9 of August, 1962, established a maximum monthly benefit of B/500 and a minimum of B/50 for disability and old age pensions.

THE INSTITUTE FOR ECONOMIC
DEVELOPMENT
(Instituto de Fomento Económico)

The Institute for Economic Development (IFE) was established in 1953 for the purpose of increasing, diversifying, and rationalizing production, and was given specific responsibility for:

1) developing agricultural and livestock production, especially with respect to contributing to better nutrition and to the development of raw materials for the industries of the country;

2) diversifying agricultural production by the introduction of new crops that would be profitable and appropriate to internal and foreign markets;

3) making possible the establishment, development, expansion, or rationalization of industries, and to aid, establish, or participate in public or private enterprises dedicated to this end;

4) strengthening Panamá's international economic position;

5) undertaking the construction of dwellings and subdivisions;

6) facilitating the acquisition of small farms and the construction of low-cost housing;

7) promoting urban development and redevelopment;

8) providing banking services in places where none are available; and

9) developing transport and communications.[4]

IFE was originally organized into three departments, namely, Commercial Banking, Development, and Urban Development, but it was relieved of the first responsibility involving banking in 1956 with the creation of the National Bank, and of the third responsibility with respect to urban development in 1958 with the establishment of the Institute of Housing and Development.

IFE was initiated with a transfer of assets from the *Banco Agropecuario e Industrial*

and the *Banco de Urbanización y Rehabilitación,* and a government subsidy of B/75,000 per month. Additional resources have been obtained from the issuance of bonds and through grants of foreign aid.

IFE's most important current activities are the administration of the agricultural price-support program, the granting of loans to farmers, the rental of agricultural machinery and equipment, the undertaking of economic feasibility studies, and the provision of educational programs and seminars.

On July 31, 1962, IFE reported assets of B/18.6 million after allowing for bad debts of B/1.5 million. About B/6 million of the assets were invested in interest-bearing loans and accounts receivable, B/9.2 million were in real estate, and B/9 million were in inventories of farm products. On the same date, IFE had a capital of B/10.4 million, long-term debt of B/3.8 million, and accounts and notes payable of B/1.8 million.[5]

The work of IFE is currently conducted by four departments: the Central Office, Department of Credit, Department of Development, and the Department of Agricultural Mechanization. The Central Office, besides handling the bulk of the administration and accounting, participates in the lending and price-support programs and maintains a Center of Industrial Development. The latter makes feasibility studies with the assistance of international agencies, and conducts seminars and engages in other educational activities that are designed to increase industrial productivity. During the first eleven months of 1961, the Central Office had receipts of B/2.38 million, its principal sources of funds being a government subsidy of B/87,500 per month, rentals from real estate, and amortization and interest on loans. During this period, IFE had also borrowed B/750,000. On the expenditure side for the period, IFE had administrative expenses of nearly B/1 million, and had made loans and investments of B/712,649.[6]

---

[4] Law No. 3, January 30, 1953, Chapter 1, Article 2.

[5] Instituto de Fomento Económico, *Informe a la Asamblea Nacional* (Panamá, October, 1962), p. 5.
[6] Instituto de Fomento Económico, *Informe de Presupuesto* (Panamá, November 30, 1961), pp. 3, 5.

TABLE 10.5

Receipts and Expenditures of the Institute for Economic Development

(Thousands of Balboas)

	January 1 to November 30, 1961	Estimate for Calendar Year 1961
Receipts		
Government subsidy	962.5	1,050.0[1]
New borrowing	750.0	750.0[1]
Sales of products	3,502.4	4,038.5[1]
Sales of services	84.1	91.8
Rentals	360.8	393.6
Loan repayments	534.3	582.9
Interest	156.5	170.7
Payments on accounts receivable	11.2	12.3
Other income	32.8	35.7
Deposits	48.0	52.4
TOTALS	6,442.6	7,177.9
Expenditures		
Wages and salaries	841.5	917.9
Operating expenses	961.3	1,048.6
Loans	756.7	1,002.7[1]
Repayments on borrowings and accounts payable	989.1	1,079.0
Purchases of products	2,654.6	3,493.7[1]
Furniture and equipment	88.7	96.8
TOTALS	6,291.9	7,638.7
		460.8
		7,177.9

[1] Less deficit on cash transactions.

Source: IFE, *Informe de Presupuesto,* November 30, 1961 and *Informe a la Asamblea,* October, 1962.

The Department of Credit makes loans to farmers, cattle-raisers, and food processors. Its loans, including those made by the Central Office, amounted to over B/1 million in 1961.[7] Of this total, 45.5 per cent was made to farmers, 37.4 per cent to cattle-raisers, and the remainder was for industrial purposes. Of 3,788 loans made in 1961, 1,964, or nearly 52 per cent, were for less than B/150, and another 44 per cent were between B/300 and B/500. Loans of over B/1000 constituted only 2 per cent of the total number, but they represented 34 per cent of the total amount loaned.

[7] *Informe a la Asamblea Nacional,* p. 82, Tables D, E, and F.

The principal responsibility of the Department of Development is the administration of the price-support program. During 1961, the Department purchased B/3.3 million worth of farm products, of which B/1.8 million were domestic products and B/1.5 were foreign.[8] These purchases are used to stabilize the prices of farm products and to assure a stable supply. Products purchased were principally rice, coffee, corn, and copra. Sales in 1961 totaled B/4.04 million of farm products, including B/453,000 drawn from inventories existing at the beginning of the year. The gross profit on sales was B/303,000.

The Department of Agricultural Mechanization is principally concerned with the rental of agricultural machinery. From January 1 to November 30, 1961, the Department received rental income totaling B/84,125.[9]

Table 10.5 shows the actual receipts and expenditures of IFE for the eleven-month period from January 1 to November 30, 1961, and estimates for the full-year's operations. Notwithstanding a government subsidy of B/1,050,000, IFE's estimated cash expenditures exceeded estimated cash receipts for calendar year 1961 by B/460,800. However, it should be noted that debt repayments were over B/1 million, and IFE's loans increased by B/367,000 over the previous year.[10]

Neither space nor time allows a detailed analysis of IFE's faults and virtues over the years. However, at least a few observations based on limited research are possible. First, it is clear that too many important, complex, and varied responsibilities were assigned to IFE when the agency was formed. The scope of responsibilities would have justified five different authorities, each administered by an outstanding executive. If one wishes to bury a socially worthwhile activity, it could not be done more effectively than to pile one arduous task upon another and ask that they be done simultaneously. Therefore, the transfer of some functions to the Institute of Housing and Urban Development and to the

[8] *Ibid.,* Table 1.
[9] *Informe de Presupuesto,* p. 3.
[10] IFE, *Informe a la Asamblea Nacional,* p. 82, Table D.

National Bank was highly desirable. By the end of 1962, consideration was also being given to the transfer of other responsibilities to new agencies. Under discussion was the transfer of the entire industrial development program to a joint private-government industrial bank, and the transfer of the Center for Industrial Development to the Ministry of Agriculture, Commerce and Industry.

IFE has several conspicuous faults. Its administration has not clearly defined the purposes of the price-support program. There have been price supports for coffee in the face of surplus world production, and price supports without quality standards for salt. There has been an inadequate development of marketing facilities, of cooperative activities, and of foreign markets. There is evidence of political influence and an emphasis on vested interest instead of national interest. Excessive timidity and ideological confusion also have contributed to IFE's difficulties.

INSTITUTE OF HOUSING AND URBAN DEVELOPMENT
(Instituto de Vivienda y Urbanismo)

The Institute of Housing and Urban Development (IVU) was created in 1958. Its functions consist of providing public housing, facilitating home ownership, and developing housing areas. Its board of directors consists of seven members, one representative each from the Panamanian Association of Engineers and Architects, the Chamber of Urban Property of Colón, the national insurance companies, the Institute of Aqueducts and Sewerage, labor organizations, and the Association of Industrialists. All members are appointed by the executive branch.

IVU receives a subsidy from the government of B/750,000 per year plus 15 per cent of the tax on the production of beer. The latter accounted for B/258,495 in 1961. In addition, during 1961 IVU received interest and rent of B/132,927, and B/260,848 as payments for administering the real estate of the Institute for Economic Development, the Free Zone of Colón, and other properties.

TABLE 10.6

Statement of Receipts and Expenditures for the Institute of Housing and Urban Development, January 1, 1961, to December, 1961

(Thousands of Balboas)

Receipts		
Sales of houses	354.7	
Interest and rent	132.9	
Fees from IFE, etc.	260.8	
Government subsidy	1,008.5	1,756.9
Expenditures		
Administration	1,221.3	
Construction and purchase of real estate	7,238.6	8,459.9
Deficit		6,703.0
Increase in debt		
Accounts receivable (increase)	1,974.0	
Bonds issued	3,306.0	
Notes payable	1,423.0	6,703.0

The accounts of IVU do not lend themselves to a simple statement of receipts and expenditures. They are described in the Comptroller General's report as bordering on anarchy.[11] The data in Table 10.6 are estimated from known receipts and changes in broad categories of assets and liabilities.

On December 31, 1961, IVU reported assets of B/16.5 million, consisting primarily of construction in process (B/6.4 million), houses and lots (B/2.4 million), land (B/3.9 million), and uncompleted contracts (B/2.6 million). It had a capital of B/5.6 million and a medium- to long-term debt of B/5.6 million. In addition, it had accounts payable and contracts obligated of B/4.7 million. IVU's balance sheet as of December 31, 1961, is shown in Table 10.7.

There can be no doubt of the importance and the need for a program such as IVU is administering. One is impressed also with the energy of its administrators and the momentum of the program. At the same time, there is no excuse for the slipshod accounting and the absence of financial controls which the Comptroller General denounced in his

[11] Contraloría General, *Informe* (Panamá, October 10, 1962), p. 103-A.

TABLE 10.7

Balance Sheet of the Institute for Housing and
Urban Development, December 31, 1961

(Thousands of Balboas)

Assets	
Cash or deposits	518.2
Accounts receivable	431.7
Other	49.7
Finished houses and lots	2,350.4
Contracts not completed	2,552.1
Construction in process	6,448.6
Accrued assets	21.3
Government bonds	54.9
Land	3,917.4
Equipment	96.7
Buildings	33.8
TOTAL	16,474.8[1]
Liabilities	
Accounts payable	2,162.3
Deposits	194.5
Accrued liabilities	305.1
Contracts obligated	2,552.1
IVU bonds	3,770.4[1]
Notes payable	1,847.5
	10,831.9
Capital	5,642.9
TOTAL	16,474.8

[1] Not shown is a bank loan commitment of B/2,518,000.
Source: Instituto de Vivienda y Urbanismo, *Informe Financiero,* December 31, 1961.

Informe. Many worthwhile public activities have been buried in their infancy by the infection of scandal, which is used by opponents to poison the public's attitude. Throwing the baby out with the bath water has been the fate of many idealistic projects that become tainted by corruption or incompetence. There is no excuse for tolerating laxity and incompetence in accounting for public funds, nor alleged corruption in executing public tasks. These faults are all the worse when they endanger an important and worthwhile task.

THE NATIONAL LOTTERY
(Lotería Nacional de Beneficencia)

In Panamá, it is said that everyone plays the lottery. More than any other government institution, it is woven into the fabric of daily existence. More than 2,500 persons find employment in the lottery, and its pot-of-gold at the end of the rainbow is a source of hope for the poverty-stricken.

The National Lottery was formally established as a semi-autonomous institution in 1914. Its board is composed of the Minister of Labor, Social Welfare and Public Health, the director of the National Bank, and representatives of hospitals, schools, and the Chamber of Commerce. In 1961, the lottery contributed B/5.8 million to the Treasury, or 9.3 per cent of the ordinary revenues of the government and more than one-half the amount raised by the income tax. Compared with 1951, the lottery has declined somewhat in relative importance. In 1951, the lottery produced a revenue of B/3.9 million, or 11.9 per cent of total revenues, and nearly as much as the income tax (B/4.1 million). Nevertheless, the revenue from the lottery increased by 49.3 per cent from 1951 to 1961 (see Table 10.8).

As a source of government revenue, the lottery raises serious questions. In the first place, it utilizes a large amount of resources. If the lottery were to exist without government sponsorship, then the fact that it utilizes a large amount of resources is irrelevant, for the resources would be used in any event. But the government, by having a financial interest in the lottery, encourages participation, and therefore helps to divert an increasing amount of resources into the lottery. By doing so, systematic private saving is discouraged. Accordingly, there should be less emphasis on the lottery and less advertising. In fact, government policy should be to "play down" the lottery, merely making it available but not encouraging it.

The lottery is also important from the point of view of political patronage. Some 2,500 persons are directly employed. The advertising expenditures give the political party in power tremendous influence over the communications media, and the other expenditures enable the party in power to confer or withhold benefits. It should be noted in Table 10.9 that salaries and other expenses

TABLE 10.8

Income and Expenditures of the National Lottery,
1951 and 1961

(Thousands of Balboas)

	1951	1961	Per-centage Increase
Net sales	B/21,687	B/33,828	56.0
Prizes paid	16,024	25,152	57.0
Ratio of prizes to sales (per cent)	(73.9)	(74.4)	00.7
Gross profit on sales	5,663	8,676	53.2
Other income	111	296	166.7
	5,774	8,972	55.4
Less commissions	−1,394	−2,183	56.6
Salaries and other expenses	−684	−1,166	70.5
Net gain from operations	3,696	5,623	52.1
Paid to the Treasury during the year	3,904	5,829	49.3

Source: Lotería Nacional de Beneficencia.

TABLE 10.9

Expenses of the National Lottery, 1961

Commissions paid	B/2,183,306
Wholesalers	600,753
Retailers	1,582,553
Number of wholesalers	52
Number of retailers	2,044
Administrative expenses	1,165,960
Salaries	436,096
Printing	401,080
Advertising	98,957
General expenses	229,827
TOTAL EXPENSES	B/3,349,266

Source: Lotería Nacional de Beneficencia.

have been increasing more rapidly than ticket sales and the contribution to the public treasury.

Data with respect to family expenditures for lottery tickets show a range of expenditures of 5.6 to 13.7 per cent of income among income classes up to B/5500. No clear evidence of correlation with income exists within the range of incomes shown in Table 10.10, but the data suggest that the purchase of tickets becomes regressive at incomes above B/3500. Assuming that prizes are distributed in the same manner as the purchases of tickets, at best the burden of the lottery is distributed proportionally until an income of B/3500 is reached and then it becomes regressive.

GOVERNMENT BANKS

Among the earlier banks created by the government were the Savings Bank (Caja de Ahorros), established in 1934, and the National Bank of Panamá (Banco Nacional de Panamá), started in 1956. The success of these two banks led to the establishment of the Popular Credit Bank (Banco Crédito Popular) in 1960 and the Cattle and Agricultural Credit Bank (Banco de Crédito Agrícola y Pecuario) in 1961. The latter two had not initiated operations as of late 1961.

The National Bank of Panamá undertakes the usual functions of a commercial bank and acts as the agent and depository of the government. On June 30, 1962, it reported capital of B/6.3 million and deposits of B/31.1 million. During the fiscal year ending June 30, 1962, it earned a net revenue of B/1.4 million. During 1961, it paid into the Treasury B/279,500 from its profits.

The Savings Bank was created to stimulate regular savings by the public. On June 30, 1962, it reported capital of B/2.4 million and deposits of B/15.5 million. During fiscal year 1962, the Savings Bank earned B/325,-273 after payment of dividends. The bank also serves as an agent in administering international aid programs. In February, 1962, it received a commitment from the Agency for International Development to the amount of B/2.5 million to facilitate the development of home ownership for moderate income families. The Institute of Housing and Urban Development will build the houses and the bank will finance the purchases.

The importance of public banks within the Panamanian monetary system is shown in Table 10.11. The data indicate that the public banks held 35 per cent of total bank deposits on June 30, 1962.

Panamá does not possess a central bank. If one should be created, the experience

TABLE 10.10

Lottery Purchases of Panamanian Families in Relation to Income

Annual Income per Family (Balboas)	Panamá City[1]		Bocas del Toro[2]		Puerto Armuelles[3]		David[4]	
	Amount (Balboas)	Per Cent	Amount (Balboas)	Per Cent	Amount (Balboas)	Per Cent	Amount (Balboas)	Per Cent
450	—	—	43.55	9.7	37.73	8.4	36.55	8.1
625	—	—	70.32	11.3	69.33	11.1	42.91	6.9
750	58.82	7.8	—	—	—	—	—	—
875	—	—	93.38	10.7	100.65	11.5	48.96	5.6
1,250	102.92	8.2	123.72	9.9	124.28	9.9	83.34	6.7
1,750	165.46	9.4	239.76	13.7	194.48	11.1	125.00	7.1
2,250	182.87	8.1	279.76	12.4	207.03	9.2	190.79	8.5
2,750	271.89	9.9	285.01	10.4	238.97	8.7	165.64	6.0
3,500	259.74	7.4	348.40	10.0	276.06	7.9	266.40	7.6
4,500	365.29	8.1	—	—	286.00	6.4	355.82	7.9
5,500	487.76	8.9	—	—	—	—	—	—
6,750	239.78	3.6	—	—	—	—	—	—

[1] 1952 figures. Coverage: 438 families.
[2] 1956 figures. Coverage: 138 families.
[3] 1956 figures. Coverage: 232 families.
[4] 1956 figures. Coverage: 333 families.

Source: Contraloría General de la República, *Estudio de los Ingresos, Gastos y Costo de la Vida, Ciudad de Panamá, 1952–1953*, second edition, 1955, p. 66.

gained by the administration of the National Bank should prove invaluable. The principal need at the moment is for an investment bank, designed to make long-term loans to industrial enterprises, to organize and participate in these firms, and to create a market for the securities of new and expanding corporations. A mixed private-public industrial development bank has been proposed, and legislation will soon be introduced for its creation. However, there is the danger in hybrid creations of this sort that the major risk will be borne by the government, and any rewards will be received by private investors. For example, it has been proposed that the private shares should receive a yield that is 6 per cent greater than the public shares, although the government would bear

TABLE 10.11

Productive Assets and Deposits of Panamanian Banks, June 30, 1962

(Thousands of Balboas)

	Productive Assets	Per Cent	Deposits	Per Cent
All banks	B/120,699.5	100.0	B/133,061.8	100.0
Public banks	46,061.0	38.2	46,600.3	35.0
Private banks	74,638.5	61.8	86,461.5	65.0

Source: Dirección de Estadística y Censo, *Hacienda Pública y Finanzas,* 2° trimestre, 1962.

the greater part of the risk. It has also been proposed that the private shares should be guaranteed a 4 per cent return during the first five years of operation. Such an inequitable participation does not afford an auspicious beginning to government participation in a private enterprise. If the government is to be a partner in such ventures, its return should be proportional to its risk.

THE GAMBLING CONTROL BOARD

Gambling is a state monopoly. The function of the Gambling Control Board is to prescribe the regulations and taxes on all games of chance, and to operate casinos and other gambling enterprises. The principal proprietary activities are the operation of the casino at El Panamá Hilton Hotel and the racetrack (*Hipódromo Presidente Remón*).

The casino at El Panamá Hilton Hotel realized a profit in 1961 of B/362,000. Gross earnings were B/671,700, salaries and related expenses amounted to B/211,200, and other expenses were B/98,500. The casino's contribution to the Treasury was B/252,000 in 1961. The Remón racetrack has experienced financial difficulties since 1957. It is a relatively large operation. In 1961, it employed about 150 persons and paid total salaries of B/296,000. It reported a net income of B/75,940 in 1961, out of which it made a contribution to the Treasury of B/25,600.

OTHER AGENCIES

Among the remaining institutions, there are those designed to promote specific industries: the Cattle Institute, the Coffee Institute, and the Tourism Institute. In general, these agencies perform functions ordinarily undertaken by trade associations, and their activities should not be subsidized by the government. Rather, agencies established to advance the interests of specific industries should be financed by taxes levied on the firms in those industries. This is now true of the Tourism Institute and the others should be similarly financed.

Two agencies were established in 1961 in the area of utility services. The Institute for Sewers and Aqueducts (IDAAN) was created as a unit of the Ministry of Labor, Social Welfare and Public Health in 1956, but was given the status of an autonomous entity in 1961. It is charged with planning, constructing, and maintaining water and sewage lines and sewage disposal facilities in the capital and its environs.

The water problem created in agriculture by the prolonged dry season should be resolved. In addition, there is a need for additional power resources. For these two reasons, the Institute for Water Resources and Electrification (IRHE) was established to study the requirements and availability of water resources, and to plan and to make recommendations for the construction of necessary facilities. IRHE received an initial grant of B/800,000 in 1962, and it expects to receive international assistance in developing its program.

SUMMARY OF RECOMMENDATIONS

1) The status of autonomous institutions should be reserved generally to proprietary activities which have the possibility of generating a self-sustaining level of revenues.

Housing, utilities, social security, banks, postal and telegraph, and similar operations tend to qualify in this respect. The status of autonomous institutions should be denied agencies that have merely control or regulatory functions, or that perform as trade associations, unless they receive revenues levied specifically on the regulated industries, or from those whose interests are promoted by the industry.

2) No single agency should be assigned several unrelated and important tasks, since there is a tendency to concentrate on one, or undertake all of them inadequately. Agricultural and industrial development should not be combined, nor agricultural and industrial lending. Educational, investigative, and proprietary activities should not be assigned to the same agency. Specialization of endeavor should be the rule.

3) All specialized agencies should be subject to the same standards of accountability as those required of any government department. Each should publish fully the state of its finances, including periodic balance sheets and statements of receipts and expenditures. These should be in necessary detail, and be audited and certified by the Controller General.

4) All specialized agencies should be divorced from political patronage. The same standards of personnel selection and job security (civil service) should apply to them as to all regular government agencies.

5) Managing the investment portfolio of the Social Security System is a governmental function. The directors of the System should be concerned with providing services to the insured and not with investments. All resources of the System should be invested in government bonds, but the purchasing power of the bonds should be maintained and the interest return should be guaranteed.

6) The advertising and propaganda of agencies charged with operating lotteries and games of chance should be severely limited. The purpose of these agencies should be to make gambling available to those who want it but not to encourage the activity.

CHAPTER 11

Fiscal Incentives for Development

INTRODUCTION

PANAMÁ HAS HAD two major laws for the stimulation of private domestic production. The first statute, Law Decree No. 12 of May 10, 1950, emphasized income tax concessions, customs duty protection, and exemptions from import taxes; its successor, Law Decree No. 25 of February 7, 1957, restricted the income tax exemption to income from foreign sales, and reduced the period of time available for customs duty protection and exemption from import taxes. This chapter is concerned with a review of the operating experience under these laws and with a consideration of ways in which the current incentive law may be improved.

A second concern, dealt with at the end of the chapter, is the policy of encouraging so-called foreign base companies. These are firms that "operate" in Panamá merely for the purpose of consummating international sales without taking physical possession of goods. Through a provision of the income tax law, the income from these sales is not construed to arise in Panamá. Thus, since Panamá exempts all income from foreign sources, these firms enjoy a permanent income tax holiday without the need for specific contracts.

LEGAL PROVISIONS OF LAW NO. 12 OF 1950 AND LAW NO. 25 OF 1957

Law No. 12 of 1950 states that it was enacted for the purpose of encouraging three types of activities: 1) agricultural and livestock production; 2) the extraction of raw materials and the utilization of forest, mineral, and fishing resources; and 3) manufacturing industries of all kinds. In an additional descriptive clause, however, the law is also extended to "the rendition of services." Thus, the statute appears to encompass all developmental activities, such as tourist hotels or commercial activities, which could be construed to be in the public interest to support under the legislation.

Eligibility for the benefits under the law was also very broad and highly discretionary, for the privileges were not confined to new industries or to new firms. On the contrary, any firm could qualify for the benefits provided that it fulfilled investment and production goals which satisfied the Minister of Agriculture, the National Economic Council, the Cabinet, and the President. The grants were also not exclusive; that is, the rights that were granted to one firm in an industry were extended to other firms in the same industry provided that these firms were willing to undertake similar obligations. Conversely, whenever an enterprise applied for a contract to undertake economic activities similar to those which already existed under protection of contract, the firm had the right to enter into a contract under the same terms as the existing contracts and for a period that would not exceed the unexpired term of the oldest contract.

Fiscal benefits under the law may be divided into two categories: taxes on foreign commerce and internal taxes. With respect to taxes on foreign commerce, three types of concessions were provided: 1) exemption of taxes on the imports of machinery, equipment, spare parts, containers, fuels, lubricants, and raw materials; 2) exemption of all taxes on the export of products; and 3) tariff protection on competitive products. Fiscal benefits within the category of internal taxes were of two types: 1) *exemption* of taxes on installations, operations, and production, and on the distribution, sale, or consumption of the firm's products; and 2) a *stabilization* or *freezing* of the tax rates for the duration of the contract with respect to the income tax, social security taxes, stamp taxes, notary fees, registry fees, and rates for public services provided by the Republic. Although not specifically included in the law, three other taxes—real property, tourism, and business licenses—have been included in some of the contracts and have been frozen for the duration of the contractual periods. These fiscal benefits may be conferred in whole or in part; that is, a particular firm may be granted all of the fiscal benefits or only part of them. Also, the benefits were available for a maximum period of twenty-five years, but they could be granted for shorter periods than the maximum.

In return for any concessions or exemptions granted, the recipient was required to assume several commitments. Among the more important of these were: 1) to invest the amount specified in the contract; 2) to sell products in the national market at wholesale prices that were not higher than those agreed upon with official agencies; 3) to give job prefer-

ence to Panamanians except in the case of certain experts and specialized technicians that the enterprise considered necessary; and 4) to favor the use of domestic raw materials.

Law No. 25 of 1957, the one currently in effect, followed the same basic pattern as the earlier 1950 development law except that it restricted the fiscal benefits in several important ways. These restrictions were undoubtedly prompted by concern over tax revenue losses. The provisions for customs duty exemptions, tariff protection against competitive products, and the exemption from export taxes were retained, but the maximum period for these benefits was fifteen years as compared to the previous maximum period of twenty-five years. Exemptions were provided for taxes on the capital of the enterprise, its installations, operations, production, distribution, and the sale of its products, but no provision was made for the stabilization of the tax rates for the duration of the contracts with respect to the income tax, social security taxes, stamp taxes, notary fees, registry fees, and rates for public services provided by the Republic. The income tax exemption for profits derived from foreign sales was retained, but with the limitations that the maximum period was fifteen years, and that the exemption was not available for the export of natural resources.

OPERATING RESULTS OF THE
DEVELOPMENT LAWS

Length of Contracts

A total of 211 contracts were issued under both the 1950 and 1957 development laws as of November, 1962. As shown in Table 11.1, sixty-eight of these contracts were issued during the seven years in which the 1950 law was in operation, while 143 contracts were processed during the six years in which the 1957 law has been in effect.

Table 11.1 also shows the length of the contracts under both laws. Under the 1950

TABLE 11.1

Contracts Issued under Law No. 12 of 1950 and Law No. 25 of 1957

Year	Number of Contracts		Length of Contracts in Years	Number of Contracts	
	1950 Law	1957 Law		1950 Law	1957 Law
1950	4		1		1
1951	6		2		3
1952	21		3		1
1953	7		4		1
1954	9		5		8
1955	8		6		
1956	13		7		1
1957		32	8		2
1958		29	9		
1959		16	10	1	4
1960		26	11		
1961		22	12		
1962[1]		18	13	1	2
	TOTALS 68[2]	143[2]	14		4
			15		33
			16		
			17		8
			18		16
			19		14
			20		9
			21		4
			22	1	6
			23	1	4
			24	3	
			25	56	14
			26	2	
			27	1	
			28	1	
			29		
			30		4
				TOTALS 67[2]	139[2]

[1] To November, 1962.   [2] Discrepancies in the totals are due to ambiguities in the data.

law, there was a marked tendency to issue contracts for the maximum period of twenty-five years permissable under the law, although seven contracts were made for less than twenty-five years and four exceeded the maximum. Ostensibly the 1957 law provided for a maximum contractual period of fifteen years. While there were thirty-three contracts issued for this maximum, twenty-seven were for less than fifteen years, but seventy-nine were for periods in excess of the maximum, four of them for as long as thirty years.

There are two explanations for the number of contracts for less than the maximum period. The first is the increase in the number of duplicate contracts in a particular industry since all contracts in the same industry must terminate on the same date. Second,

there is probably concern over tax revenue losses. There are also two possible reasons for the relatively large number of contracts issued under the 1957 law in excess of the maximum period. One is the requirement, despite the fifteen-year limitation in the 1957 law, to give firms a contract equal in length to the contracts received by their competitors under the 1950 law. Second, there is the tendency in Panamá for the Assembly rather than the Executive to authorize unique contracts, and in doing so, the Assembly often exceeds the maximum periods established in the incentive laws. For these reasons, seventy-nine out of 139 contracts issued under the 1957 law actually exceed the maximum period provided for in the law. This development, of course, defeats one of the principal ob-

jectives of the 1957 law, which was to reduce the maximum period of the contracts
from twenty-five to fifteen years.

Customs Exemptions and Tariff Protection

Grantees are invariably given the privilege of exemption from customs duties on
certain types of imports, but tariff protection
against foreign competition is less frequently
granted. Under the 1950 law, thirty-eight
out of sixty-eight firms, or 56 per cent of the
grantees, were given tariff protection; under
the 1957 law, 81 out of 139 grantees, or 57
per cent, were given protection.

Not all of the firms receiving authorization
of protection by contract actually receive
protection since the National Assembly must
act on tariff adjustments after the protection
has been authorized. However, it is estimated
by the Executive Director of the National
Economic Council that approximately 90 per
cent of the firms that are authorized to receive protection do, in fact, actually receive
protection.

The second of two chapters in this study
dealing with taxes on foreign commerce
has analyzed exhaustively the policy implications of providing particular firms with tariff
protection from foreign competition and exemptions from customs duties. For purposes
of integrating these findings and conclusions
into the over-all context of providing fiscal
incentives for economic development, they
are repeated at this point in summary form.
The salient points developed with respect to
providing tariff protection are:

1) Production and employment data show
evidence that protective tariffs have in general
assisted the development of protected industries.

2) For some protected products, there is
evidence that their prices have become competitive with respect to foreign goods, but
there are other protected products for which
prices have remained substantially above those
of foreign products. Unfortunately, products
for which duties have resulted in higher
prices are also those which are important in

lower income and moderate income budgets.

3) If the financial sacrifice on the part of
consumers could be calculated and capitalized, it would total in some cases more than
the value of the industries being protected.
The high prices in these cases have been
simply a private "tax," protecting monopolists and redistributing income from poor to
rich.

4) A protective tariff is justified if it brings
into being or accelerates the development of
a "healthy" industry, whose costs of production and prices become competitive with
levels elsewhere. On the other hand, if it
protects a "sick" industry, far from being a
gain to the economy, it actually reduces the
standard of living, and nearly always the
standard of living of low-income groups.
There is evidence that both "healthy" and
"sick" industries have been protected.

5) There are two important disadvantages
of subsidies in the form of protective tariffs.
The first is that the amount of the subsidy is
never fully known. Second, among the types
of incentives offered by the government to
stimulate economic development, only in the
case of protective tariffs is there an actual
encouragement to monopolistic practices. By
eliminating foreign competition, protective
tariffs deprive the economy of the most important mechanism assuring fair play to consumers.

The salient points developed previously
with respect to providing exemptions from
customs duties are:

1) Firms with contracts were permitted to
import free of any duties B/23.1 million of
goods in 1961, on which the duties exempted
were B/3.6 million. The fully-exempted imports of these firms amounted to 20 per cent
of total imports, while duties exempted for
these firms were nearly 29 per cent of total
import duties and fees.

The amount of exempted imports on the
part of contract firms has been growing very
rapidly. From 1952 to 1961, total exemptions
rose from B/2.7 million to B/23.1 million.
From 1960 to 1961, they rose from B/13.6
million to B/23.1 million. Duties exempted

increased from B/2.1 million in 1960 to B/3.6 million in 1961.

2) Over B/10 million of the exempted imports in 1961 were in the category of capital goods, amounting to a saving in duties for the firms of B/1.7 million; the corresponding savings in duties on the importation of raw materials and semi-manufacturers were B/2.0 million. If all industrial and mining equipment and machinery were to be placed on the free list, the cost in additional duties foregone would only be B/462,500.

3) To the extent that the saving in duties results in lower prices, the exemption from duties is a saving for consumers. But there is no assurance that all of the saving will be passed on to consumers.

4) Only capital goods, raw materials, and semi-manufactures used in the further production of goods should be benefited with exemptions. This would mean the denial of exemptions to construction materials, transport vehicles, and office machinery and equipment.

Other Tax Incentives

A great deal of difficulty was encountered in developing an inventory of firms having contracts under the 1950 law that provide for the stabilization of their income tax and other tax rates. There is no master list of these firms available in Panamá, and in addition, many of the contracts reviewed for the purpose of developing a list were found to be ambiguous. Thus, the information obtained undoubtedly has a margin of error.

A total of forty firms were found to have contracts that provide for a freeze of certain tax rates or to have special tax concessions. Seven of these firms have abandoned operations, and six have very unique contracts. Among the unique contracts, the oldest in point of time and by far the most important in terms of revenue loss is one with the Chiriquí Land Company (United Fruit Company). This contract has no terminal date and provides for a flat-rate income tax of 30 per cent. Another contract with Com-

pañía Panameña de Fuerza y Luz, a privately-owned power, light, and telephone company, exempts the firm from import duties as well as notary fees, stamp taxes, and registry fees. Moteles, S.A. and Hoteles Continentales are not subject to import duties and property taxes. Petroquímica (Golden Eagle Refinery) and Refinería Panamá are not subject to import or export taxes, consular fees, an income tax on export sales, or dividend taxes. In addition, property tax rates and public registry fees for these two firms are frozen for the duration of the contracts.

Considering only the thirty-three firms presently in existence or expected to be operating in the near future, it was determined that twenty-nine have a tax freeze applicable to six taxes or fees: the income tax, social security taxes, stamp taxes, notary fees, registry fees, and rates for public services supplied by the Republic. In addition, several firms have a tax freeze with respect to three other taxes, the authority for which, apparently, is derived from legislative action rather than the 1950 law: sixteen firms have been guaranteed a stabilization of their property tax rates, seventeen for business licenses, and ten for the tourism tax. Of the twenty-nine firms with contracts stabilizing their tax rates, twenty-eight have contracts freezing the tax rates for twenty-five years, and one firm has a ten-year contract.

Revenue Loss

Part of the cost of granting tax incentives, as in the case of protective tariffs, is not measurable. With other taxes, such as the property tax and social security taxes, the calculations are not warranted because they would be too complicated relative to the importance of the results. Therefore, consideration will be given only to the revenue loss apparent from the customs duty exemption and the stabilization of income tax rates. Reference has already been made to the cost of the customs duty exemption. Duties exempted increased from B/2.1 million in 1960 to B/3.6 million in 1961.

In estimating the loss of revenue from granting firms a freeze of their income tax rates, the records of six firms could not be obtained. As far as it is known, however, these firms are relatively small, so the results obtained in the absence of these firms should be reasonably complete. In 1961, twenty-four contract firms (including the Chiriquí Land Company) paid B/2,097,468 in income taxes, whereas if they had been fully taxable in this year their total income tax payments would have been B/3,421,207, a difference of B/1,323,739. This loss of revenue would be slightly higher if the six missing firms had been included, and it would also probably be greater in 1962 because of the adoption of higher income tax rates.

Combining the customs duties exempted of B/3.6 million in 1961 and the income tax loss of B/1.3 million for the same year, results in a total of B/4.9 million. This total, in turn, was approximately 13 per cent of total tax revenues of B/47.6 million in 1961. Making allowance for several other taxes covered by the contracts, the enactment of higher income tax rates in 1962, and a rising trend of customs duty exemptions, it appears reasonable to assume that the total revenue loss resulting from the 1950 and 1957 development laws would be about 15 per cent of total tax revenues in 1962. This appears to be a very high price to pay for tax incentives in terms of revenue foregone, especially when the relation between incentives and development activities is so tenuous.

RESTRICTION OF THE INCOME TAX CONCESSION

An issue currently debated in Panamá is whether some action should be taken to restrict the contracts issued under the 1950 law in view of their current and future drain on government revenues. These discussions have focused on the income tax concession rather than on customs duty exemptions or tariff protection, perhaps because the income tax concession is more conspicuous. It should be borne in mind, however, that some of the firms enjoying an income tax benefit are also protected from foreign competition by relatively high tariffs. If a reconsideration of their income tax concession is warranted, so also is the question of whether they should continue to receive tariff protection.

There are several reasons justifying concern over the income tax concession. The first is that the benefits are appreciable in terms of a reduction in the effective rate of the tax. Under the 1950 law, eligible firms were guaranteed that they would be subject to the income tax rate in effect at the time of receiving their contracts. Thus, firms receiving contracts from 1950 to 1952 pay taxes according to a 1946 rate schedule, and firms receiving contracts from 1953 to 1956 pay taxes according to a 1953 schedule. There is one exception to the above in the case of the Chiriquí Land Company. This firm has a special contract with the government that provides for a flat-rate tax of 30 per cent on its taxable income.

The importance of these stabilized rates may be appreciated by comparing the burdens under the 1946 and 1953 income tax schedules with those in effect during 1962. On the taxable income bracket between B/90,000 and B/100,000, the marginal rate of the income tax was 14.4 per cent under the 1946 schedule and 21.3 per cent under the 1953 schedule. By comparison, on the taxable income bracket between B/80,000 and B/100,000 under the 1962 schedule, the marginal rate is 29.4 per cent.[1]

Reference has been made to the fact that the income tax concession in 1961 resulted in a loss of revenue of approximately B/1.3 million. An important feature of this loss is that most of it is attributable to a small number of large and profitable firms. In 1961, 44.4 per cent of the loss of revenue is attributable to the unique contract with the Chiriquí Land Company, while the five most profitable firms account for 91.1 per cent of the loss, and the nine most profitable for

---

[1] See Tables 2.1, 2.2 and 2.4 in Chapter 2.

98.5 per cent. The remaining firms, quite obviously, experienced either small profits or losses. Thus, to the degree that there is a problem with respect to the loss of revenue from granting income tax concessions, it is attributable to a handful of relatively large and profitable firms.

How important are these firms in the context of the whole of the income tax system? Table 2.9 in Chapter 2 demonstrates that a relatively large segment of corporate enterprise is presently covered by income tax contracts. This table shows the declared income and the tax payments of the twenty taxpayers with the highest taxable income in 1959 and 1960. Eight of these twenty firms in 1959 had contracts freezing their income tax rates. Ranked in order of the size of their declared income in 1959, the first, fourth, fifth, tenth, eleventh, twelfth, fifteenth, and nineteenth firms had a contract covering the income tax. Of the total declared income of these twenty firms in 1959 of B/20.6 million, B/12.4 million, or 60 per cent, is attributable to firms with income tax contracts.

Making the problem even more severe is that nearly all of these firms received a twenty-five year contract under the 1950 law, with the result that their privileged status even in 1962 extends for a considerable period into the future. As Table 11.2 shows, most of the firms in 1962 were still entitled

to a freeze of their income tax rates for an additional period of fourteen to nineteen years.

Without question, a very serious mistake was made by Panamá in granting income tax concessions to some of the largest and most profitable firms in the country for a period of twenty-five years. This mistake is so apparent that the Executive has made one formal effort to restrict the benefit by proposing to the National Assembly in 1961 that all corporate dividend and interest payments should be taxable when received by individuals. In the most part, if not entirely, the motivation for this proposal was to obtain a larger income tax contribution by indirection from firms with income tax contracts.

Although the Assembly acted on the proposal, the resulting legislation [2] is so confusing that no one in Panamá, including officials in the income tax division is certain of its provisions. The law was circumscribed in two important ways. First, it applied only to contract firms, and second, it was permissive rather than obligatory. According to the law, a contract firm is given an opportunity to elect coverage under a new contract for a period of ten years, which provides: 1) that any income re-invested could be applied to reduce taxable income up to an amount which represents 75 per cent of its taxable income; and 2) the tax imposed is the difference between the tax payable by the company computed at rates specified by contract and that payable in accordance with tax rates currently in effect. The tax, however, may not exceed 60 per cent of the dividends paid.

In effect, therefore, a tax liability is established on declared dividends by firms which elect to be covered by Law No. 87, but this tax can only be collected at the rate of 60 per cent of dividends paid. This latter restriction requires the tax administration to maintain a current account of potential tax liability for a corporation, but the dividends declared establish the timing and the amount of the tax that may be collected.

TABLE 11.2

Expiration Dates and Contract Years Remaining for Firms with Income Tax Contracts

Expiration Dates of Income Tax Contracts	Number of Firms	Number of Contract Years Remaining as of 1962
1966	1	4
1975	1	13
1976	3	14
1977	4	15
1978	4	16
1979	2	17
1980	9	18
1981	4	19
1989	1	27

[2] Law No. 87 of December 28, 1961.

The above provisions of Law No. 87 are so complicated that it is desirable to present a specific illustration in order to explain more fully the determination of tax liability. This may be done according to the following example:

1) If a contract firm has a taxable income of B/1,000,000, this amount may be reduced up to 75 per cent by re-invested income. On the assumption that the full re-investment credit is taken, a taxable income of B/250,000 remains.

2) The tax on this B/250,000 is then calculated at current rates, which may be assumed for illustrative purposes to result in a tax liability of B/50,000.

3) The tax is then computed on the basis of the full taxable income of the firm and its guaranteed contractual tax rate, which may be assumed to result in a tax liability of B/100,000.

4) The tax liability of a firm under the provisions of Law 87 may be greater but cannot be less than the tax obligation under its guaranteed contractual tax rate. Thus, in the illustration above, a tax of B/100,000 must be paid. However, in the event that the tax computed at the guaranteed rate exceeds the tax under Law 87, the amount of the re-invested income which was of no value as a credit in reducing the tax (that is, the amount that reduced the tax from B/100,000 to B/50,000) may be carried over as a credit against income for three years.

5) Further, assume that the corporation declared dividends of B/150,000. The tax on these dividends (levied on the stockholders but collected by the corporation) is the difference between the tax on B/1,000,000 computed at the guaranteed rates (previously assumed to be B/100,000) and the tax on B/1,000,000 computed at the current rates (which may be assumed to be B/300,000). Thus, the tax on dividends would be B/200,000.

6) The tax on dividends, however, cannot be more than 60 per cent of the dividends declared. Thus, the tax on dividends cannot be more than 60 per cent of B/150,000, or B/90,000.

7) The difference between the computed tax on dividends (B/200,000) and the amount that may be collected (B/90,000) is carried over as a postponed tax liability for collection in the future.

These provisions were further complicated by another section of Law No. 87, which in obvious contradiction provided for the exemption of all dividends for seven years for firms electing to be covered under Law No. 87. Either this provision or the preceding one which taxes dividends would have to be rescinded. Furthermore, it is difficult to understand how firms can be expected to elect voluntarily to impose upon themselves higher taxes. If the law indeed provides for higher tax levies, why should firms elect to be covered by its provisions? If the law does not provide for higher levies, what was its purpose? It is only to be expected that no firms have elected to be covered by Law No. 87.

As Law No. 87 gives every appearance of being a dead letter on the statute books, the question should again be raised as to what, if anything, should be done about the firms with twenty-five year contracts under the 1950 development law? There are, of course, very good reasons for doing nothing. Any restrictive action, either overt or covert, will be construed by some elements of the business community to be evidence of bad faith on the part of the government. Without considering the merits of the case, they will merely damn the government for not living up to its commitments. One research report summarizes the reaction to be expected in the statement: "Whatever the merits of this case, no matter how valid the claim that the previous law provided excessive benefits, this step is regarded by many businessmen as a unilateral violation of the government's contracts with the companies concerned." [3]

Be that as it may, incurring the wrath of some businessmen, and suffering the loss of some investor morale, seems preferable to

[3] *Promoting Production in Panamá,* Continental-Allied Company, Inc., September, 1962, pp. 98–99.

a continuation of the present concessions for another fourteen to nineteen years. If these firms were of minor importance from a revenue point of view, or if their remaining period of subsidization was relatively short, the problem could be ignored. But these contract firms, as it has been shown, represent a major part of taxpaying capacity in Panamá. They are the "blue-chip" industrial enterprises, and they are owned in large part by the relatively small number of Panamanians with the greatest capacity to pay taxes. As a result, their continued income tax subsidization for another fifteen years will, to an appreciable degree, delay tax reform in general for fifteen years. This is an excessive price to pay for the sake of viewing contracts as inviolable.

Panamá has two alternatives in adjusting the income tax concession. One is to act directly and overtly by simply rescinding the contracts. To cushion the shock, each firm could be given a contract for fifteen years of income tax benefits dated from the time of receiving their contracts, which would leave most of the firms with a few more years of benefits. They could also be given the privilege of retaining their customs duties exemptions for the duration of their original contracts. But the benefits covering other taxes, like the property and social security taxes, should also be terminated.

The second approach is to combine an adjustment of the income tax concession with fundamental income tax reform by the enactment of a law that would make dividends taxable when received by individuals. This law would apply to all corporations, not just the contract firms. Since this law will have to be enacted eventually if the income tax is to be rationalized, it could be argued that it might as well be done now in order to accomplish the additional goal of resolving the problem of obtaining additional tax revenues from the contract firms. Under this solution, the contract firms could continue to receive their preferential income tax rates, but dividends paid would be taxed under current tax rates. Thus, the income tax concession

would apply only to retained earnings. This degree of preferential treatment could be justified in terms of an incentive to certain corporations to save and invest.

GUIDELINES FOR A NEW INCENTIVE LAW

Besides restricting the existing income tax concession, Panamá should give consideration to the enactment of a new incentive law, for the current 1957 law has three basic shortcomings: 1) the maximum period for contracts of fifteen years is excessive; 2) an income tax exemption should be substituted for tariff protection; and 3) the exemption of customs duties should be more restrictive. To assist in the formulation of a new incentive law, some observations will be made, first, on the general role of tax incentives. Following this, some specific suggestions for a new tax incentive law will be offered.

The Role of Tax Incentives

Although tax incentives for the stimulation of development (particularly industrial expansion) are a world-wide phenomenon in underdeveloped countries, they are viewed without enthusiasm by many professional experts. There are doubts, first, about the effectiveness of tax incentives. Unquestionably, investment responds to a multiplicity of factors, such as the size of the market, the cost and availability of skilled labor, and general economic and political conditions. In the total context of these factors that determine investment decisions, it is believed that tax concessions are of marginal importance. Tax incentives cannot be viewed as substitutes for well-conceived promotional programs, the availability of low-cost financing, the development of economic infrastructure in the form of highways, water supply, and power, and the training of labor. Given these and other basic prerequisites for development, the most that can be said for tax incentives is that they may demonstrate a government's determination to promote and encourage private enterprise, and they may be used to offset certain deterrents to investment. They may also have, to some degree, a psychological appeal to businessmen that outweighs their real significance.

But if tax concessions are to be justified as a means of compensating for other handicaps that deter investors, the question may well be asked why a direct approach to the removal of these impediments would not be more effective than tax incentives. For example, industrial development in Panamá is restricted by a regressive tax system that limits domestic purchasing power; domestic industry not receiving tax concessions is hampered by customs duties on capital goods, raw materials, and fuel; profits are subjected to a special surtax; corporations are taxed according to a progressive rate schedule; rigid depreciation allowances and an absence of loss carry-overs inhibit investment; and alternative but less desirable forms of investment, such as speculation in urban land and real estate, are encouraged through an absence of capital gains taxation. Is it not more important in terms of industrial development to provide permanent and positive incentives by the removal of these major defects from the tax system than to offer temporary and essentially negative palliatives in the form of tax concessions?

One of the most important problems in the use of tax incentives is the loss of public revenues, for the use of incentives is invariably accompanied by the need for additional funds for the developmental functions of a government. In this respect, it is sometimes argued that tax incentives do not result in a "loss" of revenue. One technical report prepared for the Government of Panamá states that: ". . . if the government grants contracts only to companies that would not undertake the investment in the absence of the contract, then there is no revenue loss even of potential revenue. Without tax benefits, the firm would not have undertaken the investment, and there would be no activity to tax." [4]

[4] *Ibid.*

This statement is logically correct, of course, but it is not possible to determine that a given investment would not have taken place but for a tax concession. While there are undoubtedly instances in which tax concessions are instrumental in a favorable decision to invest, it appears quite unreasonable to take the position that in a country like Panamá there would have been an absence of investment on the part of the exempt firms if there had been no tax incentives. And for this amount of investment that would have resulted in the absence of tax incentives, the use of incentives results in a direct loss of government revenue.

There are also certain general problems of serious proportions that must be faced in the use of tax concessions. One of these is the relative treatment to be given to different types of firms within an industry, particularly between new and growing firms and old and relatively stagnant firms. The variation among firms in this respect poses a dilemma, for if the exemption privilege is not granted to all firms in an industry, some companies are placed at a competitive disadvantage. On the other hand, if tax concessions are extended to all firms, there is a tendency for the program to degenerate into a general subsidy instead of a method of encouraging new investment.

Income tax exemptions, in particular, are a perverse type of subsidy. Income tax relief provides little assistance when it is needed most, namely, during the initial period when losses or low profits are sustained. In Panamá's case, income tax exemption during a period of low initial profits is especially gratuitous because the corporate income tax is progressive and has very nominal effective rates on low incomes. On the other hand, if the exemption period is extended to cover a period of time in which most firms become profitable, the exemption becomes meaningless in terms of need, and losses in government revenue may become substantial.

Finally, it should be mentioned that tax incentives, to the degree that they are oriented to the attraction of foreign capital, are essentially a "beggar-my-neighbor" policy. It is true, other things being equal, that a particular country like Panamá will stand to gain relative to other countries if its tax concessions are comparatively more attractive. This advantage, however, is difficult to maintain, for most underdeveloped countries are in competition for foreign capital, which makes them compete, in turn, with respect to tax concessions offered. As a result, the relatively underdeveloped countries like Panamá are placed in a position in which the more incentives they offer, the more they have to offer. At the same time, a process of increasing the liberality of incentives deprives all underdeveloped countries of a fair return from international investment, without at the same time increasing the total flow of investment. In other words, in attempting to outbid each other in tax concessions, underdeveloped countries only succeed in cutting their own collective throats.

It is for the foregoing reasons that there is a consensus of informed opinion to the effect that tax incentives should be used cautiously and prudently. It is recognized that tax incentives have a legitimate place in an over-all developmental program for the purpose of inducing resources into more desired uses and impeding their employment in less desired areas. There is justification to use fiscal policy instruments for the purpose of helping particular firms to become established and grow. Historical experience with tax incentives suggests, however, that in the absence of caution and restraint, they can result in substantial revenue losses without appreciable positive effects. The case for fiscal subsidies rests on selective and short-run assistance.

Specific Suggestions for a New Tax Incentive Law [5]

1) *Length of Contracts.* Benefits should be granted until most firms (but not all) be-

[5] In addition to these suggestions, it would be helpful to refer to a definitive study of tax concessions by K. E. Lachmann, *Industrial Promotion Laws in Central America,* United Nations, April 19, 1960.

come efficient and profitable. This period should not be less than five years or more than ten, for if it exceeds the latter the benefits are not needed by most firms and the loss of government revenues becomes excessive. In selecting between a five- or ten-year period, it is probably more prudent to grant each firm an exemption for five years rather than to have a ten-year maximum and to try to exercise discretion by granting some firms contractual periods of less than the maximum.

2) *Activities Qualifying for Concessions.* The objectives to be sought under an incentive law are additional investment and employment. Therefore, it matters little whether these objectives are accomplished by the inception of a new firm or the expansion of an old one, the production of a new product or additional output of something already produced, the development of a new industry or the expansion of an existing one. Accordingly, it is suggested that a new incentive law should not be circumscribed by provisions that limit the benefits to either new products, new firms, or new industries. It is also a mistake to try to make refined distinctions as to the degree of usefulness of particular firms, and to tailor the tax concession to each firm. Rather, all the benefits should be available to any investor who provides a reasonable assurance that additional production will be forthcoming.

It is recognized that this policy would create a competitive unneutrality in those instances in which one firm in an industry would be given benefits on the basis of intended expansion, while its competitors would be denied benefits because they did not have similar intentions. But the only alternative to this is more undesirable; that is, to grant benefits to the whole of an industry, merely because of the inception of one new firm. This would result in an undue loss of revenue and would reward firms that planned no expansion in output, or alternatively, it would mean that a new firm would have to be denied the benefits if the whole of the industry is not to be benefited.

Moreover, it should be realized that a policy of restricting the benefits to investors who have plans for additional production is not to be identified with a policy of granting exclusive contracts, for any firm in an industry would be eligible for benefits providing it is willing to undertake a *quid pro quo* for the benefits received. In this respect, the policy proposed does not differ from that followed in the 1950 and 1957 incentive laws in Panamá.

3) *Types of Fiscal Benefits.* In the total variety of fiscal incentives that may be offered, there are some grounds for making a distinction among them in terms of relative desirability. Thus, protective tariffs against foreign competition are relatively undesirable for three reasons: 1) the amount of the subsidy is never fully known; 2) there is a tendency for the protection to become permanent; and 3) Panamá's tariff wall is already high on a wide number of manufactured products.

It is also undesirable to grant exemptions of those taxes that are relatively unimportant as incentives, such as the real property tax, stamp taxes, internal excises, registry fees, and municipal taxes, or those that are earmarked for a special purpose, like social security taxes. Among the taxes used in Panamá, there remain only the income tax and customs duties that can be scored as relatively favorable for exemption purposes.

The income tax is a perverse subsidy in the sense that it provides little relief when firms need it the most, that is, the first few years in which they are in operation. In fact, an income tax exemption is inversely related to need, for it only subsidizes firms that are profitable. Nevertheless, Panamá should probably use an income tax exemption if for no other reason than it is necessary for competitive reasons and it has a somewhat irrational appeal to businessmen. However, probably more important than the income tax exemption itself are provisions for the carryover of losses and accelerated depreciation.

The principal problem with respect to the exemption of customs duties is that it can be extended to include non-essential items, with the result that the loss of revenue can become excessive. Panamá is currently suffering from this problem, for in 1961 exempted duties represented 29 per cent of total import duties and fees. The exemption of customs duties should be reserved for capital goods, raw materials, and semi-manufactures, while construction materials, transport vehicles, and office machinery and equipment should be denied exemption.

4) *Administrative Discretion Versus the Use of Rigid Criteria.* One of the more unpleasant features of a tax incentive law is the need to assess the applicants and reach a decision as to their eligibility for the benefits. This is necessary because some firms must be denied the benefits because their contributions to the economy are unlikely to warrant the granting of exemptions. The problem is rendered more difficult because most firms exaggerate their intended investment, employment, and output at the time of filing their applications.

When this problem of deciding eligibility is entirely a matter of administrative discretion, there is undoubtedly a tendency for the vast majority of applicants to be given the benefits. In the past two years in Panamá, there are only four instances in which contracts were denied. Furthermore, when there is latitude in the extent of the benefits that may be granted, it is an open invitation to political pressures and favoritism. The whole procedure also becomes exceedingly profitable for lawyers.

When technicians view these excrescences of an incentive program, they are tempted to evolve rigid semi-automatic provisions in terms of necessary employment, investment, or value-added that will exclude the unworthy automatically and without the exercise of administrative discretion. These attempts are unlikely to be successful. Because of the tremendous variety of activities covered by an incentive program, it is improbable that any single criterion or even group of criteria would prove satisfactory to exclude those who should be ineligible. In addition, there is the problem that the data submitted by the applicants are often unreliable.

This does not mean, however, that nothing can be done to limit the degree of administrative discretion. The legislation should set out in detail the considerations and standards that should guide administrative decisions. Each application should also be given a careful economic and technical analysis. To limit the area of discretion, each beneficiary may be given the same concessions. But the most important safeguard of all is to have a development law that does not provide excessive benefits.

5) *The Use of a "Positive" Approach.* A general characteristic of promotional efforts in Latin America is to be schizophrenic with respect to businessmen in general and foreign investors in particular. Incentives are offered, but gingerly and with a fear of being exploited. This apprehension may take the form of requiring a certain percentage of the labor force to be composed of domestic labor or of limiting the profits that may be earned. Often there is justification in equity for these restrictions, but it is, nevertheless, psychologically undesirable to clutter a development law with controls of various types. A more desirable approach is to be cautious with respect to the incentives offered rather than to be generous with the one hand and restrictive with the other.

6) *A General Development Law or a Tax Incentive Law?* Another tendency among Latin American countries is to include special non-tax benefits and general government measures in aid of industry within the scope of a tax incentive law. This procedure has a tendency to weaken the incentive laws by distraction, without at the same time providing an over-all program for development.

FOREIGN BASE COMPANIES AND TAX-HAVEN SUBSIDIARIES

Despite their apparent number and importance, there is a tremendous void of ignorance concerning the operation of foreign base companies in Panamá. No one has undertaken a study to determine the number of these companies, the nature of their operations, and the extent of their contributions to the economy. And because they are rather intangible and ethereal, and their fiscal respectability is somewhat under a cloud, the undertaking of research on foreign base companies is somewhat like inquiring into the "numbers" racket. As soon as a person is asked questions concerning base companies, he is inclined to become guarded in his answers as if he is being interviewed about an illegal business activity.

In the most part, the information on foreign base companies has been obtained by interviewing several persons who are directly involved in their operations. This is not the most objective source of information, but under the circumstances there was no alternative, since most of the firms are neither taxed nor regulated. However, despite this method of inquiry, there was often a consensus in the information obtained, which lends some dependability to the data.

At the outset it is necessary to distinguish between the whole gamut of corporations that avoid the application of the Panamanian income tax in some way or another and base companies as such. A figure of 10,000 "paper" companies is often mentioned in Panamá, but this number includes the total of tax-exempt legal entities. This total includes corporations formed for the purpose of creating a family trust, those organized for a single transaction, and those formed for a particular purpose, such as avoidance of inheritance taxes. It also includes shipping lines operating under the Panamanian flag and investment companies. On the other hand, if attention is centered merely on base companies as such, that is, companies organized in Panamá for the purpose of negotiating tax-free sales in the foreign market and carrying no inventory, the total number is not known but it is probably considerably less than 10,000.

A specific illustration may make the characteristics of a tax-haven subsidiary more understandable. The Joy Manufacturing Company is a United States firm specializing in the manufacture of mining machinery. This firm has manufacturing subsidiaries in six foreign countries, licensees in eight, and distributors in some seventy others. Joy International S.A., a Panamá corporation that pays no U.S. income tax until it remits dividends, is responsible for managing all subsidiaries for a fee, for the exports of all Joy products from foreign and domestic sources, and for financing overseas companies. This Panamanian firm is also exempt under the Panamanian income tax.[6]

Base companies may operate in three different ways. In the first instance, a foreign firm may establish an office in Panamá merely for the purpose of negotiating foreign sales. A few of these have rather large operations, in one case amounting to an office staff of about one hundred persons, but most firms merely rent a small office and employ a resident manager and a secretary. A second method of operating is through agents, each of whom specializes in handling the sales accounts of several base companies. Once again, the largest of these agents employs about one hundred persons, but the others are much smaller. These two types of "operating" companies—foreign firms with their own sales offices and agents—probably total from 150 to 200 firms. Finally, many base companies are represented through lawyers, and since these firms are more invisible, little is known about their number. About all that can be said is that approximately fifteen law firms derive much of their business from representing base companies. These law firms, in effect, undertake the same functions as agents.

The basic incentive for base companies to operate in Panamá, of course, is to avoid tax liabilities in their own countries. Although there appears to be a sprinkling of base companies in Panamá from most major countries of the world, the greater number are from the United States. These firms are primarily motivated by the provisions of the U.S. Internal Revenue Code that allow a

deferral of tax liabilities until earnings are repatriated. Although the foreign income provisions of the United States Revenue Act of 1962 attempted to curb the most significant areas of tax abuse and inequality in the use of foreign subsidiaries, there appear to be sufficient exemptions in the legislation so that most base companies operating in Panamá will not be affected.

On their part, the base companies are also interested in operating in a country where the atmosphere is "congenial," and where they are given the additional incentive of low or non-existent taxes. This gives them the best of both worlds: freedom of taxation both at home and abroad. Panamá was obliging in this respect, for the original Panamanian income tax law of 1941 exempted income derived from outside the Republic. In other words, Panamá adopted the territorial principle of taxing income on the basis of the source of the income rather than on the residence of the taxpayer. Thus, base companies, in order to be exempt from the Panamanian income tax, merely had to "arrange" their sales in such a way that their income was construed to arise outside of Panamá. But at times, these companies were harassed by the income tax administration on technical details. As a result, Law No. 26 of September, 1957, was passed to remove these difficulties. With this law, Panamá overtly and directly beckoned the base companies, some claim with the idea in mind of becoming the Switzerland of Latin America. And apparently this law has had some effect, for it is reported that there has been a rising tide of new incorporations since 1957.

The competition for base company business is keen. Besides such well-known tax-havens as Switzerland and Liberia in other hemispheres, Panamá faces competition closer at home from Nassau, Curaçao, Venezuela, Uruguay, Costa Rica, and a host of other countries. Panamá's success in attracting base companies is probably due more to such factors as location, relative political stability, and the advantages that the monetary and banking system have to offer, for

6 First National City Bank, *Monthly Letter,* June, 1962, pp. 67-68.

all of the countries anxious to obtain this type of business offer tax concessions.

In assessing the deliberate policy of encouraging base companies in Panamá, one can take an altruistic and social point of view in the context of the common good of all nations, or a myopic and pragmatic view of what is good for Panamá is good for Panamanians. Viewing the policy from an international perspective, Panamá is just one country among many in the business of providing a tax-haven for foreign firms. Providing these havens probably has no effect on the over-all total of foreign investment in underdeveloped countries, and therefore contributes nothing to the underdeveloped world at large. And it is certainly not conducive to a policy of harmony and cooperation among underdeveloped countries. Instead, these countries are pitted against each other, each offering more concessions to obtain the firms, but all receiving less benefits in the aggregate because of the competition.

Even from the selfish point of view of the tax-haven countries, a policy of attracting base companies is not the type of endeavor that represents the real substance of economic development. Unlike a policy of tax incentives to attract industry, base companies do not develop the natural resources of a country or result directly in appreciable amounts of employment or investment. Encouraging base companies is to be identified with a policy of attempting to achieve development the easy way and without sacrifice. As such, it is unlikely to have an important effect on development. There is not room for many Switzerlands in the world.

Nevertheless, the benefits to Panamá of encouraging base companies are not insignificant when a rough inventory is made. It is estimated that the organization process alone of a base company costs approximately B/500 for various taxes, fees, and legal services. In addition, there is an annual business license fee of B/100 paid by each base company operating an office. Companies actively operating in Panamá are estimated to employ approximately 4,000 persons. Several of the larger office buildings have been erected primarily to provide office space for the base companies. Possibly the most important advantages are to be found in the deposits of the banking system, where foreign deposits represent approximately 30 per cent of total deposits. Even though the base companies are not inclined to invest directly in Panamá, these deposits represent the means by which commercial banks can make loans, and can do so with a multiplier effect. And finally, mention should be made of "corporate tourism." Base companies bring permanent "tourists" in the form of resident managers, and an intermittent stream of other short-run tourists in the form of visiting businessmen. An attempt has been made to estimate the total of all these benefits and it appears to be about 3 per cent of the national income. This is not a spectacular contribution, but it is also not one to be dismissed cavalierly in a country with a high rate of unemployment.

Panamá's policy with respect to base companies should be one in which the benefits derived should be viewed in terms of a short-run, uncertain, and marginal advantage. It should be recognized that this type of business activity does not constitute the real substance of economic development. It should be realized, further, that base companies represent an unstable element, as their continued existence depends essentially on the tax policies of foreign governments.

Meanwhile, in the short run, Panamá could attempt to maximize the benefits to be derived from base companies. This could be accomplished in two ways. First, all "operating" base companies must pay an annual business license tax. The chapter on Other Indirect Taxes proposes a way in which this tax may be improved. Second, the schedule of fees for incorporating a business may be revised. Neither of these adjustments should be so severe as to cause a flight of the firms to more congenial climates.

At the present time, the incorporation fee is based on declared capital and has four rates. The fee is B/10 for firms with a de-

TABLE 11.3

Current and Proposed Incorporation Fees

Declared Capital (Balboas)	Current Tax (Balboas)	Current Effective Rates (Per Cent)	Proposed Tax (Balboas)	Proposed Effective Rates (Per Cent)
5,000	10	.2	10	.2
10,000	10	.1	10	.1
15,000	14	.090	20	.13
20,000	17	.085	30	.15
25,000	21	.084	40	.16
50,000	40	.080	90	.18
75,000	59	.079	140	.19
100,000	77	.077	200	.20
250,000	152	.061	325	.13
500,000	277	.055	800	.16
750,000	402	.054	1,075	.14
1,000,000	527	.053	2,000	.20
2,000,000	627	.031	2,250	.11

clared capital of less than B/10,000; B/75 for each additional B/1000 from B/10,000 to B/100,000; B/50 for each additional B/1000 from B/100,000 to B/1,000,000; and B/10 for each B/1000 over B/1,000,000. As shown in Table 11.3, the result of these declining rates is not only very modest fees, but also very striking regressivity when the tax is related to declared capital. Table 11.3 also demonstrates that the system of fees could be strengthened and rationalized by retaining the basic fee of B/10 for firms with a declared capital of less than B/10,000, but by changing the remaining fees as follows: B/2.00 for each additional B/1000 from B/10,000 to B/100,000; B/1.50 for each additional B/1000 from B/100,000 to B/1,-000,000; and B/.25 for each B/1000 over B/1,000,000.

SUMMARY OF RECOMMENDATIONS

1) The income tax concession granted to firms under the 1950 law should be restricted in one of two ways: (a) by giving each firm a maximum exemption of fifteen years; or (b) by taxing the dividends of all corporations at the personal income tax level.

2) A new tax incentive law should be enacted with the following basic features: (a) a maximum period for contracts of five to ten years; (b) the provision of income tax and customs duty exemption; and (c) only limited and short-run tariff protection against foreign competition.

3) The incorporation fees should be revised according to the schedule shown in the text.

CHAPTER 12

The Colón Free Zone

INTRODUCTION

THE COLÓN FREE ZONE was initiated by Decree Law No. 18 of June 17, 1948, for the purpose of encouraging the development in Panamá of a warehousing and distribution center for the transshipment of goods. The objective was to develop "entrepôt" trade—or the movement of goods *through* rather than originating in Panamá. The city of Colón, situated at the Atlantic entrance to the Panamá Canal offered an ideal location for this customs-free zone, for the city is literally situated at the crossroads of the world. From a locational point of view, the only shortcoming is that several firms currently operating in the zone receive and ship all of their goods by air, and the airport is forty miles from Colón. In the future, another customs-free zone situated at the airport may be desirable.

The idea of a warehousing and distribution center in Panamá is appealing, for it offers several conspicuous advantages to manufacturers in the United States and Europe with foreign sales in Latin America. By maintaining inventories physically closer to distributors, it is possible to process orders in less time and at a lower cost than if the orders were filled directly by the manufacturers. In turn, this means that customers in Latin America may carry lower inventories and make more efficient use of their capital. In

other words, a distribution center moves the manufacturer and his product closer to the market so that it can be served better. And to make the idea even more attractive, Panamá offered several fiscal incentives for participating firms.

The development of the Free Zone lagged from 1948 to 1953, with only a handful of firms taking advantage of the legislation. During this period, the zone was not centralized at one site, and particular firms could avail themselves of the provisions of the law only by establishing *zonitas,* or little free zones in their own buildings situated in the city of Colón. Each one of these *zonitas,* in effect, was a bonded warehouse, operated under customs surveillance. When the present Free Zone area was opened in 1953, all the *zonitas* were required to move to the centralized location. Thus, the actual history of the Colón Free Zone as a physically enclosed area dates from 1953.

The Colón Free Zone functions as an autonomous government agency, administered by a manager operating under the direction of a five-member board of directors. Three of the directors are appointed by the President with approval of the Cabinet and the National Assembly; a fourth member is appointed by the President from a slate of three candidates proposed by the Panamá City Chamber of Commerce, Industry, and Agriculture; while the last member is appointed by the President from a slate of three candidates recommended by the Colón Chamber of Commerce. The Board of Directors is responsible for the general operation of the Free Zone, and in particular must approve each expenditure in excess of B/5000.

Since its inception, the Free Zone has received grants in both land and money from the national government. The land includes the present site of the Free Zone, an area of thirty-nine acres, and an additional seven acres located outside of the zone known as the Fort De Lesseps area. The latter is a parcel of residential property that was transferred from the Panamá Canal Company to the national government, which, in turn, gave it to the Free Zone. At the present time, the Fort De Lesseps property is valuable to the zone only as a source of rental income, but it has considerable potential value as the land area could be enlarged by filling from its present size of seven acres to about 160 acres.

Monetary grants from the national government include two of B/150,000, the proceeds of a bond issue of B/500,000 for which the national government pays both the principal and the interest, and ten annual grants of B/100,000. These annual grants were due to expire in 1962. Thus, the total of monetary grants received as of the end of 1962 was B/1,800,000.

According to the legislation establishing the Free Zone, one-half of the annual profits was to accumulate indefinitely as a reserve fund, while the other one-half was to be paid regularly to the national government. These profits have never been shared, however, and have been used in their totality instead by the Free Zone for re-investment purposes. Through the re-investment of profits and national government grants, a public facility with a value of approximately B/8 million had been developed in the Free Zone by 1962. The comparable total for private investment in buildings and equipment is estimated by the Free Zone authorities to be B/3 million as of the end of 1962.

There are approximately 1,400 employees of private firms in the Free Zone, about 10 per cent of this number being casual or part-time workers. An additional one hundred employees work for the Free Zone authority. The total of salaries paid by Free Zone firms in 1961 was B/2,096,470, or an average of about B/1500 per worker. There is no way to calculate the indirect jobs created by the Free Zone, but these are probably considerable in such activities as dock workers and in transportation services. Many Panamanian business firms have also profited from the Free Zone, such as banks, law firms, and insurance companies. Free Zone firms in 1961 spent B/3.5 million in the Republic of Panamá for materials, merchandise, and supplies.

Firms desiring to operate in the Free Zone are required to enter into a contractual arrangement for either the rental of land on which they may construct a building, or for the rental of land and buildings provided by the Free Zone. Thus, in no case may firms own the land. The contracts for the use of land and buildings vary in length from one to twenty years, with the rental rates declining with the duration of the contract. Only the larger firms enter contracts for the maximum period of twenty years. Most firms from the United States prefer to rent buildings rather than construct their own, because they are disinclined to build on rented land, and they also prefer to operate under circumstances in which they are able to terminate operations quickly. Some firms also maintain that it is cheaper to rent than to build. Out of forty-five buildings in the Free Zone in November, 1962, thirty are owned by the zone and fifteen are privately owned.

The level of rents is established by the Board of Directors. Initially, the rent was B/0.10 per month per square meter for land, and B/0.65 per month per square meter for warehouses. In 1961, the rent for the land was increased to B/0.15 per month per square meter, and the rent for warehouses was changed to a sliding scale, decreasing with the size of the storage space and the length of the contract. For example, for 200 meters, the rent per month varies from

B/0.748 for a one-year contract to B/0.667 for a twenty-year contract; while for 1,500 meters, the rent per month varies from B/0.713 for a one-year contract to B/0.633 for twenty years.

A generous arrangement exists with respect to the extension of contracts. If a firm enters into a five-year contract, and then at the end of this period extends the contract for another five years, it is given the benefit of a reduced rate on the second five years as if the original contract were for ten years. Under these circumstances, there is very little inducement for firms to enter into long contracts. The Free Zone also guarantees not to raise the rent during the period of a contract.

All original service installations are undertaken by the Free Zone, such as water, sewers, and streets, but the tenants are required to pay for water supply, light, and power. All maintenance expenses of the rented buildings are also assumed by the Free Zone, including the provision of eight guards for patrolling the zone.

It has been a deliberate policy on the part of the Free Zone to offer warehousing facilities below the market cost as an incentive to prospective firms. This is evident in the statement published in 1954:

> In addition to the above, the rates charged by the public warehouse of the Colón Free Zone are so low, in comparison with the charges made by other firms engaged in the storage business, that even in the cases where only storage is required without the need of the other advantages, the use of the public warehouse of the Colón Free Zone is convenient and highly recommended.[1]

An attempt has been made to calculate the total cost of providing a Free Zone warehouse, including the cost of the land, buildings, capital, streets, water and sewage installations, administration, repairs, and maintenance. This calculation shows that the present level of rent for a warehouse leased for twenty years results in a net yield to the

Free Zone of only .96 per cent annually on the total cost of supplying the warehouse. It has also been determined that the cost of storage facilities in Panamá on the private market for short-run periods is approximately B/2.00 per square meter per month as compared to a cost in the Free Zone of about B/0.75.

TYPES OF FIRMS AND FREE ZONE ACTIVITIES

Firms wishing to avail themselves of Free Zone provisions may do so in three ways. First, they may establish a warehousing or processing operation for the handling of their own goods. Second, a firm may utilize the services of a warehousing firm, which will receive, store, re-package, and re-ship goods as an agent of a manufacturer. And finally, a firm may utilize facilities provided by the Free Zone itself in the form of a public warehouse.

Because there is tremendous variation in the activity of Free Zone firms, and precise information on each firm is not available, it is difficult to classify the firms in order to present a general picture of Free Zone operations. A directory issued in November, 1962, lists ninety-five operating firms, fifty-nine of which appear to operate a warehouse for the handling of their own goods, thirty-four appear to act as agents, while the remaining two firms are a commercial bank and a telegraph office. The thirty-four agents, in turn, are shown to represent two hundred and thirty firms.

It appears likely that the ninety-five operating firms have come from two sources. Probably the greater number are either Panamanian wholesalers or retailers that established operations in the zone. The wholesalers were representatives of foreign firms in Panamá and established operations in the Free Zone to continue their service of the Panamanian market, and in some cases, to develop foreign sales. About eight or ten of the Free Zone firms appear to be Pana-

[1] The Colón Free Zone, Regulations and Tariffs, 1954, pp. 9–10.

manian retailers that operate principally for the purpose of supplying their own retail outlets. The remaining firms, perhaps about one-third of the total number, are foreign manufacturers that were attracted by the Free Zone incentives to establish a genuine entrepôt trade. It is unfortunate to generalize in this manner, but there is no alternative in the absence of a careful study of each firm.

Among the total number of Free Zone firms are wide variations in activities and size. Some firms derive all of their income from foreign sales, others all of their income from the domestic market, while most have a combination of both foreign and domestic sales. Some agents represent only two or three foreign manufacturers and others as many as fifteen. Some firms combine several operations; they are engaged in entrepôt activity, but also act as a "paper company" for the negotiation of sales so that income arises in Panamá but there is no physical receipt of goods. A few firms have rather substantial work forces, but others employ no one. There are also a few businesses supplying other Free Zone firms, and some specializing in ship chandlery and sales to the Canal Zone.

About ten of the Free Zone firms are subsidiaries of large United States manufacturers. These are owned by "blue-chip" industrial concerns, as is evident from such names as the Coca Cola Export Corporation, Firestone International Co., Colgate-Palmolive (W.I.) Inc., Goodyear Western Hemisphere Corporation, Gillette Export Corporation, Pfizer Corporation, and Squibb Mathieson International. About fifty other United States manufacturers are represented through agents. These sixty United States firms, either operating a Free Zone firm in their own right or working through agents, represent the real substance of entrepôt trade. Most of the agents on the other hand, are Panamanian firms. There is also a sprinkling of English, Swiss, Japanese, Mexican, and German firms, represented principally through agents. Drug companies predominate among the larger operations because their products are small, light, and relatively high in value—the characteristics most favorable for entrepôt trade.

The public warehouse is used by from thirty to forty firms. About three-fourths of the goods entering the public warehouse is reported to be re-exported to foreign countries. But the warehouse is also used by Panamanian retailers and wholesalers for the purpose of deferring customs duties on goods destined for the domestic market, as there are no regulations prohibiting this practice.

The regulations promulgated for the Free Zone anticipated several types of activities. In addition to warehousing, re-packing, and transshipment, it was believed that some firms would undertake manufacturing, bottling, assembling, refining, and the transforming of goods. In the course of time, however, only the drug firms (and not all of these) have undertaken a re-packaging process that involves more than the breaking-up of shipments. Therefore, the total amount of value added to the goods passing through the Free Zone, except in the case of a few drug firms, is probably minimal.

Law Decree No. 2 of 1957 has accorded Free Zone firms full entitlements under the current general development law of Panamá (Law No. 25 of February 7, 1957). Despite this, however, manufacturing firms serving the Panamanian market have not located in the zone, apparently because of the cost involved in shipping their products from Colón to Panamá City, the consumption center of Panamá. And no manufacturing firms have been attracted to the Free Zone for the export of their products to foreign countries despite the availability of income tax exemption on income attributable to foreign sales. In the future, there is unlikely to be any manufacturing per se in the zone, but additional firms are likely to undertake packaging, labeling, and additional manual operations in general.

The Free Zone regulations provide for the release of merchandise under four circumstances: 1) sales to official agencies of the United States government established in the Canal Zone; 2) sales to vessels transiting the Panamá Canal that are destined for foreign ports, or that are navigating between the Republic and foreign ports; 3) exports to foreign countries by maritime or air transportation; and 4) the introduction of goods into the Republic provided that a wholesale transaction is involved. Table 12.1 shows that approximately 80 per cent of total exports by value within recent years has been destined to foreign markets, with the remaining 20 per cent released to the Canal Zone, ships in transit, and to the domestic market. The percentage of exports by value destined to the Panamanian market has averaged about 12 per cent within recent years, and was as high as 21 per cent in 1957.

There is no question that the basic rationale for a duty-free zone is to promote the transshipment of goods rather than to provide a tax-haven for retailers and wholesalers who are introducing goods into the domestic market. The development of the latter activity is undesirable for two reasons: 1) it provides a deferral of customs duties and a loss of other tax revenues without an adequate compensation in terms of higher levels of employment and investment; and 2) whenever a bonded warehouse is established for the introduction of goods into a country, it is an open invitation to smuggling activities. At the same time, it is difficult in practice to prevent a genuine entrepôt firm from selling a part of its products in the domestic market. What emerges as a policy guideline, therefore, is that Free Zone regulations should not prohibit sales to the domestic market, but there should be a conscious effort to discourage wholesalers, jobbers, or retailers that are engaged principally in supplying the domestic market. This policy could be implemented by requiring each Free Zone firm to sell a certain percentage, say 60 per cent, of its imports into the zone to foreign countries. If the Board of Directors does not have the authority to establish this requirement, it could be obtained through legislation.

The use of the Colón Free Zone by wholesalers supplying the Panamanian market, or by Panamanian retailers supplying themselves, has been a rather general practice since the inception of the zone, and it is evident from Table 12.1 that it still persists despite spasmodic efforts of control. In the early history of the Free Zone, the administrative authorities actually encouraged activities related to the domestic market. In a brochure published by the Free Zone in 1954, there is the following statement:

Inasmuch as all merchandise upon entering the Free Zone will not be required to pay corresponding import duties, it will be possible for local merchants to order large quantities of goods, which eventually will be used in their local business transactions, even when the customs tariffs on these goods are in the high bracket. The Colón Free Zone will accept the entrance of this merchandise into its public warehouse and allow partial withdrawals instead of on the total shipment. In this manner it will not be necessary to disburse a large amount of capital import duties at one time, and this will also enable the merchant to "turn over" his capital in a more productive way.[2]

It is irregular, indeed, to have an agency of the national government offer to assist firms in avoiding customs duties. According to present administrators of the zone, this policy was based on sheer expediency. In the early history of the zone, it is explained, any kind of business was needed to insure that the area would become an operating reality.

But seven years later, in 1961, the Free Zone still appears to be operating under conditions of expediency. Table 12.2 shows a classification of each firm's sales based on its percentage of foreign sales to total sales. In developing this table, sales to ships and to the Canal Zone were construed as domestic sales. The evidence shows that sixty-seven firms, or over one-half of all the firms, had less than 50 per cent of their sales destined to the foreign market in 1961, while thirty-eight firms, or about 30 per cent of all the firms, had less than 10 per cent foreign sales. Thus, about one-third of the firms were using the zone as a tax haven in a very literal sense.

[2] *The Colón Free Zone, Regulations and Tariffs*, 1954, p. 9.

TABLE 12.1

Commercial Activity in the Colón Free Zone, 1953 to 1962

Year	Imports into the Free Zone (Millions)	Exports to Panamá		Exports to Foreign Countries		Exports to the Canal Zone		Exports to Ships in Transit		Total Exports from the Free Zone (Millions)
		Value (Millions)	Percentage of Total Exports	Value (Millions)	Percentage of Total Exports	Value (Millions)	Percentage of Total Exports	Value (Millions)	Percentage of Total Exports	
1953		B/ 1.3	16.0	B/ 6.2	76.5	B/ .3	3.7	B/ .3	3.7	B/ 8.1
1954		3.3	9.3	30.3	85.1	1.0	2.8	1.0	2.8	35.6
1955		3.6	12.2	23.5	79.9	1.5	5.1	.8	2.7	29.4
1956	B /28.9	5.2	14.6	27.6	77.7	1.9	5.4	.9	2.5	35.5
1957	28.2	7.4	21.0	24.8	70.5	1.8	5.1	1.3	3.7	35.2
1958	33.0	7.5	17.3	32.5	74.9	1.8	4.1	1.6	3.7	43.4
1959	46.0	8.0	12.7	50.6	80.4	2.3	3.7	1.9	3.0	62.9
1960	54.7	9.4	12.3	62.8	81.8	2.4	3.1	2.2	2.9	76.7
1961	62.6	11.1	11.8	77.2	82.4	2.4	2.6	3.0	3.2	93.7
1962[1]	47.0	9.5	13.3	56.6	79.5	1.6	2.2	3.5	4.9	71.2

[1] January to August, 1962.   *Source:* Adapted from information provided by the Colón Free Zone.

TABLE 12.2

Free Zone Firms Classified by Percentage of Foreign Sales to Total Sales in 1961

Percentage of Foreign Sales to Total Sales by Value of Sales[1]	Number of Firms
90–100	21
80– 90	18
70– 80	6
60– 70	4
50– 60	7
40– 50	4
30– 40	9
20– 30	9
10– 20	7
0– 10	38
TOTAL	123[2]

[1] Sales to ships in transit and to the Canal Zone are considered as domestic sales.
[2] This total includes firms using the public warehouse, agents, and those handling goods on their own account.

Another undesirable development is the use of the Free Zone by firms operating principally for the purpose of servicing or supplying other firms in the zone. For example, there are four firms specializing in the sale of stationery and office equipment to other Free Zone firms. There is also one firm that provides transportation services, and another that sells insurance. Unless these firms are able to fulfill a requirement that most of their sales are destined to the foreign market, they should be denied the privileges accorded by the Free Zone legislation.

The Board of Directors has been aware of the undesirability of having firms in the Free Zone that are primarily supplying their own Panamanian retail operations. The Board has passed a resolution stating that firms with less than 60 per cent of their sales arising from foreign exports are not fulfilling the objectives of the zone, and could be forced to leave the area. There is also an article in the Free Zone regulations requiring a minimum employment by each firm of three persons. Moreover, to remove a firm which is not fulfilling the objectives of the zone, it is maintained by the Free Zone authorities that it is only necessary for the Board of Directors to pass a resolution in favor of terminating a contract. Despite these control devices, however, only one firm has been refused a renewal of its contract, and the number of firms currently using the Free Zone merely for storage purposes prompted one manager of a genuine entrepôt firm to complain that "he was surrounded by locked warehouses."

FISCAL INCENTIVES

There are four different types of fiscal advantages of operating in the Free Zone, and in the aggregate they constitute a substantial incentive. They include freedom from customs duties and consular fees, relatively low income tax rates, exemption from the national government property tax, and freedom from municipal license fees, except those on vehicles.

All goods may be introduced into the Free Zone without payment of customs duties or consular fees. Goods re-exported to foreign countries or to ships in transit continue to be exempt from import taxes, while goods released to the Panamanian market bear customs duties when they leave the Free Zone. Goods re-exported to the Canal Zone are free of duty only if they originate in the United States.

Two irregularities exist with respect to the application and administration of the customs exemption. The first is that the exemption has been extended to include all machinery, equipment, and supplies used by Free Zone firms. This appears to be an unnecessary incentive, and in addition, it provokes an evasion problem, since many of the goods introduced for use in the zone can also be used in home consumption.

Secondly, it is widely believed that there is considerable smuggling of duty-free goods into the Panamanian market. No definitive proof exists of the extent of smuggling, but certainly all the circumstances exist to encourage the activity. The Free Zone itself, although situated adjacent to the sea, has no port facilities of its own, with the result that all incoming and outgoing maritime shipments must be transported by truck between the zone and Cristóbal in the Canal Zone. Similarly, all air shipments must be transported by truck about forty miles. The existence of some Free Zone firms supplying their own retail outlets in Panamá City is also an occasion for smuggling. In the movement of these goods, hundreds of trucks and private passenger vehicles pass through the Free Zone gates each day, many of them with only a casual inspection. These opportunities for smuggling also may be supplemented by more unorthodox methods. For example, it is reported that small ships depart ostensibly for foreign ports, but land their cargoes instead on Panamanian beaches.

As would be expected, the Free Zone authorities are prone to minimize the extent of smuggling, and to maintain that they cannot be responsible for what happens after goods leave the Free Zone. This is a cavalier and short-sighted attitude. The Free Zone authorities cannot escape the responsibility for smuggling activities, since the problem would not exist if the zone was not in operation, and smuggling can be controlled best at its source. Also, the respectability and the public support of the Free Zone depend on minimizing the smuggling problem. Therefore, every effort should be made by the Free Zone administration to control the movement of contraband goods.

The simplest and most effective means of dealing with the smuggling problem is to weed out the culprits. There is no question that the vast majority of Free Zone firms operate a respectable business. There is also no question that evidence could be obtained on the illegitimate operations of the few firms involved in smuggling if a serious attempt were made to do so.

The income tax treatment of Free Zone firms is quite complicated, for it varies by the type of business activity and has been subject to change over time. First, considering those firms that actually take ownership possession of goods rather than those that act as agents, income tax liabilities were based originally on the 1946 income tax rate schedule. This schedule was not advantageous until income tax rates were raised in 1953 for all Panamanian individuals and firms, but the firms in the Free Zone continued to be taxed under 1946 rates.

With this difference in income tax burdens between Panamanian firms and those operating in the Free Zone, a problem of income tax evasion arose on the part of those Free

Zone firms that were supplying affiliated operations in Panamá. One Free Zone firm, for example, operated a food supermarket in Colón, and exaggerated the prices charged the retail store in order to maximize its Free Zone profits and minimize its tax liabilities. This practice became so prevalent that the Panamanian government in 1954 issued a decree which provided that all firms having an affiliated operation in Panamá would be subject to the 1953 income tax rates on all of their profits, whether these were attributable to Free Zone or other operations.[3] But this decree did not affect other Free Zone firms. These continued to be taxed on the basis of 1946 income tax rates provided that the goods were sold to non-affiliated Panamanian firms, the Canal Zone, ships in transit, or to foreign countries.

An important change in the method of taxing firms in the Free Zone was initiated on January 1, 1958, when a distinction was made between domestic sales and goods re-exported to foreign countries. On the income from sales made to the Panamanian market, the Canal Zone, and ships in transit, the applicable income tax rates were those adopted in 1953 instead of the 1946 schedule. The income arising from the re-export of goods to foreign countries was also made subject to the 1953 rates, but a discount of 90 per cent of the tax was permitted. Firms with both domestic and foreign sales were required to prorate their earnings for income tax purposes. This proration is at best difficult to accomplish, and for those with weak compliance habits it provides an easy opportunity for the evasion of taxes.

The change in income tax treatment based on the distinction between domestic and foreign sales had sharply different effects on Free Zone firms, depending on whether they sold to the Panamanian market or re-exported their goods to foreign countries. As shown in Table 12.3, the effect of the 1958 change was to increase the tax liability on income attributable to domestic sales by from 50 to 100 per cent, depending on the level of

taxable income (compare columns 1 and 2 of Table 12.3). But quite the contrary was the result for the income tax liability on income attributable to foreign sales, which was reduced by at least 80 per cent (compare columns 1 and 3 of Table 12.3).

The liberalization of the income tax liabilities for firms deriving a large part of their income from the re-export of goods was a tremendous bonanza for some companies. Since these firms paid their anticipated 1958 income taxes before their income tax liabilities were reduced, they received very substantial credits on their 1958 tax liabilities. These credits have been carried forward by the government since 1958 rather than being refunded to the firms, and the credits have been so substantial in some cases that by 1962 some firms are still paying their tax liabilities from a tax credit earned in 1958. In other words, for some firms the tax reduction in 1958 was so generous that it was sufficient to satisfy the tax liabilities accruing in four subsequent years.

It should be noted, also, that these firms under discussion—those that actually take ownership possession of goods—are not subject to the increases in income tax liabilities experienced by other Panamanian firms. Thus, despite the fact that income tax rates were raised in Panamá in 1961 and 1962, the Free Zone tax liabilities of these firms continue to be based on 1953 rates. As a result, a Free Zone firm, even though most of its profits may be derived from domestic sales, pays considerably less in income taxes than Panamanian firms (compare columns 2 and 4 in Table 12.3).

A problem of interpreting the income tax provisions has developed for those firms with both domestic and foreign sales. The law requires a strict segregation of sales, with domestic sales bearing the full 1953 rates and foreign sales subject to a 90 per cent reduction of the 1953 rates. It is reported that firms invariably interpreted this provision to mean that total income may be divided into two segments for income tax purposes. This means, however, that the pro-

[3] Law No. 13 of February 8, 1954.

TABLE 12.3

Comparison of Income Tax Liabilities in the Colón Free Zone and the Republic of Panamá

(In Balboas)

Taxable Income	(1) Income Tax Payments in the Free Zone 1948 to 1957[1]	(2) Income Tax Payments in the Free Zone on Domestic Sales 1958 to 1962[2]	(3) Income Tax Payments in the Free Zone on Foreign Sales 1958 to 1962[3]	(4) Income Tax Payments in the Republic of Panamá, 1962
10,000	389	450	45	602
50,000	3,529	5,000	500	6,887
100,000	9,329	14,000	1,410	19,997
200,000	24,929	38,100	3,810	45,706
300,000	41,129	65,100	6,510	93,506
400,000	57,929	84,600	8,460	135,506
500,000	74,729	141,500	14,150	177,506
750,000	119,729	209,850	20,985	293,006
1,000,000	154,729	302,850	30,285	415,506
1,500,000	260,729	506,850	50,685	630,000
2,000,000	356,729	710,850	71,850	840,000
2,500,000	452,729	914,729	91,485	1,050,000

[1] Firms paid 1946 rates, except those selling to affiliates after 1954 which paid 1953 rates.

[2] Firms paid 1953 rates.

[3] Firms paid 1953 rates with a 90 per cent discount.

gressivity of the tax is affected. A test case was made of this issue in 1961 by the Income Tax Division, and since this time firms are required to consolidate their income for tax purposes. Procedurally, this takes the form of requiring firms to calculate the tax due on their total income, subtracting from this the tax due on domestic sales, and then allowing the 90 per cent tax reduction on the remainder.

Two exceptions must now be made to the foregoing description of the application of the income tax to Free Zone firms. The first is for firms providing services, such as agents who merely handle and do not purchase or sell goods. These firms are subject to the full amount of Panamanian income taxes and to any changes in these tax rates. The second exception is for those Free Zone firms that have entered into special contracts with the national government under the terms of Law No. 27 of 1950, or its successor, Law No. 24 of 1957. These contracts, it should be noted, are separate and distinct from Free Zone contracts, for the latter only provides entitlements under the Free Zone legislation.

Contracts under Laws No. 27 of 1950 and No. 24 of 1957 accord eligible Free Zone firms a guarantee that the income tax rates in effect at the time of entering their contractual obligations will be maintained for a period of twenty years. There is also a guarantee that other taxes, such as stamp duties and certain excises, will be stabilized for the duration of the contract. A law requiring foreign firms to have a work force composed of at least 75 per cent Panamanians is also waived. On the other hand, a contracting firm must post a bond in cash or government bonds of B/10,000, which is forfeited in the event that the firm terminates its operations before the end of the contractual period.

Only seven Free Zone firms have these national government contracts. This is attributable to the amount of the bond, which makes a contract feasible only for large firms, and to the fact that most of the large Free Zone firms are owned by United States corporations, which are generally disinclined to commit themselves for a long-run period. Typically, most United States firms prefer to operate under circumstances in which they may leave the zone in the event that a change in conditions should make their operations unfavorable.

In the course of developments in the Free Zone, the firms with national government contracts have not benefited from the contractual guarantee that their income tax liabilities would not be increased. These firms all have substantial foreign sales, and, as it has been shown, the tax liabilities for all firms with income from foreign sales were sharply reduced in 1958. Thus, there is the ironical situation in which the government has entered a guarantee with a few firms to insure them that their income tax burdens would not be increased, but then has voluntarily granted a significant tax decrease. But on the other hand, the government is unable (or unwilling) to raise the tax burdens on these firms. During the period from 1958 to 1962, several excise taxes were increased, such as stamp taxes on checks, telegrams, and on bonded paper. The Free Zone firms with a national government contract were absolved from these tax increases, although they were made applicable to the other Free Zone firms. Thus, the firms with special contracts are in a rather enviable situation: they profit from tax decreases introduced in the Free Zone, but are not subject to tax increases.

The third fiscal incentive is that the whole of the Free Zone area is exempt from all taxes on real property. This includes the land itself, which is owned by the Free Zone authority, as well as all buildings, whether these are owned by the zone or by private firms.

Finally, all Free Zone firms were exempt initially from the municipal license fees levied by the city of Colón for a period of twenty years, and in compensation for this loss of revenue, the national government guaranteed to reimburse the city with an annual grant. The grant has varied from year to year, but has averaged about B/25,-000. In 1957, however, the exemption from municipal license fees was limited to those firms involved *exclusively* in foreign trade and these firms were required to pay 10 per cent of the normal license fees. According to this change, therefore, the majority of Free Zone firms would be fully liable for the payment of municipal license fees. Despite this, however, the municipality of Colón has never initiated an attempt to collect taxes from any of the firms in the zone.

Providing the Free Zone firms with an exemption from municipal taxes is an undesirable policy, for it is not an important incentive, and the city of Colón is sorely in need of revenue. On the other hand, it is shown in the chapter on Municipal Finance that the municipal license fees are extremely arbitrary and capricious. A possible solution to the present problem would be to require the Free Zone authority itself to give the city of Colón an annual grant in lieu of the application of the municipal license fees, and at the same time terminate the annual grants to the city by the national government.

POLICY CONCLUSIONS

In some respects, the development of the Colón Free Zone is impressive. In the first instance, there is no question that the decision to develop a customs-free area for entrepôt trade in Panamá is economically sound. A thriving and viable new "industry" has been developed, and its contributions to the Panamanian economy are not insignificant. A public investment valued at B/8 million has been created from relatively modest contributions from the national government, while the total of private investment in buildings and equipment is estimated to be B/3 million. The employment of 1400 persons may not sound spectacular, but anyone that has witnessed the extent of unemployment and the depressed business conditions in the city of Colón, cannot help but react favorably to the sight of these relatively well-paid workers walking out of the Free Zone gate. Thus, the shortcomings of the zone are not in concept, but in imperfections in implementation, and not in a lack of accomplishment, but in a failure to maximize the zone's contribution to the Panamanian economy.

The first set of improvements that could be introduced to the operation of the Free

Zone is based on the proposition that the zone is no longer struggling for existence, but is an established and profitable operating reality. The zone is no longer an infant industry and should not be treated as one. Therefore, the Free Zone should be given no further government subsidies, and in fact, should contribute one-half of its annual profits to the national government as the original legislation establishing the zone requires. The zone should also make a contribution to the city of Colón in lieu of the exemption granted Free Zone firms from municipal license fees, this contribution taking the place of the annual grant paid to the city by the national government. The Free Zone should find no difficulty in obtaining funds for these new obligations, if this should be necessary, by a realistic pricing of its warehouses.

The second set of improvements is based on the proposition that the fundamental purpose of the zone is to foster entrepôt trade and not to provide an opportunity for Panamanian wholesalers and retailers to avoid customs duties. For most of its history, the zone has followed a policy in attracting firms of "come one, come all," as if the principal goal was to develop the zone regardless of social consequences. This policy should be terminated by requiring that 60 per cent of the sales of each firm should be made to foreign countries. Furthermore, there is no justification for subsidizing domestic sales and those made to ships in transit and to the Canal Zone. These sales should be subject to the current amount of Panamanian income tax liabilities and not to the 1953 rates, as is presently the case.

If any activity should be provided a fiscal incentive in the Free Zone, it is the genuine entrepôt trade, but on this score it should be realized that most of the firms engaged in this activity are subsidiaries of United States manufacturers. For these firms, the principal tax incentive is a deferral of the United States tax, not the income tax subsidy provided by Panamá. In other words, for these firms the cake itself is United States tax deferral, while Panamá merely provides the

frosting. It follows from this that what is done with respect to Free Zone tax policy, within limits, is probably not controlling with respect to the attraction or retention of United States firms.

The amendments introduced in 1962 to the United States Internal Revenue Code do not appear to pose a threat to the operation of United States firms in the Free Zone. As this legislation was introduced at first to the United States Congress, the foreign earnings of United States corporations would have been taxed at full U.S. rates. However, subsequent amendments provided a number of relief provisions, principally the exclusion of earnings that are invested in underdeveloped countries.

The basic policy with respect to attracting foreign firms to the zone should be to provide sufficient incentives in order to be competitive with other areas, such as Curaçao and Barranquilla, but not to play "give-away" with the tax system. The policy of the Free Zone administrators, on the other hand, apparently is to be satisfied with a contribution from the firms in terms of investment and payroll and not to be concerned about tax revenue. This approach is undesirable. It is important to obtain a contribution in terms of tax revenue from firms engaged in entrepôt trade, for their value to the economy in other ways is limited. By the nature of their operations, their work forces are relatively small and their investments are largely in inventory. Although many of these firms have derived substantial earnings from the Free Zone, only a small proportion of the funds has been re-invested in Panamá.

In attempting to maximize the tax contribution from earnings on foreign sales, the tax reduction in 1958, whereby the income tax liability on foreign sales was reduced to 10 per cent of the 1953 rates, was a clear mistake. This reduction gave existing firms an unwarranted and unnecessary windfall gain. At the present time, the income tax liability on profits from foreign sales is only about 3 per cent of net income as compared to 52 per cent in the United States. The tax burden is also very low as compared to normal Panamanian rates. In the case of one United States firm operating in the Free Zone, a tax of B/46,644 was paid on a profit of B/1,400,921 in 1961, while the corresponding income tax for a Panamanian firm engaged in domestic business would have been B/588,387.

There is little doubt that the income tax liabilities on profits from foreign sales could be substantially up-graded without detracting from the Free Zone fiscal incentives. In the first instance, these tax liabilities should be based on the current Panamanian income tax schedule rather than on the 1953 rates. Second, it would appear that a tax reduction of about 75 per cent of the full tax liability rather than 90 per cent would provide a sufficient incentive in view of the other tax advantages offered by the Free Zone.

Recommending an increase in tax burdens for the Free Zone raises the issue of whether a change in rates would be legal in view of the many references in the Free Zone legislation to the effect that the government *guarantees* the stability of all incentives during the life of a contract. There is no question that the government has a monopoly on sovereign powers, and has the *right* to change commitments if it should decide that the provisions are not in the public interest. What is more debatable is whether it constitutes desirable developmental policy to change the ground rules in the middle of the game. On this score, it is undoubtedly true that frequent changes in incentive legislation are destructive of business confidence, and for

this reason, amendments to the Free Zone law should be kept to a minimum. On the other hand, the sanctity of contractual agreements cannot be carried to the point where the government must continue to observe terms that are clearly against the public interest. It also should be repeated that the present income tax incentives offered by the Free Zone are only of peripheral importance. United States business firms are primarily interested in the deferral of United States income taxes and sound commercial considerations, with Panamanian income tax incentives of secondary importance.

SUMMARY OF RECOMMENDATIONS

1) The subsidies granted to the Free Zone by the national government should be terminated.

2) The Free Zone should assume responsibility for the present grants given to the city of Colón by the national government.

3) Additional revenues to make possible the above two recommendations may be obtained by raising Free Zone rents.

4) To be eligible for a Free Zone contract, 60 per cent of the sales of each firm should be made to foreign countries.

5) Domestic sales, as well as those made to ships in transit and to the Canal Zone, should be subject to the current Panamanian income tax liabilities.

6) Foreign sales should be subject to a reduction of about 75 per cent of the current income tax rates.

CHAPTER 13

Municipal Finance

ALTHOUGH THERE ARE three levels of government in Panamá—national, provincial, and municipal—only the national and municipal governments are important from a fiscal point of view. According to the Constitution, provincial governors are required to act as intermediaries between the national and municipal governments, but their functions are few and their budgets insignificant. In contrast, the Constitution accords municipalities a dominant role by saying that "The State is based on a community of autonomous municipalities." [1] A municipality is defined in the Constitution as the political organization of the community, which is established in a territory determined by neighborhood relations and has sufficient economic capacity to maintain its government adequately.

Local governments must cooperate with the national government in matters relating to the achievement of social welfare. They also must comply with the Constitution and other laws and decrees of the Republic. On the other hand, the national government is required to give supporting aid to the local government whenever needed because of epidemics, grave breaches of the public order, or other matters of public interest.

Municipal power is vested in a municipal council and a mayor. The number of persons constituting a municipal council depends on the population of the district, varying from five members for communities with less than 10,000 inhabitants to eleven members for communities with more than 125,000. [2]

The municipal council represents the legislative branch, but its real functions extend to executive and administrative matters, while the mayor, though in theory representing the executive power, has rather minimal authority. The municipal council exercises some of its functions through special commissions. There may be commissions for specific purposes such as sanitation, education, public finance, economics, urbanism, and agriculture. These secondary governmental units are directly responsible to the municipal council and not to the mayor. It is through these commissions that the municipal council exercises administrative and executive functions. The authority to impose taxes, contributions, charges, and fees is also vested in the council.

The mayor has few powers. He is required to cooperate with the municipal council in improving administration, to prepare a budget showing anticipated revenues and expenditures, to appoint and dismiss certain employees, and, in general, to promote the progress of the community.

The Planning Department at the Presidency recently has encouraged the organization of planning offices at the municipal level. Four of these offices have been established and a few more are being developed. Their main functions will be to develop plans as

[1] Article 186.

[2] A district is the territory within which a municipality exerts its authority. It is also called a *municipio*.

a guide to municipal activities and to suggest desirable reforms. In fulfilling these functions, the municipal planning offices will work closely with the Planning Department at the Presidency.

In practice, municipal governments have less responsibility and authority than is accorded to them in the Constitution, principally because legislation at the national government level has not implemented the constitutional spirit. As a result, municipalities in Panamá do not have the political autonomy that is found in many other Latin American countries. In Panamá, the mayor is appointed by the national government rather than elected at the local government level, although there is ample precedent for the latter in several Latin American countries. Also, the fact that both legislative and executive powers have been given to the municipal council results in a lack of centralization in the direction of municipal affairs and to disorderly administration. Furthermore, the division of responsibilities between the councils and the mayors is not clearly defined. These factors have resulted in the national government assuming many public services traditionally considered as belonging to the municipal government in other countries, such as the provision of sewerage and water services.

Relative Financial Importance of Municipal Governments

From a fiscal point of view, municipal governments are relatively unimportant in Panamá. Their total expenditures during the period from 1959 to 1961 were at an average level of 3.7 per cent of total governmental expenditures. Moreover, 9.7 per cent of these expenditures resulted from national government grants. As mentioned previously, the reason for this relatively unimportant position of the municipalities has been the tendency of the national government to absorb traditional municipal functions, either directly or through the device of establishing autonomous or semi-autonomous institutions

for sewerage, water, fire protection, garbage removal, and the like.

An insight into the relative importance of local governments in Panamá may be gained by a comparison with the United States and Venezuela. In the United States, local governments in 1957 spent almost as much as the federal government for purposes other than defense, and nearly twice as much as the state governments. In contrast, municipal governments in Venezuela accounted for only 3 per cent of total public spending. Unlike Panamá, however, Venezuela has state governments that account for about 9 per cent of total public spending. (See Table 13.1.)

Change in Importance of Municipalities

Since 1904, when Panamá became an independent nation, the degree of autonomy of the municipal governments has been sometimes enlarged and at other times reduced, depending on prevailing political sentiments. But municipal governments in Panamá have never, until recent times, acquired the status enjoyed by local governments in many other countries, and at times, their authority has almost disappeared.

TABLE 13.1

Public Expenditures in Panamá, the United States, and Venezuela by Levels of Government

Level of Government	Panamá 1959–61 Average (In Millions of Balboas)	United States 1957 (In Billions of U.S. Dollars)	Venezuela 1958–59 Average (In Millions of Balboas)
National	81.7[1]	30.9[2]	5,300[4]
State	—	16.9[3]	530[5]
Municipal	3.1	30.7	170
TOTAL	84.8	78.5	6,000

[1] Net of grants to municipalites of B/305,000.
[2] Net of expenditures on defense and grants to state and local governments.
[3] Net of grants to local governments.
[4] Net of grants to states.
[5] Net of grants to municipalities.
Sources: Estadística Panameña, Series "E," Nos. 1 and 3, 1961; *Presupuesto de Gastos y Rentas,* 1959, 1960, 1961; Carl S. Shoup, *The Fiscal System of Venezuela, a Report* (Baltimore: The Johns Hopkins Press, 1959), pp. 313–14.

Although the Constitution of 1904 provided that municipalities were autonomous, the provincial governors were responsible for the appointment of mayors, and municipalities were prohibited from borrowing unless authorized by the National Assembly. The Constitution of 1941 reduced municipal governments to almost committees in charge of parks and festivities, creating, instead, provincial governments (*Ayuntamientos Provinciales*) that took over previous municipal functions. The Constitution of 1946, which is currently in effect, enunciated again the principle of municipal autonomy, and restored the traditional functions to municipalities. In addition, the Constitution of 1946 provided for the election of mayors through popular vote or for their appointment by the national government. Law Number 8 of 1954, however, provided for the appointment of mayors by the national government.

Specific Municipal Functions

Table 13.2 provides data on the principal functions of municipal governments. The legislative and judicial functions, together with general administration, accounted for nearly two-thirds of municipal expenditures in 1961. Education, which is the most important public service, represented one-fifth of total expenditures.

It is important to point out some peculiarities of educational services at the municipal level. First, the larger part of these expenditures results from a law which requires 20 per cent of municipal tax revenues to be allocated to education.[3] As a result, out of B/550,400 spent on education in 1961, B/520,000 was provided from special funds established by law for educational purposes. These funds are administered by two municipal committees, one for general education and the other for physical education. But on each committee, there is only one person from the municipal council. Thus, municipal governments do not have direct control over the allocation of most of their educational expenditures. The remaining expenditures on education are spent principally on public municipal libraries and grants to schools and other educational institutions, such as the national medical school, the national museum, and so forth.

Expenditures on health are determined and administered in the same way as expenditures on education. The percentage to be earmarked for health is 5 per cent of total municipal tax revenues. In 1961, out of B/83,000 spent on health, B/44,000 was derived from the 5 per cent fund established by law for this purpose, while B/39,000 was spent directly by local governments, principally on municipal dispensaries.

Social assistance, which was the third most important item of expenditures in 1961, accounted for about 6 per cent of total current expenditures. About 42 per cent of this category was spent on fire departments and on other governmental functions such as

TABLE 13.2

Expenditures of Panamanian Municipalities, 1961

Functions	Amount (Balboas)
Legislative	138,100
Judicial	210,500
General administration[1]	1,408,700
Education	550,400
Social assistance	155,700
Festivities	28,700
Sanitation	6,700
Health	83,100
Gardens and parks	15,000
Cemeteries	48,000
Aqueducts	3,200
Public markets and slaughterhouses	89,700
Garbage collection	45,900
TOTAL CURRENT EXPENDITURES	2,783,700
Public works	246,600
Public debt	17,700
Miscellaneous and not classified	143,400
TOTAL	3,191,400

[1] Includes costs of public lighting and water services that have not been segregated because of a lack of information.

Source: Based on data compiled by the Contraloría General de la República, Dirección General de Estadística y Censo.

[3] Article 121 of Law Number 8 of 1954 requires 15 per cent of municipal revenues to be spent on general education and 5 per cent on physical education.

traffic control and fire prevention. Religious associations received subsidies and grants amounting to about 8 per cent of total social expenditures. The other one-half of the expenditures on social assistance consisted of grants and subsides to a great variety of institutions, such as dispensaries, communal dining rooms and nursery schools. Other services such as sanitation, aqueducts, parks and gardens, cemeteries, and garbage collection represent a very small part of municipal current expenditures.

Expenditures on public works were B/246,-600 in 1961. Almost two-thirds of this amount was spent by two committees: one rebuilding the historical monuments of the old site of the city of Panamá, the other improving the appearance of the present city.

It is worth noting the insignificance of some services traditionally considered as important at the municipal level. The garbage collection service, for example, is undertaken by some municipalities, but not by the two principal cities in the republic, Panamá and Colón. In these two cities, the national government assumed responsibility for garbage removal after this service was discontinued by the Canal Zone authorities. There is a general impression that this service in Panamá and Colón has deteriorated rapidly in recent years. This is confirmed by a study made by the Planning Department at the Presidency on the condition of the garbage removal service in the city of Panamá. The study found that most of the equipment had become obsolete and that the efficiency of the service was at a much lower level than eight years ago when the service was provided by the Canal Zone.

Municipalities also do not assume responsibility for the building, maintenance, and repair of city streets. All of these services, instead, are undertaken by the national government. This is an undesirable procedure, and an improvement would result if all highways and streets were classified into national and municipal. The latter should be built and maintained at the municipal level, since the cities are better able to determine their own needs.

The central public markets in some municipalities, including those in Panamá and Colón, are also operated by the national government. These responsibilities once again are clearly the kind that could and should be assumed by local governments.

During the period from 1950 to 1960, the Panamanian population increased by 33.6 per cent, while municipal expenditures rose by 56 per cent. As a result, per capita municipal expenditures rose from B/2.7 to B/3.1, an increase of 14.8 per cent. In spite of this increase, the current low level of per capita expenditures is in itself an indication that municipal governments have done little to satisfy the rising need for services at the local level. Since per capita municipal expenditures rose by 14.8 per cent from 1950 to 1960, and per capita gross domestic product rose by 24.2 per cent, municipal expenditures represented a smaller proportion of per capita gross domestic product in 1960 than in 1950.

There are tremendous unfilled demands for municipal services. These demands are increasing because of population growth, the migration from rural to urban areas, and the increase in per capita income. Present educational facilities, both in quantity and quality, fall far short of what is socially necessary; streets should be widened and paved; the system of garbage collection needs to be improved; and so forth.

From the foregoing, it is apparent that municipal governments in Panamá, besides having very few functions, do not have the authority to undertake the principal ones for which they are responsible. At the minimum it would seem that municipal governments should assume most of the responsibility for primary education, health services, the construction and maintenance of city streets, and garbage removal.

If the municipalities were to accept responsibility for even the major part of these functions, total municipal revenues would have to be increased to at least B/6 million, or by about 100 per cent. For example, the construction of primary schools will require about B/3 million per annum. If health services were assumed completely by the local governments, an additional B/1 million annually would be needed. The maintenance cost alone of city streets is estimated to be B/1.5 million per annum. Garbage removal costs in the two cities of Panamá and Colón are estimated to be B/1.5 million annually.

There are two principal gains to be derived if municipal functions were extended. The first is a political one that extends from the decentralization of authority, for countries in which democracy is strong usually have divided authority among different levels of government. This dispersion of power helps to prevent a single government or clique from assuming dictatorial control. The second advantage is one of efficiency in providing governmental services. Citizens are more inclined to contribute to the support of government when they can see a direct connection between their contributions and the services provided.

But some structural changes in municipal government organization would be necessary in Panamá to realize these gains. First, it would be preferable for mayors to be elected so that they would be more responsive to the needs of the local electorate. Second, some of the administrative functions should be transferred from the semi-independent commissions to the mayors so that the latter would have greater authority and responsibility.

MUNICIPAL REVENUES

Of the sixty-three municipalities in Panamá, four have annual revenues of over B/100,000, twenty-two obtain between B/10,000 and B/100,000, and thirty-seven have revenues under B/10,000. The first group, which includes the municipalities of Panamá, Colón, David, and Barú, accounts for more than 70 per cent of total municipal revenues.

As shown in Table 13.3, municipal revenues in 1960 amounted to B/3,189,700. This total may be divided between 87.0 per cent in the form of ordinary revenues and 13.0 per cent from extraordinary revenues. Ordinary revenues, in turn, arise from several sources: 72.7 per cent of total municipal revenues from taxes. 4.0 per cent from municipal services, 3.9 per cent from municipal property, and 6.4 per cent from miscellaneous sources. Extraordinary revenues are obtained from two sources: 9.6 per cent of total municipal revenues is derived from national government grants and 3.4 per cent is from delinquent taxes.

Although only 9.6 per cent of total municipal revenues was derived from national government grants, certain cities were very de-

TABLE 13.3

Revenues of Panamanian Municipalities by Type and Province, 1960

(Thousands of Balboas)

	Bocas del Toro	Coclé	Colón	Chiriquí	Darién	Herrera	Los Santos	Panamá	Veraguas	Total
Ordinary revenues	75.6	104.8	349.9	387.0	12.1	76.7	56.6	1,646.0	62.6	2,771.3
Taxes	29.0	90.0	325.6	263.1	9.7	68.1	46.5	1,436.4	45.9	2,314.3
Indirect	25.5	72.5	321.1	230.0	9.7	53.1	42.2	1,094.2	41.6	1,889.9
Direct	3.5	17.5	4.5	33.1	.0	15.0	4.3	342.2	4.3	424.4
Municipal services	43.1	1.8	1.1	71.5	.0	.6	.0	8.8	1.2	128.1
Municipal property	1.0	10.1	18.9	37.8	1.4	5.4	8.3	29.0	12.7	124.6
Miscellaneous	2.5	2.9	4.3	14.6	1.0	2.6	1.8	171.8	2.8	204.3
Extraordinary revenues	40.3	47.1	76.0	31.6	12.0	14.7	35.9	99.4	56.7	413.7
Total revenues	115.9	151.9	425.9	423.3[1]	24.1	91.4	92.5	1,745.4	119.3	3,189.7[1]

[1] Including B/4,700 not classified in the table.

Source: Estadística Panameña, Series "E," No. 3, 1961, p. 23

pendent on the national government. For example, the municipalities in the provinces of Darién and Veraguas derived almost one-half of their total revenues from national grants, and those in the provinces of Bocas del Toro, Coclé and Los Santos obtained around one-third of their revenues from transfer payments. On the other hand, the municipalities of Panamá and Chiriquí obtained only about 5 per cent of their total revenues from the national government, and those of Colón and Herrera around 15 per cent. Taxes accounted for B/2,314,300 of total revenues in 1960. They constituted the main source of revenue in all of the provinces except Bocas del Toro, Veraguas, and Darién.

Within the category of tax revenues, indirect taxes represent 81.7 per cent and direct taxes 18.3 per cent. Indirect taxes were more important than direct in all of the provinces. In order of importance, the principal indirect taxes were those on commercial businesses, industrial activities, and services. The principal direct tax is a license tax on passenger vehicles,[4] but this levy is important in terms of revenue only in the provinces of Panamá and Chiriquí. Panamá accounted for 80.2 per cent of total tax revenues obtained from automobile licenses and Chiriquí for 8.3 per cent.

Municipal services accounted for about 4 per cent of total municipal revenues. Within this category, the supply of electricity is the most important source of revenue. However, only the municipalities in the three provinces of Bocas del Toro, Colón, and Chiriquí derive revenue from this source. The second most important source of revenue from municipal services is the supply of water, but the total revenues from this source is from municipalities in the province of Chiriquí.

Revenues from municipal property accounted for 3.9 per cent of total municipal revenue. Collections are derived principally from the sale of municipal property. Revenues from salt extraction are important only in the provinces of Los Santos and Coclé. Rental

income from the use of municipal property, such as forest resources, sand deposits, and salt mines, is significant only in a few provinces.

REVENUE ANALYSIS

From the foregoing analysis of expenditures and receipts, it is apparent that the municipal governments must receive much greater tax revenues if municipalities are to fulfill an expanded role in supplying governmental services. At the present time, approximately 85 per cent of the municipal tax revenues collected in the cities of Panamá and Colón are derived from two levies—49 per cent from vehicle license taxes, and 36 per cent from taxes on commercial and industrial establishments. The remainder of this chapter will be devoted to an analysis of these two taxes in order to evaluate their potential for further development. A concluding section will consider possible new taxes that could be adopted by the municipalities.

Vehicle License Taxes

Each municipality levies its own vehicle license fees. Research has not been undertaken on all these schedules of fees, but based on a survey of the ones used in the cities of Panamá and Colón, it appears likely that much could be done to improve the present schedules throughout the Republic. Taxes on vehicles imposed in these two municipalities are basically the same. As a result, reference will be made only to those fees levied in the city of Panamá, but the analysis and recommendations probably have general applicability.

Two types of vehicle taxes are levied: 1) an annual tax of B/2 on both commercial and private vehicles; and 2) a transit tax on private and commercial vehicles. These transit taxes, shown in Table 13.4, consist of a schedule of rates varying according to the size, type, and use made of the vehicles. The

---

[4] Taxes on commercial vehicles are classified as indirect taxes.

TABLE 13.4

Vehicle License Taxes in the City of Panamá

Type of Vehicle	Monthly Rate	Annual Rate
Moved by Mechanical Power		
Automobiles used for rental purposes		
5 passengers or less	B/ 1.50	B/ 15.00
7 passengers	2.50	24.00
Automobiles for private use		
5 passengers or less	2.50	24.00
6 to 7 passengers	3.50	34.00
Buses		
10 passengers or less	4.00	40.00
11 to 22 passengers	5.00	50.00
More than 22 passengers	7.00	70.00
Trucks		
Up to 1 ton	4.00	40.00
1 to 2 tons	5.00	50.00
2 to 3 tons	7.00	72.00
3 to 5 tons	11.00	110.00
5 to 10 tons	18.00	180.00
Over 10 tons	24.00	240.00
Trailers		
For private automobiles	1.75	17.50
For commercial use		
Up to 1 ton	2.00	20.00
1 to 2 tons	2.50	25.00
2 to 3 tons	3.50	35.00
3 to 5 tons	5.50	55.00
5 to 10 tons	9.00	90.00
Over 10 tons	12.00	120.00
Motorcycles		
Private use	1.00	10.00
Commercial use	1.50	15.00
Automobiles for private use owned by employees of the Canal Zone	—	5.00
Demonstration plates	—	25.00
Change of automobile motors	—	1.00[1]
Transfer of ownership	—	1.50[1]
Moved by Animal or Human Power		
Coach	2.00	24.00
Small carts	—	1.00
Carts	—	5.00
Bicycles		
Rental	—	5.00
Other	—	2.00
Bicycles owned by employees of the Canal Zone	—	1.00

[1] For each application.

rates have been established, apparently, with the intention of distributing the tax burden among vehicles in accordance with their use of the streets and highways.

Vehicles propelled by mechanical power are divided into seven groups. There is a lower rate for automobiles used for rental purposes (B/15 to B/24 annually) as compared to vehicles in private use (B/24 to B/34). This means that a Volkswagen or any similar small car bears a tax of B/15 (rental) or B/24 (private), while a Chevrolet bears a tax of B/24 (rental) or B/34 (private). Buses are subject to annual taxes varying from B/40 to B/70, depending on passenger-carrying capacity. Taxes on trucks vary with weight from B/40 to B/240 annually, while trailers are taxed at one-half the rates for trucks. Taxes on motorcycles vary with use, with B/10 imposed for private use and B/15 for commercial. Private vehicles owned by employees of the Canal Zone are taxed at the low rate of B/5 annually.

These fees are irrational on several counts. There is no justification for taxing vehicles used for rental purposes at lower rates than those that are privately owned and operated. While it is rational to tax small vehicles at a lower rate than large ones, the distinction between the two should not be based on passenger-carrying capacity. Monthly rates should be eliminated. There is also no justification for the low tax on vehicles owned by employees of the Canal Zone.

But more important than these faults is the level and graduation of the fees. In Panamá, as in other underdeveloped countries, there is a tendency for middle and upper income groups to indulge in an undue amount of conspicuous consumption that is not compatible with generally accepted economic and social goals. One of the more important forms of this consumption is the ownership of expensive vehicles. And if a society is to tolerate the ownership of a Mercedes Benz or a Thunderbird by some persons, while others are without shoes, the least that should be done is to levy steeply progressive taxes on the ownership and operation of expensive vehicles. In this way, conspicuous consumption will be restrained, and to the degree that it persists notwithstanding the heavier tax levies, the revenues obtained through higher taxes may be used for social purposes.

Several objections may be made to this proposal, but all may be rebutted. It may be argued, first, that the taxation of income or wealth is a more appropriate method of introducing progressivity into a tax system. This is true in principle, but compliance and enforcement difficulties with respect to the income tax in Panamá are so severe that an attempt must be made to supplement the progressivity of the income tax by introducing progressive elements into other taxes. It may also be argued that the purchase of expensive automobiles may be curbed by custom duties, denial of import permits, or foreign exchange controls. To some degree, this is attempted in Panamá through relatively high custom duties on expensive vehicles. But this policy is not effective and needs supplementation through some other device. This is clearly evident by the number of luxury-type automobiles in use.

Finally, it could be argued that a progressive license fee based on the value of vehicles is in conflict with the generally accepted theory of highway finance, which holds that vehicles should be taxed according to the benefit principle. According to this principle, vehicles should bear a burden in proportion to the use or benefit received from highway use, and the revenues derived therefrom should be dedicated to the construction and maintenance of highways. This principle, however, seems inappropriate in Panamá for two reasons. First, the benefit principle would lead to much higher tax imposts on commercial vehicles, and this would be undesirable in a country in which transportation is one of the severe impediments to economic development. Second, if all vehicle taxes were dedicated to highway use at the local level, municipal governments would be denied a source of revenue that is sorely needed for

other purposes besides road and street development.

A system of progressive license fees could be introduced by the adoption of the schedule shown in Table 13.5. This schedule would be applicable to all new vehicles, but a depreciation allowance would be permitted of 10 per cent of the new car value for each year of vehicle age. Thus, a new vehicle purchased for B/5000 would be valued for tax purposes after one year at B/4500, and so forth. Vehicles would not be depreciated to a value lower than B/1000, and the minimum tax on all vehicles would be B/24, which is the current tax rate on small privately-owned vehicles in Panamá. All passenger vehicles, whether for rental or private use, would be subject to the same tax schedule.

If this tax were introduced, the tax levy on a Volkswagen (Model 113), with a new car value of B/1,975, would be increased from the current rate of B/24 to B/45. After the vehicle was five years old, the tax would be B/28, and after six years, B/24. The tax on a Chevrolet (Bel Aire), with a new cost of B/3,675, would be increased from B/34 to B/107. This tax would decrease to B/24 after nine years of vehicle age. A new Cadillac valued at B/8,885 would be taxed at B/365 in the first year as compared to B/34, and this tax would decrease to B/188 in the fifth year of vehicle age and to B/24 in the tenth year of age. Admittedly, these are precipitous increases in tax rates. But can it be argued that a person who can afford to pay B/8,885 for a new Cadillac could not afford to pay B/365 for a license fee?

To implement the tax, it would be desirable for the national government to issue an ordinance each year specifying the value for tax purposes of all new vehicles. It would also be desirable to have uniform tax rates throughout the Republic to prevent vehicle owners from registering their vehicles in municipalities where the tax rates might be lower in the absence of uniform rates.

In addition to this progressive schedule of fees, several other reforms should be introduced in order to develop a more equitable

TABLE 13.5

Proposed Tax Schedule for Automobiles

Value	Tax Rates
B/1,001 to B/1,500	B/ 24 plus 2.0 per cent on excess over B/1,000
B/1,501 to B/2,000	B/ 34 plus 2.5 ” ” ” ” ” B/1,500
B/2,001 to B/2,500	B/ 46.50 plus 3.0 ” ” ” ” ” B/2,000
B/2,501 to B/3,000	B/ 61.50 plus 3.5 ” ” ” ” ” B/2,500
B/3,001 to B/3,500	B/ 79.00 plus 4.0 ” ” ” ” ” B/3,000
B/3,501 to B/4,000	B/ 99.00 plus 4.5 ” ” ” ” ” B/3,500
Over B/4,001	B/121.50 plus 5.0 ” ” ” ” ” B/4,000

and rational system of license fees. The favorable tax treatment accorded vehicles owned by employees of the Canal Zone should be eliminated. A more serious problem is the number of vehicles exempt from the tax. At the beginning of 1962, there were 1,842 vehicles exempt from the tax in the city of Panamá, of which 1,116 were exempt because they were owned by the national government and 359 were not taxed because they were owned by public officials. The remaining exemptions were 207 granted to diplomats, 64 to consular employees, and 53 to deputies of the National Assembly. There is reason to believe that these exemptions, because of their number, have been given with undue liberality, but even if they have not, there is no justification to exempt government vehicles and those owned by public officials. Probably the most unjustified exemption is one given to employees of newspapers, of which there were 43 in 1962.

Finally, there is a collection problem that should be resolved. The total of delinquent license taxes has increased from B/32,000 in December, 1960, to B/67,000 in September, 1962. Reports of delinquent taxes are forwarded for collection at the end of each month to the transit office of the national government. Since a license tax on vehicles is relatively easy to enforce, there is no excuse except lassitude for the increase in the amount of delinquent taxes.

Taxes on Commercial and Industrial Establishments

The second important source of tax revenue at the municipal level is a business license tax levied on commercial and industrial establishments. In the municipalities of Panamá and Colón, there are thirty different taxes on commercial establishments and twenty-six on different types of industrial activities. Table 13.6 presents a sample of these taxes. In most cases, these taxes are established within a range. For example, wholesalers in the city of Panamá may be assessed within a range of B/10 and B/100 per month, and hotels from B/25 to B/150 per month. Although these taxes are payable monthly, a reduction of 10 per cent is given if the payments are made annually and in advance.

These taxes on commercial and industrial establishments are so inequitable and arbitrary in concept and application that they represent a throwback to the Middle Ages. To illustrate, in the city of Panamá, why should sausage factories be subject to a tax of from B/25 to B/250 when soap factories are taxed within a range of B/10 to B/100? Why should retailers selling Panamanian goods be taxed from B/1 to B/25, while retailers selling foreign goods are taxed from B/1 to B/50? Clothing firms fall within a tax range of from B/25 to B/100, but clothing firms manufacturing only trousers are taxed from B/10 to B/25. Soft drink manufacturers are taxed from B/250 to B/300, but dairies are taxed only from B/25 to B/100. This type of arbitrary taxation, without any relationship to income, sales, payroll, capital, or other relevant base of taxation is little better than the salt and window taxes of the Middle Ages.

Another disadvantage of this system is that it is often possible to tax a business under two different classifications. For example, a retailer is assessed a higher tax if he sells only foreign goods. But if a retail store sells both domestic and foreign goods, should the tax be based on the sale of domestic or foreign goods? The schedule of fees abounds with ambiguities similar to this one, which results in discrimination and confusion.

The assessments within the tax ranges are also arbitrary and inequitable. The determination of the tax levy is based on two factors: 1) the capital invested by the firm, which is declared each year when the business pays a license tax (patente) to the national government; and 2) visual observation of the business by inspectors at the municipal level. The reports on invested capital are an objective factor, but they do not permit a distinction to be made between firms with low and high ratios of sales to capital. But this is not the heart of the problem. What essentially determines the tax due within the range established by law is the relationship between the inspector and taxpayer. This situation is an open invitation to bribery and corruption.

Judged by any criterion of sound taxation, the taxes on commercial and industrial establishments fall short of acceptability for a progressive and enlightened system of taxation. They are not directly related to a relevant basis of taxation, such as sales, property, or income, and are therefore arbitrary and inequitable. And because the base of taxation is so vague, they are difficult to administer equitably. The only substantial argument that can be presented for their retention is that they are productive of revenue, and this defense is not controlling because there are alternative sources of revenue that could be substituted for these taxes. Therefore, Panamá should give serious consideration to the elimination of these taxes on commercial and industrial establishments and to the adoption of substitute forms of revenue.

TABLE 13.6

Taxes on a Sample of Commercial and Industrial Establishments in the Municipalities of Panamá and Colón

	Monthly Tax Rates	
	Panamá	Colón
Commercial Establishments		
Commission merchants	B/10–B/100	B/ 5–B/100
Distributors		
Foreign firms	B/10–B/100	B/ 5–B/100
National firms	B/ 5–B/ 50	B/ 5–B/100
Insurance companies	B/25–B/ 50	B/ 50–B/100
Candy and pastry shops	B/ 5–B/ 25	B/ 2–B/ 10
Pawn shops	B/75–B/150	B/ 50–B/100
Wholesalers	B/10–B/100	B/ 30–B/150
Retailers		
Selling Panamanian goods	B/ 1–B/ 25	B/ 1–B/ 25
Selling foreign goods	B/ 1–B/ 50	B/ 1–B/ 50
Barbershops, per chair	B/ 1	B/ 1–B/ 3
Hotels	B/25–B/150	—
Restaurants	B/ 2–B/100	B/ 5–B/ 15
Industrial Establishments		
Sawmills	B/ 5–B/ 25	B/ 10–B/ 50
Soft drink manufacturers		
First category	B/300	B/50
Second category	B/250	B/50
Sausage factories	B/25–B/250	B/ 1
Dairies	B/25–B/100	B/ 20–B/ 50
Soap factories	B/10–B/100	B/ 5
Clothing firms	B/25–B/100	B/ 5
Clothing firms manufacturing only trousers	B/10 B/ 25	B/ 5
Coffee manufacturers	B/ 5–B/ 25	B/ 5
Cement manufacturers	—	B/400–B/600
Steel mills	—	B/ 25–B/100

Possible New Taxes

In Panamá, as in the Central American countries, the property tax traditionally has been a source of revenue of the national government. This development is probably in part attributable to the small geographic size of the country as well as to the tendency toward centralization of governmental authority and functions. By contrast, in the United States and many other countries, the property tax is the backbone of the revenue system at the local governmental level.

Since the time that the property tax was first imposed in Panamá, certain striking social changes have taken place. One of these is the rise of large urban centers and the consequent need for very substantial increases in revenues in order to provide additional services at the local government level. The property tax is an appropriate tax to fulfill these rising demands for municipal services. Besides being productive of revenue, the property tax serves other social objectives. First, the tax is a means of recouping some of the appreciation in land values for the benefit of society. Second, since municipalities encompass agricultural as well as urban land within their jurisdictions, the property tax can be a means of exacting a larger tax contribution from the agricultural industry. And finally, the property tax can be a means of stimulating the use of uncultivated land.

At the present time, the property tax is very under-developed as a source of revenue for the national government. As a result, it would be possible, and, in fact, desirable for both the national and municipal governments to tax property as a source of revenue. This can be accomplished through what is known as a "tax supplement." Under this system, the national government would continue to assess and collect the property tax, but the municipalities would be permitted to levy an additional rate to the property tax at their own discretion. For example, the existing property tax rates for the national government currently vary from three-fourths to one and one-half per cent. The municipalities could be given the authority to increase these rates up to 100 per cent of their present levels. This procedure has the advantage that the arduous task of administering the property tax would remain with the national government, but the municipalities would have the right of self-determination with respect to imposing taxes on their own citizens.

Another reason why this system would be desirable in Panamá is that a large proportion of the agricultural land is presently not assessed, and even in the cities, much must be done to improve assessments. Therefore, for the foreseeable future, property tax administration must remain a responsibility of the national government.

Alternatively, a tax supplement for the benefit of the municipalities would be possible by using the income tax rather than the property tax. Under this system, the municipalities would be permitted to levy an amount, say up to 10 per cent, to the income tax liabilities of all taxpayers with residence within their political jurisdictions. This supplement is similar to a surtax. With an expected income tax yield of approximately B/15 million in 1962, a 10 per cent surtax on all income tax payments for the benefit of municipalities would yield about B/1.5 million.

SUMMARY OF RECOMMENDATIONS

The municipalities of Panamá are mere fiscal appendages of the national government. They need to be given additional responsibilities as well as greater revenues. Progress toward these goals could be accomplished by the adoption of the following recommendations:

1) It would be preferable for mayors to be elected so that they would be more responsive to the local electorate.

2) Some administrative functions should be transferred from the semi-independent commissions to the mayors so that the latter would have greater authority and responsibility.

3) Municipal governments should assume most of the responsibility for primary education, health services, the construction and maintenance of city streets, and garbage removal. The assumption of these responsibilities would require at least a doubling of municipal revenues.

4) A new schedule of vehicle license fees should be adopted. This schedule should be progressive with respect to the value of vehicles and uniform throughout the Republic.

5) The taxes on commercial and industrial establishments are extremely inequitable and arbitrary and should be abandoned. They should be replaced by either a property tax or income tax "supplement."

Index

A

Agriculture: extent of, 2; planned development of, 3; land tenure and use, 67–68; taxation of land, 67–75; revenue from taxes, 72–74; private ownership of land, 73

Alcoholic beverages: taxes on, 5, 16, 142–54; duties on, 102, 143–45; illegal traffic in, 106–8, 152; structure of liquor industry, 143; types of taxes, 143–45; administration of tax, 145; revenues from, 145; production of beverages, 146; beer, 147; retail establishments, 147; wholesale establishments, 147; shipments to Canal Zone, 149–52; policy conclusions, 152–54; recommendations for, 154

Amortization costs, 9

Appeals in tax cases, 23, 50

Appraisers of estates, 81

Assessments: of net worth, 50, doomage, 52; for property tax, 64–67; of rural property, 68–72

Auditing of taxes: procedure of, 48–50; personnel for, 53

Automobiles: duties on, 100; vehicle license taxes for, 203–6

Autonomous agencies: activities of, 14, 16, 155–69; Social Security System, 155, 158–62; Institute for Economic Development, 155, 163–65; Institute for Housing and Urban Development, 155, 165–66; banks, 155, 167–68; National Lottery, 156, 166–67; Gambling Control Board, 168; recommendations for, 169

B

Banks: government, 155, 167–68

Bearer shares, 86

Beer: tax on, 147

Bonds: government, exemption of, 86

Budgetary contributions and loans, 4

Business: taxation of, 19, 29, 37, 39–41, 45, 140; property taxes for, 63; subsidies to, 99, 115; incorporation fees, 135, 184; license fees, 138–39, 184; foreign base companies, 182–85; municipal taxes on, 206–7

C

Campesinos: taxation of, 72

Canal: value of, 2

Canal Zone: income tax in, 37–38; merchandise purchased in, 103; contraband problems in, 105–6; liquor shipped to, 149–52

Capital gains: taxes on, 19, 41–43

Capital requirements; exemptions affecting, 122

Catastral Comisión, 61, 65, 74, 81

Cattle Institute, 155, 169

Charges and fees, 135–36

Chiriquí Land Company, 72, 175

Cigarettes: taxes on, 136

Coffee Institute, 155, 169

Collection: of income tax, 54; of property tax, 74–79; of inheritance and gift taxes, 83–84

Colón Free Zone: activities in, 5, 16, 155, 186–97; contraband problems in, 108–10, 192; rental contracts in, 187; commercial activities in, 188–91; types of firms in, 188–91; regulations in, 189–90; undesirable development in, 190–91; income tax in, 192–93; fiscal incentives in, 192–95; policy conclusions, 195–97; recommendations for, 197

Commerce, foreign. See Foreign commerce

Construction: exemptions for, 61, 62–63

Consumption taxes, 136–38

Consular fees, 93, 192

Contraband. See Smuggling

Contractual arrangements with government, 118–19, 171–73, 180, 194–95

Corporations. See Business

Council, municipal, 198

Customs duties. See Import duties

D

Debt: amortization costs of, 9; floating, 9; and Social Security System, 9, 10; public, 9–10

Deductions from income tax, 21–22, 46

Delinquency in property taxes, 75

Depreciation and taxes, 22, 46

Development program: agrarian reform, 3; health problems, 3; housing needs, 3; educa-

FISCAL SURVEY OF PANAMA:
PROBLEMS AND PROPOSALS FOR REFORM

JOINT TAX PROGRAM OAS/IDB

designer:	Edward D. King
typesetter:	Monotype Composition
typefaces:	Bodoni, Times Roman
printer:	Universal Lithographers
paper:	Perkins and Squier F
binder:	Moore & Co.
cover material:	Columbia Riverside Linen